Contents

INTRODUCTION

MARXIST CRIMINOLOGY AND SOCIAL JUSTICE   13

Social Justice/Criminal Justice

The Maturation of Critical Theory in Law, Crime, and Deviance

BRUCE A. ARRIGO, Ph.D.

California School of Professional Psychology

Institute of Psychology, Law and Public Policy

LIVERPOOL JMU LIBRARY

3 1111 00959 6220

West/Wadsworth

I(T)P® An International Thomson Publishing Company

Belmont, CA • Albany, NY • Boston • Cincinnati • Johannesburg • London • Madrid • Melbourne
Mexico City • New York • Pacific Grove, CA • Scottsdale, AZ • Singapore • Tokyo • Toronto

LIVERPOOL JOHN MOORES UNIVERSITY
Aldham Robarts L.R.C.
TEL. 051 231 3701/3634

Dedication
For my parents Tony and Rita:
In the hope that I might someday find as much justice in society
as they find, everyday, love in their lives

Criminal Justice Editor: Sabra Horne
Development Editor: Dan Alpert
Assistant Editor: Claire Masson
Editorial Assistant: Cherie Hackelberg
Marketing Manager: Mike Dew
Project Editor: Jennie Redwitz
Print Buyer: Karen Hunt

Permissions Editor: Susan Walters
Copy Editor: Laura Larson
Illustrator: Carole Lawson
Cover Design: Sandra Kelch
Cover Image: © 1998 PhotoDisc, Inc.
Compositor: Thompson Type
Printer: Webcom Limited

Printed in Canada
1 2 3 4 5 6 7 8 9 10

For more information, contact Wadsworth Publishing Company, 10 Davis Drive, Belmont, CA 94002, or electronically at http://www.wadsworth.com

International Thomson Publishing Europe
Berkshire House
168-173 High Holborn
London, WC1V 7AA, United Kingdom

International Thomson Editores
Seneca, 53
Colonia Polanco
11560 México D.F. México

Nelson ITP, Australia
102 Dodds Street
South Melbourne
Victoria 3205 Australia

International Thomson Publishing Asia
60 Albert Street #15-01
Albert Complex
Singapore 189969

Nelson Canada
1120 Birchmount Road
Scarborough, Ontario
Canada M1K 5G4

International Thomson Publishing Japan
Hirakawa-cho Kyowa Building, 3F
2-2-1 Hirakawa-cho, Chiyoda-ku
Tokyo 102, Japan

International Thomson Publishing Southern Africa
Building 18, Constantia Square
138 Sixteenth Road, P.O. Box 2459
Halfway House, 1685 South Africa

All the essays in this book were written specifically for this book with the exception of "The Prophetic Meaning of Social Justice" by Richard Quinney, which is copyrighted by Richard Quinney and used by permission.

Library of Congress Cataloging-in-Publication Data

Arrigo, Bruce A.
    Social justice/criminal justice : the maturation of critical theory in law, crime, and deviance / Bruce A. Arrigo
        p. cm. — (The Wadsworth contemporary issues in criminal justice series)
    Includes bibliographical references and index.
        ISBN 0-534-54558-0 (pbk.)
    1. Social justice. 2. Criminal justice, Administration of.
3. Criminology. I. Title. II. Series: Contemporary issues in crime and justice series.
HM216.A74   1998
303.3'72—dc21   98-20988

PROPHETIC CRITICISM AND SOCIAL JUSTICE   **71**

ANARCHIST CRIMINOLOGY AND SOCIAL JUSTICE   **91**

POSTMODERN FEMINIST CRIMINOLOGY AND SOCIAL JUSTICE 109

SEMIOTICS AND SOCIAL JUSTICE 129

CONSTITUTIVE CRIMINOLOGY AND SOCIAL JUSTICE   150

CATASTROPHE/TOPOLOGY
THEORY AND SOCIAL JUSTICE

QUEER THEORY AND SOCIAL JUSTICE

❖
_____

Foreword

ocial Justice/Criminal Justice appears at a time when the field of criminology is settling into a sustained focus on empirical research to establish
the causes of crime and test corresponding policy implications to determine how crime can be reduced. This is a trend of which I strongly approve.

But this type of empirical research, useful as it is, often makes certain implicit assumptions: it examines the causes of crime and tests policy implications only within the context of existing social structural arrangements. The
reason for this is rather straightforward: empirical research requires measuring
observable phenomena. A phenomenon that can be observed and measured
necessarily exists within the context of what already exists—the world as we
know it. One cannot observe and measure phenomena that would exist in a
world that itself does not already exist.

To the extent that criminologists confine themselves to this type of empirical research, they simply cannot think creatively about larger issues in our
field. Using terms from Quinney's chapter, they necessarily are stuck with
"what is" and locked out of "what ought to be." In particular, they have no
systematic way of thinking about what is captured in the term *social justice.*

Social science in general has historic roots in the ministry, and in its early
days many social scientists were "do-gooders" who overtly used theory and
research to try to make a better world (however they defined that). Like other
social sciences, the field of criminology has not entirely severed itself from
these roots. Rather, even the most empirically oriented criminologists see
themselves and their work in the context of trying, at least at some level, to
make the world a better place. For most of us in the mainstream, however,
this is a deep and somewhat hidden background to our work that we do not
overtly acknowledge.

Critical criminologists, in contrast, bring that somewhat hidden background right out to center stage and, by focusing on what ought to be, refuse
to confine themselves to examining what already is. This is the reason critical
criminology is not part of mainstream criminology. It is also why mainstream
criminologists can find it difficult to relate to critical criminology, vaguely un-
comfortable to think about. It can be much easier to ignore the whole thing.

Critical criminologists therefore have always paid a price for their obsti-
nate insistence on looking at the larger picture. I do not expect that the publi-
cation of this book will suddenly change that basic situation.

But this book will serve an important function for the field. It provides a
comprehensive sweep of critical criminology, with a focus on the implications
these theories have for the concept of social justice. The book appears to me

to be without equal in the scope and quality of its coverage in this area. In addition, it is tied together with very strong introduction and conclusion chapters, along with the introductions to each individual chapter. These provide a framework for understanding what is often difficult material for those who are not familiar with it. The overall result is a book that both serves a purpose for the field and makes a substantial argument to it.

I like some chapters better than others. But each chapter challenged me. Each chapter confronted me. Each chapter made me think about what I do as a criminologist and why I have chosen some paths rather than others in my professional career. I hope every criminologist reads and thinks about this book.

Thomas J. Bernard
State College, PA

ACKNOWLEDGMENTS

I am indebted to many people for the completion of this project. I especially want to thank five doctoral students. Three of them worked tirelessly on the chapter edits and master glossary. They insisted on making the prose more accessible and student-friendly. These students include Peter Patch, Kristi Wagner, and Kim Ewing. Jennifer Santman contributed significantly to the final proofing of the manuscript and the creation of the index. A fifth student, Carol Fowler, developed the index.

I would like to thank the following reviewers for their helpful suggestions: Gregory Barak, Eastern Michigan University; Thomas Bernard, Pennsylvania State University; Robert Bohm, University of Central Florida; Mona Danner, Old Dominion University; Miriam DeLone, University of Nebraska; Frank Horvath, Michigan State University; Peter Kraska, Eastern Kentucky University; Paul Mazerolle, University of Cincinnati; Thomas Tomlinson, Western Illinois University; Edward Tromanhauser, Western Illinois University; and Sheila VanNess, University of Tennessee at Chatanooga.

I also want to thank the staff at Wadsworth, especially Sabra Horne and Kate Barrett. They supported this project from beginning to end and recognized its importance for an undergraduate (and graduate) audience. Wadsworth's series editor, Todd Clear, deserves recognition. He had vision enough to understand that the field of criminal justice was in desperate need of a critical text on social justice.

Finally, I want to thank the Critical Criminology Division of the American Society of Criminology. The membership continues to be inspirational for me. They realize that ours is a task of raising consciousness first and then moving to social change second. Hopefully, in some small but meaningful way, this anthology speaks truth to their wisdom.

Bruce A. Arrigo

❖

About the Authors

Bruce A. Arrigo is professor of forensic psychology and criminology and director of the Institute of Psychology, Law, and Public Policy at the California School of Professional Psychology–Fresno. He has written extensively in the areas of critical criminology and social theory, mental illness and offender rehabilitation, feminist jurisprudence and psychoanalysis, and homeless studies and deviance. His recent articles have appeared in such periodicals as *Criminal Justice and Behavior, Justice Quarterly, Journal of Offender Rehabilitation,* and *Crime, Law, and Social Change.* Arrigo has published two books: *Madness, Language, and the Law* (1993) and *The Contours of Psychiatric Justice* (1996). Together with T. R. Young, he is completing *The Dictionary of Critical Social Science* (in press). Arrigo is also the editor for the peer review quarterly *Humanity and Society.*

Gregg Barak is professor of criminology and criminal justice and former department head of sociology, anthropology, and criminology at Eastern Michigan University. Prior to coming to EMU, he was professor and chair of the Department of Criminology and Criminal Justice at Alabama State University where he was the recipient of the Dean of the College of Arts and Sciences Award for Excellence in Research and Creativity in 1991. Barak was the program chair for the annual meetings of the Academy of Criminal Justice Sciences in 1993 when the theme was "Class, Race, and Gender." He has also been a deputy editor of *Justice Quarterly* and the book review editor for *Social Justice.* Throughout the O. J. Simpson criminal trial in 1995, Barak was an expert commentator for 107.1 FM radio in Ann Arbor. From this has emerged the anthology *Representing O. J.: Murder, Criminal Justice, and Mass Culture* (1996). He is also the editor of three other anthologies: *Crimes by the Capitalist State: An Introduction to State Criminality* (1991); *Varieties of Criminology: Readings from a Dynamic Discipline* (1993); and *Media, Process, and the Social Construction of Crime: Studies in Newsmaking Criminology* (1994). Barak has authored *In Defense of Whom? A Critique of Criminal Justice Reform* (1980) and *Gimme Shelter: A Social History of Homelessness in Contemporary America* (1991), which was selected by the American Library Association for its Choice List of Outstanding Academic Books for that year. His latest work is *Integrating Criminologies* (1997).

Jeff Ferrell is an associate professor in the Department of Criminal Justice at Northern Arizona University. He received his Ph.D. in sociology from the University of Texas at Austin. His research and professional interests include the intersections of criminal and cultural processes, the development of qualitative research methods in criminology and criminal justice, and criminological theory. He is the author of *Crimes of Style: Urban Graffiti and the Politics of Criminality* (1996) and lead coeditor, with Clinton R. Sanders, of *Cultural Criminology* (1995).

Stuart Henry, Ph.D. is Professor and Chair of Sociology at Valparaiso University, having previously taught at Eastern Michigan University for eleven years. Before coming to the United States in 1984, he taught at Nottingham Trent University in England and had previously held research positions at Middlesex University and London University. He has studied marginalized knowledges found in informal institutions including mutual aid groups, informal economies, nonstate systems of discipline and social control, and cooperatives. Most recently he has examined the relationship among social norms, private discipline, and public law. His research has been funded by the National Science Foundation, the Economic and Social Research Council, and the Federal Emergency Management Administration. He has published over sixty articles in professional journals or as chapters in books and encyclopedias. Henry has authored, coauthored, or edited fourteen books on various aspects of crime, deviance, and social control, including *Self-Help and Health* (1977), *The Hidden Economy* (1978), *Private Justice* (1983), *The Informal Economy* (1987), *The Deviance Process* (1993), *Employee Dismissal* (1994), *Social Control* (1994), *Criminological Theory* (1995), *Constitutive Criminology: Beyond Postmodernism* (1996), *Essential Criminolgy* (1998), and *The Criminology Theory Reader* (1998). He serves on the editorial board of *Theoretical Criminology* and *Law and Society Review*. He has received several teaching and research awards, including the State of Michigan Teaching Excellence Award (1990) and the Eastern Michigan University Distinguished Faculty Scholarly-Creativity Award (1994).

Nancy C. Jurik is associate professor of justice studies at Arizona State University. She received her Ph.D. in sociology in 1980 from the University of California, Santa Barbara. At ASU she teaches courses in feminism and justice, justice theory, women and social control, economic justice, and women and work. In 1995, she was selected by the ASU graduate student council as an outstanding faculty mentor to graduate students. She has published research on women and crime and on gender issues in the workplace. She recently published a book with Susan Ehrlich Martin entitled *Doing Justice, Doing Gender: Women in Law and Criminal Justice Occupations* (1996). Her current research focuses on women and men in home business and on microenterprise loan programs in the United States.

Michael J. Lynch is an associate professor in the criminology department at the University of Southern Florida and director of the Ph.D. program. Broadly defined, his interests include questions related to social, racial, class, and gender justice. His articles have appeared in a diverse range of journals, including the *Journal of Research in Crime and Delinquency, Justice Quarterly, Crime, Law and Social Change, Social Justice,* and *Journal of Criminal Justice Education.* He is the author/editor of six books and currently coedits the journal *Social Pathology.*

Peter K. Manning is professor of sociology and criminal justice at Michigan State University. In Oxford, he was a visiting fellow and research fellow at Wolfson College, a fellow of Balliol College (1982–1983), and a senior research officer at the Centre for Socio-Legal Studies (1984–1986). He has published twelve books—the most recent being *Organizational Communication* (1992)—and numerous articles and chapters in scientific publications. His research interests are in organizational analysis and criminology, with special interest in fieldwork and qualitative methods. His recent research examines legal decision making (with Keith Hawkins), nuclear safety regulation, and private security. He is named in *Who's Who in America* and *Who's Who in the World.*

Dragan Milovanovic is a professor of criminal justice at Northeastern Illinois University, Chicago. He has published extensively in the sociology of law and criminology. His books include *The Sociology of Law* (1994), *Postmodern Law and Disorder* (1992), *Weberian and Marxian Analysis of Law* (1989), *Chaos, Criminology, and Social Justice* (1997), and *Postmodern Criminology* (1997). He has also coauthored or coedited several recent books: *Constitutive Criminology* (1996); *Race, Gender and Class in Criminology* (1996); *Legality and Illegality* (1995); and *Thinking Critically About Crime* (1997). He was the recipient of the Distinguished Achievement Award, 1992–1993, from the Division on Critical Criminology of the American Society of Criminology for his critical scholarship and service.

Hal Pepinsky teaches in the Department of Criminal Justice at Indiana University, Bloomington. His most recent books include *Myths That Cause Crime* (with Paul Jesilow; 1992), *The Geometry of Violence and Democracy* (1991), *Criminology as Peacemaking* (coedited with Richard Quinney; 1991), and *We Who Would Take No Prisoners: Selections from the Fifth International Conference on Penal Abolition* (coedited with Brian MacLean; 1993).

Richard Quinney is professor of sociology at Northern Illinois University. He has written extensively in the areas of crime, law, justice, community, and peace. His books include *The Social Reality of Crime* (1970); *Critique of Legal Order* (1973); *Class, State, and Crime* (1977); *Social Existence* (1983); *Providence* (1985); and *Criminology as Peacemaking* (with Hal Pepinsky; 1991). His most recent work explores the relationship among prophetic thought, existentialism, and morality. Autobiographical reflections are contained in *Journey to a Far Place.*

Katheryn K. Russell is an associate professor of criminology and criminal justice at the University of Maryland, College Park, where she completed her Ph.D. She received her undergraduate degree in legal studies from the University of California at Berkeley. Her law degree is from Hastings Law School (University of California). Russell's teaching, research, and writing have been in the areas of criminal law, sociology of law, and race and crime. Her 1994 article "The Constitutionality of Jury Override in Alabama Death Penalty Cases," published in the *Alabama Law Review,* was cited by the U.S. Supreme Court in *Harris v. Alabama* (1995). Russell has also taught at the American College of Law (Washington College of Law), City University of New York Law School, Howard University, and Alabama State University. She interned at the Southern Poverty Law Center and the American Civil Liberties' Reproductive Freedom Project. She is a member of the American Society of Criminology, the Academy of Criminal Justice Sciences, and the

American Bar Association. Russell's book *The Color of Crime: Racial Hoaxes, White Fear, Black Protectionism, Police Harassment and Other Macroaggressions* was published in 1998.

Brett Stockdill recently completed his Ph.D. at Northwestern University in sociology. He is a queer activist, writer, and educator living in Los Angeles. Until recently, he was a member of ACT UP (Aids Coalition to Unleash Power), sat on Chicago's Issues Committee, and taught in the Department of Sociology at Northwestern University. He is currently doing AIDS-related mental health research in the Department of Sociology at the University of California, Los Angeles.

Paul Stretesky is completing work on his Ph.D. in the School of Criminology and Criminal Justice at Florida State University. His areas of interest include methods of research, environmental justice, critical criminology, and hate crimes. His current research is entitled "Waste Wars: Hazardous Waste, Environmental Justice and Race: The Case of Florida." It examines the spatial distribution of hazardous waste sites in light of race and class relations.

Nancy A. Wonders is a sociologist and an associate professor of criminal justice at Northern Arizona University. Her scholarship focuses on the relationship among social inequality, law, and justice. Some of her publications include "Determinate Sentencing: A Feminist and Postmodern Story: in *Justice Quarterly, 13* (December 1996), 301–338; and "Gender and Justice: Feminist Contributions to Criminology," in Gregg Barak (Ed.), *Varieties of Criminology: Readings from a Dynamic Discipline* (with Susan Caulfield; 1993). Other publications that have appeared in journals and books address topics such as violence against women, the role of the state in law creation and policy formation, sexual harassment policy, and integrating gender in the criminal justice curriculum.

T. R. Young is a founding member of the Red Feather Institute in Weidman, Michigan. He has been a university professor and, most recently, a visiting lecturer at the University of Pittsburgh, the University of Colorado, Texas Women's University, and Vermont University. He has written extensively in the areas of sociology, social psychology, and philosophy of science. His recent books include *The Drama of Social Life: Essays in Post-Modern Social Psychology* (1990) and *Chaos Theory and the Drama of Social Change: Essays in Postmodern Philosophy of Science* (1992). With Bruce A. Arrigo, he is completing a book on chaos theory and postmodern criminology.

Introduction

Some Preliminary Observations on Social Justice and Critical Criminology

BRUCE A. ARRIGO

SOCIAL JUSTICE/CRIMINAL JUSTICE: IDENTIFYING THE ISSUE

The criminal justice apparatus is large and, in many ways, difficult to manage. Part of this difficulty is related to the system's commitment to *justice*. We recognize this commitment when lawbreakers are arrested, when suspects are prosecuted, and when felons are incarcerated. But this fidelity to justice is not always so clear. The conditions under which the criminal justice system maintains an effective administration of law enforcement, criminal court, and correctional practices can and does get bogged down in a number of competing, sometimes even conflicting, circumstances.

These contradictory circumstances are witnessed every day in a variety of ways. For example, as citizens we may question the social, political, and economic conditions that justify an officer's use of deadly force during a fleeing suspect's arrest, that lead a defense attorney to zealously represent factually guilty suspects, and that promote fundamental liberty interests for convicted and incarcerated killers. Indeed, at times we may believe that the criminal justice system produces policy outcomes or other programmatic initiatives that essentially satisfy the interests of police, court, and/or penal agencies (that is, the "system") while failing to satisfy the needs of the public.

I contend that this very dilemma is at the core of what makes the American criminal justice system so controversial. The dilemma is both profound and unrelenting. On the one hand, there is a need to produce sound, criminal justice outcomes. On the other hand, there is a need to legitimize essential, social justice tenets. Balancing the interests implied in this tension is not so easily accomplished.

The Orenthal James Simpson double-murder case is an excellent example of this problem. The entire trial (including the criminal verdict) raised a number of basic questions about whether the system works. Clearly, one could argue that, on balance, based on the collection and presentation of evidence, the skill of the respective litigators, the wisdom of the judge's assorted trial rulings, and the soundness of the jury process, the system fulfilled its responsibility. The acquittal of Mr. Simpson represented the fruits of a criminal justice apparatus that, although not perfect, did its job. However, one could also argue that the evidence collected and presented was incomplete (some evidence was suppressed), that some litigators cared only about winning, that the judge's decision making was unduly influenced by the media, and that the jury verdict was a sham (too many members were understandably tired with a case that took entirely too long). Thus, the acquittal of Mr. Simpson was a vivid reminder of a system that, for the most part, failed to understand the needs of the citizens it presumes to serve.

In this illustration, criminal and social justice appear incompatible. But this polarization is not evident in every instance. Convictions like that of Jeffrey Dahmer, the Wisconsin man convicted of sexually abusing, dismembering, and eating the body parts of several of his victims, and Susan Smith, the South Carolinian convicted of drowning her own children, tell us that the criminal justice apparatus can and does produce outcomes that reflect the collective conscience of our society. However, it is precisely because so many instances arise in which the differences between the administration of the system and the appreciation of the public seem irreconcilable that understanding the role of social justice in the criminal justice apparatus becomes a matter of worthwhile investigation.

SOME HISTORICAL BACKGROUND
ON (SOCIAL) JUSTICE

Understanding the relationship between social justice/criminal justice is fundamental to this project. Thus, some introductory comments on the meaning of justice are warranted. Certainly most would agree that the concept of "justice" is by no means easy to interpret or simple to discern. This has been the case throughout the history of Western thought and civilization. Early Grecian philosophers such as Socrates, Plato, and Aristotle wrestled with the essence of justice, producing often vague and impractical definitions.

Subsequent philosophers and social commentators such as Aquinas, Kant, and Mill advanced more exacting meanings for the construct of justice, but they, too, were unable to provide workable and testable models to regulate successfully human social behavior. For example, Aquinas's often cited maxim is as follows: "justice is giving to one that which is one's due." This so-called "distributive" form of justice is undoubtedly a good sound bite; however, it is not a functional solution to the vagaries of complex civic life. The same problem is contained in Kant's ethical formalism where that which is "just and proper" must be so categorically; otherwise the behavior should be deemed immoral. Thus, according to Kant, all killings are unjust whether they occur during time of war, in self-defense, or as a criminal justice response to convicted pedophiles, rapists, and murderers. John Stuart Mill offered a more utilitarian approach to justice. His vision hinged on what produced the greatest good for the greatest number of people. Unlike Kant, defining what was just was based on the *consequence of behavior* (for instance, happiness, wealth, prestige) and not on the *act* itself (for example, killing).

These definitions and others akin to them are inadequate. In large part, they represent grand or totalizing theories about the content of justice without detailed reference to specific events that fundamentally challenge the day-to-day effectiveness of any one approach. This discrepancy has led to more recent attempts at defining this very elusive construct. These efforts focus on the question of equality (justice) and its absence in society (inequality) (for example, Hayek, 1960; Nozick, 1974; Rawls, 1971). At the core of several of these theories is a detailed critique of the role of capitalism, legal authority, communitarianism, legitimacy, democratic liberalism, and social change (Kamenka, 1979). Many of the chapters explore these themes to some greater or lesser extent.

More contemporary analysts of justice are prone to comment on its many forms (for example, technical, retributive, substantive, procedural) (Young, 1981). Criminal justice scholars are uniquely equipped to address the notion of justice and what it embodies in relationship to crime, social control, law, deviance, and punishment. Typically, these observations are in response to how the police, court, and correctional systems (and their representatives) promote or fail to promote the administration of justice. Thus, it should come as no surprise that this anthology squarely considers the meaning of justice in relation to matters of criminal and legal practice. I contend that this is a necessary and essential juncture for fostering both fruitful and targeted dialogue on the state of social justice in American society. Further, this dialogue is key to better comprehending where and how social justice/criminal justice are compatible, incompatible, or, in the extreme, irreconcilable.

SOME HISTORICAL BACKGROUND
ON CRITICAL CRIMINOLOGY

This book, then, is an effort to learn something more about social justice. To understand its meaning and significance in our lives, each contributor focuses on a unique perspective. Critical approaches to criminology frequently address criminal justice issues, and defining social justice is certainly one of them. *Critical theory* in criminology is not to be confused with *critical criminology* (Groves & Sampson, 1986; Sykes, 1974). The former represents a very broad and rich intellectual tradition in the history of Eurocentric thought traced to the Frankfurt Institute for Social Research in Germany and notable scholarly collectives in France. Critical criminology refers to an elaboration or reconceptualization of Marxist theory as applied to the sociology of crime and delinquency (Melossi, 1985).

Many critical perspectives appear in criminology. Not all of them are reflected in the pages that follow. Clearly, to construct a single text inclusive of all approaches simply would not be possible. The orientations described here, however, are considered by many in the field to represent the major, "cutting edge" points of view. In other words, careful attention was given to the selection process. Fueling this process was a concern for incorporating those essential viewpoints that have influenced, deepened, or challenged our understanding of law, crime, and deviance during the past two decades. All of the perspectives in this anthology have had such an impact.

The decision to not make sense of social justice through the prism of critical theory in criminology is deliberate. This orientation is only partially consistent with several of the chapters, and where it is developed it is not essential to the overall thrust of these respective sections. Critical theory is concerned with the "eclipse of reason" (Groves & Sampson, 1986, p. 560)—that is, the crisis in how we define justice, freedom, equality, and happiness based on subjective rather than objective distinctions. Critical theorists such as Horkheimer (1974), Marcuse (1960), and Habermas (1975) address this predicament in their various critiques of culture and science. Interestingly, the critical theory tradition draws notable inspiration from Karl Marx and his analysis of capitalism and the importance of reflective praxis and meaningful social change (Groves & Sampson, 1986, pp. 560–564). Several contributors raise questions about reason, culture, and science but do so indirectly in their particular assessments of social justice. For example, the chapters on semiotics, postmodern feminism, anarchist criminology, and chaology are influenced by developments in critical theory as applied to criminology; however, there is no full-blown analysis of this relationship in any one of these sections.

The decision to make sense of social justice through the lens of critical criminology is also calculated. This branch of criminology is itself a rather recent phenomenon (Lynch & Groves, 1989). Varieties of it can be traced to the works of such figures as Taylor, Walton, and Young (1973), Wright (1973), Platt (1974), and Quinney (1970, 1974). What each of these early commentators shared was a profound commitment to the genuine vitality and contemporary utility of Marxist thought, particularly when interpreting issues concerning crime and justice. Thus, many, though not all, of the ideas contained in the chapters are about resurrecting and rethinking Marxist criminology with a unique "twist," so to speak.

The contributions of Marx are not immediately or directly evident in several chapters. The theoretical strains of peacemaking, topology/catastrophe theory, semiotics, queer theory, and so forth, are good illustrations of this point. Nevertheless, the authors for these chapters do share many of the intellectual convictions of a Marxist-informed analysis. Questions concerning social change, inequality, the problems of capitalism, repression, and so on, are, at times, only thinly embedded in these chapters; however, these macrolevel issues are at the core of what each writer describes.

Because Marxism is, in part, an important jumping-off point for many, though not all, contributors, it is useful to consider the historical development of critical criminology. It is also important to provide a blueprint of sorts for the maturation of critical criminology as a way of grounding the reader in how the traditions described in each chapter evolved and, in some areas, function interdependently. Again, I hasten to add that not all chapters owe complete allegiance to the theoretical insights of Marx. The more broadly conceived field of critical theory is also folded into the writings of several authors. Thus, readers should take note of the fact that, for my purposes, Marxism is a convenient point of departure from which to comprehend, albeit incompletely, the various criminological strains of thought developed in the anthology as applied to the issue of social justice.

As Figure 1 demonstrates, Marxist thought is consequential for those writing within the tradition of critical criminology. The first level identifies the distinction between *instrumental* and *structural* Marxism. This distinction essentially determines what forces are responsible for how society functions. It also includes how issues pertaining to law, crime, and deviance work. Instrumentalists believe that the economy (or in Marx's terms the *base*) determines how laws are enacted, how crimes are constructed, and how deviance is defined. Thus, for example, arrest, prosecution, conviction, and incarceration rates are fundamentally dictated by changes in the economic well-being of a given society. As prosperity increases, criminal justice problems diminish. As prosperity decreases, criminal justice problems intensify.

Structural Marxists are not entirely sympathetic to the interpretation of instrumentalists. They believe that other, relatively autonomous forces operate in society. These forces shape or determine how society functions. Such things as politics, morality, personal beliefs, and education are recognized as *spheres of influence*. Marx himself was to refer to the totality of these factors as the *superstructure*. Thus, multiple factors contribute to how law, crime, and deviance are understood and embodied within the social fabric of a given culture.

What both instrumental and structural Marxists have in common, however, is the central role of struggle. In other words, both branches of Marxism maintain that the unfolding drama representing our lives is essentially about conflict. Struggle and conflict here imply a scarcity of resources over which members actively compete. They also refer to the acquisition of tangible power sufficient to ensure that the interests of certain groups find legitimacy in the law, protecting (perhaps insulating) such collectives from criminal prosecution or other forms of marginalization. The dilemma that both instrumental and structural Marxists see, of course, is that there can only be some winners and a lot of losers in such a society. At the sociological level, this win-loss dynamic produces structural inequalities (that is, gender, race, class disparities). At the psychological level, this win-loss dynamic produces frustration, repression, and alienation. Thus, both structural and instrumental Marxists agree that change is necessary and, indeed, inevitable.

Level 1	Instrumental Marxists			Structural Marxists	
Level 2	Anarchists	Conflict (Quinney, 1970)	Commodity-Exchange		Structural Interpellationist
Level 3	Left Realists	Socialist Feminists	Postmodern Criminology	Critical Race Theorists	Peacemaking	Anarchists/ Abolitionists
			Critical Eclecticism			

FIGURE 1 Development of Critical Criminology

The instrumental/structural distinction can be traced directly to the voluminous writings of Karl Marx and his associate, Frederick Engels. Both drafted many of their more influential papers during the mid- to late 1800s. The current resurgence in Marxist criminology in North America, however, surfaced during the turbulent decade of the 1960s and established institutional support across college campuses during the revolutionary decade of the 1970s (Lynch & Groves, 1989, pp. 2–3). The second level of Figure 1, then, represents the birth of a new criminology, a critical criminology—one in which society itself was said to foster, create, and sustain crime, victimization, and oppression (Taylor, Walton, & Young, 1973, 1975; see also Bohm, 1982, for more on the distinctions among varieties of critical criminology).

Critical scholars during this period were divided into three main divisions. Anarchists recognized the ravaging and demoralizing effects the state wielded producing economic devastation for many citizens (Tifft & Sullivan, 1980). Wedded to the instrumental Marxist critique, their response was to dismantle the system, produce stateless (and classless) societies, and promote mutual aid and shared responsibility among communal members (Kropotkin, 1902, 1913).

Conflict criminologists, especially those like Richard Quinney (1970), were concerned for the *social reality of crime*. In other words, criminal justice policies related to law, order, crime, punishment, victimization, and deviance were merely definitions developed by people (authorities) who possessed the power to shape, enforce, and administer such policies. "Crime is a judgement made by some about the actions and characteristics of others" (Quinney, 1970, p. 16). Thus, matters of justice, due process, equity, and fairness were less the product of economic forces and less the product of institutional constraints (for example, education, the family, politics, religion) but were, instead, the result of those who marshaled the most power and control.

During the late 1970s, structural Marxist criminologists were also increasingly divided over the relationship between the base and the superstructure and the regulatory influence that one had over the other. Two varieties of structural Marxism developed: commodity-exchange and structural interpellation. The commodity-exchange form (also known as capital logic) was originally developed by Pashukanis (1978/1924) and based on Marx's (1967) work in volume 1 of *Capital*. On the North American front, much fruitful Marxist analysis resulted from Pashukanis's insights (for example, Balbus, 1977a, 1977b; Beirne & Sharlet, 1980; Fraser, 1978; Milovanovic, 1981).

Pashukanis explains how commodities (for instance, one basket of hay, two bushels of apples, three loaves of bread) are transformed when sold in a marketplace. The marketplace here represents the economy. What happens is that all products have natural or intrinsic value. This natural value includes the amount of work and time it takes to harvest or make a commodity and the satisfaction one feels having harvested or made the product. When a commodity enters the marketplace, the intrinsic *use value* is replaced with an equivalent *exchange value* (for example, one loaf of bread = two sticks of butter).

The same is true today. An elite baseball player is a free agent. The player is looking for a starting role on a professional team. Thus, he is a commodity. All of his athletic abilities and all of the work and sacrifice it took for him to acquire these skills and to experience some heartfelt satisfaction are equated with (exchanged for) a certain dollar amount.

As commodity-exchange advocates contend, the problem with this version of structural Marxism as it functions in contemporary society is that money becomes the ultimate arbiter of value. But money masks and conceals the differential amounts of labor required to make products. When consumers purchase, say, a stereo, they are not aware of what amounts of time, labor, and personnel costs as well as parts, manufacturing, and distribution problems go into the construction of the stereo. These things disappear in the marketplace. They are brought under the neutralizing form of money. The concrete dimension of existence and experience is replaced by the abstract. The qualitative aspects of human social interaction are substituted with quantitative ratios. The realities of work, leisure, ritual, and celebration are replaced by their suggested monetary forms or equivalents. Thus, for commodity-exchange Marxists, economic value plays a more important role in determining how society functions.

There are also the structural interpellationists. These Marxists examine the effects of the superstructure's spheres of influence in codetermining the economic relations of our society. Thus, the spheres of influence that are significant include the political, the ideological, and the economic. These three forces are said to have collective effects in producing social phenomena or events in life. Indeed, according to structural Marxists, the base is, at best, the determinant of reality but only in the last instance. Contributions from Althusser (1971) and Poulantzas (1973) have substantially informed several subsequent critiques on the nature of law, crime, and deviance (for instance, Esping-Anderson, Friedland, & Ohlin, 1979; Milovanovic, 1986, 1987) from a structural interpellationist perspective.

Structural interpellationists maintain that with the increasing complexities of advanced, monopoly capitalism come new and different forms of state regulation. This state regulation addresses various economic crises that may or may not lead to some legitimation crises (Habermas, 1975, 1984, 1987). In other words, people can and do withdraw their commitment from the economic system and the rule of law. For example, the volatile effects following the first jury verdict of the officers prosecuted for the beating of Rodney King signaled how people in economic distress could angrily react to judicial decisions. The infamous cry "No justice, no peace" aptly summarizes the King problem and the problem structural interpellationists identify.

Embedded in this dilemma, however, is the *position* one assumes. In other words, with state-regulated capitalism, one's *status* as inmate, mental patient, doctor, welfare recipient, displaced worker, judge, addict, juvenile delinquent, business entrepreneur, and so forth, is instrumental in determining what rights will be honored in law and elsewhere. Here, the state finds itself balancing the needs of individuals against the demands of an ever-increasing, technologically driven economy. In early competitive capitalism legitimation was maintained by the inherent "justice" of marketplace practices and commodity-exchange. Justice was done through the natural process of trading goods. In advanced or late capitalism, however, the state apparatus confronts a different problem. One's position or status is more closely aligned with the effects of the super-structure and not the operation of the base. For example, when one appears before a criminal court of law as a defendant, one can only communicate through the code of the court. We call this code *legalese*. To present one's case from outside this (judicial, not economic) sphere of communication is to risk objection by opposing counsel and to risk a sustainable ruling by the judge. One's case, then, potentially becomes nonjusticiable, *according to the law.*

Capital logic Marxists recognize that many forces determine the function-ing of society; however, they ultimately conclude that the economically pow-erful cause, administer, and sustain the operation of it. Structural interpellationists, too, recognize that many (competing) forces regulate society, but they ultimately conclude that the "cause" of things (for example, court rulings, a death row inmate's execution, the firing of a patrol officer) is always multiple. Political, legal, economic, and ideological factors exert pressure. For these Marxists, the origin of events in society is never reducible to fundamen-tal economics.

The next level of analysis in Figure 1 represents the current grouping of critical criminological scholars. Many, though not all, of the contributors write from within one or more of these traditions. Parenthetically, I have intention-ally chosen not to include a chapter on Left realism because this movement now represents the mainstream response to British imperialism perpetrated up to the mid-1970s (MacLean, 1991; Young, 1987). Thus, it can no longer be viewed as a peripheral form of criminological inquiry, particularly in relation-ship to its version of social justice.

Each chapter includes some historical background on the development of that theory's unique critical criminological perspective beyond (or indepen-dent of) the previous outline. At times, this information is prominently fea-tured within the chapter's narrative. At other times, reference to the historical antecedents of the criminological theory are presented in the chapter's ab-stract. In either case, I do not need to comment on such matters here. How-ever, it is important to note that critical eclecticism is a viewpoint not identified within any one critical camp. Criminological theorists embracing this orientation are, by definition, inclined to incorporate ideas from among the various critical perspectives. They roam the field, so to speak. They bor-row some ideas from peacemaking and others from postmodernism, and still others from socialist feminism and so forth. To that end, they are inclined to "push the envelope" when it comes to understanding passionately issues in law, crime, and deviance.

IN SEARCH OF SOCIAL JUSTICE:
SOME PRELIMINARY OBSERVATIONS

Defining social justice through critical criminology can, in part, be facilitated by considering the possible relationship between it (social justice) and criminal justice. There are only two prospects. It may be that there is no such thing as social justice. In other words, critical criminology may show us how police, court, and correctional decision making function to maximize system outcomes while minimizing the collective conscience or social will of society. Alternatively, it may be that there is something called social justice as identified through the lens of radical criminology. In this model, socially just tenets would be acknowledged through the administration of the criminal justice apparatus. This model is represented by four forms. Figure 2 depicts the operation of these forms.

As Figure 2 indicates, the forms of social justice vary rather remarkably. They can be summarily explained as follows. First, social justice is a starting point. Notions of fairness, equity, proprietorship, due process, and so forth, anchor the criminal justice system. Police, court, and correctional practices begin with such notions and endeavor to express them through various institutional practices. Second, criminal justice is the starting point. The system wields its effects and, when working effectively and efficiently, produces outcomes that reflect, that mirror, the interests, aspirations, needs, and sentiments of the general public. Third, there is social justice, but it is essentially incompatible with criminal justice. In other words, though the system endeavors to produce results, it does so to the near exclusion of those for whom the apparatus was designed. The operation of the American criminal justice system, then, largely fails to protect and serve the goals of a just society as embodied and expressed by its citizenry. Fourth, there is social justice, and it routinely interacts with criminal justice. Sometimes social justice precedes criminal justice. Sometimes criminal justice precedes social justice. Further, this interactional process produces, at times, points of convergence: outcomes that simultaneously represent the demands of the system and the needs of the public.

Each chapter, then, tells us something more than what social justice is or is not. Each chapter tell us what social justice is in relationship to criminal justice. This additional feature of the anthology is significant. The analysis offered by the contributors represents an effort to deepen our understanding of law, crime, and deviance. In other words, beyond offering different critical criminological perspectives from which to interpret the meaning of social justice, each chapter considers how its unique interpretation relates to or furthers our knowledge of criminal justice.

Form	Relationship to Criminal Justice		
1	Social Justice	$\longrightarrow$	Criminal Justice
2	Criminal Justice	$\longrightarrow$	Social Justice
3	Social Justice and Criminal Justice	= =	Criminal Justice and Social Justice
4	Social Justice	⇄	Criminal Justice

FIGURE 2 Forms of Social Justice in Critical Criminology

ORGANIZATION OF THE BOOK

It should be somewhat obvious that the nature of this anthology is such that it is largely ideological. In other words, each chapter is an argument, a polemic, about what social justice is (in relationship to criminal justice) informed by a particular critical criminological viewpoint. One theme organizing the anthology is a commitment to theoretical rigor and sound polemical inquiry. This is a book filled with ideas. This is not a criticism of the anthology but simply a statement of what the reader can expect.

Another theme weaving the text together is some statement(s) on social justice. Perhaps a better way to say this is that the reader can expect to read about *types of justice*. For some, the notion that there are or may be many *justices* will be a bit unsettling. For others, this realization will be liberating. I am not simply suggesting that different people will have different perspectives on social justice. Instead, what I am suggesting is that, for many contributors, the notion of social justice per se will not be fixed or static or certain; rather, it will be a more dynamic expression of events and actors subject to the social, economic, and political forces that shape ideas and issues pertaining to law, crime, and deviance.

Certain features to the anthology, however, are constant. They, too, warrant some review as they contribute to the text's overall organization. First, each chapter includes some historical or background material situating the critical perspective described within the larger field of theoretical criminology. Second, each chapter includes an identification of several, core assumptions related to the theory presented. These assumptions include such things as the role of the state in constructing definitions of crime; the importance of language in privileging certain dominant worldviews; the persistence of patriarchy (that is, male-saturated culture) in creating and sustaining institutional realities in law that oppress women and other minorities; and so forth. Third, each chapter includes an identification of several, essential principles that represent the theory under review. These principles will, at times, be similar for various contributors; thus, readers should expect to see some similar ideas reappearing throughout the anthology.

Stylistically, organizational themes give further definition to the anthology. Contributors have endeavored to keep their citations and references to a minimum. The aim is to reach the largest possible constituency and to make some rather complex ideas as reader-friendly as possible. What references are used within each chapter are contained at the end of that chapter under a separate heading. Further, contributors rely upon topical examples to illustrate their ideas. The use of case law, crime stories/events, controversial criminal justice figures, and the like, are significant. These illustrations help contextualize the otherwise more abstract material.

Related to the theme of simplicity and accessibility is the importance of facility. By facility I mean the extent to which the chapters are structured to help navigate students through some murky, uncharted, and/or difficult waters. Accordingly, at the end of each chapter, a list of discussion questions is provided. These queries represent a guide to students (and teachers), highlighting some of the more noteworthy ideas developed by the contributors.

One final point on the organization of *Social Justice/Criminal Justice*. Each chapter represents an ideological frame of reference, so readers should feel comfortable to canvass any one chapter and understand how that particular critical perspective addresses the question of social justice. However, it is also important to have a more integrated understanding of critical social justice. In other words, it is meaningful to know what general position critical criminology takes on the issue of defining social justice. This matter is explored in the concluding chapter. That last chapter, then, represents a synthesis of all the material that precedes it. Several thematic points developed in the separate chapters will be brought together. Thus, for the first time, readers will be provided with a comprehensive interpretation of what critical social justice is and how it is distinguishable, if at all, from criminal justice as informed by critical criminology.

REFERENCES

Althusser, L. (1971). *Lenin and philosophy and other essays*. New York: New Left Books.

Balbus, I. (1977a). Commodity form and legal form: an essay on the relative autonomy of the law. *Law and Society Review, 11,* 571–587.

Balbus, I. (1977b). *The dialectics of legal expression*. New York: Sage.

Beirne, P., & Sharlet, R. (1980). (Eds.). *Pashukanis: Selected writings on Marxism and law*. New York: Academic Press.

Bohm, R. M. (1982). Radical criminology: An explication. *Criminology, 19*(4), 565–589.

Esping-Anderson, G., Friedland, R., & Ohlin, E. (1979). Class struggle and the capitalist state. In R. Quinney (Ed.), *Capitalist society*. Homewood, IL: Dorsey.

Fraser, A. (1978). The legal theory we need now. *Socialist Review, 8,* 164–166.

Groves, W. B., & Sampson, R. 1986. Critical theory and criminology. *Social Problems, 33*(6), 558–560.

Habermas, J. (1975). *Legitimation crises.* Boston: Beacon.

Habermas, J. (1984). *The theory of communicative action. Vol. 1: Reason and the rationalization of society* (T. McCarthy, Trans.). Boston: Beacon.

Habermas, J. (1987). *The theory of communicative action. Vol. 2: Lifeworld and systems: A critique of functionalist reason* (T. McCarthy, Trans.). Boston: Beacon.

Hayek, F. (1960). *The constitution of liberty.* Chicago: University of Chicago Press.

Horkheimer, M. (1974). *Eclipse of reason.* New York: Seabury.

Kamenka, E. (1979). What is justice? In E. Kamenka & A. Erh-Soon Tay (Eds.), *Justice* (pp. 1–24). London: Arnold.

Kropotkin, P. (1902). *Mutual aid.* Boston: Extending Horizons Books.

Kropotkin, P. (1913). *The conquest of bread.* New York: Blom.

Lynch, M., & Groves, W. C. (1989). *A primer in radical criminology* (2nd ed.). Albany, NY: Harrow.

MacLean, B. (1991). In partial defense of socialist realism. *Crime, Law, and Social Change, 15,* 213–254.

Marcuse, H. (1960). *Reason and revolution.* Boston: Beacon.

Marx, K. (1967). *Capital.* New York: International.

Melossi, D. (1985). Overcoming the crisis in critical criminology: Toward a grounded labelling theory. *Criminology, 23,* 193–207.

Milovanovic, D. (1981). The commodity-exchange theory of law: In search of a perspective. *Crime and Social Justice, 16,* 41–49.

Milovanovic, D. (1986). Juridico-linguistic communicative markets: Towards a semiotic analysis. *Contemporary Crises, 10,* 281–304.

Milovanovic, D. (1987). The political economy of "liberty" and "property" interests. *Legal Studies Forum, 11,* 267–293.

Nozick, R. (1974). *Anarchy, state and utopia.* New York: Basic Books.

Pashukanis, E. (1978). *Law and Marxism: A general theory* (C. J. Arthur, Ed.). London: Ink Links. (Original work published 1924)

Platt, A. (1974). Prospects for a radical criminology in the U.S. *Crime and Social Justice, 1,* 2–10.

Poulantzas, N. (1973). *State power and socialism.* London: New Left Books.

Quinney, R. (1970). *The social reality of crime.* Boston: Little, Brown.

Quinney, R. (1974). *Critique of legal order.* Boston: Little, Brown.

Rawls, J. (1971). *A theory of justice.* Cambridge, MA: Harvard University Press.

Sykes, G. (1974). The rise of critical criminology. *Journal of Criminal Law and Criminology, 65,* 206–213.

Taylor, I., Walton, P, & Young, J. (1973). *The new criminology: For a social theory of deviance.* New York: Harper & Row.

Taylor, I., Walton, P., & Young, J. (1975). *Critical criminology.* London: Routledge & Kegan Paul.

Tifft, L., & Sullivan, D. (1980). *The struggle to be human: Crime, criminology and anarchism.* Orkney: Cienfuego.

Wright, E. O. (1973). *The politics of punishment: A critical analysis of prisons in America.* New York: Harper & Row.

Young, J. (1981). Toward a critical theory of justice. *Social Theory and Practice, 7,* 279–302.

Young, J. (1987). The task facing a realist criminology. *Contemporary Crises, 11,* 337–356.

Radical Criminology and Social Justice

R adical criminology is a version of Marxist criminology. In this article by Lynch and Stretesky, a radical criminological analysis is used to further understand what social justice is. The authors describe several basic Marxian assumptions on the material nature of society (Marx's economic theory) and assumptions about human nature (how people behave). They argue that social justice is about providing for the economic needs of members within a society. Further, they emphasize the importance of similar life chances and opportunities that produce equal treatment for each person. According to Lynch and Stretesky, radical criminologists actively seek solutions to the presence of social injustice. Aside from treating people equally, radical solutions or reforms support what Lynch and Stretesky call "affirmative action plans" and an end to "crime-producing poverty." For them, social justice is something radical criminologists strive to achieve and/or maintain. Social justice concerns eclipse criminal justice responses. Thus, criminal justice represents a subset of the issues that make up social justice.

1

Marxism and Social Justice

Thinking About Social Justice, Eclipsing Criminal Justice

MICHAEL J. LYNCH AND PAUL STRETESKY

L ike other criminologists, radical criminologists are committed to a number of beliefs, and like other criminologists, these beliefs affect their view of the world. To be sure, radical criminologists have a different set of beliefs than more traditional criminologists and owe a great debt to Karl Marx and his system of thought. Thus, before beginning our discussion of social justice, we would like to make our position (our beliefs) on the issue of social justice explicit so that it is not misinterpreted. This view was well summarized by Ward (1973) when he wrote that radicals possess "a firm belief that the wretchedness of much of humanity is unnecessary and that [this wretchedness] cannot be eliminated within the framework of existing society" (p. 3).

There is nothing hidden in this statement. It implies that the troubles people experience today (for example, unemployment, homelessness, environmental pollution, racism, sexism) are the result of the way society is organized and that these troubles are not, as Mills (1959) noted, of their own making. It is true that people tend to interpret a bad turn of events as their own fault, or as "personal trouble." When a person loses a job, for example, he or she does not think of the structural relationships that made them expendable (such as corporate downsizing, the shift in production to foreign markets, increased mechanization) or of the thousands of others experiencing the same plight. They see themselves as alone and isolated. In reality, however, the person is not alone. Modern life is a constant struggle, and it is not this way because people do not work hard enough or because, as a society, we have limited resources. Life is a struggle because we have failed miserably at the task of implementing a plan that ensures social justice for all members of society. Increasingly, it seems impossible to institute such a plan within the confines of society as it exists today. Thus, the essential task is reorganizing society so that social justice can be achieved. How that is to be accomplished will be discussed later in this chapter. For now, let us turn to a discussion of what we mean by the term *social justice*.

THINKING ABOUT SOCIAL JUSTICE

When people think of social justice, they tend to think of tomorrow. Social justice is, in their view, a task for tomorrow—something that will happen after we take care of the problems of today. For the majority of (traditional) criminologists and politicians, contemporary questions about justice are typically defined as belonging to one or more of the following limited sets of issues: rising rates of violent or property crime; burgeoning prison populations and prison overcrowding; lax punishments due to early release and unserved time; soft sentences, a lack of deterrence in law and the mis- and underutilization of responses such as the death penalty; the expansion of drug use and drug smuggling; an increase in gang membership and gang-related acts of violence. To be sure, these are not trivial issues. Yet, as a group, many mainstream criminologists and politicians are wrong when they express the opinion that these are the most important issues of the day and that we can take care of social justice issues tomorrow, after these types of "pressing" and "immediate" criminal justice issues are solved. Since there are always "pressing" problems, tomorrow never seems to arrive, and questions concerning policies that promote social justice have successfully been put off indefinitely. Further, what escapes the mainstream perspective is the connection between economic *in*justice and crime; that is, crime cannot be addressed in a meaningful manner without first addressing the ways in which our economic and social system is unjust and the ways in which those injustices produce criminality.

Most politicians and criminologists are content to wait until tomorrow to address the "bigger" issues of social and economic inequality that plague our society. However, there are no more tomorrows. Tomorrow exists for the hopeful, for those who imagine experiencing a better way of life in the near future. For many, this circumstance, this possibility (a better way of life), has been erased by a world economic system that is stagnant for the majority of its participants. There are no more tomorrows for people who live in a world where the following images may be seen and where people must live out a ghostly existence as the figures that occupy the bodies these scenes describe:

> Homeless men, women, and children shuffle by on the street, sleep on sewer grates for warmth when the police do not move them along, search people's trash for food and clothing, and sell their bodies to eat. They build cardboard shantytowns and disappear into alleys, down unused subway tunnels and into the dark as daylight breaks.

> A pregnant juvenile with AIDS is serving time in a local lockup. She comes from an urban neighborhood where drug and alcohol abuse is prevalent. She lives in a home without running water and cannot afford to treat her medical condition. Her arrest provides her with the first prenatal examination of her pregnancy.

> A child cries from hunger. Tears swell in her eyes and stream down her face. She is only partially clothed, and has not had a well-rounded meal in

several months. Her mother goes hungry to provide the child with mea-ger meals.

A Vietnam veteran with a steel plate in his head and a portion of his brain missing waits on a line to receive some free food. His veteran's disability check keeps his ex-wife and children clothed and fed. He, however, has nothing. But he shares his free food—a few two-day-old donuts—with a homeless family with small children.

A forest in a distant country disappears, chopped and burned to the ground so that the land may be used to fuel industrial production some-where across the globe. In the process, hundreds of species of plants and animals become extinct, and human and animal ways of life are forever altered. The barren land erodes, the nutrient rich soil, useful for growing crops, washes into the river and out into the ocean. The land becomes a desert, forces changes in the lifestyle of the people who are indigenous to the area, threatening their meager existence. Agricultural peoples are dispossessed of their land and forced into poverty and starvation by brutal and violent methods enforced by state militia so that powerful corpora-tions may raise cattle en masse and provide beef to a segment of the world's consumer market.

Tens of thousands migrate from their native lands, establishing make-shift living spaces on mountainsides. Cold and hungry, these people—men, women, and children, old and young—live in a desperate situation, the victims of violence, sniper fire, and unsanitary health conditions.

These are but a handful of the real and appalling images from *our* world that negatively impact human beings (and nature) and involve questions related to social justice. These are *real,* everyday images; they are not fantasies of our, your, or someone else's imaginations. They exist today and now; they have existed for a thousand yesterdays. Open your eyes, look around, and you will see them. Many exist in the city or area in which you live, within the bound-aries of "great," "economically superior" nations such as the United States or England. Others are hidden away in countries you rarely consider as being re-lated to your life. Each of these images is very distant from us *only* to the ex-tent that we refuse to recognize them as real and meaningful consequences of the way life is organized in modern social, political, and economic systems of production and consumption: as outcomes of class, race, and gender relations.

All of these images have two things in common. First, each depicts ways of life, behaviors, and actions that have been created by the types of social, eco-nomic, and political systems in which we live—systems of living we actively construct and reconstruct by the way we live. Second, these images are all ex-amples of social injustice. And it is only by seeing these injustices—by coming face to face with the realities that our modern way of life has created—that we can come to understand what social justice is and why there is a need to pro-mote it.

By social justice we mean two things. First, a society exhibits social justice when it (a) provides for the needs of the members of society and (b) when it treats its peoples in an equal manner. In turn, equal treatment implies that people are provided with more than quantitatively similar outcomes; they must be provided with similar opportunities and chances to choose from among a constellation of possible life paths, each of which is respected and valued (Carnoy, 1994; Lynch & Patterson, 1996). In this view, equal treatment is more than an ideology or belief that people should be treated equally. It is an outcome verifiable through observation (Ryan, 1982). These observations may be empirical or qualitative. Whatever method of assessing equality we choose, the method of observation must be constructed so that it is sensitive to the discovery of unequal treatment.

Second, when we examine societies that do not exhibit social justice, we cannot be satisfied simply to critique the injustice we see. We must seek solutions or find mechanisms that promote and generate social justice. In doing so, we ask ourselves a number of questions. How, for example, can we create a society where people do not go hungry? Where they can get honest, meaningful work that provides a decent standard of living when they want it? Where they can live in housing devoid of rats, lice, and vermin? Where people do not have to prey on one another, through "legitimate" and "illegitimate" means to gain economic security or generate status and feelings of self-worth? Where race, gender, and class do not affect their opportunities, life chances, life choices, and life course? These are the types of questions important to any discussion of social justice.

To be sure, these questions eclipse the study of criminal justice, and it is good that they do. Criminal justice is a subset of the issues that make up the domain of social justice. It is our contention that we cannot understand criminal justice unless we are willing to grapple with the larger questions and issues embedded within the meaning of the term *social justice*.

In the remainder of this chapter, a social justice perspective that draws on Marxian insights will be discussed. Before this can be done, however, we need to review some of the observations Karl Marx used to understand class-based societies and the types of alienation and exploitation found there. We will also update this view to include gender- and race-based considerations.

MARX: BACKGROUND AND ASSUMPTIONS

In this section, we review the history and assumptions Karl Marx used to examine society. We then use this material to discuss his view of social justice and the way this perspective has affected the responses to crime constructed by some criminologists.

Personal Background

Marx was born in Germany in 1818. His father, a "liberal," believed in the humanistic portion of the revolution in thought known as the French Enlightenment. The elder Marx was concerned with society's less fortunate, the inherently unfair disparities in wealth created by people, and principles of democratic governance. During this period, class conflicts (battles and riots between the owners of machinery and the laborers of such machinery) were commonplace. Monarchies were challenged and replaced. This was the world that influenced the young Marx's mind (Garaudy, 1966).

Marx began to work through the contradictions he saw in the world early in his university education. He consumed then rejected the views of the leading German philosopher of the day (Hegel) and, in so doing, created a theory of society that was an inversion of Hegelian philosophy. For Hegel, life was a working out of the problem of estrangement and absolute spirit. In Hegel's view, estrangement existed because people confronted objects as being outside themselves, as having an objective and independent existence. This was not a necessary condition of life but, rather, a misunderstanding of the relationship between people and objects. In fact, Hegel believed that things were not independent of people but that things existed in the mind. Things, in other words, were mental constructs, and one reason people were estranged from things was that they treated them as real and external objects. But, each person did not construct their own mental images. The mental image each person constructed reflected the images found in an ideal or "absolute" mind (similar to the view found in Plato's philosophy). In other words, the way we perceived things was a reflection of "the heavens" or an "absolute spirit"—the one mind in the universe that thinks and constructs perceptions. This view of things is also know as "objective idealism" (Joad, 1957).

Marx's System of Thought

In contrast to Hegel's idealism stands Marx's materialism. For the sake of simplicity, we divide Marx's system of thought into two parts: his assumptions about the material nature of society, which encompasses his economic theory, and his assumptions about human nature. We begin with Marx's economic perspective, turn to his views on human nature, and relate these to other questions such as alienation and social justice in a following section.

Marx's Economic Theory To begin, Marx rejected Hegel's view that the things we saw were mental constructs. In its place he substituted materialism, the idea that those things that exist are real (matter) and independent of people's minds. Thus, in contrast to Hegel's theory of history as thought, Marx created a theory of history based on real social (class) relationships. For Marx, these real social relationships were found first in *class,* which defined how people related to one another, and second in the conflicts between these classes. Thus, for Marx, class became one of the most important organizational features of society and a construct that would have to be addressed in any study related to human society.

Class was defined by a person's (or group's) relationship to the *means of production* and the *mode of production.* These three portions of Marx's theory—class, the mode of production, and the means of production—make up what is often referred to as the *infrastructure,* the economic base (system) of society. A society's infrastructure was important in Marx's view because it set the limits of the social system, often referred to as the *superstructure* of society. That is, Marx argued that each economic system was able to support a specific set of social relations. The way in which law, education, family and kinship networks, government, and even crime were organized was directly related to the way the economic system was organized. For this reason it is important to take a closer look at the different components that make up a society's economic system.

As we noted earlier, an economic system is composed of the mode, means, and relations of production. The mode of production defined the *kind* of economic system on which a society was built. For example, a society might be based on a feudal, mercantile, or capitalist system of producing. Each system contained *structural* forces or consistent organizational features that limited the way society was organized socially.

Each mode of production was also modified by the means of production peculiar to that society. The means of production defined *how* production was carried out in a society. For example, production could be machine based or technological, or it might be based on manual labor. A means of producing could also be defined in terms of agricultural or factory production. Thus, this would mean that there might be a difference between a capitalist system of agrarian (agricultural) production and a capitalist system of industrial production, which would explain differences between the social organization of nations.

How people related to the means of production defined their *class* position. For example, if a group controlled the means of production through ownership, they would be defined as the owning class. Under feudalism, in which production was land based, the owning class consisted of the lords and kings. Under capitalism, those who own factories and other *primary* means of production are defined as capitalists. Those who operated or worked the means of production were under the direct control of the owning class. In feudalism, not only were the serfs or working class directly controlled by the lords and kings; they were property, being part of the land possessed by the owning class. In a capitalist system, workers are still controlled by the owning class, although the control appears less pervasive.

Class relationships or class positions are important because they also indicate the amount of wealth and power possessed by different classes. Historically, economic power has always translated into political power, and the group that controls or owns the means of production also controls the rules and often the rulers (if they are not the rulers themselves!).

Although the economic system of a nation was important because it defined *how* people actually lived, it was unable to give us any clues as to the appropriateness of such forms of economic and social organization for human beings. In other words, examining social and economic organization does not, by itself, answer the question of whether these forms of organization are useful for achieving our human potential. To answer such a question, it is necessary to have a theory about human nature. The next section addresses Marx's theory of human nature.

Marx's Theory of Human Nature   One could argue that the most basic assumptions underlying Marxian theory are assumptions about human nature (for an overview, see Marx, 1964/1844). Marx felt that humans were social beings, produced, in some sense, by their surroundings. This means that our actions, thoughts, and feelings are at least partly determined by our relationship to others and the physical world in which we live. Marx also believed that humans were creative beings. Creativity was part of our unique human "essence," and it was this essence that separated us from other living creatures. Marx felt that as creative beings, we have a natural desire to use our creativity to produce objects through labor. Laboring—for ourselves and in a way determined by our own needs (defined socially)—is what made people human.

Unlike the position taken by objective idealists, Marx argued that to learn how people relate to each other, one must first examine how people relate to their material world. Marx believed that human labor was the median between individuals and the material world in which they live. Labor is, after all, the only means we have of creating what we can imagine from our physical surroundings. How we go about creating those things, however, may be different depending on when and where we live. Marx concluded that all people in all societies relate to their material environment via their labor; however, not all societies organized labor in the same way. For example, labor is organized differently in tribal societies, feudal societies, and capitalist societies. Thus, the people living in one type of society would go about obtaining items such as food and clothing much differently than individuals living in another type of society.

Marx pointed out that no matter how labor is organized in a society, that society still required rules and laws to bind people together, it still required government to supervise people, and it still required philosophy and religion to inspire people. Marx claimed that the way labor is organized influences superstructures in our society such as the types of law, the types of religion, the types of philosophy, and the type of government. It follows, then, that understanding how labor is organized within a given society would allow one to predict how the superstructures in that society are arranged (Marx, 1973/1857, 1984/1859, 1989). Thus, Marx believed that the organization of labor is meaningful because it lies at the very base of society. He called this foundation the "economic structure" or the "mode of production" (see previous section).

Finally, Marx also believed that we are cooperative beings and that we must work together to create the things we need to survive. Though these basic assumptions about human nature may seem far removed from a discussion about social justice, they are important concepts in Marxian theory and as such form the foundation for a discussion of social justice.

MARX AND SOCIAL JUSTICE

How do Marx's theories of society and human nature help us decide whether a society is unjust or, more important, help us prevent forms of social injustice from occurring? In this section we introduce three important concepts—alienation, exploitation, and marginalization—which Marx (1974/1867) used to demonstrate and discuss the effects of class inequality in a capitalist society. Taken together, we believe these terms are synonymous with the concept of social injustice.

Recall that one of Marx's most basic assumptions about human nature is that individuals are creative beings that need to show their creativity through labor and that we are social and cooperative beings that must work together to produce the things we need to survive. If we think about the way labor is organized in capitalist societies, we realize that some members of society must sell their labor to survive. For example, most of us must work for others so that we may purchase things like food, clothing, and shelter. When we exchange our labor for wages, the exchange is rather one-sided. In this exchange we do not, for example, retain the right to determine when we work, what we will produce, how much we are paid, or how we will produce it. In other words, we do not make the rules about working—such rules are made by employers. For Marx, such conditions of laboring were inherently *alienating* because they transformed the only thing we owned (our creativity, our labor) into an object that we must sell to another. In the process of selling our labor, we lose control of a significant activity that makes people human. For example, we can conjure up images of the uninterrupted toil of a laborer who mindlessly but quickly affixes bolts to unrecognizable pieces of machinery as they roll by at a steady, but speedy, pace on an endless conveyer belt. This worker has become alienated from that which is produced, unable to take satisfaction in his or her creation, perhaps having no knowledge of the end product. As Marx points out, in this way the working class is transformed into "mere appendages of flesh upon a machine of iron." While this image is certainly abhorrent it is how millions live and, it is without a doubt a form of social injustice.

As if alienation alone were not horrid enough, laborers in capitalist societies are simultaneously *exploited* by capitalists. Perhaps the best way to explain what Marx meant when he wrote about the "exploitation of the proletariat" is to explain another of his concepts: surplus value (for example, Marx, 1974/1867, pp. 312–531; Sweezy, 1942, pp. 56–74; Volkova & Volkov, 1986).

According to Marx, the value of a product is equivalent to the value of the raw materials, the tools and machinery used up, and the labor time required to create the product. If everything has a value equal to the sum of its parts, how do the capitalists make a profit? The answer is simple: the capitalists' profits comes from *unpaid labor.* The process of extracting unpaid labor from workers begins when workers, who have labor to sell and must sell that labor to survive in a capitalist system, enter into a contract with the capitalist, who purchases labor as a commodity. The "trick" that, so to speak, occurs here is that the capitalist, not the worker—the buyer, not the seller—defines the conditions of labor such as the length of the working day. This is important, because it is by redefining the working day that the capitalist is able to appropriate surplus value. The explanation of this phenomenon is as follows.

Left to their own or in a "natural" state, workers will produce as much as they need to sustain themselves (and their family unit) and will cease laboring when the day's task is completed. That is, generally workers will cease to labor when "*reproduction requirements*" (the minimal requirements necessary to sustain life in a given cultural context) have been met. Workers who have contracted with the capitalist to work an entire working day, however, cannot stop working at their own option because they are required by contract to work a minimum number of hours. Thus, even when workers have reached a point where they have produced what is needed for their survival, they must continue to work. The labor workers produce beyond what is required to sustain themselves, labor that goes to the capitalist, is called *surplus labor.* This free or surplus labor produces *surplus value* (the value beyond that required to replenish the worker and the materials of production). Surplus value is the source of profit for the capitalist. Thus, capitalists have every incentive to increase the surplus extracted from the labor process. The way this is done has important ramifications for workers and will be discussed more completely later. For the moment, we wish to finish our discussion of worker exploitation.

Marx argued that the degree of working-class exploitation could be measured by the *rate of surplus value,* which was defined by a ratio of paid to unpaid labor. The higher this ratio, the greater the exploitation of the worker. The current average rate of surplus value for manufacturing industries in the United States exceeds 400 percent. This means that workers currently produce commodities valued at more than four times the wages they receive. This extra value (the surplus) belongs to the capitalist, not the class who has produced it.

Many myths about worker productivity can be addressed by spending a few moments contemplating the meaning of this current rate of surplus value. For example, the current rate of surplus value for U.S. industries is *three times higher* than the 1954 rate (Perlow, 1988, pp. 45–50, 512). What this means is that U.S. workers produce *three times more* than they did forty years ago relative to the wages they are paid. They are also exploited, as we noted earlier, three times more. These figures indicate that, contrary to popular opinion, contemporary U.S. workers are *more productive* than their counterparts were forty years earlier.

A lack of productivity and profit is often cited, however, by U.S. corporations as a reason for moving plants and manufacturing to other nations. Yet, this is clearly not the case. American workers are very productive and also highly exploited. They are not, however, superexploited, as are workers in other nations where nonunionized (unorganized) laborers with lower reproductive expenses accept much lower wages than U.S. workers. We bring up this issue because, as we shall see later, this problem is central to questions of social justice. For the moment, we wish to return to the production of surplus value to round out our discussion.

The rate of surplus value can be increased in several ways. Under contemporary circumstances, the most important is the use of technology that intensifies human labor. Such technology replaces human labor with machine labor, making the remaining labor more efficient. As a result, fewer workers produce more goods, and the total value of the goods increases while the sum paid in wages decreases. This leads to an increase in the rate of surplus value. More important, every increase in the use of technology that replaces human labor creates a *surplus population* of unemployable laborers. In short, to increase profit, capitalists increase the rate of surplus value. The method for accomplishing this increase shrinks the available number of jobs and minimizes the ability of workers to obtain employment. As an example, we need only look at major industrial centers such as Detroit, once the center of the U.S. automotive industry. Not only have U.S. auto manufacturers moved production overseas to lower labor costs, but they have increasingly relied on technological innovations that replace human laborers. Giant machines rather than people build automobiles, and the unemployment rate in Detroit has skyrocketed.

The production of a surplus population is a widespread phenomenon in the United States. For example, between January 1993 and December 1995, the U.S. Bureau of Labor Statistics reported that 3.8 million workers were displaced from their jobs. This figure represents an increase in job displacement of 700,000 workers from the subsequent reporting period of January 1991 to December 1992. In the four-year period of January 1991 to December 1995, more than 7 million American workers lost their jobs. Some found better jobs, some equivalent jobs, some worse-paying jobs, and some remained unemployed in an economy with a shrinking number of career and trade opportunities. Income distributions from recent years also speak to the increase in the marginalization of the American public. By 1991, the lowest 20 percent of income earners—one of every five people—took home less than 5 percent of all the income earned. In contrast, the top 20 percent of income earners had to scrape by on the nearly 45 percent of the income they were able to take home (Reiman, 1995, pp. 27–30). The picture is even worse when disparities in wealth are at issue. For example, in 1988, the wealthiest 1 percent of people in the U.S. owned 42 percent of all wealth (Perlow, 1988, p. 52), leaving 58 percent of the wealth to be distributed—unevenly—among the remaining 99 percent of the population.

What is even more shocking is an examination of these figures with respect to race and gender. On average, African-American families earn about 64 percent of what white families earn (Carnoy, 1994), while the average woman makes about 70 percent what the average male is able to earn. Thus, the process of producing a surplus population of economic marginalized people clearly is most fully felt by minorities, the lower class, and women. And, to be sure, such wage, wealth, and employment differentials are the stuff of which social (in)justice is made. These are the kinds of issues that radicals have made central to their justice and crime reform platforms.

CRIMINAL "JUSTICE"
AND CLASS STRUGGLE

When we look at the criminal justice system, what do we see? Radicals see a
system of class control and oppression. One reason they see this picture is because they look at *who is controlled by this system and who is omitted from this form
of control*. Without a doubt, the criminal justice system controls the lower
classes. As Reiman (1995, p. 133) notes, about 45 percent of the U.S. prison
population was not employed full-time when arrested, and 69 percent earned
less than $10,000 in the year prior to their arrest. Inmates are over two-and-
one-half times more likely to earn less than $10,000 per year compared with
persons in the general population and four times more likely to be unemployed (Reiman, 1995, p. 134). The figures are even worse when comparisons
involve jail inmates and the general population (for example, Lynch & Groves,
1989, chapter 9). Clearly, then, jails and prisons seem to house the most economically marginal in our society (Goldfarb, 1969).

This story of who is controlled by criminal justice is also a story, often an
unread story, of who is omitted from this system of doing justice. The rich
and powerful, when they are controlled, are subjected to less stigmatizing rules
and regulations of agencies such as the Food and Drug Administration (FDA),
National Highway Traffic Safety Administration (NHTSA), the Environmental Protection Agency (EPA), Occupational Health and Safety Administration
(OHSA), Consumer Product Safety Commission (CPSC), and so on. These
administrative agencies rarely use the criminal penalties that some of them can
access to control corporate criminality. Many are staffed by people who were
once top executives in the industries they police and oppose regulation of corporate activities (Burkholz, 1994; Claybrook, 1984; Glantz, Slade, Bero,
Hanauer, & Barnes, 1996). Some, of course, claim that corporations are not
subject to the same social control practices because their behavior is less costly
and less violent than the activities of street criminals. Such an understanding
of corporate criminality is, to put it plainly, wrong. First, the costs of corporate crime are several times (minimally) higher than the costs of all street
crimes. Second, these crimes—which include but are not limited to such
things as the production and marketing of unsafe and deadly products and
drugs, unsafe and deadly working conditions, unsafe and deadly elimination of
chemicals and chemical products into illegal landfills, rivers, and streams—are
as, *if not more,* violent than ordinary one-on-one crimes of violence such as
homicide. Third, corporate violence is *more likely* than ordinary crime to reap
massive violence—that is, to have multiple victims (for example, Frank &
Lynch, 1992; Reiman, 1995; Simon & Eitzen, 1993). All of this means that
the poor and powerless are more likely to be punished, and punished severely,
for crimes that are less serious than those committed by the rich and powerful.

In sum, it is evident from what has been said so far that two systems of
doing justice operate in our nation: one for the poor and powerless, and one
for the rich and powerful. The connection between class and the ways in

which we do justice cannot be denied, nor, it seems, can the idea that criminal justice is part of the way class struggle is mediated. Beyond this, it might also be that different levels of power and wealth, different class positions, provide different motivation and opportunities to commit crime—and very different types of crime at that. In short, class seems to be associated with the way systems of social control *react* to people and the types of crime people commit. In other words, people's reactions to their situations, crime included, are structured in ways that affect the types of choices they are able to make (Groves & Frank, 1993).

RADICAL REFORM:
TOWARD SOCIAL JUSTICE

From the preceding discussion, it should be evident that when Marxists talk about social justice, they are talking about a broad set of ¡   ₃s that are grounded in economic relations. Also, it should be clear th₂   ₋ types of reforms preferred by Marxists will have a tendency to affec ₋rime and justice indirectly, through reform of economic relations. This preference, however, does not mean that those interested in the Marxist perspective must avoid making suggestions concerning the ways in which criminal justice and law can be reformed. Indeed, Marxist criminologists have made a number of important suggestions about such issues (for example, Michalowski, 1985, pp. 405–413; Platt, 1982a, 1985; Reiman, 1995, pp. 30–31, 179–194). In what follows, we examine several suggestions for achieving social justice. The first type is aimed at the broadest level of economic equality. The second is targeted at a more restricted level. The final issues addressed are, in some sense, the narrowest as they relate directly to crime and criminal justice.

Level 1

Earlier, we noted that social justice existed in a society when it both provides for the needs of the members of society and treats its people equally. Nations with high levels of poverty, unequal distributions of wealth, increasing homelessness and unemployment, variable rates of infant mortality or disease based on social class, variable dropout rates based on social class, and variable income levels dependent on race or gender, and so forth, are doing a *very poor job* of ensuring social justice. The United States, for example, ranks high on all of the dimensions noted here and thus can be said to have a very poor record of ensuring social justice for its citizens. This occurs despite legal and constitutional claims contained in important U.S. documents that supposedly assure social justice and equality regardless of race, class, or gender.

In addition to such obvious problems as these are the issues of social justice in relation to the exploitation and alienation of the workforce raised in previous sections of this chapter. These are the broadest social justice issues with which Marxists deal. How exactly are these conditions to be corrected?

Marx argued that social injustice would be addressed by members of the working class themselves when they arrived at that point in history where they understood how and in what ways they were exploited at work and alienated from their true status as human beings. When such conditions emerge, a blood revolution would occur designed to wipe the working class's oppressors from the face of the Earth.

The fact that such a revolution has *not* occurred in places like the United States does not mean that such a revolution will never occur. It simply means that either (a) the working class, taken as a whole, has never achieved the type of consciousness needed to generate a large-scale revolution or (b) specific key concerns have been addressed that have successfully forestalled revolution for the time being. Most certainly, key periods of worker revolt have occurred in the United States. These revolts have been suppressed by force through the use of police (Platt, 1982b) or, alternatively, have lost momentum through owner/worker concession. The conditions for further revolt still exist, however. These are evident in such measures as the rate of surplus value and the marginalization process discussed previously. Thus, one way to deal with this type of injustice is to create rules that govern profit taking by corporations, distribution of salaries within corporations, and even rules of ownership of corporations. For instance, worker-owned or cooperative businesses, in which laborers own, manage, control, and evenly distribute profits, would go a long, long way in diminishing the exploitation and alienation of the working class.

Level 2

The reforms just reviewed are broad-based reforms. More immediate and intermediate revisions can be made to improve social justice. Included here are what has been labeled as "affirmative action" plans. Today, affirmative action has a bad name and is seen as depriving white males of equal opportunity. Nothing could be further from the truth (Carnoy, 1994; Lynch & Patterson, 1996).

Over the past decade, women and African Americans have dramatically increased their educational levels and now have an educational attainment equivalent to that of white males. Yet, compared with white males, African Americans and women on average earn less in similar occupations, are fired more often, and generally occupy positions of lower prestige. The lack of economic power for these groups translates into a lack of political power also. Thus, there is an obvious need for programs that grant African Americans and women the same types of opportunities for success available to white males. "Affirmative action" plans such as these are the kind of immediate and intermediate reforms Marxists fashion when promoting social justice.

Level 3

To simplify this discussion, we will draw directly on materials from Reiman (1995, pp. 179–194). His reforms are not only useful but instructive in the ways in which they connect criminal justice reform to social justice.

For the most part, a cursory reading of Reiman's reforms sounds like the reforms that might be offered by any criminologist. They include such things as let the punishment fit the crime; legalize the production and sale of illegal drugs, and treat addiction as a medical problem; enact and enforce stringent gun control laws; develop correctional programs that promote rather than undermine personal responsibility and that enable inmates to become productive citizens; and narrow police and judicial discretion to promote equal treatment. These suggestions, however, are intimately connected to two additional conditions, without which the preceding reforms will have no effect. These additional conditions are (a) put an end to the crime-producing poverty in our midst, and (b) establish a more just distribution of income and wealth, making equal opportunity a reality for all Americans.

CONCLUSION

This chapter has addressed the most basic issues surrounding questions of social justice as situated within a Marxist perspective. Consequently, we have been unable to fully flesh out a complete program of radical social justice, and this chapter should not be considered a definitive discussion of these issues. Readers are instructed to review some of the materials cited within this chapter, listed in the reference section.

Further, we would also like to point out that we have not addressed a number of concerns that Marxists have added to the class-based theory that informs their position on society in recent years. In particular, this brief review has not addressed in any significant way issues of racial or gender oppression that currently structure the world (Schwartz & Milovanovic, 1996).

What we have laid out, then, are some perplexing and long-standing problems that relate to achieving social justice. The remaining problem is achieving social justice. We hope that some of you are motivated to take up this task.

REVIEW QUESTIONS

1. According to a radical criminologist, what is social justice? Is there a connection between criminal justice and social justice?

2. Pick one of the images presented in this chapter, and describe how that image relates to the issue of social justice.

3. Why is Marx's theory of surplus value important in discussing the issue of social justice?

4. Define the terms *alienation* and *exploitation,* explaining how these relate to the extraction (or rate) of surplus value.

5. Why are issues related to race, gender, and class important to considerations of social justice? Which of these has been emphasized by Marxists? In what ways are

Marxists attempting to include other issues related to social justice?

6. Discuss some policies that might be useful for reorganizing society so that life chances are both meaningful and more evenly distributed.

7. What are the relations of production? How does understanding the relations of production within a given society aid in examining and understanding social justice?

8. In this chapter, the authors make their commitment to radical beliefs quite evident. What are their beliefs? How do these beliefs affect

their conclusions? Do you think that other criminologists hold beliefs that affect the way they view the world?

9. Imagine some of the things you have witnessed in your life that violate your sense of social justice. Discuss these with your classmates in an open forum.

10. What assumptions did Marx make about human nature? How might these assumptions have affected his view of what was wrong with society?

REFERENCES

Burkholz, H. (1994). *The FDA follies*. New York: Basic Books.

Carnoy, M. (1994). *Faded dreams*. Cambridge: Cambridge University Press.

Claybrook, J. (1984). *Retreat from health and safety*. New York: Pantheon.

Frank, N., & Lynch, M. J. (1992). *Corporate crime, corporate violence*. Albany, NY: Harrow & Heston.

Garaudy, R. (1966). *Karl Marx: The evolution of his thought*. New York: International.

Glantz, S., Slade, J., Bero, L. A., Hanauer, P., & Barnes, D. E. (1996). *The cigarette papers*. Berkeley: University of California Press.

Goldfarb, R. (1969, November). Prisons: The nation's poorhouses. *New Republic, 15–17*.

Groves, W. B., & Frank, N. (1993). Punishment and structured choice. In G. R. Newman, M. J. Lynch, & D. Galaty (Eds.), *Discovering criminology*. Albany, NY: Harrow & Heston.

Joad, C. E. M. (1957). *Guide to philosophy*. New York: Dover.

Lynch, M. J., & Groves, W. B. (1989). *Primer in radical criminology*. Albany, NY: Harrow & Heston.

Lynch, M. J., & Patterson, E. B. (1996). Thinking about race and criminal justice: Racism, stereotypes, politics, academia and the need for context. In M. J. Lynch & E. B. Patterson (Eds.), *Justice with prejudice* (pp. 1–18). Albany, NY: Harrow & Heston.

Marx, K. (1964). *The economic and philosophic manuscripts of 1844*. New York: International. (Original work published 1844)

Marx, K. (1973). *Grundrisse*. New York: Vintage. (Original work published 1857)

Marx, K. (1974). *Capital. Vol. 1*. New York: International. (Original work published 1867)

Marx, K. (1984). *Critique of political economy*. New York: International. (Original work published 1859)

Marx, K. (1989). *Precapitalist economic formations*. New York: International.

Michalowski, R. (1985). *Order, law, and crime: An introduction to criminology*. New York: Random House.

Mills, C. W. (1959). *The sociological imagination.* New York: Oxford University Press.

Perlow, V. (1988). *Super profits and crises.* New York: International.

Platt, T. (1982a). Crime and punishment in the United States: Immediate and long term reforms from a Marxist perspective. *Crime and Social Justice, 18,* 38–45.

Platt, T. (1982b). *The iron fist and the velvet glove.* San Francisco: Synthesis.

Platt, T. (1985). Criminology in the 1980s: Progressive alternatives to law and order. *Crime and Social Justice, 21/22,* 191–199.

Reiman, J. (1995). *The rich get richer and the poor get prison.* Boston: Allyn & Bacon.

Ryan, W. (1982). *Equality.* New York: Vintage.

Schwartz, M. D., & Milovanovic, D. (Eds.). (1996). *Race, gender and class in criminology.* New York: Garland.

Simon, D. R., & Eitzen, D. S. (1993). *Elite deviance.* Boston: Allyn & Bacon.

Sweezy, P. M. (1942). *The theory of capitalist development.* New York: Modern Paperback Readers.

Volkova, T., & Volkov, F. (1986). *What is surplus value?* Moscow: Progress.

Ward, B. (1973). *The radical economic world view.* New York: Basic Books.

Socialist Feminist Criminology and Social Justice

S ocialist feminism is one of several feminist approaches to the study of crime. Similar to Marxist thought, it examines the economic arrangements in a capitalist society that give rise to social inequality. In addition, however, socialist feminists study how the organization of capitalism is saturated within a male culture. According to representatives of the theory, these organizing principles result in male dominance over women, a patriarchal system of social and economic inequality, and a gendered form of crime and justice. Jurik's chapter explores several of the basic assumptions and principles of socialist feminist thought. It also includes summaries of related feminist analyses both supportive and opposed to the socialist feminist agenda in criminology and other disciplines. Jurik maintains that socialist feminists specifically call for the elimination of capitalism and patriarchy. Social justice requires a dramatic rethinking of how social institutions function and how interpersonal relationships unfold. In this regard, social justice is not an end point or a variation of criminal justice but rather a starting point from which to address the gendered dimensions of law, crime, and deviance.

2

Socialist Feminism, Criminology, and Social Justice

NANCY C. JURIK

As one of several "feminist" approaches, socialist feminism has been highly influential both as a theory and as a movement. Socialist feminism identifies two equally important sources of women's systematic subordination to men in Western society: (1) the economic organization of capitalism and (2) the cultural system of patriarchy that produces men's dominance over women. Socialist feminist work has generated an interest in the interplay between economic arrangements and gender relations in framing social inequality.

Over the past three decades, the study of women, crime, and law has exploded onto the criminological scene. Although rarely the focus of explicit discussion within criminology, socialist feminist concerns have inspired feminist analyses of the relationships among gender, class, race-ethnicity, criminality, victimization, and law. Socialist feminist–inspired research pushes criminology beyond its often narrow criminal/legal justice focus to address broader concerns of social and economic justice for women and men alike.

This chapter describes the history and contribution of socialist feminism to the study of crime, law, and social justice. It begins with a historical overview of the perspective, and then turns to discussion of basic theoretical assumptions and principles. Examples from social science research on crime, law, and criminal justice further elaborate the principles of socialist feminist theory. A critique of this theory provides the background for understanding recent moves away from it as a total explanation of crime and gender justice. The conclusion highlights the continuing implications of socialist feminism for understanding criminal and social justice.

For purposes of presentation, this chapter presents socialist feminism as a more or less unified approach. However, it also acknowledges the diversity and conflict that have always been part of socialist feminist theorizing. The discussion reveals the considerable overlap between socialist feminism and other theories, both feminist and nonfeminist.

Thanks to Gray Cavender, Julie Cowgill, Marjorie Zatz, and Belinda Herrera for their helpful suggestions on earlier drafts. Thanks also to Meda Chesney-Lind, James Messer-schmidt, and Natalie Sokoloff for helpful conversations about this project.

In this chapter, studies and theories are cited as examples when their themes generally are consistent with those of socialist feminism. The authors of each study do not necessarily refer to their approach as socialist feminist.

HISTORY OF SOCIALIST FEMINISM AND SOCIALIST FEMINIST CRIMINOLOGY

A history of socialist feminism requires some background on the women's movement. This review will focus on U.S. feminist history; however, similar movements occurred in England and Europe at about the same time (see Humm, 1992).

Women's Movement

The first women's movement, referred to as first wave feminism, occurred in the late nineteenth and early twentieth centuries. First wave feminism grew out of the movement to abolish slavery (Davis, 1981) and activism to help the poor (Freedman, 1981). Although initially directed at a range of issues affecting women, first wave feminism came to focus primarily on political rights, especially gaining women the right to vote. After women gained suffrage in 1920, the movement subsided. However, writings from this movement inspired leaders of a second wave of feminism, which began about 1967.

The 1960s was a period of economic boom that stimulated increasing expectations for success and achievement for all. Related to these expectations, it was also an era of declining birth rates and postponement of marriage. This social and economic climate contributed to women's sense of relative disadvantage when they compared themselves with men. Second wave feminism emerged during this period. It drew its initial membership from women working in the civil rights, student, and antiwar movements of the 1960s. Women gained an increased sense of political efficacy from their work in these progressive social movements but were denied power and leadership positions. Women asked that the fight against women's oppression be included as part of movement goals and that they be allowed to assume more leadership roles. In 1967 and 1968, after their demands were repeatedly rejected, many white women (and some women of color) left antiwar and civil rights activities to form women-only consciousness-raising groups. The women's liberation movement grew out of these gatherings (Echols, 1989).

Although sharing a common desire to overcome women's systematic subordination to men, the women's movement was composed of different and often conflicting segments. Liberal feminists focused on extending to women the same formal legal rights as those of men, including the equal opportunity to compete with men in existing social, economic, and political institutions. They formed the National Organization for Women (NOW) and worked toward the passage of an Equal Rights Amendment (ERA) to the U.S. Constitution. Radical feminists believed that only the extensive transformation of major societal institutions could eliminate women's subordination (Firestone, 1970).

However, divisions also emerged within radical feminism about the primary causes of women's oppression and whether feminists should continue to work with male-dominated leftist movements. Initially, two principal divisions emerged within radical feminism: "feminists" and "politicos." Feminists focused more on the personal dimensions of women's oppression and on the active role of men and male-dominated institutions in maintaining that oppression. They emphasized personal and cultural avenues for change. Politicos charged that feminists focused too much on male-female interpersonal dynamics and neglected structural forces of oppression like capitalism and imperialism. Although they felt betrayed and undermined by male radicals, politicos embraced the analysis of the New Left and continued to work as activists against the Vietnam War. They explicitly rejected the contention of feminists that feminism was an inherent critique of class relations and that women's liberation included socialism (Philipson & Hansen, 1990).

Although they disagreed on many issues, feminists and politicos shared many projects, including work for abortion on demand, battered women's shelters, and free, quality child care (Philipson & Hansen, 1990).

Emergence of Marxist Feminism and Socialist Feminism

Politicos, also termed Marxist feminists, at first emphasized that women's oppression was an outgrowth of class exploitation under capitalism. They drew their analysis from arguments by Karl Marx (1967) and Frederich Engels (1972) that women's subordination originated with the development of private property and men's control over it. This analysis suggested that capitalist expansion would eventually force all women into full-time labor force participation. The incorporation of women into the workforce would lead to the demise of the nuclear family. The disappearance of family demands would make men and women workers equal. Equality would cause men and women to recognize their common predicament as workers and to unite in the overthrow of capitalism (Zaretsky, 1976).

Gradually, some Marxist feminists concluded that prioritizing capitalism over patriarchy as the source of women's oppression was wrong. They observed that in socialist societies in Latin America and Eastern Europe the elimination of capitalism had not meant the end of patriarchy (Bengelsdorf & Hageman, 1979; Stacey, 1979). They also doubted that capitalism would lead to the disintegration of the family or that it would automatically end women's subordination to men. They tried to develop a theory to bridge Marxism with feminism and a social movement to unite socialist and women's liberation groups. Their socialist feminist perspective emphasized the dual roots of women's subordination: the economic organization of capitalism and the cultural organization of patriarchy (Eisenstein, 1977, 1979; Hartmann, 1976; Jaggar, 1983; Mitchell, 1971; Sokoloff, 1980; Young, 1989).

Between 1969 and 1975, socialist feminists formed seventeen women-only independent community organizations ("unions") in several major U.S. cities (Hansen, 1986). These unions produced both socialist feminist scholarship and activism. Their activism focused on unionizing women workers and developing alternative women's institutions (for example, women's health collectives, abortion/contraceptive counseling centers, domestic violence shelters).

A general decline of leftist movements in the 1970s and divisions within the socialist feminist community led to the end of women's unions around 1976 (Hansen, 1986). Many members who were women of color felt that the unions were dominated by white feminist concerns. Lesbian feminist members felt oppressed by the focus on relations with men and assumptions of heterosexuality among members (Combahee River Collective, 1979). Union members were disillusioned by the failure to recruit significant numbers of working-class women to their ranks. Despite the end of its activist heyday, socialist feminism remained a viable theory in the fields of sociology, women's studies, and criminology. However, in the 1980s, the fall of socialism in Eastern Europe, the wave of conservatism in the United States and Western Europe, and continuing conflicts within feminism caused the decline of socialist feminism as an explicit and distinct form of feminist theorizing (Eisenstein, 1990; Smart, 1995).

Socialist Feminism and Criminology

Within criminology, socialist feminism emerged as an influential perspective in the late 1970s. Until the mid-1970s, criminology and criminal justice were overwhelmingly dominated by studies about the etiology of and response to men's crimes. Even perspectives critical of mainstream "positivist" criminology (such as labeling and Marxist theories of crime) continued to ignore women's criminality and victimization (Messerschmidt, 1993).

Beginning in the mid-1970s, feminist-inspired analyses drew attention to the neglect of women and the bias in male-centered theories of crime and criminal justice (Smart, 1976). Early notoriety came with liberal feminist research on purported changes in the criminality of women (Adler, 1975; Simon, 1975). These studies posited an association among the women's liberation movement, changes in employment opportunities available to women, and reported increases in the frequency and severity of women's crimes. The media hype surrounding liberal feminist research on women's liberation and female criminality converged with an increasing number of scholarly attacks on mainstream criminology to generate a wave of research on women criminals and victims (see Cavender, 1995; Daly & Chesney-Lind, 1988). This research included radical feminist critiques of both male-centered and liberal feminist criminologies (Klein, 1973; Rafter & Stanko, 1982; Smart, 1976). Radical feminist critiques concentrated on the effects of patriarchy on women's crime and victimization (Dobash & Dobash, 1979; Stanko, 1985). Other critiques were informed by both radical feminist theory and Marxist-inspired radical criminology. These studies focused on the effects of capitalist political-economic organization and class exploitation on women's criminality and victimization (Klein & Kress, 1976; Schwendinger & Schwendinger, 1983).

Gradually, feminist criminologists systematically integrated concerns about class and gender into their work (Rafter & Natalizia, 1982). Some socialist feminist criminologists were activists in New Left and socialist feminist unions (Cavender, 1996; Klein & Kress, 1976). Within criminology, socialist feminist ideas informed empirical research and theorizing up until the late 1980s, but a socialist feminist theory of crime was not formally introduced until 1986 (Messerschmidt, 1986). Like other New Left social movements and early socialist feminist unions, socialist feminist criminologists focused on the integration of theory and practice to build a more just society.

By the early 1990s, some criminologists and legal scholars recommended a move away from socialist feminism and toward newer approaches (Messerschmidt, 1993; Smart 1984). Despite its decline as an explicit feminist approach, socialist feminist principles continued to inform research in criminology and law (see Danner, 1996).

MAJOR ASSUMPTIONS
OF SOCIALIST FEMINISM

Like other theories, socialist feminism includes implicit and sometimes unstated arguments—that is, assumptions. Socialist feminists make assumptions about human nature, the relationship between individuals and society, the best methods for knowing about the world, the role of values in social theory, the likelihood of worldly progress, and the relationship between law and justice.

Like Marx, socialist feminists assume that human character is socially and historically determined. The economic organization of society, its mode of production (feudal, capitalist, socialist), form societal institutions such as family, religion, and government. These institutions and one's location in the organization of production (as a wage worker or owner/capitalist) determine human consciousness and behavior.

Historical changes in the organization of production gave rise to changes in social institutions and human character. Marx referred to this perspective as historical materialism. Historical materialism implied that the observable character of human beings emerged from economic change and development throughout history; human character was not inherent in the genetic composition of human beings.

Marx and Engels argued that production and reproduction were central to understanding society. However, neither fully discussed the dual role of production and reproduction as determining factors in history. Focusing on production and class relations, they treated reproduction and gender relations as derived from class relations. They described the division of labor between men and women in society as "natural."

Socialist feminists believe that the social organization of reproduction is just as important as the mode of production in shaping social institutions and human consciousness. Men dominate women's reproductive labor through the system of patriarchy. Reproductive labor includes giving birth to children as well as child rearing and other unpaid household labor necessary to "reproduce" the workforce of society. Patriarchal beliefs dictate that women are responsible for most reproductive tasks. In contrast to Marx, who assumed that divisions of labor between men and women were natural, socialist feminists assume that these arrangements were *socially constructed*. Marx had often critiqued other social ideologies for accepting existing arrangements as "natural" and therefore inevitable. Socialist feminists drew on this Marxian critique to question the fairness of the existing gender division of labor.

Thus, for socialist feminists, women are *made*, not born. The productive and reproductive relations in society determine individual identity. Some socialist feminists rely on gender role theory to explain the transmission of patriarchal values to individuals. These roles are the outgrowth of power relations in patriarchal capitalist societies. Gender identity is produced by childhood socialization patterns common to male-dominated capitalist societies: boys learn to be aggressive and competitive; girls learn to be passive and nurturing. Accordingly, individuals learn socially approved feminine and masculine roles. Some socialist feminists rely on psychoanalytic methods to explain how women and men unconsciously channel natural drives for self-fulfillment but instead learn to accept and behave in ways that accord with male dominance. Even these perspectives, which allow for some notion of inherent biological or psychological drives, view gender inequality as socially created rather than inborn. Capitalism and patriarchy enslave women and prevent them from realizing their potential as productive and creative human beings.

Socialist feminists assume that societal notions of gender roles are widely disseminated and accepted throughout society. Their theories imply that women share a common position of disadvantage, which gives them unique insights into the problems of capitalism and patriarchy. Thus, socialist feminists seek to understand women's standpoint and use it to inform their theory and activism.

Socialist feminists borrow their methodology for investigating the human condition from both Marx and radical feminists. They apply Marx's dialectical approach to trace how tensions and contradictions in the systems of reproduction and production have led to corresponding changes in class and gender relations over time. Like radical feminists, they rely on women's consciousness-raising for insights into women's common experience of exploitation and oppression.

Socialist feminists reject views that theory should or could be value neutral. They use Marx's concept of praxis to argue for the merging of theory with practice. Socialist feminists seek to go beyond understanding women's position; they aim to improve it.

Implicit in their merging of theory and practice is a belief, also drawn from Marxism and radical feminism, that society can and will evolve toward a more just system. Socialist feminists believe that a total theory of class and gender oppression is essential for the struggle to move society toward class and gender equality.

Clearly, the socialist feminist vision of justice references more than simple obedience to formal legal codes. Socialist feminists are highly critical of legalistic views of justice. A just society can only be accomplished through the elimination of both capitalism and patriarchy and through the radical transformation of social institutions and relationships.

PRINCIPLES OF SOCIALIST FEMINISM

Our historical overview and discussion of assumptions prepares us for a presentation of the major principles of socialist feminist theory. A later section will apply these principles to the study of crime, law, and criminal justice.

The major argument of socialist feminist theory is that gender inequality is caused by exploitative systems of production and reproduction. Thus, capitalism and patriarchy converge to produce gender inequality.

Patriarchy emerged in precapitalist horticultural societies in which a male head had authority over the family, including the work and marriages of its members. Although in precapitalist societies a gender division of labor already existed, the household was the center of production. With the development of capitalist industrialization and the emergence of wage labor, capitalism interacted with patriarchy to produce some important changes in class and gender relations. As capitalists organized mass production, the factory and not the home became the production center. Initially, everyone (men, women and children) went out to work, but gradually workers, social reformers, and even some capitalists argued for the removal of women and children from the harsh, dangerous conditions of factory life. Male-controlled unions fought for and won "protective legislation" that restricted or removed women and child laborers from factory jobs. Capitalists eventually agreed to pay men a "family wage" that would be large enough to support their wives and children. The family wage designated men as the sole breadwinners and satisfied capitalists' desires for a more stable, healthy workforce. Despite the widespread ideology that all men could earn enough to keep their wives at home, many nonunionist whites, men of color, and men in Third World countries never received a family wage.

Women were exploited because they provided free, reproductive labor in their homes. Their labor advantaged men and the capitalist system. This labor of childbearing, child rearing, and other household work reproduced the workforce by providing care for present and future workers (that is, husbands and children). Reproductive labor was often unnoticed or viewed as insignificant by husbands, children, and capitalists. Women's primary responsibility for reproductive labor either kept them out of, or minimized their opportunities in, the public world of paid work and politics.

Socialist feminists note that women were denied control over their sexuality and reproduction. Men's control of these domains was accomplished through social institutions and the constant threat of male violence. Economic pressures due to low wages and restricted employment opportunities and social, cultural, and legal regulations pressured women to seek men's protection in heterosexual, monogamous, nuclear families. Laws limited women's access to effective contraception and abortion.

Patriarchal ideologies about women's domestic responsibilities also shaped women's paid labor in the productive sphere. Women were defined by their reproductive roles so that their paid employment often mirrored the support, service, and caregiving roles that they so long assumed at home. They were paid less because this "help" and "support" work was viewed as less skilled than work that men typically did. Women's paid work was also viewed as secondary to that of men. These ideologies emerged from the gendered division of productive and reproductive labor and justified paying women lower wages than those of men.

The undervaluing of women's paid labor also allowed capitalists to keep men's wages low by threatening to hire women to replace them. This threat occurred throughout the history of industrialization and served to promote men's antagonism toward working women. Men often bound together to keep women out of unions and out of traditionally male jobs. Management has used men's fears of being replaced by women workers to deny raises or to extract other concessions. Socialist feminists emphasize the collection and analysis of women's experience as essential for elaborating the workings of capitalism and patriarchy in contemporary society. Women's experiences were typically ignored by male-dominated activists and social scientists. Borrowing from Marx's discussion of workers as the revolutionary class and from radical feminists' emphasis on consciousness-raising, socialist feminists regard women's standpoint as the best start for developing a revolutionary consciousness and analysis. However, their analysis does not stop with women's experiences; it includes a historical analysis of societal economic organization and institutions that gave rise to women's experiences.

Socialist feminists differ on the amount of autonomy that they accord the systems of patriarchy and capitalism. Some argue that patriarchy is a cultural manifestation of economic inequality; a second group believes that capitalism and patriarchy are two autonomous but mutually influencing economic systems; a third group argues that capitalism and patriarchy are two sides of a single economic system that exploits women. Regardless of the exact relationship between them, patriarchy and capitalism are fundamental causes of women's subordination.

Socialist feminists acknowledge racism as a third system of oppression working with capitalism and patriarchy. They argue that racist and imperialist ideologies serve to further stratify both patriarchy and capitalism and thereby to divide workers. Although they always acknowledge it as important, socialist feminists have never sufficiently developed the analysis of racism or fully integrated it into their theory.

Socialist feminist–inspired criminology focuses on the dual effect of class and gender relations in framing criminality, criminal justice, law, and resulting social injustices. Like Marxist and other critical criminologists, socialist feminists challenge theories that explain crime as the outgrowth of individual genetics or psychology. They analyze crimes as the outgrowth of social and economic inequalities within patriarchal capitalist society. Even individual motivations for crime—which might include economic need, acquisitiveness, insecurity, selfishness, anger, a desire for excitement, resistance, or rebellion—are linked back to cultural manifestations of capitalism and patriarchy.

Socialist feminists argue that criminal justice responses to victims have been shaped by the class, gender, and race of the victim and criminal. The criminal justice system is riddled with patriarchal views of women, especially lower-class women and women of color.

Law is also viewed by socialist feminists to be heavily influenced by class and gender interests. Like the criminal justice system, law tends to protect the position of elite, white males. The standpoints of women and the poor are typically ignored or misinterpreted.

Socialist feminist analyses of law and criminal justice require that they attend to the role of the State (federal, state, and local government) within patriarchal and capitalist societies. Some socialist feminist analyses assume that the State was simply the reflection of capitalist and patriarchal interests, while others describe the State as also having the power to shape patriarchy and capitalism. They show that the State constitutes a powerful interest group with its own dynamics. The application of socialist feminism to the study of crime, criminal justice, and law will be considered in the next section.

MARXIST AND SOCIALIST FEMINIST CRIMINOLOGY APPLICATIONS

Appearing in the late 1970s and early 1980s, Marxist feminist criminological writings were precursors to socialist feminist criminology. Marxist feminist scholars seek to incorporate some of the ideas of radical feminism into radical or Marxist criminology. Marxist criminology draws on the political, philosophical, and economic analyses of Marx (see Zeitlin, 1967) and Engels (1972), as well as the work by Willem Bonger (1916), the first scholar to apply Marxist ideas to criminology.

In one of the first Marxist feminist analyses, Klein and Kress (1976) examined women's "unique economic and social position" in modern capitalist society. They described women's position as "rooted in the sexual and maternal aspect of female life" (p. 35). Another Marxist feminist analysis by Balkan, Berger, and Schmidt (1980) described women's crime and victimization as the outgrowth of gender role socialization processes that occur in capitalist society. Schwendinger and Schwendinger (1983) linked the extent and nature of rape to changes in economic conditions and class struggles across the history of Western capitalist societies.

Davis's (1981) Marxist feminist analysis of rape demonstrated the differences in legal recognition of rape along racial lines. The history of slavery shaped images of African-American women and men that differed from images of white women and men. Black men and women were not allowed to marry or form traditional families. Moreover, to extract the greatest possible profit from the labor of slaves, black women were exempted from myths of feminine delicacy and purity. Slaveholders often described black women as "loose women" and "whores." Black men were portrayed as excessively virile and as desiring the slave master's woman. These images shaped popular and criminal justice perceptions of rape. Davis argued that rape charges have been indiscriminately aimed at black men, guilty and innocent alike. In contrast, white masters' rapes of black women, which were part of the sexual coercion and economic domination of U.S. slavery, were rarely recognized by the criminal justice system. Davis criticized feminist scholarship (for example, Brownmiller, 1976) for accepting and perpetuating the myth that black men most often rape white women. Feminists also failed to analyze the distinct situation of black women victims of rape. Davis revealed the unconscious racism that permeated many feminist analyses of rape.

Marxist feminist criminologists were criticized for using overly deterministic models of the mode of production's effect on individual behavior, on the State, and on other social institutions (Messerschmidt, 1986). Some feminists charged that Marxist feminist criminologists failed to devote enough attention to the analysis of patriarchy and women's reproductive roles (Dahl, 1987). Patriarchy became a simple offshoot of the class relations of production.

A unifying theme of socialist feminist–inspired criminological and legal studies is a more equal emphasis on class and gender relations for understanding crime, law, and criminal justice. Subject matter for socialist feminist analyses includes research on the criminality of women and men, women's victimization, the gendered nature of law, and the treatment of women in the criminal justice system. In the following section are several applications of socialist feminist analyses to each of these areas. The implications of this scholarship for understanding social justice will be considered at the end of this section.

Linking Crime and Criminal Justice
to Patriarchy and Capitalism

Messerschmidt (1986) has provided the most explicit and formal statement of a socialist feminist theory of crime. He aims to explain the crimes of men and women who are members of different classes. He argues that reproduction and production are equally important in structuring society and individuals. The gendered division of labor gave rise to differing patterns of gender role socialization and thus to unique masculine and feminine identities. Masculine character structure requires self-confidence, independence, competitiveness, a drive for dominance, aggressiveness, and even violence; feminine character structure demands patience, understanding, sensitivity, passivity, dependence, nurturance, and nonviolence (p. 40). These character differences prepare women and men for the different types of labor that they have to perform.

Gender-based divisions of labor and personalities converged with class-based opportunities to determine the frequency, nature, and motivation of crimes that men and women commit. Elite men have the greatest opportunity to commit the most socially harmful crimes. These include white-collar and corporate crimes such as price fixing, toxic waste, and the production and marketing of dangerous products. Elite men's motivations for crimes include competitive pressures, aggressiveness, and a drive for dominance. Working-class men have fewer opportunities to commit corporate crimes with large-scale harm but plenty of opportunity to commit street crimes such as violent assault, hustling, theft, or property damage. Their motivations include frustration, a sense of economic deprivation, and economic need. At times, they vent anger and frustration or seek dominance by victimizing women.

Messerschmidt (1986) argues that women are more heavily supervised and controlled; few women occupy positions of corporate power. Thus, in contrast to men, women have less opportunities for either street or corporate criminal opportunities. Given women's subordinated and isolated position, they tend to commit less serious crime such as nonviolent theft (for example, shoplifting, fraud) or prostitution. These crimes are an outgrowth of societal roles and economic opportunities for women. Miller (1986) uses an analysis of class struggle and patriarchal relations to explore the experiences of women engaged in criminal hustling activity like prostitution. An analysis of the impact of federal and local policies on women and their criminality is an important component of Miller's work. She explains increases in U.S. women's criminal hustling activity as the result of economic conditions and government policies that worsened the position of women during the 1970s and 1980s. Single women of color with children are the most severely disadvantaged and the most visible in Miller's observations of street hustling. She argues that the women hustle to generate income; it is a form of work for them. However, their hustling *labor* is still heavily controlled by men. Thus, patriarchal relations, capitalism, and State policies frame women's work/crime activities.

In her analysis of the criminal careers of thirty-nine British women, Carlen (1988) also attributes apparent increases in women's criminality to the increased poverty of women during the era of Thatcher economics and social policy. Many of the women in her sample had been battered, sexually victimized, and/or economically disadvantaged as children. These experiences converged with their early imprisonment to minimize their hope of obtaining the womanly benefits of the love or labor of a male breadwinner. They had less to lose when using crime as a solution to their economic or emotional needs.

State policy also figures prominently in Carlen's analysis. She argues that different modes of social regulation produce differences in women and men's criminality and in criminal justice responses to their offenses. "When women do break the law, those from lower socio-economic groups are more liable to criminalization than are their middle class sisters" (p. 5).

Women's Victimization

Feminist analyses of women's victimization have covered issues of sexual harassment, rape, domestic violence, and child abuse. Socialist feminist analyses direct attention to the interplay between capitalism and patriarchy in women's victimization experiences and in official responses to them.

In a later, more socialist feminist work, Klein (1982) analyzes wife battering as the extreme end of a continuum of inequality in heterosexual marriage. She argues that this arrangement is the outgrowth of the historical interplay between patriarchy and capitalism. Historical changes from feudalism to capitalism moved the center of production from the home to the factory. Although these changes gradually brought more political rights for women, they also meant the increasing privatization and isolation of family and home life. While many poor women work full-time, family ideals center on housewives as nurturers and consumers, and husbands as breadwinners. Correspondingly low wages for women reinforce women's economic dependence on men. Cultural images of women as sexually vulnerable or as nagging wives are widely disseminated by the media. These conditions, combined with the frustrations experienced by many men in the workplace, make battering behavior a frequent effect of the social relations of women's domination. Klein emphasizes that battering is not simply the aberrant manifestation of psychopathic individuals. It is an extreme but recognizable outcome of life in patriarchal capitalist society.

Davis (1993) offers a structural analysis of the victimization of young homeless girls and its implications for the social control of women. She traces homeless girls' high rate of victimization to contemporary gender, age, social class, and race–ethnic relations. Recent economic crises, urban dislocation of the poor, feminization of poverty, increased restrictions and punitiveness in social welfare, and public and police concerns with law and order have heightened both the likelihood of homelessness and the danger faced by homeless women and girls. Davis argues that homeless girls are increasingly the victims of street violence, theft, and police harassment. Economic conditions of inflation and deteriorating job opportunities, and the fear of victimization, also force many girls and women to remain in homes where they are being victimized.

Davis's analysis elaborates the role of the State in dealing with the victimization of homeless girls. State efforts to intervene ultimately fail because of (1) an inadequate investment of state resources, (2) a focus on individual rather than systemic change as the solution to homelessness, and (3) the State's ultimate support of the patriarchal relations and privacy within the family.

A Black Socialist Feminist Approach

Rice (1990) has criticized feminist criminology for its unified description of "women's experience," suggesting a broader socialist feminist approach to consider the effects of gender, class, and race simultaneously. She describes black women as the "dark figures" of criminology: their experiences have been overshadowed by attention to white women and black men. Other women of color and women from developing countries also have been noticeably absent from the past two decades of feminist criminology.

Feminist criminologists' descriptions of femininity have failed to recognize the historical and contemporary differences in the cultural experiences and socialization patterns between black and white women. Black women have more often been single, heads of households, and had to adopt corresponding traits of independence and self-reliance that were not as necessary for middle-class, married white women. Despite assertions that women have been imprisoned more for their different and unacceptable lifestyles than for their criminal records, few feminist criminologists have analyzed how this generalization might uniquely affect black and white women. Rice also criticizes feminist criminologists' assertions that women's crimes are infrequent and of trivial nature. She argues that these generalizations are not necessarily true of black women. Although white feminists have noted the high rates of criminal victimization among black women, they have failed to sufficiently analyze the degree to which attacks on black women have been related to racism as well as to sexism.

White feminist criminology has treated all women as equally oppressed and all men as uniformly oppressive. Rice (1990) calls for more dynamic models of the relations between oppressors and oppressed in racially structured, patriarchal, capitalist societies. The significance of race and racism must be integral to feminist criminological analysis.

Applications Summary

The examples discussed in this section connected women's experiences of law and the criminal justice system to life in patriarchal, capitalist, and racist societies. In addition to making class, gender, and race-ethnic relations central, they also question historically taken-for-granted concepts in the study of crime and criminal justice. They challenge images of offenders as clearly distinct from victims, of the family as a safe haven, and of the law as offering protection or neutral mediation.

In addition, these studies have highlighted the importance of systematic analyses of the State's law-making and law-enforcing activities and its integral links to patriarchy and capitalism. They have shown that the State is seldom a neutral mediator or protector of women, nor is it merely a disseminator of the "people's will." In socialist feminist analyses, the State has increasingly been viewed as more than a simple reflection of capitalist interests. Along the lines of post-Marxian critical theories, the State has also been portrayed as exerting its own determining influence on the economic organization of society (Scranton, 1990).

A central theme in these analyses, and of socialist feminism more generally, has been that problems of crime, law, and criminal justice cannot be solved without attention to broader social justice concerns. Social justice ultimately requires the elimination of capitalism, patriarchy, and racism through the systematic transformation of major institutions and of citizens themselves (Cain, 1990; Rice, 1990).

CRITIQUES OF SOCIALIST FEMINISM
AND CONTEMPORARY TRENDS

Socialist feminism has been instrumental in integrating concerns about gender and economic inequality into feminist scholarship on crime, law, and criminal justice. However, during the 1980s, criticisms of socialist feminism mounted to the point that many concluded it was no longer a viable framework for feminist analysis (Eisenstein, 1990; English, Epstein, Haber, & MacLean, 1985; Smart, 1984). A discussion of the major criticisms of socialist feminism clarifies the direction of feminist analyses in the 1990s and beyond.

The success of the "marriage" between Marxism and radical feminism has been questioned by many socialist feminists (see Sargent, 1981). They conclude that the socialist feminist project was so strongly influenced by Marxist categories of class, labor, and production that a truly feminist reconstruction was not possible (Landry & MacLean, 1993; MacKinnon, 1989; Smart, 1995, pp. 132–133; Young, 1990b, pp. 21–35).

Socialist feminist analyses have often failed to question the usefulness of Marxian class analysis for women who are simply assigned to the class of their husbands or fathers. The Marxist-inspired focus on women's labor also means that socialist feminists have never sufficiently analyzed the significance of men's control over women's sexuality or its significance for women's subordination. Despite the efforts of some socialist feminists to give equal weight to both systems, many describe patriarchy as the cultural-ideological manifestation of the economic base of capitalism (Mitchell, 1971, 1974). Marx's emphasis on production over reproduction continues to dominate much socialist feminism.

Generally, critics have attacked as overly simplified the socialist feminist position that the mode of production determines cultural and political institutions (Smart, 1995). In response, some neo-Marxian and some feminist analyses emphasized the capacity of the State and cultural forces to shape the mode of production (Althusser, 1969; Landry & MacLean, 1993; Williams, 1980). Socialist feminist criminology has made significant contributions toward conceptualizing the State as an active determinant of gender relations and economic conditions (Davis, 1993; Messerschmidt, 1986).

Critics have questioned the overall usefulness of the concept of patriarchy within radical and socialist feminist work. They have charged that radical and socialist feminist analyses ignore the significant historical, cultural variations in the domination of men over women (Acker, 1989, Messerschmidt, 1993). Descriptions of patriarchy are drawn from contemporary Western industrial societies. Several analyses that posit cross-cultural differences or changes in patriarchy over the course of history are not consistent with prevailing historical and anthropological evidence (see Messerschmidt, 1993). Too often, patriarchy is portrayed as a universal, invariant, and total system of male domination over women. Although some socialist feminists (for example, Walby, 1991) have tried to develop dynamic accounts of the contradictions and changes in patriarchy over time and within a given society, many feminists have abandoned the term altogether (Acker, 1989; Messerschmidt, 1993).

Socialist feminism in general, and its criminological applications in particular, also have been criticized for adopting overly deterministic models of patriarchy and capitalism (Smart, 1990; Messerschmidt, 1993). There is little room to explain instances in which women and men resist gender and class oppressions.

Feminists have attacked socialist feminists' use of gender roles to explain differences in men and women's behavior (Lopata & Thorne, 1978; Martin & Jurik, 1996; Messerschmidt, 1993). Gender role analysis ignores differences in what constitutes appropriate masculine and feminine behavior across time, generation, class, race-ethnic groups, and cultures. It also poses dichotomies of masculine versus feminine conduct that ignores the overlap between the character and behavior of men and women (Connell, 1987; West & Fenstermaker, 1995; West & Zimmerman, 1987). Critics charge that socialist feminism relies too heavily on several dichotomies, such as man/woman, capitalist/worker, and production/reproduction. Excessive use of dichotomies obscure variation within and overlap between categories (Young, 1990a). Subtle nuances are lost with the productive/reproductive dichotomy. For example, many reproductive activities such as child care are now paid and thus constitute productive labor. The capitalist/worker dichotomy also obscures the complexity of modern class society.

Moreover, the reliance of socialist feminism on "women's experience" as an intellectual concept and organizing tool makes the theory insufficiently flexible to grasp the myriad of experiences belonging to women across the socially constructed lines of race, class, sexual orientation, age, nationality, and physical ability. Just as socialist feminist theories of patriarchy often paint a monolithic image of man, so the category "woman" and her experience also was too unified to last. More recent socialist feminist analyses have recognized the diversity of women's experiences (Danner, 1996; Rice, 1990).

During the 1980s, a wave of conservatism in the United States and England coupled with the failure of socialism in Latin America and Eastern Europe led socialist feminists to question their analysis. Women in socialist countries such as Cuba and Nicaragua reported that they had been forced to prioritize socialism at the expense of feminism (Chincilla, 1994). Long-range goals of socialism also appeared overly idealistic and even irresponsible in the face of the escalating poverty, sexism, racism, homophobia, and other violence facing socialist and nonsocialist nations (Eisenstein, 1990).

Socialist feminists have repeatedly drawn attention to the importance of racism as a system of oppression. Nevertheless, they replicate Marx's failure to develop a systematic and fully integrated analysis of racism (Davis, 1981; Joseph, 1981; Rice, 1990). Interest has increased in theoretical writings by U.S. women of color and Third World women that critique universalizing notions of women's experience (Collins, 1990; Mohanty, Russo, & Torres, 1991; Rice, 1990). This scholarship has challenged generalizations about women that have been based on white women's experiences alone. For example, rather than viewing the home and reproductive labor as the source of their oppression, African-American women have often regarded their home as a respite from the racist exploitation that they experience in the paid workforce.

Within criminology, scholarship by women of color has pointed out the dominance of white women's experiences in feminist generalizations about women's crimes and victimizations. The experiences of women of color in the criminal justice system are framed by both racism and sexism. Coming to grips with these differences among women requires a paradigm shift that can consider concrete situations as well as their larger social structural and historical contexts (Messerschmidt, 1993; Rice, 1990; Richie, 1996).

Interest in poststructural and postmodern critiques of total theories of society and of grand theories of social change/progress, including Marxism and socialist feminism (Barrett, 1991; MacDonald, 1991; Smart, 1995, p. 7), has also grown. Postmodern-inspired analyses have even challenged the scientific orientation of socialist feminist scholarship. Smart (1995, pp. 10–11) and others (for instance, Harding, 1987) have argued that feminism must abandon the truth claims that are a part of the social scientific agenda: "The core element of postmodernism is the rejection of one reality" (Smart, 1995, p. 45). Smart has argued that the new agenda must be to deconstruct—that is, to show the contradictions and inconsistencies in existing truth claims.

However, not all feminist scholars have accepted a focus on deconstruction alone. Some scholars have argued for approaches that incorporate key socialist feminist concerns but are more mindful of differences among women and men, of the power of culture and the State to shape economic organization and individual consciousness, and of the ability of individuals to resist oppressive social arrangements (Landry & MacLean, 1993; Martin & Jurik, 1996; Messerschmidt, 1993; Rice, 1990; Scranton, 1990; Sumner, 1990).

Some (for example, Hennessy, 1993; Landry & MacLean, 1993) have used the term *materialist feminism* to refer to a variety of feminist works that examine the relationships and contradictions among consciousness, ideology, production-reproduction of material life, and human conformity-resistance. These factors are viewed as equally important and mutually determining. A materialist feminist agenda emphasizes the use of historical analyses to gather *partial* truths that vary across gender, class, race-ethnicity, sexual orientation, nation, and other conditions. The knowledge gained from such investigations requires constant negotiation, dialogue, and revision.

Unlike much of postmodernism, materialist feminism and feminist race approaches focus more on political struggle (Landry & MacLean, 1993). A politics informed by these approaches consists of partial, temporary, and multiple alliances around particular issues (Collins, 1991; Haraway, 1985; Young, 1994). Social progress is not seen as inevitable but as possible with continued struggle (Cain, 1990; Landry & MacLean, 1993).

CONCLUSION

Materialist feminism, feminist race scholarship, and other "post–socialist feminist" theories constitute more than semantic distinctions (Epprecht, 1994). They represent the dynamic and ever-changing nature and vitality of feminist scholarship. While incorporating many socialist feminist concerns, these feminist writings of the 1990s have moved through and beyond socialist feminism (Eisenstein, 1990).

In recent years, some feminist scholars have even moved away from the discipline of criminology because its subject matter is too narrowly focused on the causes and control of crime (Smart, 1995). Within such a narrow perspective, social justice becomes a secondary concern to criminologists. For example, social justice becomes a means to reduce crime. Even worse, social justice may be seen by mainstream criminologists as the outgrowth of criminal justice: more effective enforcement of existing laws leads to greater social justice.

Other feminist scholars endeavor to educate uninformed criminologists about significant insights gained from feminist theory and research (Daly & Chesney-Lind, 1988). The outcome of the struggle to use feminist and socialist feminist ideas to transform the disciplines of criminology remains uncertain (Scranton, 1990). However, socialist feminism continues to instill in feminist-oriented studies of crime, law, and criminal justice a consideration of gender, class, and increasingly of race dynamics (see Rice, 1990). Feminist scholars continue to challenge narrow concentrations on crime causation and crime control.

Socialist feminist analyses locate crime, law, and criminal justice as dimensions of a much larger and more important picture: that of social justice. They demonstrate that gender, racial-ethnic, and economic equality are central to theorizing and activism toward a fair and just society. Hopefully, this contribution will inspire scholarship and service in the decades to come.

REVIEW QUESTIONS

1. What historical conditions led to the rise of second wave feminism?

2. What aspects of radical feminism and Marxism do socialist feminists try to merge?

3. What is the role of women's experience in a socialist feminist analysis?

4. How do socialist feminists explain the criminality of women?

5. Describe criticisms of socialist feminism with regard to its analysis of race and class.

6. What insights about social justice does a socialist feminist perspective offer?

7. How is a materialist feminist perspective similar to yet different from a socialist feminist analysis?

REFERENCES

Acker, J. (1989). The problem with patriarchy. *Sociology, 23,* 235–240.

Adler, F. (1975). *Sisters in crime: The rise of the new female criminal.* New York: McGraw-Hill.

Althusser, L. (1969). *For Marx* (B. Brewster, Trans.). London: Penguin.

Balkan, S., Berger, R., & Schmidt, J. (1980). *Crime and deviance in America: A critical approach.* Belmont, CA: Wadsworth.

Barrett, M. (1991). *The politics of truth: From Marx to Foucault.* Cambridge: Polity.

Bengelsdorf, C., & Hageman, A. (1979). Emerging from underdevelopment: Women and work in Cuba. In Z. Eisenstein (Ed.), *Capitalist patriarchy and the case for socialist feminism* (pp. 271–295) New York: Monthly Review Press.

Bonger, W. (1916). *Criminality and economic conditions*. New York: Little, Brown.

Brownmiller, S. (1975). *Against our will: Men, women, and rape*. New York: Bantam.

Cain, M. (1990). Towards transgression: New directions in feminist criminology. *International Journal of the Sociology of Law, 18*, 1–18.

Carlen, P. (1988). *Women, crime, and poverty*. Philadelphia: Open University Press.

Cavender, G. (1995). Alternative approaches: Labeling and critical perspectives. In J. Sheley (Ed.), *Criminology* (2nd ed., pp. 349–368). Belmont, CA: Wadsworth.

Cavender, G. (1995). We matter: The lives of girls and women [Interview with M. Chesney-Lind by G. Cavender]. *American Journal of Criminal Justice, 19:1*, 287–301.

Chinchilla, N. S. (1994). Feminism, revolution, and democratic transitions in Nicaragua. In S. B. Jaquette (Ed.), *Women's movements in Latin America* (pp. 177–191). Denver: Westview.

Collins, P. H. (1991). *Black feminist thought*. New York: Routledge.

Combahee River Collective. (1979). A black feminist statement. In Z. Eisenstein (Ed.), *Capitalist patriarchy and the case for socialist feminism* (pp. 362–372). New York: Monthly Review Press.

Connell, R. W. (1987). *Gender and power*. Stanford, CA: Stanford University Press.

Dahl, T. S. (1987). *Women's law*. Oslo: Norwegian University Press.

Daly, K., & Chesney-Lind, M. (1988). Feminism and criminology. *Justice Quarterly, 5*, 497–538.

Danner, M. (1996). Gender inequality and criminalization: A socialist feminist perspective on the legal social control of women. In M. Schwartz & D. Milovanovic (Eds.), *Race, gender, and class in criminology*. New York: Garland.

Davis, A. (1981). *Women, race, and class*. New York: Vintage.

Davis, N. (1993). Systemic gender control and victimization among homeless female youth. *Socio-Legal Bulletin, 8*, 22–31.

Dobash, R. E., & Dobash, R. (1979). *Violence against wives*. New York: Free Press.

Echols, A. (1989). *Daring to be bad: Radical feminism in America 1967–1975*. Minneapolis: University of Minnesota Press.

Eisenstein, Z. (1977). Constructing a theory of capitalist patriarchy and socialist feminism. *The Insurgent Sociologist, 7*, 3–17.

Eisenstein, Z. (Ed.). (1979). *Capitalist patriarchy and the case for socialist feminism*. New York: Monthly Review Press.

Eisenstein, Z. (1990). Specifying U.S. feminism: The problem of naming. *Socialist Review, 20*, 45–56.

Engels, F. (1972). *The origin of the family, private property and the state*. New York: International.

English, D., Epstein, B., Haber, B., & MacLean, J. (1985). The impasse of socialist feminism: A conversation. *Socialist Review, 79*, 93–110.

Epprecht, M. (1994). Is socialist feminism passe? A review essay. *Marxism, 7*, 138–146.

Firestone, S. (1970). *The dialectic of sex: The case for feminist revolution*. New York: Bantam.

Freedman, E. (1981). *Their sister's keepers: Women's prison reform in America, 1830–1930*. Ann Arbor: University of Michigan Press.

Hansen, K. V. (1986). Women's unions and the search for a political identity. *Socialist Review, 86*, 67–95.

Haraway, D. (1985). A manifesto for cyborgs: Science, technology, and socialist feminism in the 1980's. *Socialist Review, 80,* 65–107.

Harding, S. (Ed.). (1987). *Feminism and methodology.* Philadelphia: Open University Press.

Hartmann, H. (1976). Capitalism, patriarchy, and job segregation by sex. *Signs, 1,* 137–169.

Hennessy, R. (1993). *Materialist feminism and the politics of discourse.* New York: Routledge.

Humm, M. (Ed.). (1992). *Modern feminisms: Political, literary, and cultural.* New York: Columbia University Press.

Jaggar, A. (1983). *Feminist politics and human nature.* Totowa, NJ: Rowman & Allenheld.

Joseph, G. (1981). The incompatible ménage à trois: Marxism, feminism and racism. In L. Sargent (Ed.), *Women and revolution* (pp. 91–108) Boston: South End.

Klein, D. (1973). The etiology of female crime: A review of the literature. *Issues in Criminology, 8,* 3–30.

Klein, D. (1982). The dark side of marriage: Battered wives and the domination of women. In N. Rafter & E. Stanko (Eds.), *Judge lawyer victim thief: Women, gender roles, and criminal justice.* (pp. 83–107) Boston: Northeastern University Press.

Klein, D., & Kress, J. (1976). Any woman's blues: A critical overview of women, crime, and the criminal justice system. *Crime and Social Justice, 5,* 34–49.

Landry, D., & MacLean, G. (1993). *Materialist feminisms.* Cambridge, MA: Blackwell.

Lopata, H., & Thorne, B. (1978). On the term "sex roles." *Signs, 3,* 718–721.

MacDonald, E. (1991). The trouble with subjects: Feminism, Marxism and the questions of poststructuralism. *Studies in Political Economy, 35,* 43–71.

MacKinnon, C. (1989). *Toward a feminist theory of the state.* Cambridge, MA: Harvard University Press.

Martin, S. E., & Jurik, N. (1996). *Doing justice, doing gender: Women in law and criminal justice occupations.* Newbury Park, CA: Sage.

Marx, K. (1967). *Capital. Vol. 1.* New York: International.

Messerschmidt, J. (1986). *Capitalism, patriarchy, and crime.* Totowa, NJ: Rowman & Littlefield.

Messerschmidt, J. (1993). *Masculinity and crime.* Totowa, NJ: Rowman & Littlefield.

Miller, E. (1986). *Street women.* Philadelphia: Temple University Press.

Mitchell, J. (1971). *Women's estate.* New York: Vintage.

Mitchell, J. (1974). *Psychoanalysis and feminism.* New York: Vintage.

Mohanty, C., Russo, A., & Torres, L. (Eds.). (1991). *Third World women and the politics of feminism.* Bloomington: Indiana University Press.

Philipson, I., & Hansen, K. (1990). Women, class, and the feminist imagination. In K. Hansen & I. Philipson (Eds.), *Women, class, and the feminist imagination* (pp. 3–40). Philadelphia: Temple University Press.

Rafter, N. H., & Natalizia, E. (1985). Marxist feminism: Implications for criminal justice. In B. Price & N. Sokoloff (Eds.), *The criminal justice system and women* (pp. 465–484). New York: Boardman.

Rafter, N. H., & Stanko, E. (Eds.). (1982). *Judge lawyer victim thief: Women, gender roles, and criminal justice.* Boston: Northeastern University Press.

Rice, M. (1990). Challenging orthodoxies in feminist theory: A black feminist critique. In L. Gelsthorpe & A. Morris (Eds.), *Feminist perspectives in criminology* (pp. 57–69). Philadelphia: Open University Press.

Richie, B. (1996). *Compelled to crime.* New York: Routledge.

Sargent, L. (1981). *Women and revolution: A discussion of the unhappy marriage between Marxism and feminism.* Boston: South End.

Schwendinger, J. R., & Schwendinger, H. (1983). *Rape and inequality*. Beverly Hills: Sage.

Scranton, P. (1990). Scientific knowledge or masculine discourses? Challenging patriarchy in criminology. In L. Gelsthorpe & A. Morris (Eds.), *Feminist perspectives in criminology* (pp. 10–25). Philadelphia: Open University Press.

Simon, R. J. (1975). *The contemporary women and crime*. Washington, DC: National Institute of Mental Health.

Smart, C. (1976). *Women, crime, and criminology: A feminist critique*. London: Routledge.

Smart, C. (1984). *The ties that bind*. London: Routledge & Kegan Paul.

Smart, C. (1990). Review of James Messerschmidt, *Capitalism, Patriarchy and Crime. Contemporary Crises, 11,* 327–329.

Smart, C. (1995). *Law, crime, and sexuality: Essays in feminism*. Newbury Park, CA: Sage.

Sokoloff, N. (1980). *Between money and love: The dialectics of women's home and market work*. New York: Praeger.

Stacey, J. (1979). When patriarchy kowtows: The significance of the Chinese family revolution for feminist theory. In Z. Eisenstein (Ed.), *Capitalist patriarchy and the case for socialist feminism* (pp. 299–354). New York: Monthly Review Press.

Stanko, E. (1985). *Intimate intrusions: Women's experience of male violence*. London: Routledge.

Sumner, C. (1990). Foucault, gender and the censure of deviance. In L. Gelsthorpe & A. Morris (Eds.), *Feminist perspectives in criminology* (pp. 26–40). Philadelphia: Open University Press.

Walby, S. (1990). *Theorizing patriarchy*. Cambridge, MA: Blackwell.

West, C., & Fenstermaker, S. (1995). Doing difference. *Gender & Society, 9,* 8–37.

West, C., & Zimmerman, D. (1987). Doing gender. *Gender & Society, 1,* 125–151.

Williams, R. (1980). *Problems in materialism and culture*. London: Verso.

Young, I. M. (1989). Beyond the unhappy marriage: A critique of dual systems theory. In L. Sargent (Ed.), *Women and revolution* (pp. 43–69). Boston: South End.

Young, I. M. (1990a). *Justice and the politics of difference*. Princeton, NJ: Princeton University Press.

Young, I. M. (1990b). *Throwing like a girl and other essays in feminist philosophy and social theory*. Bloomington: Indiana University Press.

Young, I. M. (1994). Gender as seriality: Thinking about women as a social collective. *Signs, 19,* 713–738.

Zaretsky, E. (1976). *Capitalism, the family and personal life*. London: Pluto.

Zeitlin, I. (1967). *Marxism: A re-examination*. New York: Van Nostrand Reinhold.

Peacemaking Criminology and Social Justice

Peacemaking criminology challenges us to think about the presence of violence and democracy in society and in our lives. It considers how people, in the midst of conflict, build trust, community, and peace rather than distrust, separatism, and war. One form of conflict is crime. Crime can be as local as the harm caused by spousal abuse or as global as international warfare. Pepinsky argues that peacemaking criminology endeavors to forge meaningful, humane relationships between victims and offenders, between friends and enemies within situations of conflict. This peacemaking process entails a deliberate effort at "educating *for* peace." Educating for peace acknowledges power with others as opposed to power over others. Educating for peace is about mediating power imbalances. It is about listening empathically to people who need a forum in which to openly speak about their anger and frustration. Failing this, we must accept that the violent, destructive, and crime-ridden behavior others engage in is a mechanism for the expression of unexamined pain. Thus, peacemaking in criminology and criminal justice is about resituating everyone, from offender to victim, from prosecutor to defense attorney, from police officer to probation officer, into a larger social fabric of mutual respect and love. Through open communication, we foster greater security and social control in our lives and society. Social control, then, is a return to peace and a return to justice.

3

Peacemaking Primer

HAL PEPINSKY

My general theory on the difference between how we create violence and how we create peace is well referenced and spelled out in *The Geometry of Violence and Democracy* (Pepinsky, 1991). The text that follows, which I call a peacemaking primer, is my translation as of the end of the summer of 1995. In it, I address the question of how to turn peacemaking theory into practice, evaluating the empirical results that followed from the testing of my propositions. Ultimately, I found that my own intervention in conflicts served to create peace, safety, and security more than war, distrust, and planned coercion.

HISTORICAL BACKGROUND

My first book, *Crime and Conflict: A Study of Law and Society* (1976), had proved unpublishable in the United States when a British press put it out. The book won critical notice from British law-in-society folks for representing U.S. pragmatism. In it, I proposed crime control legislation in the two penultimate chapters there. I soon recognized that those proposals were dangerously misguided. I have always accepted as a scholarly mandate that my proposals be tested in practice. Further, I recognized that the analysis and findings in my first theoretical statement were obtusely stated and obscure. Frankly, this was due to being too busy trying to legitimize my paycheck at the expense of plainly and honestly pursuing this research objective: distinguish what I now call "warmaking" (read "violence") and "peacemaking" (read "democracy" and "responsiveness") (Pepinsky, 1991).

In 1976, I was proposing policies for "crime control" to be empirically tested. Interestingly, the exemplary projects I cited in support of my propositions later turned out to be ephemeral successes. In 1995, I proposed ways for people to build trust (rather than distrust) in the midst of conflict, build community (rather than hardened separation between our personal enemies and ourselves), and make peace (rather than war).

Similar to oral history among aboriginal peoples told by elders to children, in my "enlightened" professional world I still find personal stories of conflict to be the most authoritative data sources for distinguishing what works (that is, what creates a feeling in which people act safer and more secure around others) from what does not (what leaves people feeling they have to be guarded with and harsher to those whom they distrust).

PEACEMAKING ASSUMPTIONS

The power of organized force to kill wounds and dictates our social agenda. This is a product of imbalanced participation from those voices affected by that force; that is, the quieter and more hidden the voices of those most hurt by force are, the freer the violence is to feed upon itself and multiply into our daily lives. As Tifft and Markham (1991) argue, the power of violence experienced daily through our intimate social exchanges is paralleled only by that power that is ordered and ratified by those who, in good social Darwinist fashion, survive in this ethos to become national and corporate leaders.

It is commonplace in the language of chaos theory that we become more or less secure all at once at every political level of our lives (from our homes to the cabinet or board meeting room), on a social plane or attitude that chaologists call "fractals." In other words, at all levels of social interaction we find multiple forms of discourse or language (Wagner-Pacifici, 1994). These discourses operate *differently* among those living in the *same* society, organization, or institution. For example, if people are involved in global conflict, the same "war," so to speak, will be found in the bedrooms of our communities. The war, however, will assume a different language. We can hear or read the difference in the words used, the questions asked, the stances taken in everyday communication. We speak of "time-outs" and "grounding" in homes and schools for children, or "indefinite confinement" and "life without parole" for adolescent or young adult prison inmates, or "annihilation" and "extermination" of entire villages when people cannot be conscripted into military service during wartime. This is the larger theoretical frame in which this primer asks, "What do I do that contributes to an attitude of peace among those causing others tremendous, concerted pain and fear? What do I do to stop the process of human separation or exclusion of victims and offenders, friends and enemies, from 'normal,' participative social discourse?"

PRIMARY DATA SOURCES

People learn to experiment with putting peacemaking theory into practice in everyday life. As people begin to calculate their own attitude in relation to others' attitudes in conflicting situations, they learn to reposition themselves by balancing or mediating opposing forces. This process makes adventure and learning out of what in the warmaking attitude may be recalled as a frustrating or meaningless experience. The following situation illustrates this concept.

I received a faculty mass mailing asking that interested parties sign up and speak to community groups via the Indiana University Global Speakers Bureau. I was put in touch with a sixth- to eighth-grade social studies teacher with a problem. Her sixth-graders could not understand why they needed to learn about ethnic conflict, notably in Bosnia. She asked me to discuss the importance of global ethnic conflict for them during a fifty-minute presentation in the school cafeteria.

When I arrived at the school, the teacher quickly informed me about the all-Caucasian/Christian student body, the faculty and administrators, and what specific behavioral problems and/or threats individual children posed. During our discussion, she cited overhearing negative things being discussed within a boys' bathroom down the hall. Apparently, some eighth-grade boys had been known to engage in activities such as throwing small sixth-grade boys in toilets. Before entering the cafeteria, I checked out the bathroom. It was squeaky clean with the exception of little spots on the wall above the urinals. On closer inspection, these spots were the minute, carefully placed contents of one or more persons' noses.

Thus informed, I began my presentation by providing a short, introductory lecture to the several dozen students, focusing on what I had been asked to do. I told them I had gone abroad and had lived most recently in an East African Muslim neighborhood. I also said that every time I went abroad, I studied ethnic conflict in other times and places. This increased my awareness of the ethnic conflicts I was in the midst of at home and aided me in learning new ways to deal with them. I told them that my goal, by the end of our time together, was for them to have admitted they harbored deep-seated ethnic conflicts of their own. They had the choice of acting the way people in Bosnia had done, which led to war on one another, or learning to do better than the "grown-ups" in making peace with their problems. Much shouting and exuberance ensued, as students struggled to gain my attention. Those most noticeable were mainly boys whom other students later identified as sitting at the troublemakers' table. Soon I addressed the topic of the bathroom and asked how they would propose to clean up the bathrooms if they were an adult like myself and in charge of the school.

After much discussion, two main points emerged. First, some older boys were doing things far worse than I had cited (for example, urinating on the toilet paper). Second, someone would have to clean it up, either because it had to be done or because it was their job, as in the case of a janitor. They even went on to elaborate on what I knew to be tried-and-tested adult military solutions. Examples ranged from enforcing people to log into the bathroom to installing surveillance cameras (which as one student pointed out might "accidentally" get moved out of position). One boy even called out the idea of setting booby traps.

During our discussions, I discovered that two students had family members going to Bosnia for the NATO peacekeeping force. I assured them that efforts were being taken to educate individuals on safety measures and that I hoped no one got hurt, but three to four million booby traps were buried in Bosnia. This situation was due to generals and national leaders who truly applied these solutions.

Eventually, I pointed out to the students that they were presenting me with an enormous problem, which angered many of them. Despite the various ideas they offered on how to fix the bathroom problem, it was getting worse instead of fixed. I asked whether anyone could imagine anything all the people in the room could do who wanted the problem fixed.

Finally, from behind me, softly enough that I had to ask her to repeat herself, a student I will rename Lisa said, "We could take turns cleaning the bathrooms ourselves and choose who did it in a lottery." I expressed delight with that idea. The din of ideas on catching the culprits continued to elicit my response of "It will not work." Finally, one young man called out in frustration, "You keep telling us our ideas won't work. Okay, tell us what *will* work!" My reply was in support of what Lisa had proposed, adding that I would like to try her idea. At this point, there was a chorus of "Yeah, Lisa!" followed by a big round of applause.

I summed up the experience by giving them credit for learning the difference between making war on ethnic conflict and making peace with it. Their situation involved conflict between local children from "good families" and children who had moved in from the big city. They were praised for their honesty regarding their anger and frustration, while keeping in mind the Anabaptist mutualist premise that truth and honesty in crisis are the foundation of trust. This is the essence of community (Cordella, 1991). The students took a problem that had the potential to degenerate into further violence and instead became active in fixing it themselves.

In a follow-up thank-you call with the teacher, I summarized the plan the students had created themselves once they set their minds to the task. The teacher, who sounded quite enthused at the idea of students assuming responsibility for keeping the rest rooms clean, informed me she would take the idea to her principal. She also shared my appreciation of the role of gender in this conflict. A quiet, well-behaved girl was the first to see how to manage the problem as others who should or could have done so did not. The level and spontaneity of the applause she earned meant that the children appreciated how to make peace when they truly listened to the quieter voice among the oppressed class.

This was a case of what Bystydzienski (1993) calls "women transforming politics" and what Brock-Utne (1985, 1989) calls "educating *for* peace." This differs from the warriors' version of peace studies, "educating *about* peace."

Regardless of what happened the next day at the school, I knew that on the previous day I had empirically validated the power of thinking like a peacemaker to a group of students and teachers whom I happened to meet. This talk was educational as it demonstrated why the students needed to be interested in the ethnic conflict in Bosnia to avoid making the same mistakes in their own lives. When another teacher apologized for the children being rowdy, my reply was simply that the best any of us can aspire to as a teacher is to create a single, halfway memorable moment in a class period together. In this case, the children saw and felt the connection between their own problems and ethnic conflict in Bosnia, much more readily than those adults to whom I have tried to explain it since.

To those who find themselves in a warmaking frame of mind, my approach to teaching students about why ethnic conflict is important might appear to have occurred as a reckless, stream-of-consciousness improvisation. In my peacemaking frame of mind, I tried to reduce my agenda to a level that provided meaning without determining direction and followed the four steps to

making peace, steps I lay out and reiterate elsewhere in this chapter. At any
moment, where I chose to listen, where I chose to roam across the cafeteria,
and how I chose to respond were consciously calculated in relationship to
where I stood among a group of suspicious, angry, fearful, little people institutionalized to be pitted against big people who also were in the room. I was
surprised at what was happening. Overall, in the field of academic inquiry, it
was strong experimental evidence in support of a whole variety of peacemaking propositions.

PRINCIPLES OF PEACEMAKING:
MEDIATING POWER IMBALANCES

Peacemaking is one of two ways we have of approaching social control. "Social control" refers to achieving a sense of greater trust and social safety among
one's associates, as manifested in the feeling of being happier and more secure
in the next moment than at present. The other approach is what I call "warmaking." Warmaking entails the belief that our social insecurity and danger
can be traced to identifiable persons who act out of evil or psychopathic motives, individually or in groups. The first task in making war on one's social
insecurities is to identify one's enemies by establishing their blame and subduing their evil ways. This can be accomplished by killing them, separating them
from the social fabric in which they live, or intimidating them into remaining
in their proper place and conforming to the social roles their betters prescribe
for them.

It is customary to maintain in peacemaking that all our social danger arises
from imbalances of power to blame and subdue one another among those
whose actions affect our lives. In the peacemaking frame of mind, all imbalances of power *over* (as opposed to *with*) others are defined as "violence." A
state of peace, by contrast, manifests itself as harmony or resonance in human
interaction. In this state, each of us can honestly tell others how their actions
empower or threaten our security without the threat of isolation. At one extreme, we are increasingly aware that imbalances of power are global, as between megacapitalist corporate associations and poor women and children of
color. We see ever increasing urgency in mediating, cutting across, and reducing these imbalances for the very sake of human survival. At the other extreme, we are keenly aware of endemic interpersonal power imbalances. In
recent years, through association with victims and survivors, I have become
aware that live warfare has been waged against women and children at home
for more than four millennia, since the rise of national political patriarchies,
beginning on a grand scale in Egypt. At its most gruesome, this warfare extends to endemic ritual homicide and cannibalism against the smallest and
most vulnerable among us, especially infants and children.

It is also agreed in peacemaking that anyone's capacity for achieving social
control, safety, and security rests exclusively on one's power to choose among

one's own options for how to act next in any social setting. Ultimately, all peacemaking entails having the self-possession to live social life through a series of four thought/action steps. In this section I define these peacemaking steps.

The first step involves taking enough time to review one's own feelings and impulses to provide oneself with *choices*. My friend Bill Breeden, a peace activist who is the only individual to serve jail time for the Iran-Contra affair, illustrates choice by suggesting the following: "It is human nature for us to be born with the urge to poop in our pants. It is also human nature for us to quickly learn how to suppress this urge in order to put our poop in the right place so we may enjoy the happy company of other human beings. It is human nature for us to have conflicting urges. All of our conscious power to live and learn together rests on our capacity to recognize we do have choices."

The second step of thought and action is to *choose* to identify and introduce oneself to those persons most blamed and subdued in whatever violence threatens them the most. The third step involves making a conscious attempt to draw these victims out, listen to what scares and threatens them the most, and hear what they would like to have happen next. The fourth step entails joining with the voiceless or subdued in confronting the greatest power holders in a given situation who threaten and ignore the needs and interests of weaker people (the subdued and/or blamed). Through this process, one becomes an advocate for the less powerful. This, ultimately, is how one *mediates* power imbalances.

By incorporating these peacemaking steps into one's social interaction, social power is tilted back onto itself like on a teeter-totter. Mediation requires listening empathetically and respectfully to the power holders' response and ultimately listening most carefully and respectfully to one's harshest or most immediate critics. As one learns what the "opposing" parties' interests are, one's own direct and vicarious experience of choice(s), when discussed in relationship to the choices of others, can assist the conflicting parties in developing a repertoire of options.

Ultimately, peacemaking presupposes that there is nothing more or less to becoming more socially secure together than for each of us to exercise our own power to live by these four steps. These four steps can be used as an alternative to blaming and attacking one's enemies. I have noticed that the only practical, manifest evidence we receive of whether any of us has even taken the first step of choosing to act out peacemaking's four steps, instead of blaming and attacking, lies in the second step. If you can recognize that power imbalances alone are enough of a problem for motivation to understand and speak on behalf of victims, you are most likely in a peacemaking frame of mind. By contrast, when I or someone else is in a violent frame of mind, I notice that the victims on whose behalf one speaks are abstractions instead of real people with whose problems and outlook one has personally become involved. A common corollary of such evidence of being in a warmaking frame of mind is that one will remain stoic and avoid describing one's own problems.

In addition to choosing whom to be around, peacemaking is also a matter of being prepared, unlike my critic, to acknowledge power imbalances in the relations that personally matter the most. Quinney (1991) argues that our capacity to end suffering rests on our capacity to acknowledge the suffering of others. Quinney is a practicing Buddhist, and in his essay he refers to the life power that comes from acknowledging the suffering of others as "compassion." There are many words for compassion in all political and religious traditions, including secular humanism ("justice"). One major source of current inspiration for peacemaking in criminal justice is indigenous customs for responding to what we otherwise call "crimes." This can be seen in the new juvenile justice acts in New Zealand and Australia (Consedine, 1995).

Denial or avoidance of getting into one's own victimization is the looking-glass self of failing to get close to other victims *as* victims. Later I try to explain the proposition that it is self-defeating to try and coerce or threaten anyone into acknowledging and confronting others' and one's own victimization. But among those of us prepared to validate victimization, we see ourselves as making choices that our warmaking friends claim they do not have. This is all we will ever know until someone's references to victimization become personal. Norwegian scholar Nils Christie (1981) is renowned among criminologists for observing, succinctly, that insofar as we allow ourselves to know anyone in many personal respects, we lose our capacity to inflict pain on them. This includes knowing and acknowledging the painful or shameful sides of ourselves in balance with acknowledging our positive value in the lives of others.

I find myself in a warmaking frame of mind constantly to this day. The greater my capacity to listen and accommodate those most threatened by my own actions, the faster I can correct my own threats to their security. In addition, this reflects threats to my personal security in the social fabric we share.

Letting oneself make, apologize for, and address one's own mistakes quickly becomes its own reward to anyone who attempts to acknowledge the personal victimization of others. If I notice others allowing themselves to become personally and publicly close to victimization, I inform them with confidence they will never be able to turn back. For example, in a feminist justice seminar I teach, students have frequently written letters to me stating their surge in awareness of sexism and ageism on television, in print media, and in others' comments. Once the suffering of power imbalances has entered far into consciousness, it is impossible to repress. It will be expressed through leftist/liberal guilt, self-pity, and/or recrimination against those who should be attending to victimization but are failing to do so.

Awareness of victimization haunts many people who are close to me. It has led several friends to commit suicide and others to give up completely on belonging to any social fabric. One friend was forced by her father into many horrors, including killing and eating people. She states as long as you remain in this position, you remain a "victim." When you can cease blaming yourself for your own victimization by shamelessly and freely discussing it with others, and when you confront your worst personal nightmares, you become a "survivor." In addition, you gain command of choosing how to discuss and respond to your oppressors.

Those who have been sufficiently loved and validated during and after victimization are capable of achieving self-esteem. We commonly feel a practical and moral need to pass on our own sense of security to others. Power holders who persist in systematic violence or abuse lack this gift of personal validation by others as much as despairing victims. Thus, I notice that concerted, happy peacemakers (survivors) readily mix appreciation for power holders' openness and strength with the criticism of power holders' actions. Further, such peacemakers avoid character attacks when confronting power holders with the pain and fear they are causing. We all need and deserve personal validation. Our own safety and those of all victims rest on the personal validation of redeeming qualities and actions among abusers as much as among victims. As others have acknowledged, abusers are victims too. When you are trying to weave oppressors and victims back into a trustworthy social fabric, everybody deserves personal respect and compassion.

I try not to dwell on criticism of warmaking in this chapter. Like Canadian Quaker criminal justice activist Ruth Morris (1995), I want to stress the safety and security benefits of making peace. This chapter is less a complaint than a celebration of the fruits peacemaking offers us all. I expect to continue to be challenged by critics who find peacemaking unreal. I thank the honest critics who already have helped me appreciate how unreal and incomprehensible peacemaking seems. I recognize even in myself at every social moment the lingering question of whether trying to achieve social control by making war or peace is the real utopian fantasy.

Peacemaking is the art and science of weaving and reweaving oneself with others into a social fabric of mutual love, respect, and concern. This is one of two ways, or attitudes, with which one may enter any social interaction. The other attitude is that of working to win wars against personal enemies, those one tries to identify, isolate, and subdue for the sake of one's own and one's loved ones' safety. This attitude is called warmaking. We are all familiar with the art and science of warmaking. For example, we are all familiar with deterrence. It is quite common to apply the science of deterrence to our own children. Some may believe that swiftness and sureness of sanction are more important than, and in conflict with, severity of punishment. Others believe that the overwhelming mastery of right we demonstrate by severity of punishment creates a safer environment for all. Regardless of the side we take in any warmaking debate, the debate itself is a ritual of public discourse familiar to people particularly in the United States.

By contrast, little is written in public debate regarding ways to get along to talk about making peace. Bystydzienski (1993), a student of women in politics, and many of our feminist friends have raised awareness that peacemaking dialogue is found disproportionately among politically marginalized groups. This includes women in all populations, and Native American and African-American traditionalists. Peacemaking is the language of people who cannot take action against anyone else for the problems they share with their loved ones. In patriarchal discourse, we blame single mothers for the sins and poverty of their children. When on that pretext we deny aid to dependent children, the mothers are left to battle against all "public welfare" forces to feed and shelter their children. They cannot afford to indulge in recrimination. They cannot imagine feeding their children by blowing up the welfare office. Rage has to be translated into action. The children need to eat. This is known among feminists as "women's ways of knowing" (Brock-Utne, 1985, 1989). I find peacemaking to be practiced in its highest form, both as mastering an art and as having learned much from sad and frustrating experiences, among such heroic child caregivers and others who are publicly abandoned. Those surviving on the edge tend to find peacemaking a necessity.

The following story illustrates the peacemaking process in action. A divorced woman was a survivor of repeated rape by an older brother and grandfather. She had renounced the alcohol and drugs she retreated into during adolescence. As an adult, she encouraged many others to advocate for children's rights. For several years, the woman purposely refrained from legal protest against her ex-husband on behalf of the children. Apparently, the children's father had repeatedly attacked and raped them during prior, unsupervised visits. As is true with thousands of cases like hers, it is likely that if she made any formal move to even have visitation supervised, she would probably lose all contact with the children. By failing to launch a legal war on behalf of her children, she continues to help them recover from whatever fear and pain they suffered on visits. She calculates her children have now grown big and united enough to fend off attacks by the father.

From a warmaking frame of mind, she is morally bound to report the abuse and mandate for the state to give their father "consequences." She has certainly weighed that option. When she or anyone takes a peacemaking approach, all the rage and impulses for legal redress that others would share is present. She knows as a divorced custodial mother, she will, in patriarchal discourse, be blamed first for whatever goes wrong. In adopting the attitude of peacemaking, this mother has weighed and discussed all of these feelings and options with her children. She sees as her primary duty doing not a ritual public display of what good intentions require but what in fact will give her children the greatest sense of security and control over the threat of abuse that she and they gather together. Talk of reporting and pressing for prosecution has become a distraction to her—something she is quite willing to explain and talk over, something she has with pure practicality thought through. There is no doubt she is angry and blames this man for hurting their children. She is also aware that although blaming someone else may feel right, her children stand overwhelming odds of losing what safety they now enjoy if she acts on that feeling. Unless measures are taken, which theoretically and empirically are highly improbable in this legal world, it will not do her children any good for the abuse to be reported so she can feel she did the right thing.

The attitude of peacemaking is one of self-possession—the same kind that keeps us from pooping until we get to the toilet. It is necessary to reflect on one's own multitude of contradictory feelings and desires in an attempt to sort out the confusion. In addition, one must look beyond immediate impulses to foresee the results of such actions. In this frame of reference, taking action against others who assault or who do not live up to their responsibility is a waste of energy; it only allows those who anger you to take over your remaining capacity for personal control.

This chapter is all about social control. Ultimately, social control means weaving oneself and others of concern more tightly and intimately into a social fabric grounded in honesty and trust. When violence threatens to remove individuals from such a social fabric, the task is to identify where trust and personal empowerment can be created among a range of possibilities by one's own next action.

When someone is either engaging in violence or allowing it to happen, there are no empirical, practical grounds on which to trust the offender to refrain from reoffending all by him- or herself other than that person's demonstrated empathy and understanding of the pain and terror visited upon the victim. This does not mean that a "honeymoon period" occurs marked by guilt. Rather, it is the capacity to verbalize how the victim(s) felt when control was lost. It is also that conscious, publicly expressed and practiced self-awareness that unlocks us from any of our own patterns and cycles of violence, or from those visited upon us from violent "caregivers."

TRUST AND ITS ENEMIES

We perpetuate a lie upon ourselves when we adopt the warmaker's premise that there are two ways to trust an offender: (1) watch and contain him or her, or (2) do nothing. It is also a lie that anyone ever merits being trusted now and for all time, unconditionally. Trust has to be consistently reciprocated and renewed to stay alive. Furthermore, peacemaking presumes that betrayal of trust and violence can begin to come from any of us at any time. Our capacity for reweaving victims and offenders back into social security among us rests in confronting it openly and promptly to ensure this lapse does not reoccur.

Our entire capacity for helping—that is, to do what it takes to make individuals feel safe from any threat of violence—rests on allowing ourselves a moment of reflection. During this time, options are considered as to where and how to express our urge to hurt those who anger us. In the next moment, that of action, the course of greatest safety lies in the immediate confrontation of the pain and fear people feel in the situation. In the peacemaker's frame of reference, the potential for violence in the next moment is the sum of power imbalances underlying the discourse regarding the violence that has already taken place.

Reweaving victims, offenders, and bystanders back into a trustworthy social fabric is threatened by power imbalances. The task at hand is to identify those imbalances and take the most fundamental one at hand and mediate it. It is important to first speak with and draw out the weakest voices. In this situation, I look for who spoke last and for the smallest, quietest party in the group. This is an operating definition for how to identify and listen to victims first. As an attempt to create a safe atmosphere for the victims to express their anger, one may feel obliged to explain oneself and one's feelings. Instead, simply listening and understanding what the victim does with his or her story in the next instance is the role the peacemaker assumes. The decision of what to do next and of how to say it rests with the victim, not the listener.

During this moment of listening and understanding, one's greatest enemy is the inner voices, let alone outer ones, telling the person to step in and solve the victim's problems. Fighting other people's battles is a warmaking premise; having the ability to balance physically and emotionally oppressive voices and acts aids victims in gaining control over the expression of their experiences. Trust emerges only from what we decide to do ourselves, not from what we decide for others.

INSTITUTING PEACE

After what I call "looking down" by listening to the quietest and most isolated voices of the apparently least heard, one may offer to tell the victim's story with his or her permission. Gandhi preached *satyagraha,* "holding truth," which refers to refusing to cooperate with power imbalances. Confrontation can turn from passively listening to actively going to the oppressor to voice concerns and invite response. I call this "dumping up."

In sequence, peacemaking in the face of violence requires as its first four steps (1) reflecting on one's own feelings; (2) introducing oneself to the apparently weakest, or quietest, victim (recognizing that ultimately all violence is in some way a form of retaliation for one's own sense of victimization); (3) listening to the victim's fear and pain and attempting to understand and empathize; and (4) offering ways one might confront the people in power next.

Once, as a guest lecturer in a graduate seminar, I spoke of the kind of self-discipline peacemaking requires. One graduate student tried to side with me. Another student (who apparently did not accept the peacemaking philosophy) sitting beside me with his wife passed prolonged suffering at the fellow student's arrogance and threatened to break his jaw. After the event, I explained to both of them what I observed. When the first student backed off from verbal retaliation and taunting following the second student's threat, I knew the second student was now at virtually no risk to swing at his oppressor because he had said how he felt openly in front of others instead. Violence breaks out when we cannot safely express and be validated first for our anger and fear. Cycles of violence take hold of us precisely as the underlying fears of ourselves remain unexpressed beforehand. So when I am self-possessed enough to hold out hope and continue trying for peace, I welcome honest, open, public utterances of anger and frustration. I welcome heating up debate to its angriest, most fearsome sources, because the sooner and more directly the anger and fear are released, the safer we all become. It is absurd to my peacemaking mind to ask young, angry students to tone down their rhetoric. Better to welcome the rhetoric and take the time to discuss it. The alternative is forcing people to endure and hide their fears until they explode into blind acts of pain and devastation.

Although I am aware of my own defensiveness and sometimes give way to it, when someone verbally attacks me and blames me for something, it is by now virtually reflex for me to appreciate that the anger is where I can face it. It is no longer paradoxical to me that severely abused and threatened children and adult survivors and victims are remarkably forgiving, albeit seldom forgetting, because they know they feel reduced to taking what comfort they can get.

A corollary is that if you persist in trying to make peace with victims that you encounter, you will probably soon enjoy the satisfaction of hearing that something very small and insignificant to you has transformed a victim into an active, significantly safer, survivor. For example, one friend of mine spent years as a political prisoner. He told me that a one-page letter I wrote to a judge after the judge turned down his habeas corpus request eventually carried enough weight simply by its existence to make his parole board release him. He credits me for his release from prison.

From a warmaking perspective, the letter I wrote took less than an hour to write and send. It put me at no personal risk and was a worthless, insignificant action that was legally quashed. From a peacemaking perspective, the fact that I had written such a letter gave me more sense of having made a difference in someone's life than most of us receive in a lifetime.

PERILS OF PEACEMAKING

Peacemaking requires confronting our most basic denial first in the face of violence. We who have been attempting to consciously make peace with violence have learned from victims and survivors that the world is far more dangerous and corrupt than warriors ever acknowledge as they lead us into battle.

We know it to be an elemental natural law of fear translated into organized action that those we let fight our battles for us are likely to become more violent, dangerous, and oppressive than the enemy we send them off to fight. It is mundane reality to me that though police officers and soldiers are diverse and defy stereotypes on the whole, police, soldiers, and judges are more dangerous and in need of more watching, requiring more explanation for their actions than the subjects of their law enforcement. For instance, I am currently more wary of actions FBI agents take than of actions militia members take. This implies condemnation of no one. It is merely a watchful attitude. I feel obliged to be open and forthright about my areas of distrust.

When you opt to attempt peace rather than war in the face of violence, you accept that your exclusive duty is to identify where among power imbalances you find yourself and decide what control you will take. Any talk of who else ought to be doing it lies outside this realm of discourse. Instead, it is in the realm of going through life deciding who to entrust to play God and to take care of our victims and offenders for us.

While in peacemaking, one acknowledges far more injustice, pain, and fear than when at war. Although one recognizes that no program or leader is likely to come forward and sweep away the most fearsome threats to our sense of personal and social security, one would do well to make peace because of the personal trust, security, and validation that exists there. I regard all programmatic promises that injustices and social problems will be "solved" as false and dangerously misleading. Any time and attention we invest in seeing someone else's program as complete is time and attention taken away from deciding what to do with the victims and offenders who are personally close.

Indigenous people and the Old Testament tell us that significant change in any political culture takes seven generations of concerted, personal, intergenerational transmission of peacemaking. As I discovered from my own inquiry into the Norwegians' transition from the Viking military empire to the post-Napoleonic "tight social fabric culture, this transformation took a generation squared—that is, twenty-odd generations of twenty-odd years apiece" (Pepinsky, 1991, p. 64).

Meanwhile, I have noticed that peacemaking allows my friends and I to feel more personally and socially secure in a shorter time. I do not need to pay a therapist because I find people who will let me vent and then validate me for free. I have friends who grow their own food and build their own homes. They would take me in if I were bedridden and provide for me no matter what my situation might be. This provides me with much security regarding my future if I should be in need.

As a child, I admired twentieth-century socialist lawyer Clarence Darrow, who was my motivation throughout law school. There, and in intervening years, I have by degrees given up my faith in the rule of law. It is not only that the relatively absolute power we give lawgivers and law enforcers tends to corrupt these power holders absolutely. It is that imposing a preexisting law or rule on someone literally amounts to letting one's prejudices override one's capacity to hear the many and various explanations and desires parties have.

The healing and trustworthy exercises of personal responsibility we seek in every crime or civil wrong requires precisely that those we can trust have their own ways of responding to the threat, the fear, and the pain at hand. The self-possession to make peace rests on being prepared to be guided by what the parties desire or have done, not on what some distant legislators imagined might turn out to be in their best interests. I gain a sense of security from having only those rules of law prevail that free and open evidence and dialogue over the threat at hand. (Thus, I am inherently fond of insisting on rights provided by public records, freedom of information, sunshine laws, and open meeting laws.) Anthropologists report that many indigenous tribunals begin by letting complainants and the accused take turns expressing their feelings, fears and wants freely, unrestrained by rules of evidence. This is how all peacemaking proceeds.

THINKING GLOBALLY, ACTING LOCALLY

Insofar as I believe in peacemaking enough to enjoy its fruits, I attend to interests at hand, knowing legal positions can be adjusted once the interests are brought out into the open. Harvard law professor and renowned international mediator Roger Fisher calls this process "getting to yes." Similar to deterrence in warmaking thought, what makes us more or less secure at the interpersonal level is no different from what makes international leaders and power figures come to terms or continue to send out their troops. Our capacity to create trust, security, and peace rests on being self-possessed enough to listen, empathize, and be guided by honest, open expression of the real, most fundamental interests and fears at hand. All a warmaker can hope for in a "crackdown" is to impose social restraint and bottle fear, anger, and defiance for the moment. Either people can adjust, or in a moment as long as a generation, a nation brought together by a charismatic figure like Gandhi or Tito can degenerate into attempted genocide, into fighting over national boundaries.

It is my fate to have grown up in a country that formally became the most globally hegemonic military/economic empire. Humanity cannot survive a higher military victory than that which the United States gained in World War II. Humanity cannot survive the consumption and waste of the Earth's resources as the average U.S. inhabitant consumes. We cannot evolve into everyone surviving at the present U.S. level of consumption. If we try hard enough, we will die trying. If we acknowledge such attitudes and appropriately adjust them, we may live and prosper globally as never before.

In making war, one tends to rely on prophecies as to which opposing forces will prevail. The hope for human survival rests exclusively on personal human capacity to let go of retaliation and gain greater measures of self-possession. Then and only then, figuratively and literally, can we stop defecating on one another. This degree of attention to one's own social control takes energy. It is harder to listen to quiet voices and to notice quiet despair when you let rage and fear take over your own conscious attention. Peacemaking rests on our capacity to act like the putative martial arts master who ceases fights before they begin. I cannot fathom how adding any form of heat to conflict creates safety. For example, if someone pointed a gun at me, I would like that person to know I am safely unarmed.

I find often that it is best to attend to other matters during times when others in a dispute are not (yet) taking care of their own business. I constantly and consciously restrain my own impulses to follow up when others do not get back to me or are not doing something they indicated they would. By now, in virtually any dispute in which I become involved, long intervals pass before I will receive notice of how outcomes took place or how they were arranged.

Native American traditionalists tell us we have a primary duty to enjoy life. Marilyn French tells us all peace and justice follow from the honest pursuit of personal fulfillment and happiness. I say all social security arises from the experience of trust and happiness. In my long period of trying to figure out how we achieve social control, how we genuinely achieve trust and social security, I have found that enjoying one's right to be open and honest, feeling and doing what one will instead of what one must, lies at the root of all security. That is the primary reinforcer of my commitment to trying to make peace.

There is no sense in acting out of moral obligation to make peace other than taking time to reflect and introduce oneself and seeking to hear what silent voices have to say. We sew trust into our social fabrics when the threads we weave into our dialogue carry no strings of demand that someone fulfill our expectations rather than her or his own. When self-possession gives way to attempting to possess the soul of anyone else's actions and to relying on others to live out one's own expectations, our capacity for control is lost to the fatalistic playing out of roles of the requited lover or victim of another's malfeasance or nonfeasance.

The happy surprise of allowing others to come through for us in unantici-pated, wondrous ways comes only when we let go of our own urge to make others do the right thing or give us our due. Moreover, any act that is done because someone else thinks or might think it is the right thing to do is a lie. Honesty is the force that keeps all threads of any social fabric from breaking. I can trust only when I perceive that someone has honestly chosen what he or she wants to do, not because he or she must do it. We cannot be trusted to continue doing what we must when our surveillance of one another drops. A goal of peacemaking is to manage to do without surveillance.

The late medical missionary, Thomas Merton, called failure to "say our own 'yeses' and 'nos'" as the source of all human violence. If a decision is made not to intervene in helping someone, or if a decision is made to inter-vene to impose a reward or punishment on someone, this is not peacemaking. Peacemaking requires having the honesty and respect to say quite openly, "I'm doing this because it makes me feel good and because anything else I can see doing would make me feel worse. If this be punishment, I hope to god it hurts." I ought to be prepared to laugh at any suffering I inflict or regret it enough to describe the pain and fear I have caused and take steps to do other-wise when similarly provoked in the future.

To illustrate, I sat beside one fellow during a campus disciplinary hearing. The president of the hearing body announced to my friend that he was con-sidered likable by the hearing officers; thus, their finding that he engaged in an evil deed was nothing personal. However, they believed he was the kind of person who would do what he did, and, accordingly, the rules dictated that he be "held" responsible (which, of course, denied him any room for assuming responsibility for his own response to the problem).

This hearing officer sent chills down my spine. As the world of how peace is *truly* rather than purportedly secured, I recognize that no single person or group is a greater obstacle to peace than any other. Where once I blamed judges or reporters for failure to do what was required by law or otherwise, I no longer expect them to be any different from any other group of us who feel powerless. Power holding carries its own fear of failure to do one's duty, which means that in a political culture dominated by warmaking discourse, power holders will become as personally un-self-possessed as those they op-press and violate. This has been the case since the Nuremberg war crime trials. In these trials it was globally recognized that acting on someone else's feelings or agenda, or following someone else's orders, was the surest way to give in to the impulse to hurt and kill people.

STRATEGIC ISSUES

Given that meaningful changes in the culture sufficient enough to make judges, offenders, journalists, police officers, victims, attorneys, and the like, more reli-able overall will take generations, the change *we* create by doing what it takes to make peace with anyone, anywhere, anytime is a logical starting place for all of us. In any interaction, we gain control by looking past the difficulties of the moment confronting us, tempering our urges to lash out or to say the polite and proper thing with conscious self-awareness of what tenor of response we can anticipate. I offer this simple illustration of control. Compare how much you need to brake and how tightly you have to grip and move the steering wheel as you roll through an exit ramp from an expressway. If you look only at the road directly in front of your car, rather than focusing your eyes at the most distant point or exit ramp ahead, you will fight for control the first way and by contrast cruise comfortably through the curve the other way.

Control requires taking the time to acknowledge feelings and consider the difference between bashing an enemy versus taking time for introduction and listening to the thoughts and feelings of the other side. Peacemaking requires being self-possessed enough to determine which of the four steps in peace-making comes next and how it will be accomplished. It is important to let go of concern for making things happen and instead choose a response to what is happening. Herein lies the only power to attain personal safety and security for yourself and others.

Although others may want to know where I stand, it is important not to plead ignorance or to impose my opinions and feelings on others. Not even the smallest child, from a peacemaking vantage point, deserves that kind of patronization. Holding back honest misgivings about what others tell me or ask me is not only a disservice to and devaluation of myself; it also forecloses anyone else from addressing my concerns in relation to the concerns of others except through blind luck. I become trustworthy with anyone insofar as I convey empathy and that my actions accommodate the other's concerns. This happens when we both hear where I stood before, and then account for, in the other person's terms, how far I have listened and shifted my position.

I do not have to call anyone names. I do not have to presuppose that any-one's response to me will confirm my prejudices against his or her trustwor-thiness. I can choose my words carefully to connote no more than my own feelings and (dis)inclinations. I can attend to threats to the honor of someone I will confront and can balance criticism and fears with mention of things I trust and value. However, I cannot take for granted I am trusted and not lied to by those who do not know roughly where I stand.

There are several benefits to having faith in one's own capacity to make peace. This faith leads one (1) to pause, reflect on, and survey the range of our own feelings as we enter any conflict; (2) to introduce where our interests lie at the moment we seek information from another, including among conflicting parties; (3) to first "look down"; and (4) to then "dump up" if possible with uncompromising, open honesty about what we fear and trust, acting always in the name of our own feelings and judgments alone, with reference to others but without attributing our own actions to any of them.

This is all peacemaking entails. I cannot determine what I need to do in any conflict until I have listened to what other parties know and feel about the situation and until these other parties indicate what interests are guiding their response. Any prior speculation about what needs to happen is harmless as long as I keep the speculation in the idle perspective it deserves, practically speaking. When I let my duty to my own promise of "consequences" or let someone else's rules take precedence over stopping, looking, and listening to parties' own honest accounts of themselves in the situation at hand, I may win the war but will lose all my power to learn from the parties how they and I can comfortably weave a social fabric in harmonious concert. I lose my entire capacity to make my world safer for myself and others in the reality of each conflictual moment I face. I become prisoner to the performance of others and prisoner to engaging in my own "societally" given script. I am reduced to acting like any pure machine, and I become a threat to everyone's security, including my own. I fail to notice that even I am hurting others; I lose my capacity to care and respond.

No one ever deserves abuse. My capacity to make peace rests ultimately in taking care of myself. Insofar as I let people unfairly impose their help on me or act in this capacity, I transform their role. They now have to take care of my problems as well as their own. If I am tired in a struggle, I should withdraw from it until I feel emotionally and physically strong enough to resume my efforts. No real construction of peace depends on any single person to make it happen; and when peace breaks out, it is the concertedness of everyone's resonant and mutually accommodating actions that makes it so.

PROSPECTS FOR PEACE

Insofar as we create trust and true security by making peace with one another despite the warmaking systems in which we live and work, our warmaking systems will die down from disuse by definition. In the field of criminal justice, everyone seems to want to know what we can do with all of our prisoners. I know from experience that by the time victims have significantly healed and gained renewed security from even the most violent of crimes (for example, repeated rape), everyone involved has moved past the view that a $100,000 maximum-security cell is needed to confine a formerly violent and possibly future violent assailant. This would tear the offender profoundly and physically from any social fabric. There are too many other straightforward ways to weave victims and offenders into social fabrics to fear that the offender will just be abandoned to her or his destructive obsessions.

CONCLUSION

After years of researching on the complex literature of crime and punishment, and of war and peace, this is all that remains of what I know of how to achieve social control. People cannot talk, listen together, and fight one another at the same time. Peacemaking is a matter of injecting doses of conversation into our social space—conversation that embraces the greatest victims and most powerful oppressors of the moment at the same time. The sooner the conversation begins, the less likely explosive and violent relations will develop. The sooner dialogue commences, the sooner power imbalances will be mediated, and the sooner peace will be made. This chapter is but a guide to starting and carrying out such conversations.

REVIEW QUESTIONS

1. What does "social control" mean in this text? How does it compare with what "social control" means to you?

2. What differences are there between how social insecurity and danger are viewed when one takes a warmaking or peacemaking approach to social control?

3. What is the ultimate objective of the art and science of peacemaking, and how does that contrast to the ultimate objective of warmaking?

4. What is the significance of trust and honesty in peacemaking?

5. What are peacemaking's four steps?

6. In what respects may peacemaking be said to be both a more pessimistic and optimistic approach to social control than warmaking?

7. Where might you begin to try making peace?

REFERENCES

Brock-Utne, B. (1985). *Educating for peace: A feminist perspective*. New York: Pergamon.

Brock-Utne, B. (1989). *Feminist perspectives on peace and peace education*. New York: Pergamon.

Bystydzienski, J. (1993). *Women transforming politics*. Bloomington: Indiana University Press.

Christie, N. (1981). *Limits to pain*. Oxford: Martin- Robertson.

Consedine, J. (1995). *Restorative justice: Healing the effects of crime*. Lyttleton, NZ: Ploughshares.

Cordella, J. P. (1991). Reconciliation and the mutualist model of community. In H. E. Pepinsky & R. Quinney (Eds.), *Criminology as peacemaking* (pp. 30–46). Bloomington: Indiana University Press.

Morris, R. (1995). *Penal abolition: The practical choice.* Toronto: Canadian Scholars' Press.

Pepinsky, H. E. (1976). *Crime and conflict: A study of law and society.* Oxford: Martin-Robertson/Academic.

Pepinsky, H. E. (1991). *The geometry of violence and democracy.* Bloomington: Indiana University Press.

Quinney, R. (1991). The way of peace: On crime, suffering, and service. In H. E. Pepinsky & R. Quinney (Eds.), *Criminology as peacemaking* (pp. 3–13). Bloomington: Indiana University Press.

Tifft, L., & Markham, L. (1991). Battering women and battering Central Americans: A peacemaking synthesis. In H. E. Pepinsky & R. Quinney (Eds.), *Criminology as peacemaking* (pp. 115–153). Bloomington: Indiana University Press.

Wagner-Pacifici, R. (1994). *Discourse and destruction: The city of Philadelphia versus MOVE.* Chicago: University of Chicago Press.

Prophetic Criticism
and Social Justice

P rophetic criticism raises questions about what it means to authentically live in society. To fully "be" is to move in the direction of that which is demanded of each of us. Quinney's essay links the political-economic thought of Karl Marx with the prophetic theology of Paul Tillich. Specifically, Quinney is interested in the relationship between our existence and our essence, between what "is" and what "ought" to be, and how this divide can be bridged. This interest is applied to the question of defining justice in contemporary capitalist society. Quinney argues that the way people talk about justice is an indictor of the quality of their existence. Thus, the meaning of justice is socially constructed. Further, he suggests that a culture's expression of justice can reduce the chasm between our existential situation and our essential nature. In contemporary capitalist society, however, justice is defined mostly through laws. This definition of justice subjects it to the survival needs of the capitalist system. Quinney further explores his notion of justice when considering the problem of crime. The needs of the contemporary capitalist system regarding issues of crime and criminal justice are to promote and maintain law and order. Justice in crime-related practices, then, is expressed through punishment—that is, deterrence, retribution, repression, and incapacitation. Quinney, however, suggests an alternative view of justice, a prophetic interpretation that calls for the humanization of work, the democratization of the economy, and the elimination of all oppression. Prophetic justice is the link between what "is" and what "ought" to be, the bond between our existential conditions and our essential natures. In this context, social justice is a reclaiming of "being" rooted in history yet demanded by God.

4

The Prophetic Meaning
of Social Justice

RICHARD QUINNEY

HISTORICAL BACKGROUND

The conditions of our existence provide the setting for the possibilities of creation and fulfillment. Karl Marx (1963) noted that our future is to be made "under circumstances directly encountered, given and transmitted from the past" (p. 15). We are thus the products of our culture and the creators of it. While our daily struggle is of both transforming the existing order and removing conditions of oppression to an authentic existence, a new social order will emerge only out of the productive forces and contradictions of the old order. History is made both subjectively and objectively, as the result of conscious struggle *and* as the development of the economic mode of production.

Our destiny, moreover, is directed by the powers of our origin. As the theologian Paul Tillich (1977) reminds us, in the prophetic tradition of Jewish and Christian thinking, the symbol of providence expresses to us "the confidence that what is not utterly removed from what should be; that in spite of the present lack of fulfillment, being is moving in the direction of fulfillment" (p. 108). The unity of the "is" and the "ought" is expressed in our prophetic understanding. Both Marx and Tillich reaffirm for us the prophetic tradition. Being moves in the direction of that which is demanded.

The basic question asked in both Marxism and prophetic theology is the relation between existence and essence—that is, between our existential situation and our essential nature. In the theology of Tillich, consistent with the existential Marx, three fundamental concepts characterize the problem of existence and essence. The first is the Latin phrase *Esse qua esse bonum est,* which is a basic dogma of Christianity. It means "Being as being is good" or, in the biblical mythological form, "God saw everything that he had created, and behold, it was good." The second statement is the universal fall, fall meaning the transition from this essential goodness into existential estrangement from oneself, which happens in every living being and in every time. The third statement refers to the possibility of salvation. We should remember that salvation

---

This essay is adapted from Richard Quinney, *Class, State, and Crime,* 2nd ed. (New York: Longman, 1980).

is derived from *salvus* or *salus* in Latin, which means "healed" or "whole," as opposed to disruptiveness (Tillich, 1959). These three considerations of essential goodness, existential estrangement, and the possibility of something else through which the cleavage is overcome, necessarily point to the fundamental nature of our contemporary condition.

In the contemporary historical situation, under capitalism, our essential being is deprived. The separation of existence and essence is the tragic condition of human life in capitalist society. The contemporary capitalist world is caught in what Tillich (1948), going beyond Marx's materialist analysis of capitalism, calls a *sacred void,* the human predicament on both a spiritual and a sociopolitical level. Among the vacuous characteristics of present civilization are (1) a mode of production that enslaves workers, (2) an analytic rationalism that saps the vital forces of life and transforms all things (including human beings) into objects of calculation and control, (3) a loss of feeling for the translucence of nature and the sense of history; (4) a demotion of our world to a mere environment, and (5) a hopelessness about the future.

From the existential condition of capitalist society emerges the possibility of a transformation that will allow us to achieve the full potential of our being. Because the conditions under which we live in capitalist society divorce us from our essential nature, a transformation of the world becomes necessary (Avineri, 1969). The socialist demand is confirmed by our being. "The promise of socialism grows out of the analysis of being itself" (Tillich, 1959, pp. 202–249).

In closing the separation between existence and essence, we create a reality in which our wholeness is more fully realized. Through human praxis the unity of production and product, subject and object, and spirit and matter becomes known. We become the subjects (the "movers of history") in the world we create. Thus, Kosik (1976) observes, "the world of reality is not a secularized image of paradise, of a ready-made and timeless state, but is a process in which mankind and the individual *realize* their truth, i.e., humanize man" (p. 7). The specifics of truth are not given and preordained; they are constructed in the process of searching for the unity of being in the world. Being essentially human is realized in the course of consciously transforming our human history, always with an image of what it is to be truly human and spiritually whole.

Being human in the world is thus a social and moral endeavor. In the human praxis of transformation, we create a world of shared meanings and actions in bridging the gap between existence and essence. As human beings we construct a language of communication charged with the moral meaning of our being. The categories of human language contain and presuppose definite forms of life (Gadamer, 1975). Thus it is that justice, one of the most significant terms in any language, is a fundamental key to the form of life in a society. The substance of the term certainly differs from one society to another and from one class to another within a society. However, in the varying conceptions of justice, the character of social and moral life is registered and conducted.

The way we talk about justice—that is, the concept of justice we consciously hold—is a guide to the state of our being. And our commonsense notion of justice is a most important part of the process of transforming our social and moral world, of resolving the separation between our existence and the essence that may be realized. That notions of justice may actually increase the separation is the contradiction and the moral failure built into some societies, especially that sense of justice found in contemporary society.

JUSTICE IN CAPITALIST SOCIETY: BASIC ASSUMPTIONS ABOUT JUSTICE

Justice is an absolute statement of an ideal. Nevertheless, justice as an ideal rests on a concrete historical foundation. In practice, justice is inevitably shaped by social reality: it is an integral part of the social, economic, and political structure of society. Rather than being removed from the material world, justice plays a crucial role in establishing and reproducing social order.

Nowhere is justice more important, both in theory and practice, than in capitalist society. The concept of justice has evolved with the development of capitalism. At each stage of economic development, the particular notion of justice has been tied to the material basis of production, playing a part in securing the existing order. The struggle between classes, central to developing capitalism, is regulated by capitalist justice. Justice in capitalist society, today as always, is an ideological and practical instrument in the class struggle.

The notion of justice we conventionally know is an accumulation of ideas formed in the course of the development of capitalism. However mystified, justice is a social norm that is a directive for guiding human action (Bird, 1967). Actions are judged in terms of the directive, and justice is dispensed according to some notion of equality for people in similar situations. But as social norm, following our Greek heritage, justice complies with the interests of the stronger, mainly with the needs of the ruling class as expressed in law.

Although justice is to be applied to individual cases, the general objective is the promotion of social order. As thus conceived, individualistic needs and social order are combined to form the "healthy" whole:

> The problem of justice is closely related to the problem of a healthy order of society. It is concerned with the healthfulness of the parts as well as with sound condition of the whole. These two aspects of justice are, of course, inseparable. If the needs and aspirations of the individuals composing society are reasonably taken care of by the system of justice, and if reciprocal concern for the health of the social body exists among the members of society, there is a good chance that a harmonious and flourishing society will be the result. (Bodenheimer, 1967, p. 8)

In capitalist society, the healthy order is the one that primarily benefits the capitalist class—that is, the class that owns and controls the productive process.

To our contemporary mind, questions of justice are generally restricted to a consideration of "equal justice" and severely limited even within that realm. Again following the Greek path, justice originates in the belief that equals should be treated equally *and* unequals treated unequally (Ginsberg, 1965). In practice this has come to mean that discrimination in dispensing justice for infractions should not occur beyond what is justified by relevant differences. This leaves wide open such questions as the concrete meaning of equality, the social reality of equality and inequality, the existence of class conflict and state power, and the struggle for a better society beyond a narrow sense of justice.

Justice in contemporary capitalist society equates the limited idea of equal justice with the formulation and administration of positive law. Capitalist justice, in other words, is made concrete in the establishment of legal order. All notions of goodness, evil, and the earthly kingdom become embodied in capitalist law. Everyday life questions of justice are confined to whether the law is arbitrarily administered. Justice is grounded, not in some alternative idea of social good or natural order but in the survival needs of the capitalist system. Judgment is now in the hands of legal agencies of the capitalist state. Legality and the "rational" administration of the law have become the capitalist symbols of justice.

In recent years, in response to a crisis in the legitimation of capitalist institutions as well as the more general crisis in the capitalist system, there has been renewed interest in the concept of justice. Such diverse presentations as Rawls's (1971) *A Theory of Justice* and Nozick's (1974) *Anarchy, State, and Utopia* attest to the chaos in our thinking about justice. Both philosophical treatises are in defense of some version of capitalism. Serious academic attention is being directed to the philosophical underpinnings for modern capitalist society. However, Marxist critiques, theories, and practices are beginning to emerge.

The current theories of justice are rooted in the moral and political problems generated by advanced capitalism. The solutions presented by Rawls and Nozick are within the liberal bourgeois tradition. Nevertheless, while Nozick adopts a pure form of laissez-faire capitalism, today called "libertarianism," Rawls bases his discussion on a philosophy of the liberal welfare state. Justice for Nozick is a world of separate individuals, with individual rights, who exist and act irrespective of being in society. From this "state of nature" follows the right to property, a free market of competition, and very little interference from a "minimal state." Rawls's theory of justice, while similarly attentive to the freedom of individuals to achieve their own good, considers the principles necessary to govern the distribution of the means to achieve individual goods. It is the modern welfare state that assures and regulates this distribution.

Rawls bases his theory of justice on a hypothetical condition where rational people live in an "original position." There is consensus on the principles of living together, a liberal agreement of what is important for the fulfillment of individual goals. Omitted from this individualistic view are the realities of class conflict, exploitation, and ruling-class power (R. Miller, 1974; Nagel, 1973). Moreover, the "original position" is neutral toward values that emphasize cooperative relations between people and collective or communal activity. Opposed is any conception of society that sees human life as the collective achievement of a social good.

The liberal version of justice in capitalist society selectively and necessarily excludes a socialist vision of social order. The essence of liberalism is a society made up of autonomous units that associate only to further individual ends. Capitalist market relations are the paradigm for justice in the liberal philosophy of justice (Barry, 1972). An alternative theory of justice in society, one based on cooperative and collective action, must be found in socialist philosophy. This is a philosophy worked out in the course of socialist practice.

THE RISE OF CRIMINAL JUSTICE:
PRINCIPLES OF (CRIMINAL) JUSTICE

The capitalist notion of justice is most explicitly represented in the application to the problem of crime. Since the mid-1960s, with the increasing crisis of capitalism, official and public attention has focused on rising crime and its control. A solution to the crisis has become simply that of fighting the domestic enemy—crime. In a presidential message to Congress in 1965, the "war on crime" was launched. President Lyndon Johnson (on March 8, 1965) declared that "we must arrest and reverse the trend toward lawlessness," suggesting that "crime has become a malignant enemy in America's midst." Congress responded by enacting the Omnibus Crime Control and Safe Streets Act, noting in its opening statement (1969) the scale of the project:

> Congress finds that the high incidence of crime in the United States threatens the peace, security, and general welfare of the Nation and its citizens. To prevent crime and to insure the greater safety of the people, law enforcement efforts must be better coordinated, intensified, and made more effective at all levels of government.

A new form of crime control was being established in capitalist society. Not only was the war on crime intensified by legislation, presidential commissions, and policy research by liberal academicians, but the capitalist state was now instituting a new system of domestic control. Especially with the newly created federal agency, the Law Enforcement Assistance Administration (LEAA), with appropriations amounting to millions of dollars, all levels of government were involved in planning and implementing an apparatus to secure the existing capitalist order (see Quinney, 1974, pp. 95–113).

In the process, a new terminology was being created, that of criminal justice. Theoretically, the terminology updates the ideology of "law and order." But adding to the conventional image, the terminology of criminal justice recognizes the new emphasis being placed on maintaining the existing order through the tools and agencies of the capitalist state. In practice, criminal justice represents an innovation in control—indeed, the establishment of a new system of control, a "criminal justice system." With the euphemism of criminal justice, a new system of control has been established and (at the same time) justified. Today we are all attuned in one way or another to criminal justice.

With the war on crime and the development of a new criminal justice system, there emerged the new field of criminal justice research and education. The need for criminal justice research was expressed by the President's Commission on Law Enforcement and Administration of Justice in 1967. Congress responded by establishing the National Institute of Law Enforcement and Criminal Justice through a provision in the Omnibus Crime Control and Safe Streets Act of 1968. The National Institute provides a mechanism for initiating and coordinating criminal justice research on a national level, providing resources beyond those already furnished by other federal agencies, such as the Center for Studies of Crime and Delinquency at the National Institute of Mental Health.

Since its creation in 1968, the activities of the National Institute of Law Enforcement and Criminal Justice have grown considerably in scope. The Crime Control Act of 1973 further expanded the role of the National Institute by giving it authority to (1) develop training programs for criminal justice personnel; (2) create an international clearinghouse for the collection and dissemination of criminal justice information, including data on acts of crime; and (3) evaluate programs and projects. The criminal justice system in the United States was increasingly being rationalized through the introduction and application of a new scientific technology of criminal justice.

Recognizing that the new technology requires an educated and indoctrinated personnel, academic programs in criminal justice have developed rapidly in the last two decades. These programs have had the effect of changing the social sciences. Courses that consider the phenomenon of crime, such as criminology courses taught in sociology departments, now give more attention to criminal justice and in many cases have adopted the criminal justice and administrative perspective. Furthermore, some criminal justice programs have grown out of former social science courses. At some colleges and universities, courses in the sociology of crime have been shifted to the criminal justice curriculum. The modern move to criminal justice, in other words, is shaping the nature of our lives and minds in many ways. We are in an age of criminal justice.

The criminal justice movement is a state-initiated and state-supported effort to rationalize mechanisms of social control. The larger purpose is to secure a capitalist order that is in grave crisis, likely in its final stages of development. The criminal justice system will surely be modified in response to further problems generated by late capitalism. Technological as well as ideological solutions will be attempted. There will be greater efforts at criminal justice planning to develop a comprehensive system of criminal justice. Not only will the traditional agencies of the law be systematized, involving the police and the courts, but more emphasis will be on the prevention of crime.

In addition, alternatives to the existing criminal justice agencies are being proposed and implemented. Cases are to be diverted from the courts, and new agencies ("noncriminal justice institutions") will process cases formerly handled by the police and the courts. This leaves the criminal justice system free to deal with serious offenses against the state and the economy. At the same time, it allows a wide range of social behavior subject to surveillance and control by the state. Criminal justice is expanding, and in the process it will make further changes to provide greater control within the capitalist order.

Finally, the state is initiating the "participation" of the citizenry in crime control. Public concern about crime is being channeled into approved kinds of responses. The public is thus being enlisted into the criminal justice system. In cities large and small, citizens have been organized to fight crime by (1) encouraging victims to report all crimes and testifying against the accused, (2) helping the police by patrolling their own neighborhoods, (3) serving as auxiliary police or sheriff's reserves, (4) keeping watch on neighbors' homes, (5) reporting suspicious activities in their neighborhoods, (6) securing their own homes from crime, (7) educating children to obey the laws and respect the police, (8) keeping watch on courts to spot judges who are soft on crime, and (9) demanding stronger anticrime laws.

We are all to be a part of the criminal justice system. However, the official programs for citizen participation are being contradicted by initiatives being taken by people outside state-sponsored programs. Built into the state efforts at citizen participation is a dialectic that supports autonomous community action removed from state control. Developing alongside the criminal justice system is a grassroots approach that is beyond the design of the state. The dialectic undoubtedly will advance in coming years. Community actions themselves will be subject to criminal justice.

CRIME AND PUNISHMENT:
WHAT IS SOCIAL JUSTICE?

The social, political, and economic events of recent years in the United States, and in the whole of the capitalist world, have forced social theorists to new formulations about the nature of the crisis in social order. A Marxist theory provides a critique of the crisis in capitalist societies. Meanwhile, conventional social theory seeks intellectual and policy solutions that attempt to preserve the existing order.

One of the crucial points at which conventional social theory is being revised is in reference to crime and criminal justice. Crime has come to symbolize the ultimate crack in the armor of the existing social order. Given the modern pessimism that social problems cannot really be solved without drastically altering the established order, controls must be instituted to protect "our society." Therefore, recent thinking about crime, combined with proposed policies, have to be taken seriously as containing notions for the revision of social theory.

Several books about crime and criminal justice, and considerable empirical research, are providing important ideas for the formulations that would secure the capitalist order. These works bridge the interests of a range of social scientists including sociologists, economists, criminologists, legal behaviorists, and policy scientists. That most of these books are grounded in a moral philosophy, attending particularly to a notion of justice, makes their appearance even more important. What is emerging for the conventional social theorists, then, the theorists who would preserve the established system, is a new philosophy and likely a revised social theory for advanced capitalist society.

Most social theorists postulate some notion about the nature of human nature. For Wilson (1975), a "clear and sober understanding of the nature of man" is required not only for purposes of theory but for "the proper design of public policies" (p. xi). Human nature and subsequent policy are simply conceived: "Wicked people exist"—"Nothing avails except to set them apart from innocent people" (p. 209). Crime, in all its reification, thus provides the metaphor for our human nature; crime represents human nature in its "less attractive" form. To think about crime as Wilson does is to advance one possible notion of being human and one possible way of controlling that nature.

Moreover, being wicked (and criminal) is a *rational* choice. In all our affairs, following this image, we are self-interested people rationally pursuing what is best for ourselves and, perhaps, our families. We are rational in the capitalistic, individual, and economic sense. Our criminality, according to the economic statement on crime explicitly stated in an influential article by Becker (1968), is utilitarian: "A person commits an offense if the expected utility to him exceeds the utility he could get by using his time and resources at other activities" (p. 176). The obvious solution coming from the rational-utilitarian model is to deter crime by raising the risks of crime.

The notion of the capitalist (rational and utilitarian) individual gives support to the renewed interest in deterrence as social policy. Research by sociologists seeks to establish the importance of "certainty" and "swiftness" of punishment in deterring crime (see Tittle & Logan, 1973). In addition there are legal and philosophical works, such as *Deterrence* by Zimring and Hawkins (1973). In this book, legal scholars lend their weight to the new utilitarianism, arguing that the purpose of the criminal sanction is to deter criminal acts. This is accomplished by declaring and administering pain in cases of noncompliance to the legal code of the existing order. While the book contains an elaborate framework for empirically determining the "deterrent effect" of punishment, the overall thrust is to make deterrence (that is, punishment) "morally tolerable."

Although the traditional dichotomy between liberal and conservative may yet distinguish responses to some issues, when discussing crime and criminal policy, the distinction is of diminishing importance. The practical possibilities of punishment characterize the modern debate. What binds Wilson's thinking to the scheme of Zimring and Hawkins (1973), and these works with van Den Haag's (1975) conservative argument in his book explicitly called *Punishing Criminals,* is the contemporary justification for further instituting punishment in the capitalist state. As the "rehabilitation" ideal proves itself bankrupt in practice, liberals and conservatives alike (all within the capitalist hegemony) resort to the utilitarianism of pain.

New emphasis is given to the prison as a place of punishment. Morris (1974) furnishes "general principles under which imprisonment may be part of a rational criminal justice system" (p. 2). Although some forms of rehabilitation may be attempted within the prison of the future, mainly in a "facilitative" capacity, the principal objective of the prison is to punish the criminal. Morris thus writes, "In my view, penal purposes are properly retributive and deterrent. To add reformative purposes to that mix, as a purpose of the sanction as distinct from a collateral aspiration, produces neither clemency nor justice" (p. 58). Morris then tries to justify imprisonment as a rational form of control, providing a moral as well as rational framework for incarceration. Justice and rationality are thus linked.

With works and ideas such as these, combined with the sociological research that seemingly gives support, we have the reconstruction of a reality that takes as given the existing social order. Rather than suggest an alternative order, one based on a different conception of human nature, political economy, and social justice, the authors present us with schemes that merely justify further repression within the established order. The solutions being offered can only exacerbate the conditions of our existence.

It is with such convoluted rationality that Wilson turns his thinking to an epistemology of causal and policy analysis. In this discussion, Wilson (1975) lays bare the elements of the new utilitarianism that increasingly characterizes both government policy and social theory. After reviewing traditional theorizing about crime, Wilson (pp. 48–54) argues that such theorizing about the "root causes" of crime fails as it cannot "supply a plausible basis for the advocacy of public policy." Policy based on causal analysis commits the "causal fallacy," which assumes "that no problem is adequately addressed unless its causes are eliminated." Public policy, therefore, should be directed to conditions that can more easily and deliberately be altered. A "policy analysis," as opposed to causal analysis, is accordingly addressed to those conditions that can be manipulated to produce the desired change. That is, for the reduction of crime, the policy analyst focuses on those instruments of control (primarily relating to deterrence) that will "at what cost (monetary and nonmonetary) produce how much of a change in the rate of a given crime."

Hence, policy analysis for the new criminal justice is grounded, in theory and practice, in individual utilitarianism. Wilson (1975) writes, "The policy analyst is led to assume that the criminal acts *as if* crime were the product of a free choice among competing opportunities and constraints. The radical individualism of Bentham and Beccaria may be scientifically questionable but prudently necessary" (p. 56). The infrastructure of early capitalism is being revitalized to confront the problems of late capitalism.

The policies that follow from this version of reality emphasize deterrence and incapacitation. For Wilson there is little the police can do in reducing crime, since the police are not the crucial agency in the system. Moreover, rehabilitation does not deter crime. The best that rehabilitation can do is to isolate and incapacitate. Wilson (1975) states, "of far greater importance are those agencies that handle persons once arrested and that determine whether, how soon, and under what conditions they will be returned to the communities from which they came. These agencies are the criminal courts and the correctional institutions" (p. 163). And the function of the courts is not so much to determine guilt or innocence but, in fact, to decide what to do with criminals. Thus, what is needed is "good" sentencing—that is, dispositions that "minimize the chance of a given offender's repeating his crime," considering also the "effect any given sentence will have on actual or potential offenders" and the extent to which the sentence gives "appropriate expression to our moral concern over the offense" and conforms "to our standards of humane conduct" (p. 164).

Such sentencing, Wilson (1975) continues, should increase the probability of imprisonment, since this seems to deter crime. While severity of penalties "cannot be the norm," certainty of punishment must be. The court system, therefore, is where legal control is best concentrated and dispensed. Nevertheless, Wilson warns, in giving some attention to the problem of civil liberties, we in the United States must be willing to "accept both a higher level of crime and disorder and a larger investment in the resources and facilities needed to cope with those who violate the law and, despite our procedural guarantees, are caught by its agents" (p. 182).

The resurgence of interest in crime and punishment is characterized by an even larger problem. In spite of the elaborate legal, philosophical, and behavioralist arguments presented in recent books and articles on crime and punishment, the works lack critical understanding. The thoughts are grounded within the sensibility of the existing conventional order. What we are given— whether in Wilson's thinking about crime, Morris's proposal for imprisonment, Zimring and Hawkins's scheme for considering deterrence, or Gibbs's (1975) *Crime, Punishment, and Deterrence*—is a defense of punishment. The latter work, in spite of all its theoretical and empirical specification, revises the possibility of deterrence as sound social policy. But, more to the point, in these texts we are given a defense of punishment that is to be applied within our unique historical context, in the protection of a social order based on late capitalist development. Punishment becomes the solution when our vision is confined within the problem itself. Being both proposed and adopted in policy is the "new justice model" based on punishment, which is expressed in mandatory sentencing, "flat time," and the like (for a critique, see Platt & Takagi, 1977). Social theory, if not public policy, should be capable of more than this.

This new justice model was represented in the influential report of the Committee for the Study of Incarceration (Von Hirsch, 1976). The report, titled *Doing Justice,* combined the work of lawyers, philosophers, historians, and social scientists over a period of several years. Couched in the language of punitive reform, the purpose of the report was to create a "fairer and less brutal penal system." The criminal sanction of punishment (mainly the length of the prison sentence) was to be limited, but the aim of the report was nevertheless to provide a rationale for punishment. Rather than question the nature of the society in the first place, a scheme of punishment was designed to serve the ends of the existing society. In proposing a justice for the present and the future, there was a return to the justice of the past:

Some of our conclusions may seem old-fashioned. To our surprise, we found ourselves returning to the ideas of such Enlightenment thinkers as Kant and Beccaria, ideas that antedated notions of rehabilitation that emerged in the nineteenth century. We take seriously Kant's view that a person should be punished because he or she deserves it. We argue, as both Kant and Beccaria did, that severity of punishment should depend chiefly on the seriousness of the crime. We share Beccaria's interest in placing limits on sentencing discretion. (p. 6)

Moreover, punishment was defended on grounds of its deterrent effect and also according to the value that those who are defined as criminal deserve to be punished. The penalty was a penalty deserved based on the seriousness of the past conduct of the "criminal" and the seriousness of the act in question. Rehabilitation (or any attempt to change behavior) was rejected in favor of a penalty for the behavior. The sentencing system of criminal justice became technically rational: "Graded levels of seriousness [were] established, and the guidelines [specified] which offense categories belonged to which seriousness level" (p. 99). Such was (and is) the nature of reform at the present stage of capitalist development.

When it comes specifically to justice, the revitalization of conventional social theory is restricted to a limited historical version of it. For Wilson (1975), in his thoughts about the death penalty, justice is reduced to whether the death penalty subscribes to considerations of "fitness and fairness" (p. 184). Similarly, for Morris (1974) in his defense of imprisonment, justice is a matter of "desert," as "the maximum of punishment that the community extracts from the criminal to express the severity of the injury his crime inflicted on the community as a condition of readmitting him to society" (p. 74). Morris, in drawing from Rawls's rationalistic treatise on justice (a variant within the utilitarian tradition), determines the extent of criminal punishment and imprisonment according to what is "deserved" by the offender's crime.

All of these writings subscribe to a combination of two unique notions of justice. They conceive of justice as protecting acknowledged "rights" within the current order and as distributing punishment according to desert. The new justice model dispenses justice (that is, punishment) for the purpose of preserving the capitalist social order and in accordance to what the offender deserves in the pursuit of rational action. This notion of justice is appropriate for the capitalist order; it assumes a hierarchy of rights and competitive social relations.

There is an alternative to capitalist notions of justice. In sharp contrast to the new justice model (which is actually a mixture of old justice) is the idea of justice as distribution according to *need*. D. Miller (1974) suggests that this latter form of justice is appropriate for a society based on cooperative social relations, a communal society, and a developing socialist society. It assumes that human beings behave (or are capable of behaving) cooperatively and altruistically without the use of financial rewards or penal sanctions. Although not likely to be found in capitalist societies, this notion of justice nevertheless has its own tradition. It is found in early and latter-day communal and religious movements, with basic elements present in socialist countries today.

As capitalist society continues to develop its own contradictions and crises, the contrasts between divergent conceptions of justice become evident. What we are witnessing in recent theories and practices of criminal justice is an attempt to reestablish a justice appropriate to a former age, a justice that ignores historical development but that would seemingly preserve the contemporary capitalist order.

However, our human development is also a struggle for a social justice. Beyond the conventional notions of crime and punishment is the creation of a new social order. In question is not merely the extent of justice, but what kind and under what conditions. Now we are beginning to attend to a socialist sense of justice.

A CRITIQUE OF CAPITALIST JUSTICE

The classic dichotomy about the meaning of justice dominates contemporary social science and ethical discourse. That dichotomy is found in the debate between Socrates and Thrasymachus that Plato chronicles in the first book of the *Republic* (Pitkin, 1972). When the question "What is justice?" is posed, Thrasymachus responds that "justice is the interest of the stronger," elaborating that what is regarded as just in a society is determined by the ruling elite acting on its own interest. Later Socrates gives his formulation of justice as "everyone having and doing what is appropriate to him"—that is, people trying to do the right thing.

Obviously, Thrasymachus and Socrates are talking about two different problems. Whereas Thrasymachus is giving us a factual description of how justice actually operates, Socrates is telling us about what people think they are doing when they attend to that which is called "justice." There is justice as an ideal of goodness and justice in practice in everyday life. Justice as officially practiced in contemporary society is the idealized and practical justice of the capitalist state. The question for us, then, given a Marxist understanding of the class and state character of capitalist justice, is how do we attend to correct action and the creation of a better life?

The general concept of justice serves the larger purpose of providing a standard by which we judge concrete actions. We critically understand the actions of the capitalist state, including the administration of criminal justice, because we have an idea of how things could be. Critical thought and related actions are made possible because we transcend the conventional ideology of capitalism. Because we have a notion of something else, a socialist life, we refuse to accept capitalist justice either in theory or in practice. Critical thought, as Arendt (1971) has noted, allows us to interrupt all ordinary activity, entering into a different existence: "Thinking, the quest for meaning, rather than the scientist's thirst for knowledge for its own sake, can be felt to be 'unnatural,' as though men, when they begin to think, engage in some activity contrary to the human condition" (p. 424). In talking and thinking about how things could be, we engage in thoughts and actions directed to the realization of a different life. Arendt adds that only with the desiring love of wisdom, beauty, and the like, are we prepared with a kind of life that promotes a moral existence. Only when we are filled with what Socrates called *eros,* a love that desires what is not, do we attempt to find what is good. In critical and collective effort, we change our form of life and alter the mode of social existence.

If any body of thought has a notion of truth and beauty, of how things could be, it is that of Marxism. In fact, Marxism is the philosophy of our time that takes as its primary focus the oppression of capitalist society. It is an analysis that is historically specific and locates contemporary problems in the existing political economy. Marxist theory provides, most importantly, a form of thought that allows us to transcend in theory and practice the oppression of the capitalist order.

Marx avoided the use of a justice terminology (McBride, 1975; Wood, 1972). He steered away from justice talk because he regarded it as "ideological twaddle" and detracting from a critical analysis of the capitalist system as a whole. Both Marx and Engels were in fact highly critical of the use of the justice notion, employed as a means of mystifying the actual operation of capitalism. At the same time, they found a way to critically understand capitalism that carried with it a condemnation that goes beyond any legal notion of justice. Thus, Marxist analysis provides us with an understanding of the capitalist system, a vision of a different world, and a political life in struggling for that society.

According to Marx and Engels, the problem with the concept of justice, as used in capitalist society, is that it is fundamentally a *juridical* or legal concept. As such, the concept is restricted to rational standards by which laws, social institutions, and human actions are judged (Wood, 1972). Moreover, this restricted analysis fails to grasp the material conditions of society. Instead, human life is to be understood in terms of the productive forces and relations of society, with the state as an expression of the prevailing mode of production (Marx, 1970). To focus on the juridical nature of social reality is to misunderstand the material basis of reality. An analysis limited to legalistic questions of justice systematically excludes the important questions about capitalist society.

The critique of capitalism for Marx is provided in the very form of the capitalist system. Capitalism rests on the appropriation of labor power from the working class. Capital is accumulated by the capitalist class in the course of underpaying the workers for products made by their labor. The capitalist mode of production depends on "surplus value," on unpaid labor. Capitalism itself is a system of exploitation. The servitude of the wage laborer to capital is essential to the capitalist mode of production. Marx's condemnation of capitalism and the need for revolutionary action is based on the innate character of capitalism, on an understanding of capitalism as a whole and on its position in human history.

We have thus moved out of the classical dichotomy between value and fact. In developing a Marxist analysis, value and fact are integrated into a comprehensive scheme. Values are always attached to what we take to be facts, and facts cannot exist apart from values. As Ollman (1971) observes in his discussion of Marx's method:

> It is not simply that the "facts" affect our "values," and our "values" affect what we take to be the "facts"—both respectable common sense positions—but that, in any given case, each includes the other and is part of what is meant by the other's concept. In these circumstances, to try to split their union into logically distinct halves is to distort their real character. (p. 48)

In a Marxist analysis, the description of social reality is at the same time an evaluation. Nothing is "morally neutral" in such an understanding. The description contains within itself its own condemnation and, moreover, a call to do something about the condition. The critique is at once a description of the condition and the possibility for transforming it. All things are in relation to one another, are one in the other.

Nevertheless, the more critical and general sense of justice will not disappear from philosophical and everyday discourse. That the terms *justice* and *social justice* continue to move us is an expression of their innate ability to join our present condition with an ultimate future. In our human struggle for existence, and for beauty, we will create the essential meaning of justice.

PROPHETIC JUSTICE

The roots of our contemporary world, in spite of capitalist relations and extreme religious secularity, are firmly placed in the Judeo-Christian apprehension of human existence and fulfillment. We have an image of our essential nature and the possibilities for our human existence. But this essence has become separated from the conditions of this world; it is contradicted by human existence. The cleavage between reality and essence can be overcome only by human action. The modern historical consciousness, in other words, is derived from the historical thinking of the Judeo-Christian prophetic tradition. Through the dynamics of history, we experience the meaning that guides and transcends our history. History and the trans-historical (time and the eternal), support our human existence.

Rooted deeply in the prophetic tradition is the urge toward justice in human affairs. This urge becomes the will of divine origin operating in history, providing the source of inspiration to all prophets and revolutionaries (Dombrowski, 1936). The identification of religion with political economy can be seen in the Hebrew prophets, who looked on all history as the divine law in human life. The highly ethical religion of the Old Testament prophets and the New Testament Jesus sees human society from the perspective of a holy and just God who forgives human beings but also judges them. The prophetic soul is hopeful and optimistic in the "confidence that God will form a better society out of the ashes of the present world" (Dombrowski, 1936, p. 26). The future in this world is built on the prophetic impulse that necessarily transcends this world.

Our prophetic heritage perceives the driving force of history as being the struggle between justice and injustice. We the people, in a covenant with God, are responsible for the character of our lives and our society and for the pursuit of righteousness, justice, and mercy. The social and moral order is consequently rooted in the divine commandments; morality rests on divine command and concern rather than on the relativity of reasonableness. We seek to realize a divine concern and command, the essence of perfect justice and love. The prophetic presence is real: "God is a living entity, closer than one's hands and feet, not a philosophic or theological abstraction" (Magnin, 1969, p. 108).

Prophecy thus proclaims the divine concern for justice. The idea and belief that "God is justice" means the divine support and guidance for such human matters as the demystification of conventional thought, the humanization of work, the democratization and socialization of the economy, and the elimination of all forms of oppression (Soelle, 1976). Apparent material issues are thus conceived in terms of the transcendent, adding the necessary element that is missing in a strictly materialist analysis. Prophetic justice is both sociological and theological. In fact, the dialectic of the theological and the sociological gives the prophetic its power as a critique and an understanding of human society.

To the prophets of the Old Testament, injustice (whether in the form of crime and corruption or in the wretched condition of the poor) is not merely an injury to the welfare of the people but a threat to existence. Moral comprehension, in other words, is rooted in the depth of the divine. This is a sense of justice that goes far beyond our modern liberal and legal notions of justice. For the prophets, the worldly virtue of justice is founded on the understanding that oppression on earth is a humiliation of God. Righteousness is not simply a value for the prophet; it is, as Heschel (1962a) observes, "God's part of human life, God's stake in human history" (p. 25). The relation between human life and the divine is at stake when injustice occurs. Justice is more than a normative idea; it is charged with the transcendent power of the infinite and the eternal, with the essence of divine revelation.

For the prophets, justice is like a mighty stream, not merely a category or mechanical process. In contrast, Heschel (1962a) states, "the moralists discuss, suggest, counsel; the prophets proclaim, demand, insist" (p. 215). Prophetic justice is charged with the urgency of the divine presence in the world. "Let judgment roll down like waters, And righteousness like a mighty stream" (Amos 5:24). In Heschel's (1962a) phrase, "what ought to be, shall be!" demonstrates that prophetic justice has a sense of urgency and depth (p. 213).

Justice, or the lack of it, is a condition of the whole people. An individual's act expresses the moral state of the many.

> Above all, the prophets remind us of the moral state of a people: Few are guilty, but all are responsible. If we admit that the individual is in some measure conditioned or affected by the spirit of society, an individual's

crime discloses society's corruption. In a community not indifferent to suffering, uncompromisingly impatient with cruelty and falsehood, continually concerned for God and every man, crime would be infrequent rather than common. (Heschel, 1962a, p. 16)

Prophecy is directed to the whole world as well as to the inner spirit of the individual.

The purpose of prophecy, and of prophetic justice, is to revolutionize history. Divine compassion is expressed in our time. The call is personal: "And what does the Lord require of you but to do justice, and to love mercy, and to walk humbly with your God?" (Micah 6:8). And we are all judged collectively in the presence of corruption and oppression:

> From the heavens Thou didst utter judgment;
> The earth feared and was still,
> When God arose to establish judgment
> To save all the oppressed of the earth. (Psalm 76:9)

The possibilities of life are neither wholly economic nor wholly political; they are also religious. Whereas the socialist struggle is necessarily temporal and in this world, the expectant goal is trans-historical and eternal.

We live in an era that tends to reject the claims of a religion-based prophetic theology. In his study of the Hebrew prophets, Heschel (1962b) notes that "owing to a bias against any experience that eludes scientific inquiry, the claim of the prophets to divine inspiration was, as we have seen, *a priori* rejected" (p. 192). A scientific rationality based entirely on empirical observation of this world excludes the prophetic critique of our existential estrangement from essence. History and its concrete conditions, accordingly, are bound solely by time; there is little that would guide us beyond the mortality of our earthly selves. This also means that an evaluation of our current situation is bound by the particular historical consciousness that comprehends nothing beyond itself. Not only have we silenced God, we have silenced ourselves before our own history. But, remembering our heritage, we begin to recover the prophetic in our lives and in our understanding of history.

The prophetic meaning of justice is in sharp contrast to the capitalist notion of justice. Distinct from capitalist justice, with its emphasis on human manipulation and control, prophetic justice is a form of address that calls human beings to an awareness of their historical responsibility and challenges them to act in ways that will change the existing human condition. Human fulfillment is found in the exercise of moral will in the struggle for a historical future. The pessimistic character of a deterministic and predictive materialism is overcome in the prophetic hope for a humane and spiritually filled existence.

Through the prophetic tradition, a tradition that is present also in the prophetic voice of Marxism, a meaning of justice that can transform the world and open the future is once again emerging. Marxism and theology are confronting each other in ways that allow us to understand our existence and consider our essential nature. The human situation, no longer completely bound by time, is "elevated into the eternal and the eternal becomes effective in the realm of time" (Tillich, 1971, p. 91). Reconciliation and redemption are realized through an apprehension of the eternal.

REVIEW QUESTIONS

1. What are some of the tensions between the political economic thought of Karl Marx and the prophetic theology of Paul Tillich?

2. What role does contemporary capitalism assume in creating and sustaining the form of justice in our society today?

3. Based on this chapter, define justice in relationship to the problem of crime in society.

4. What are some of the limitations of contemporary definitions of justice when considering the problem of crime?

5. What is prophetic justice?

6. How does prophetic justice differ from some of the other definitions discussed in this chapter?

7. What role do individuals assume in creating and sustaining prophetic justice?

REFERENCES

Arendt, H. (1971, Autumn). Thinking and moral considerations. *Social Research, 38,* 417–446.

Avineri, S. (1969). *The social and political thought of Karl Marx.* London: Cambridge University Press.

Barry, B. (1972). *The liberal theory of justice: A critical examination of the principal doctrines in a theory of justice by John Rawls.* New York: Oxford University Press.

Becker, G. S. (1968, March–April). Crime and punishment: An economic approach. *Journal of Political Economy, 76,* 169–217.

Bird, O. A. (1967). *The idea of justice.* New York: Praeger.

Bodenheimer, E. (1967). *Treatise on justice.* New York: Philosophical Library.

Dombrowski, J. (1936). *The early days of Christian socialism in America.* New York: Columbia University Press.

Gadamer, H.-G. (1975). *Truth and method.* New York: Seabury.

Gibbs, J. R. (1975). *Crime, punishment, and deterrence.* New York: Elsevier.

Ginsberg, M. (1965). *On justice in society.* Baltimore: Penguin.

Heschel, A. J. (1962a). *The prophets.* Vol. 1. New York: Harper & Row.

Heschel, A. J. (1962b). *The prophets.* Vol. 2. New York: Harper & Row.

Kosik, K. (1976). *Dialectics of the concrete.* Dordrecht: Kluwer.

Magnin, E. R. (1969). The voice of prophecy in this satellite age. In H. M. Orlinsky (Ed.), *Interpreting the prophetic tradition.* Cincinnati: Hebrew Union College Press.

Marx, K. (1973). *The eighteenth brumaire of Louis Bonaparte.* New York: International.

Marx, K. (1970). *A contribution to the critique of political economy* (M. Dobb, Ed.). New York: International.

McBride, W. L. (1975, April). The concept of justice in Marx, Engels, and others. *Ethics, 85,* 204–218.

Miller, D. (1974, December). The ideological backgrounds to conceptions of social justice. *Political Studies, 22,* 387–399.

Miller, R. (1974, Winter). Rawls and Marxism. *Philosophy and Public Affairs, 3,* 167–191.

Morris, N. (1974). *Future of imprisonment.* Chicago: University of Chicago Press.

Nagel, T. (1973, April). Rawls and justice. *Philosophical Review, 82,* 220–234.

Nozick, R. (1974). *Anarchy, state, and utopia.* New York: Basic Books.

Ollman, B. (1971). *Alienation: Marx's conception of man in capitalist society.* New York: Cambridge University Press.

Pitkin, H. F. (1972). *Wittgenstein and justice.* Berkeley: University of California Press.

Platt, T., & Takagi, P. (1977, Fall–Winter). Intellectuals for law and order: A critique of the new realists. *Crime and Social Justice, 8,* 1–16.

Quinney, R. (1974). *Critique of legal order: Crime control in capitalist society.* Boston: Little, Brown.

Rawls, J. (1971). *A theory of justice.* Cambridge, MA: Harvard University Press.

Soelle, D. (1976, Fall). Review of *Marx and the Bible* by Jose Miranda. *Union Seminary Quarterly Review, 32,* 49–53.

Tillich, P. (1948). *The Protestant era.* Chicago: University of Chicago Press.

Tillich, P. (1959). *Theology of culture* (R. C. Kimball, Ed.). New York: Oxford University Press.

Tillich, P. (1977). *The socialist decision* (F. Sherman, Trans.). New York: Harper & Row.

Tittle, C. R., & Logan, C. H. (1973, Spring). Sanctions and deviance: Evidence and remaining questions. *Law and Society Review, 7,* 371–392.

United States House of Representatives. (1965). *Crime, its prevalence, and measures of prevention: Message from the 89th Congress, 8 March 1965.* Document No. 103. Washington, DC: U.S. Government Printing Office.

United States Statutes at Large. (1969). Omnibus Crime Control and Safe Streets Act, 1968. Public Law 90-351. Washington, DC: U.S. Government Printing Office.

van Den Haag, E. (1975). *Punishing criminals: Concerning a very old and painful question.* New York: Basic Books.

Von Hirsch, A. (1976). *Doing justice: The choice of punishments: Report of the Committee for the Study of Incarceration.* New York: Hill & Wang.

Wilson, J. Q. (1975). *Thinking about crime.* New York: Basic Books.

Wood, A. W. (1972, Spring). The Marxian critique of justice. *Philosophy and Public Affairs, 1,* 244–282.

Zimring, F. E., & Hawkins, G. J. (1973). *Deterrence: The legal threat in crime control.* Chicago: University of Chicago Press.

Anarchist Criminology
and Social Justice

n the following article, Ferrell explains that anarchists reject all forms of definitive knowledge claims. He argues that various points of view are equally valued when understanding an event or interpreting an experience. Thus, anarchism is more of an ongoing process than an eventual end point—that is, a constant spiral of change, reconstruction, and an openness to both. This openness to change is a recognition that ambiguity is the essence of life. We witness such ambiguity in our institutions, in our relationships, in our very identities. Ferrell describes this ambiguity in the context of "enjoying and embracing difference." Difference, and the unpredictability associated with it, allows people to be themselves, taking greater responsibility for what they do, than if external authority figures regulated their conduct by imposing conformity. Anarchist theory also calls for the establishment of small, decentralized neighborhoods that are self-shaped and self-governed. This fosters local participation and more direct action for communal change and self growth. Ferrell then applies the anarchist philosophy to the issue of crime and social justice. Anarchist criminologists reject fixed laws or regulations. These are the trappings of an inflexible injustice, the costuming of external, though hidden, authority. Anarchist criminologists also reject the rigidly imposed categories of "criminal," "delinquent," "mental patient," and so forth. Labels such as these unnecessarily reduce the diversity that individuals embody, erode the fabric of community, and stifle the fluid process of justice making. Ferrell argues that social justice exists when people respond to emerging community needs flexibly and humanely. There is no predetermined script, no permanent, rigidly prescribed formula here. Social justice exists when tolerance for difference among individuals and between groups prevails. In this way, it is negotiated directly and locally by people apart from the state-sponsored criminal justice apparatus. Indeed, it is the state-regulated system that, according to the author, needs to be dismantled because of the unequal, control-driven social relations it seeks to establish. Thus, for Ferrell, social justice is both retrospective (responding to existing crime problems) and preemptory (challenging the conditions that give rise to the existing crime problems). The anarchist vision of social justice is therefore a dynamic process, working to curtail the expanding inequality and centralized authority of the criminal justice system both before and after such harm occurs.

5

Anarchist Criminology
and Social Justice

JEFF FERRELL

HISTORICAL BACKGROUND

Anarchism cuts like a jagged line through contemporary social and intellectual history. In 1871, citizens of Paris launched an "unplanned, unguided,
formless revolution" (Edwards, 1973, p. 10) that held Paris for seventy-two
days; during that time they staged a "festival of the oppressed" that came to
be known as the Paris Commune. A century later, in 1968, French students
and workers again revolted. Spurred on by a loosely organized Situationist
movement, they attacked the French government and the controlled, consumer society of which it was a part, plastering the streets and universities
with prankish slogans like "Work Is the Blackmail of Existence" (think about
it), "The More You Consume the Less You Live," and "Boredom Is Always
Counterrevolutionary."

In Russia the same sorts of ideas and actions have bubbled to the surface
over the past hundred years or so. Around the time of the Paris Commune,
the Russian anarchist Peter Kropotkin was calling for revolt against the state
and its mechanisms of control, and another Russian anarchist, Michael
Bakunin, was working with Karl Marx and others to organize revolutionary
activity in Europe. Indeed, anarchists like Nestor Makhno helped win the
Russian revolution of 1917 and, when later betrayed by the Bolsheviks, revolted against them as well. As a Russian anarchist leaflet proclaimed in 1921,
"People of Petrograd, your first task is to destroy this government. Your second is not to create any other" (Avrich 1973, p. 163). In the 1930s, anarchists
in Spain likewise rebelled and were able to create self-managed urban and
agrarian collectives until they were destroyed by the same sorts of fascist forces
that would slaughter millions in World War II a few years later.

In the United States anarchist politics also has a long history. From rowdy
individuals like Emma Goldman and Alexander Berkman, to defiant organizations like the Industrial Workers of the World (the Wobblies, an "anarcho-
syndicalist" union that joked, sang, rode the rails, and along the way won
strike after strike in the early twentieth century), anarchists have carried on a
long and disrespectful battle against the rich, the powerful, and the pious. In
the United States, Great Britain, and elsewhere, this jagged line of anarchist
resistance continues into more contemporary confrontations as well. The punk

movement that began in the 1970s, for example, emerged directly out of the Situationist politics of its founders and was anarchic in both intention and practice. Promoting the notion of "DIY" (do it yourself), the movement spawned cacophonous and eclectic styles, self-produced fanzines, and an angry army of cranked-up, three-chord garage bands. When the Sex Pistols wailed "I wan-na be an-ar-chy!" they were not joking. Then again, knowing Malcolm McLaren, Johnny Rotten, and other punks, they probably were—but the joke had a punchline, and it was all about anarchy.

Anarchist thought has not only motivated Wobblies, Situationists, and punks but has also been a part of critical scholarship. From the early theoretical and political battles between Marx and Bakunin over the nature of radical organization, to more contemporary scholars like eco-anarchist writer Murray Bookchin and philosopher of science Paul Feyerabend (whose motto is "the only principle that doesn't inhibit progress is: *anything goes*"; 1975, p. 23, emphasis in original), anarchist ideas have helped shape critiques of power and domination in modern society. Within critical criminology, anarchist perspectives have likewise helped develop a critical analysis of the state, the law, and legal authority. Early anarchist writers like William Godwin (1971/1793) and Peter Kropotkin (1970/1927, 1975/1886) launched some of their most scathing and sophisticated attacks against the state and its apparatus of legal control (see especially Kropotkin's essay on "Law and Authority"). More recently, criminologists Harold Pepinsky (1978; Pepinsky & Jesilow, 1984; Pepinsky & Quinney, 1991), Larry Tifft (1979; Tifft & Sullivan, 1980), and I (Ferrell 1993, 1994, 1995) have attempted to develop an anarchist criminology that can both critique centralized, state legal authority and imagine more flexible and humane alternatives to it.

But, of course, the presence and influence of anarchism in contemporary politics or scholarship cannot be measured simply by the number of anarchist organizations, anarchist books, or even openly anarchist political revolts. As must already be obvious, anarchism is rooted not so much in identifiable organizations or clear political victories as it is in an ongoing process of defying dogma, negating calcified or constricting social arrangements, and defiantly putting concern for humanity ahead of respect for authority. In this sense, all sorts of playfulness, defiance, or resistance can be seen as carrying the flavor of anarchism: a high school student who cares more about creative learning than about the seating chart or the dress code, a worker who fights to help colleagues succeed rather than being forced to compete against them, a parent who defies the rules of the welfare bureaucracy to feed the kids. And in this sense, to borrow Marcus's (1989) lovely phrase, anarchist ideas and practices constitute a sort of "secret history of the twentieth century," a current of creative, playful vitality flowing under and against rules, regulations, and structures of authority. Toward the end of *The Grapes of Wrath,* as Tom Joad readies to leave, his mother asks him, "How'm I gonna know 'bout you?" He tells her, "I'll be all aroun' in the dark. I'll be everywhere—wherever you look. Wherever they's a fight so hungry people can eat, I'll be there. Wherever they's a cop beatin' up a guy, I'll be there" (Steinbeck, 1939, p. 436). So it is with anarchism—around in the dark somewhere, running through all those moments where human decency, compassion, and creativity struggle against privilege, authority, and intolerance.

BASIC ASSUMPTIONS

Any attempt at creating a list of anarchist assumptions should probably begin with that most basic of anarchist assumptions: there can be no definitive list. The anarchist rejection of political, legal, or religious authority incorporates a rejection of epistemic authority as well—that is, a rejection of the notion that any person or institution should embody and enforce final knowledge, certainty or truth. Put in a more positive way, anarchism embraces and encourages *epistemic uncertainty*—in other words, multiple interpretations and perspectives—and works to create situations in which a variety of viewpoints can coexist. This disavowal of enforced truth, this celebration of variety and diversity, thus pits anarchists against all sorts of authoritarians whose goal is a single, enforced perspective. But it also shapes the nature of anarchism itself. It means that there is no definitive list of anarchist assumptions and not much desire on the part of anarchists to create one. In fact, it implies that, while you may find much to learn from others who have experimented with defying authority or attempting self-governance, you will also want to remember to do it yourself.

That being the case, we can look at some general orientations that flow through the writings of Peter Kropotkin and Emma Goldman, through the street politics of Situationists and punks, not to discover the rules of anarchism but simply to see what these orientations suggest about authority and lived alternatives to it. As we will see, these orientations imply that, amidst the diverse ways of living that anarchism embraces, there is some sense of ways not to live as well. Thus, anarchism contains a certain odd balance between tolerance of alternatives and intolerance for those who would limit them. As we will also see, these orientations begin to suggest the shape that social relationships, and even social justice, might take within anarchist arrangements.

BASIC PRINCIPLES

As already implied, anarchism operates less as a set of fixed principles than as an ongoing process of discovery, change, and reconstruction. By its very nature, anarchism rejects the notion that change is a necessary evil, a period of temporary uncertainty to be endured before arriving at the next end point or conclusion. Instead, anarchism values change for its own sake. It understands and embraces the notion that day-to-day life is an ever-emerging process and at its best—when not confined within straightjackets of work, fear, or legal oppression—a spiral of new possibilities unwinding in directions we can hardly imagine. Rather than trying to stop this process—or worse, trying to undo change and go backward toward the illusion of certainty—anarchism celebrates this process as one that embodies growth, learning, and discovery. Anarchism advocates throwing away the map and driving until you get lost, just to see where you end up. It emphasizes a process not directed toward some preset end point or goal but simply toward the sorts of possibilities that sometimes emerge beyond ourselves and our own limits. Anarchism echoes the Clash's defiant slogan from the 1970s: "The future is unwritten and waits to be inscribed."

It is worth noting, though, that embracing this point of view means embracing change not just externally or abstractly but in our own daily lives. If we want to keep moving and emerging, we have to be willing to tear down ourselves, our institutions, and our ideologies (including anarchism!), and then to reinvent them time and again. In one of the hallmark insights of anarchism, the Russian anarchist Michael Bakunin (1974) said, "The passion for destruction is a creative passion, too" (p. 58). This notion carries all sorts of wonderfully dangerous and subversive implications; in the present context, it implies that we must be willing to discard habits, beliefs, and identities if we are to keep them from becoming dead museum pieces that inhibit new ideas and understandings. Further, it implies that our own identities—personal, professional, sexual—are never finished products but always projects under construction within a broader process of inventing and reinventing ourselves and others. For our institutions, our beliefs, and ourselves, certainty constitutes dead weight, change an ongoing emergence of possibility.

For anarchism, embracing change also means embracing *ambiguity*. In fact, the notion of ambiguity incorporates both of the anarchist themes seen so far: epistemic uncertainty (multiple viewpoints and understandings, with none certain or final) and the ongoing process of change. Ambiguity might be thought of as the flavor of anarchism, or perhaps the atmospheric fog out of which anarchist projects emerge. Ambiguity, uncertainty, confusion—all constitute fertile ground for new ideas and identities and, at their best, overwhelm any attempt to achieve final solutions or final authority. Thus, like the process of change, a state of ambiguity is not a problem to be overcome by sorting people, perspectives, and identities into their proper categories but rather a pleasure to be embraced and enjoyed for its indeterminate possibilities. For many traditional legal, political, and academic perspectives, the goal is to make sense of it all. For anarchism, as for Talking Heads, the goal is the opposite: to stop making sense.

Notions of fluidity and ambiguity in turn begin to suggest an anarchist sense of *human relations* and *human community*. For anarchists, relations among people work best when they are emergent and open to possibilities; when roles like "leader" and "follower," "teacher" and "student" are adopted only temporarily or, even better, are lost within a fog of ambiguous identities. Against all too common situations of strictly structured, authority-oriented relationships in which "everyone knows his or her place"—at work, in the family, in the prison—anarchists propose poorly organized relationships in which no one quite knows anyone's place. For anarchism, then, a sense of community develops not from regimented patterns of predictable behavior or common bonds of similarity but from a loose and inclusive federation of difference. Significantly, this sense of an eclectic, varied, and ambiguous anarchist community goes beyond the usual notion of "tolerating" differences among people, to a sense of enjoying and embracing differences. As anarchists, we do not just put up with people whom others might see as weird or offbeat, as outside the usual frameworks of propriety, or whose ideas or identities challenge our own sense of who we are; instead, we revel in the strange unpredictability of it all and enjoy the experience of being knocked a bit off center by their presence. Thus, within an anarchist community, the greater the differences, the greater the possibility for mutual enlightenment and for mutual growth away from the stultifying comfort of certainty and similarity. Anarchist communities provide a safe haven for the outsiders, a comfortable fit for the misfits—and not just for "their" sake but for the sake of everyone involved.

Within an anarchist community, then, people of all sorts are both more free to be themselves, and at the same time more directly responsible for themselves and others, than they are in situations regulated by external authority. This sense of anarchist community as shared experience, as a living fabric of social relations woven tightly enough to care for others but loosely enough to preserve their differences, has surfaced in a variety of anarchist ideas. Kropotkin, for example, argued that our humanity develops not from ruthless competition or conquest but from the principle and practice of *mutual aid* within communities of people. Other anarchists have emphasized what has variously been called *regionalism, localism,* or *decentralization.* These terms allude to what we might call the politics of scale—that is, the sense that the very size of communities, groups, or organizations in part defines what is possible within them. In speaking of localism and decentralization, anarchists argue that communities must be small enough for people to directly participate in them if these communities are not to become abstract structures of external authority. And in this sense, modern nation-states like the United States destroy possibilities for real participation and real community not only because they are governed by the worst sorts of petty tyrants and fawning greedheads but simply because they are too damn big. It follows that, for anarchists, "representational democracy" as practiced in the United States—the vesting of authority and power in others who claim to represent us in worlds well beyond our own—is a contradiction in terms. Real, lived participation and self-governance, and real social change, come about not through politicians, lawyers, or "leaders" but from doing it yourself—from what anarchists have long called *direct action.*

All of this—the embracing of epistemic uncertainty, the pleasure in ongoing processes, the enjoyment of ambiguity and difference, the demand that communities be self-shaped and self-governed—of course leads to that orientation for which anarchism is perhaps best known: its in-your-face *defiance of authority.* In standing for ambiguity, diversity, and human community, anarchism stands against those who would destroy diversity, enforce conformity, and confine others within the narrowness of their own ignorance. Throughout the history of anarchism, this dialectic has been played out; the sort of gentle, embracing tolerance described so far has been complemented by a militant intolerance for authoritarians of all sorts. Anarchists have consistently confronted—in the world of ideas and in the streets—Nazis and neo-Nazis, gay bashers, racists, corporate thugs, and other cowardly bullies, and equally so politicians, religious zealots, and other people and organizations set on enforcing tight-sphinctered truth claims and suffocating moral mandates. In this sense, anarchism opposes not just authority but also fundamentalism; that is, it opposes any orientation, whether embodied in Pat Buchanan, the Ayatollah Khomeni, or the pope, that enforces a claim to fundamental truth and absolute knowledge. And, in this sense, anarchists take it as their ongoing mission to undermine authority and discredit fundamentalism wherever they find them. As I have written elsewhere (Ferrell, 1993), the anarchist goal is to "make the authorities out to be the dangerous fools that they are" (p. 192).

ANARCHIST JUSTICE
AND SOCIAL JUSTICE:
INTEGRATION AND APPLICATION

Embedded in the orientations just seen is a sense of what shapes social justice might take under anarchism. Fluidity and process, ambiguity and uncertainty, diversity and community, direct action outside and against authority—these themes suggest not only a way of living beyond the usual constipations of alienated work, regimented schooling, and orchestrated consumption but a way of justice much different from that which undergirds contemporary arrangements of state power and legal authority.

As a starting point, we can contrast the vitality of a justice process organized around fluidity and change with the stifling unresponsiveness of a justice system organized and administered around vast collections of laws, codes, and regulations. Within a traditional state model, justice is achieved by establishing laws or regulations, and then applying them evenly and unflinchingly across subsequent situations and identities. For anarchists, though, this model guarantees not equal justice but rather, inflexible injustice. This is especially the case when preestablished rules are placed ahead of emerging needs and situations. Godwin (1971) argued in 1793 that "law tends, no less than creeds, catechisms and tests, to fix the human mind in a stagnant condition, and to substitute a principle of permanence, in the room of that unceasing progress which is the only salubrious element of mind" (p. 275). In 1886, Kropotkin (1975) likewise found the law's "distinctive trait to be immobility, a tendency to crystallize what should be modified and developed day by day" (p. 30). In other words, fixed laws and regulations presume a permanent and predefined solution to problems that are in reality never permanent but rather caught within ongoing processes of human life, historical change, and ambiguous morality. And if this was apparent in 1793 and 1886, it is apparent in the late 1990s as well:

- The law says no sleeping in public, but at the moment I am tired, I missed my train, I have no money for a room, and, anyway, I promise to stay out of the way.

- The law prohibits theft of private property, but in this particular case, that scrap metal will do the homeless woman collecting it more good than it will the contractor who owns it.

- The law prohibits vandalizing private property, but this graffiti mural is being painted on a semiabandoned building once owned by a local family and now owned by an absentee corporation headquartered a thousand miles away.

- Regulations prohibit giving final exams early, but all of us in the class agree that, given the emerging rhythm and pace of the class, its best to take it now.

As these and countless other examples begin to show, fixed codes of law and handbooks full of regulations time and again mask external authority behind abstractly benign pronouncements about prohibition and prevention and at the same time grind against the exigencies of emerging human situations.

In place of a preconfigured model of justice lodged in unbending laws and fixed regulations ("Sorry, son, but the rules are the rules"), anarchist criminologists like Larry Tifft (1979; Tifft & Sullivan, 1980) propose a fluid and responsive form of social justice organized around direct action and emerging needs. Within a broad commitment to community and to mutual aid, just solutions to problems would emerge as the problems themselves emerge ("retrospectively," as Tifft says) and would then be worked out flexibly and humanely among those involved. In effect, anarchists argue that we should keep the best interests of the community in mind—keep in mind that others matter as much or more than we do—and then go about our business. While this approach will certainly not solve all problems, it will alleviate many. And when it does fail, when problems develop, so too can solutions—not solutions authoritatively preordained in anticipation of problematic behavior but rather solutions tentatively worked out in the ongoing give-and-take of human interaction. So, from an anarchist viewpoint:

- Sleep in public all you want. If such sleeping becomes a problem at some point for reasons of safety or sanitation, the community can work with those involved—ideally, by creating better jobs, better shelters, and other alternatives rather than by criminalizing those for whom a park bench has become a bed.

- Scrounge around, squat in an abandoned building if you need a place to stay, decorate it with graffiti, "take what you need and leave the rest"— but keep in mind others' needs for shelter, survival, and privacy, too. The technicalities of private property or legality matter less in the long run than the overall well-being of the community.

- Give or take an exam whenever the class decides, or decide not to take it at all. If problems arise for particular classes or particular students, they can be worked out among teachers, students, and others. And after the solutions have served their purpose, do not codify them as rigid rules; instead, throw them away, and move ahead to different possibilities, problems, and solutions.

If an anarchist sense of justice avoids presorting emerging human situations through rigid rules and regulations, it also avoids sorting people into rigid categories of identity and status. In other words, anarchists embrace ambiguity as an essential component in a vital and fluid process of justice. If, as argued here, people and their identities are always caught in an ongoing process of development and discovery, then rigid, long-term legal categorizations of them—"criminal," "juvenile delinquent," "convicted felon"—can only serve to inhibit this process, to create boxes out of which people will find it difficult to climb. As part of seeking justice retrospectively and situationally, anarchists thus attempt to respond to people as situated actors, as individuals and groups caught in sometimes difficult situations, rather than as stereotypical embodiments of categories like "good" or "evil," "law-abiding citizen" or "criminal" (see Wieck, 1978). In other words, anarchist justice seeks to alleviate harm and restore community in problematic situations, while at the same time acknowledging the ambiguous relations we all have toward one another and toward law and legality. Thus, if we find kids engaged in violence, we attempt to rehabilitate them and their sense of mutual respect for each other and their community, but without categorizing or treating them as "incorrigibly violent juvenile offenders." If we encounter an accusation of theft, we perhaps confront the accused with the consequences of the (alleged) theft and attempt to restore a balance between individual need and community good, while at the same time recognizing that a formal label of "thief" would unjustly segregate this person from the many other people who have also stolen now and again without such consequences. A popular baby's toy incorporates balls of various sizes and colors in a common chamber; when the toy is shaken, the balls all rattle down and are sorted by color and size into separate compartments. So it is with the model of justice within the present criminal justice system; the system operates as a vast (and vastly unjust) sorting machine that uses law and punishment to sort people into predefined and all too permanent compartments of legality and illegality. Anarchists suggest that, in seeking a fluid and humane justice, we turn the toy upside down and remix the differences.

Anarchist justice seeks to "remix the differences" not only for the sake of preserving fluid and ambiguous identities but for the sake of defending and protecting diversity. Many a police patrol car has written on its side "To Protect and Serve." Within existing legal and social arrangements, though, this motto has most often meant protecting the interests of the privileged and serving the narrow agendas of political domination and ethnic or sexual intolerance. Anarchist justice would stand this situation on its head—that is, would imagine a fluid system of justice designed to serve and protect not any one group but instead the differences and diversity within and between all groups. Rather than enforcing laws that regulate or criminalize diverse sexual practices and orientations, anarchist justice would battle to protect and encourage all sorts of different (and ambiguous) sexualities. Rather than setting up a juvenile (and adult) justice system that has traditionally enforced narrow gender roles for girls (Chesney-Lind, 1989), anarchist justice would promote and protect a wide range of gender roles for girls and boys, women and men. Rather than criminalizing free expression on the Internet (as has recently been done), anarchist justice would promote diverse, self-regulating cyber-communities open to all sorts of expression. Rather than waging "war" on drugs and drug users, anarchist justice would declare peace, decriminalize many forms of drug use, and trust individuals and small groups to decide on appropriate measures and amounts.

Anarchist justice thus promotes Feyerabend's notion that "anything goes," but with an interesting twist. Anarchist justice works to protect each person's freedom to think, say, or do anything—right up to the point where that person's activities begin to limit the same freedom for others. In other words, for anarchists, anything goes, except denying that anything goes for everyone else. Or, to put it another way, anarchist justice is tolerant of most everything—except intolerance (Tifft, 1979; Ryan & Ferrell, 1986). So, under an anarchist model, the legal (and religious) enforcement of morality is abolished; people are free to believe in whatever they like, to find pleasure where they may, to pursue whatever odd or quirky paths their lives may take. At the same time, though, they are also responsible for the freedom of others, for learning to tolerate, protect, and even appreciate ideas, styles, and pleasures not their own. Here we see again the sense of community sketched previously—community loosely woven together out of the diverse interests and identities of those involved. And here we see that anarchist justice promotes and protects not just individual freedom and diversity but a community of diversity, a collective commitment to free ideas and free people.

Here we also see again the anarchist commitment to direct, community-level human relations. Anarchist justice is in a way street justice—certainly not in the usual street tough, "Dirty Harry" sense but in the sense that justice is best negotiated directly by people and groups, on the streets and in the neighborhoods, outside the constipation of a centralized, state-sponsored criminal justice system. As Tifft (1979) says, "Justice must be warm, must be living . . . face to face justice is an outgrowth of life" (p. 398); in Goldman's (1969) terms, it is "a living force in the affairs of our life, constantly creating new conditions" (p. 63). If we are to create human justice outside the external, enforced structures of law, though, we must at the same time knit (back) together human communities around mutual aid and mutual respect; we must create and re-create loose but supportive federations of people, groups, and ideas in which this sort of justice can take shape (see Michalowski, 1991, pp. 36–37). In this context Bookchin (1986; see also Dolgoff, 1974) thus speaks of "libertarian municipalism"—that is, "the anarchic ideal of decentralized, stateless, collectively managed, and directly democratic communities . . . rooted in the nonhierarchical ethics of a unity of diversity, self-formation and self-management, complementarity, and mutual aid" (p. 10).

On the way to these sorts of communities and this sort of justice, we must as best we can also quit relying on the law and law enforcement agencies for protection, resolution, or retribution. Recently, a superior court judge granted a restraining order against a three-year-old child accused of bullying another three-year-old at a playground. Asked where she got the idea to file for a restraining order, the mother of the (allegedly) bullied child answered, "The police"—who also encouraged her to file an assault and battery complaint (Thompson, 1996). While almost laughable in its perversity and inappropri- ateness, such a case reminds us of an important insight: calling the cops on your noisy neighbors, relying on restraining orders, filing suits and counter- suits, and so forth, while at times necessary and understandable under the pre- sent system, can only have the ultimate effect of both strengthening the power and authority of centralized state law and further disabling possibilities for mutual aid and face-to-face justice outside its grip. If we can begin to loosen the law's grip on our lives and wean ourselves from a reliance on it, though, we are likely to discover forms of justice among ourselves more fluid, ambigu- ous, and uncertain, and also more directly humane and communal, than those framed by legality and authority. We are likely to find ourselves at the same time more free and more responsible. As before, the ghost of Tom Joad:

> I been thinkin' how it was . . . how our folks took a care of themselves, an' if they was a fight they fixed it themselves; an' they wasn't no cops wagglin' their guns, but they was better order than them cops ever give. I been a-wonderin' why we can't do that all over. (Steinbeck, 1939, p. 435)

It will, of course, take more than a reduction in the number of police calls or restraining orders against three-year-olds, though, to get there from here. As always, protecting diversity and building community means confronting head-on the sorts of centralized authority and social inequality that stand in the way of such projects. Earlier, Bakunin's (1974, p. 58) notion that "the pas- sion for destruction is a creative passion, too" was seen in the context of emerging identities. In the present context, it suggests that we must destroy present structures of authority and inequality if we are to create room for more fluid and humane arrangements, and possibilities for anarchist justice within them. We can hardly expect to achieve community justice in a society where communities are increasingly torn apart by pervasive unemployment and en- forced economic decay. We can hardly expect to honor diversity in a society shot through with racial and sexual discrimination and racist and sexist politi- cal arrangements. We can hardly ask our friends and neighbors to forego what little protection centralized state law affords, to make peace with those around them, if they see only growing inequality and violence in their own lives and others'. Anarchist justice can only evolve as does social justice; it must be part of broader confrontations with inequality—in the mean streets, in the alien- ated workplace, within the patriarchal family—and of a larger transformation in the unforgivably vast inequalities under which more and more of us are crushed. If, as Godwin (1971, p. 270) says, "the more there is in any country of inequality and oppression, the more punishments are multiplied," then an abandonment of law and punishment will require above all else an overturn- ing of inequality and oppression. No justice, no peace; no peace, no justice.

In this sense, anarchist justice is both retrospective justice, evolving in re- sponse to lived situations and problems, but also preemptory justice—that is, an approach that seeks to remedy not only immediate problems but the social conditions that spawn them. Although it is important to ask, "How can we find justice after one person murders or robs another?" it is perhaps more important to ask, "How can a just society lessen the incidence of murder and robbery?" If we accept the present society's arrangement around domination, inequality, and centralized authority, and the phenomenally high rates of crime and violence that such arrangements spew forth, it makes little sense to then ask how anarchism might respond. Under such arrangements, any response will at best be partial and inadequate. Anarchist justice proposes instead a radical dismantling of present arrangements—radical in the sense of attacking pervasive injustice as rooted in institutional and economic inequality, and in everyday situations of dominance and subordination.

As must by now be clear, anarchist justice also proposes a radical abolition of state law and state authority. Anarchists certainly stand with those abolitionists who call for the dismantling of the prison, and for the more general dissolution of "punitive justice," as inhumane institutionalizations of vengeance and retaliation. But beyond this, anarchist justice calls for the abolition of all centralized legal and political authority, for breaking up the state's monopoly on the "administration of justice." It seeks to build decentralized, community-level processes of justice in place of a current criminal justice system that operates as a "state-protection racket" (Pepinsky & Jesilow, 1984, p. 10), extorting cash and conformity from those unlucky enough to be caught up in it. In the interest of decentralizing power and preempting injustice, it seeks to break open those cozy arrangements through which state authorities mask and facilitate white-collar crime and themselves engage in various forms of state criminality against dissenters, outsiders, and the environment. To paraphrase H. L. Mencken, anarchists realize that, in seeking justice, comforting the afflicted always necessitates afflicting the comfortable. To again recall Bakunin, anarchists understand that justice incorporates a dialectic between the creation of diverse communities and the destruction of structured intolerance and injustice. And so, in the same way that anarchism stands against authority, anarchist justice stands against the law.

RECONSIDERING ANARCHIST CRIMINOLOGY AND SOCIAL JUSTICE

The various threads of anarchist justice—fluidity and ambiguity in solving problems and resolving troublesome identities; direct protection of freedom and diversity within tolerant, responsible communities; direct confrontation with centralized authority and institutionalized inequality—thus position anarchist justice far outside contemporary conceptions of legal justice. Perhaps more important, they position anarchist justice in direct opposition to the ongoing operations of the contemporary criminal justice system and its authoritarian constructions of legality and illegality. As already seen, an anarchist sense of justice does not simply suggest that certain modifications in the criminal justice system are needed; it suggests that the system itself is flawed to the point of contributing to far greater social harm than that it alleviates. Significantly, it further suggests that these flaws of the criminal justice system are interwoven with the failings of a society both organized around authoritarian relationships and day-to-day domination and at the same time torn apart by vast and growing inequalities.

A social order that generates astronomical levels of violence and aggression, and an ever-growing criminal justice machine as its primary response, fails doubly. The first failure is one of social and cultural organization. From an anarchist viewpoint, a society saturated with violent crime—in its households, in its factories, in its streets, on its television sets—can hardly dismiss such violence as aberrational, as an accident of individual pathology or historical change. Instead, it must recognize such criminal violence as the predictable product of authoritarian control and interpersonal domination.

Violent crime in this sense exists not as an exception to social norms and social controls but rather as a dramatic manifestation of the violence and objectification woven into the normative fabric of an authoritarian social order. An economy constructed from manufactured desires and built on the backs of minimum-wage workers produces not only obscenities of opulence and poverty but regular incidents of theft, robbery, and shoplifting. An economic and legal system that time and again privileges the abusive power of transnational corporations over the interests of local communities produces not only predictable patterns of occupational danger and environmental destruction but also workers who turn to the destruction of corporate property, or even themselves, in response. A society that sacrifices the days and nights of parents, and the futures of their children, to such a system promotes not only street gangs and other surrogate associations among the young but a sense of desperation and hopelessness that undergirds all sorts of criminal adventures. A social and cultural system that celebrates the violent power of men and the seductive subordination of women produces not only a sad collection of bullies and bimbos but daily eruptions of sexual assault and domestic violence. A social order infested with sexual intolerance and ethnic discrimination spits out not only patterns of social and economic inequality but a rising tide of violent hate crimes and daily degradations.

The second failure is one of response to these patterns of violence. Not surprisingly, the same social order that promotes crimes of violence and domination responds to them with yet other forms of violence and control. Not surprisingly, "justice" in such a society is defined in terms of institutionalized authority and control, measured punishment and retribution. From an anarchist perspective, though, such arrangements of justice alleviate crime and violence less than they perpetuate the very conditions under which they occur. From this perspective, the rule of state law prevents vengeance, violence, and retaliation less than it institutionalizes them in the operations of the criminal justice system. Thus, like peacemaking criminologists (Pepinsky & Quinney, 1991), anarchist criminologists argue that justice can never come from "wars" on gangs, drugs, and crime; from criminalizing and imprisoning larger and larger portions of the population; from legitimating violence and aggression as alleged solutions to violence and aggression. Justice can only come from more humane, fluid, and tolerant social relations—social relations that undermine the sorts of authority, domination, and control that undergird both violent crime and the conventional criminal justice response to it.

If we cannot find a way to move toward such relations, we will surely continue to be caught in expanding webworks of inequitable and authoritarian control and growing spirals of violence, crime, and retribution. Clearly, the contemporary machinery of criminal justice, as mobilized in various "wars" on crime and otherwise, disproportionately and systematically criminalizes outsiders—ethnic minorities, young people, and the poor—and constructs them as "enemies" to be fought and conquered in the name of justice. In this way, the "justice" administered by the criminal justice system in fact serves to exacerbate preexisting inequalities and to perpetuate the violent injustices that they incorporate. Moreover, as labeling theorists have demonstrated time and again (for example, Becker, 1963), and as anarchist notions of process and ambiguity remind us, the confinement of individuals and groups within these categories of legal stigmatization and punishment only retards the possibilities for human development and puts in motion a downward drift of lost humanity and wasted lives.

But, of course, this machinery of legalized injustice, though most directly dehumanizing those pushed to the bottom of an inequitable social system, in turn further dehumanizes the system itself, and all those caught within it. As legal categories and controls proliferate in the absence of human communities and face-to-face justice, they confine more and more of daily life for all of us—in the street or the office, the city or the suburb—and at the same time disable the emergence of informal relations and extralegal reconciliation. As criminalized individuals descend into cycles of legal control and lived resentment, so too does the larger society descend into mean-spirited cycles of fear, retaliation, and legal retribution from which no one is free.

Clearly, the contemporary criminal justice system, and the legalized conceptions of justice that it enforces, cannot break these cycles; they can only contribute to them. But we can break them—if we can find in and among ourselves the courage to confront centralized authority and expanding inequality, the willingness to build communities around tolerance and diversity, and, most of all, the passion for ambiguity, uncertainty, and change.

CONCLUSION

To many, the development of anarchist social relations and anarchist justice as alternatives to the present society may seem unimaginable. If so, two ideas are probably worth considering. First, do anarchism's own limitations render it unimaginable, or does the present system of order and authority, by setting the terms of the debate and the frameworks of our perception, render anarchism and other alternatives literally "unimaginable" or "unthinkable"? Certainly, systems of authority operate not only through legal controls and physical punishment but by constructing and promoting particular perceptions of crime, justice, and even ourselves. Given this, our inability to imagine alternatives, or to imagine that alternatives can work, may tell us more about the power of the present system than about the alternatives themselves. And given this, it is no doubt in our interest to think the unthinkable, to stop making sense; as Cohen (1988) says, "to be realistic about law and order must mean to be unrealistic (that is, imaginative) about the possibilities of order without law" (p. 228).

Second, it is indeed unlikely that anarchism and anarchist justice can ever be attained in any final or absolute form. In fact, we might hope that this is the case. A perspective shaped by concepts of process and ambiguity operates best when it keeps to those concepts—that is, when it remains itself an unfinished and ongoing project, never fully possible but always full of possibility. And besides, whether or not anarchism is fully realizable, it certainly seems better to err on the side of freedom, kindness, and diversity than on the side of authority, retribution, and inequality. We have marched in the latter direction long enough, and with all the wrong results.

At its best, then, anarchism and the process of justice that flows from it constitute a sort of dance that we make up as we go along, an emerging swirl of ambiguity, uncertainty, and pleasure. Once you dive into the dance, there are no guarantees—only the complex rhythms of human interaction and the steps that you and others invent in response. So, if you want certainty or authority, you might want to sit this one out. As for the rest of us: start the music.

REVIEW QUESTIONS

1. What basic orientations or themes run through anarchism and anarchist justice? In what ways are these orientations different from, or even opposed to, other models of justice? In what ways are they similar?

2. Ambiguity is commonly seen as a negative state of affairs, to be resolved or overcome. How is ambiguity redefined in a positive light within a model of anarchist justice? Do you agree that ambiguity and uncertainty can have positive effects?

3. How would an anarchist community actually function? What practical measures would be necessary

to move toward anarchist justice within such a community? If the classes you are now taking were reconstructed around an anarchist model, how would they be different?

4. Anarchist justice incorporates the notion that we should protect and promote diversity and difference among people—that "anything goes." Within the model of anarchist justice, though, where are the limits to this notion that "anything goes"? Where would you set the limits?

5. Anarchism and anarchist justice are known for their defiance and disavowal of authority, legal and

otherwise. Why does anarchism stand so firmly against authority? From an anarchist viewpoint, what is wrong with certainty and authority?

6. Why is anarchist justice never finally attainable? From an anarchist perspective, why is this failure to achieve finality in fact a success?

REFERENCES

Avrich, P. (1973). *The anarchists in the Russian revolution*. Ithaca, NY: Cornell University Press.

Bakunin, M. (1974). *Michael Bakunin: Selected writings* (A. Leaning, Ed.). New York: Grove.

Becker, H. S. (1963). *Outsiders: Studies in the sociology of deviance*. New York: Free Press.

Bookchin, M. (1986). Theses on libertarian Municipalism. In D. I. Roussopoulos (Ed.), *The anarchist papers* (pp. 9–22). Montreal: Black Rose Books.

Chesney-Lind, M. (1989). Girls' crime and woman's place: Toward a feminist model of female delinquency. *Crime and Delinquency, 35,* 5–29.

Cohen, S. (1988). *Against criminology*. New Brunswick, NJ: Transaction.

Dolgoff, S. (Ed.). (1974). *The anarchist collectives: Workers' Self-Management in the Spanish Revolution, 1936–1939.* New York: Free Life.

Edwards, S. (1973). *The communards of Paris: 1871.* Ithaca, NY: Cornell University Press.

Ferrell, J. (1993). *Crimes of style: Urban graffiti and the politics of criminality*. New York: Garland.

Ferrell, J. (1994). Confronting the agenda of authority: Critical criminology, anarchism, and urban graffiti. In G. Barak (Ed.), *Varieties of criminology* (pp. 161–178). Westport, CT: Praeger.

Ferrell, J. (1995). Anarchy against the discipline. *Journal of Criminal Justice and Popular Culture, 3*(4), 86–91.

Feyerabend, P. (1975). *Against method*. London: Verso.

Godwin, W. (1971). *Enquiry concerning political justice* (K. Codell Carter, Ed.). London: Oxford University Press. (Original work published 1793)

Goldman, E. (1969). *Anarchism and other essays*. New York: Dover.

Kropotkin, P. (1970). *Kropotkin's revolutionary pamphlets* (R. N. Baldwin, Ed.). New York: Dover. (Original work published 1927)

Kropotkin, P. (1975). *The essential Kropotkin* (E. Capouya & K. Tompkins, Eds.). New York: Liveright. (Original work published 1886)

Marcus, G. (1989). *Lipstick traces: A secret history of the twentieth century*. Cambridge, MA: Harvard University Press.

Michalowski, R. (1991). "Niggers, welfare scum, and homeless assholes": The problems of idealism, consciousness and context in Left realism. In B. D. MacLean & D. Milovanovic (Eds.), *New directions in critical criminology* (pp. 31–38). Vancouver: Collective.

Pepinsky, H. E. (1978). Communist anarchism as an alternative to the rule of criminal law. *Contemporary Crises, 2,* 315–327.

Pepinsky, H. E., & Jesilow, P. (1984). *Myths that cause crime* (2nd ed.). Cabin John, MD: Seven Locks.

Pepinsky, H. E., & Quinney, R. (Eds.). (1991). *Criminology as peacemaking*. Bloomington: Indiana University Press.

Ryan, K., & Ferrell, J. (1986). Knowledge, power, and the process of justice. *Crime and Social Justice, 25,* 178–195.

Steinbeck, J. (1939). *The grapes of wrath*. New York: Viking.

Thompson, C. (1996, March 8). Sandbox "bully," 3, hauled into court. *The Arizona Republic* (Associated Press), A1, A22.

Tifft, L. (1979). The coming redefinition of crime: An anarchist perspective. *Social Problems, 26,* 392–402.

Tifft, L., & Sullivan, D. (1980). *The struggle to be human: Crime, criminology, and anarchism.* Orkney, U.K.: Cienfuegos.

Wieck, D. (1978). Anarchist justice. In J. R. Pennock & J. W. Chapman (Eds.), *Anarchism* (pp. 215–236). New York: New York University Press.

Postmodern Feminist Criminology and Social Justice

P ostmodern feminism maintains that the stories we tell—in the way that we tell them—are an important part of how we know the world, people in it, and even ourselves. This means that there is no one, best way to understand. Instead, there are multiple points of view that express our unique history, culture, and identity. Wonders applies this thinking to the question of defining social justice. She offers a brief history on the development of both feminist and postmodern thought, highlighting their respective areas of divergence and convergence. Wonders recognizes that neither feminism nor postmodernism is a unified system of inquiry. However, she broadly asserts that feminists regard gender as an important organizing principle of social life, whereas postmodernists believe language structures our daily existences. According to Wonders, feminism demonstrates the gender inequality operating in many criminal justice practices, and postmodernism reminds us of the injustices perpetuated through dominant stories about the world, stories that invalidate other and alternative ways of knowing. This point leads her to a discussion of how both theories are compatible. She contends that feminism and postmodernism offer a critique of objectivity, focus on process, recognize the centrality of identity and difference, and present a new conception of power. Functioning as the cornerstones of an emerging theory, postmodernism and feminism are always contingent, local, and relational. Social justice is a discourse, a narrative, that cannot be tied to the limited point of view of the legal order or the rigidly enforced code of the criminal justice system. Social justice, then, is a departure from universal or "totalizing" truths. It is a script in the making in which notions of crime, law, and deviance are never absolute.

6

Postmodern Feminist Criminology and Social Justice

NANCY A. WONDERS

The child wanted to swing. The world looks different from a swing, sometimes smaller, sometimes faster, sometimes just better. But as the path she was walking along left the woods and opened up onto the playground, she saw that, like the day before and the day before that, the swings were all taken. Not a single swing was free. It was amazing to the girl how often this had happened. How often she had come to this place wanting to swing, only to be disappointed. Although she did not yet know the word for injustice, it was an injustice to her. The child turned and walked away with sad eyes and a heavy heart.

BEGINNING AGAIN

One of the hallmarks of both feminism and postmodernism is the common focus on storytelling and narrative as a way to understand the world. Storytelling is valued, in part, because it challenges conventional ways of knowing about the world and traditional understandings of expertise. A story can be told by anyone. And, though some stories are better than others, what makes one story better than another depends in part on who is reading the story. Some prefer true crime stories; some prefer tales of romance or comedy. Because the value we place on a story depends in part on who we are, it is impossible to determine the "best" story for everyone. Similarly, in this chapter I will not attempt to discover the "truth" about social justice, but I will try to explain why a postmodern and feminist perspective offers a different "story" about social justice, a story that will not suit everyone but that I and others have found to be more inclusive, more useful, and more honest.

In this chapter, I argue that the story about social justice that can be told by drawing on both feminism and postmodernism is a better story than the one told by either perspective standing alone. I will begin by describing some important differences between the two perspectives or points of divergence that emerge from their unique histories. I will then explain what postmodernism and feminism have in common—what I call points of convergence between the two perspectives. I will describe why it is useful to consider these perspectives together. Most important, I will discuss the implications of postmodernism and feminism for social justice and criminal justice.

At the outset it is important to say clearly that there is no single feminist perspective and similarly that there is no unified postmodern perspective. Instead, as this book reveals, many different kinds of feminism and many different versions of postmodernism exist. Thus, any claim to represent "postmodernism" or "feminism" in its entirety is sure to be an exaggerated claim. Indeed, some postmodern theorists argue that it is not possible to summarize the field at all, since postmodernism is a response against "totalizing" theory or efforts to explain the world in a unified and unifying way. Obviously, then, my goal is less ambitious. What I will do is sketch out some of the ways that the conceptual histories of these perspectives diverge and converge. In the process some versions of feminism and postmodernism will be emphasized more, some less.

Because the bridge between feminism and postmodernism has only recently been built, the history of postmodernism and feminism is necessarily brief and would include only a few criminologists. Instead, it is appropriate to provide a short history of feminism, followed by another of postmodernism to discover how the divergent histories of these perspectives have led to a convergence of thought and perspective. This process will facilitate the reader's understanding of ways that these two perspectives can work together to create a new vantage point from which to view criminal justice and social justice.

DIVERGENT HISTORIES

Feminism

The emergence of feminism within the United States was both a cause and a consequence of the movement for women's liberation, because feminism developed as a form of social criticism as well as a social movement (Fraser & Nicholson, 1988). As social criticism, feminism provides an analysis of the causes of women's oppression and advances theories and strategies for integrating women into power structures within our society. As a social movement, feminism has served as the organizing vehicle for people working toward economic, political, and social equality for women in particular and for eliminating sexism and gender inequality more generally. Feminism, then, refers to a set of theories about women's oppression and a social movement to create equality for women.

The effort to detail the sources of women's inequality and to develop strategies for remedying it has created tremendous diversity within feminism. The number of feminist perspectives continues to grow, reflecting different points of view about the causes and consequences of gender differences, as well as different understandings of social change. Thus, today we have liberal feminists, Marxist feminists, radical feminists, socialist feminists, black feminists, materialist feminists, and many others (see Jurik in this volume for more information about feminism). Although many would agree with the broad commitment of feminism to work toward equality for women, this theoretical diversity sometimes causes confusion, leading some to reject all of feminism because they reject certain perspectives within it. Whereas some have criticized feminist theory for this theoretical variation and apparent lack of agreement, many others have argued that it is the rich variation within feminism and its openness to diverse ideas that give it its strength (Caulfield & Wonders, 1993).

Though feminism is far from unified as a theory, it is fair to say that all feminists do share a primary focus on gender as an important organizing principle of social life. Because of the centrality of gender, some feminists can be criticized for their inattention to other sources of inequality, including race and class. Other feminists can also be criticized for their tendency to essentialize gender—that is, to make the differences between women and men seem natural and inevitable, although the majority of feminists argue that gender is not biological but is created through social interaction. Still, no other perspective has done as much to raise societal consciousness about the oppression of women and gender inequality. Additionally, feminists have contributed enormously to our understanding of social justice by exploring the linkages between gender and the law, the state, crime, and victimization. In the field of criminology, feminists have been credited with raising societal consciousness about violence against women (Caringella-MacDonald & Humphries, 1991; Ferraro, 1989), the link between masculinity and crime (Messerschmidt, 1987, 1993), the differential treatment of girls and women by the justice system (Chesney-Lind, 1989; Rafter, 1985), the barriers faced by female justice workers (Belknap, 1996; Martin & Jurik, 1996), and many other social issues that were previously ignored by scholars and policy makers.

Like all social theories, feminism has strengths and weaknesses. Interestingly, as some scholars have discovered, many of these weaknesses can be mitigated by taking advantage of the strengths of postmodern theory.

Postmodernism

Postmodern theory began first in Europe, but its impact extended throughout the United States during the 1980s and 1990s. Postmodernism originated as a critique of philosophy and modernity by intellectuals in France and Germany (Rosenau, 1992). In the United States this critique was taken up by academics in many disciplines, but particularly literary critics in English departments.

Postmodern criticism has been directed at a number of features of contemporary society, but perhaps the most significant feature is the role that language plays in constructing reality. Postmodern theorists, such as Derrida, Baudrillard, and Lyotard, argue that reality does not exist in an objective sense; instead, it is constructed through social interaction via the medium of language. Language and the meanings attached to signs and symbols construct the world as we know it via "texts." Texts may be books, poetry, or other written works, but events in the world may also be understood to be texts since all written material and all events need to be "read" or understood by each individual—and we all read "texts" differently from one another. As Cornell (1991) writes, " 'Text' here is meant to refer not only to a literary text, but also to an established context of meaning through which we read ourselves" (p. 108).

For postmodern theorists, to understand the world and to change it, then, requires the "deconstruction" of language, signs, symbols, and texts. "Deconstruction involves demystifying a text, tearing it apart to reveal its internal, arbitrary hierarchies and presuppositions" (Rosenau, 1992, p. 120). Deconstruction requires an analysis of texts or events that does not take their meaning for granted but instead recognizes that meaning is always in the process of being created through social interaction.

Deconstruction plays a central role in postmodern thought, since it is the vehicle for both social criticism and social change. Through critical analysis of a text's or event's meaning, an opening is created for a new understanding or interpretation of the same text or event. Because meaning is inherited from the past, deconstruction gives people today a chance to interpret the world differently, to give new meanings to old events—indeed, to tell the story of history and of the present from a new vantage point. Because the concept of deconstruction can be somewhat abstract, it may be helpful to illustrate using the following passage written by Butler (1992) in which she deconstructs a statement (and common attitude) about rape:

> The defense attorney in the New Bedford gang rape case asked the plaintiff, "If you're living with a man, what are you doing running around the streets getting raped?" The "running around" in this sentence collides grammatically with "getting raped": "getting" is procuring, acquiring, having, as if this were a treasure she was running around after, but "getting raped" suggests the passive voice. Literally, of course, it would be difficult to be "running around" and be "getting raped" at the same time, which suggests that there must be an elided passage here, perhaps a directional that leads from the former to the latter? If the sense of the sentence is "running around [looking to get] raped," which seems to be the only logical way of bridging the two parts of the sentence, then rape as a passive acquisition is precisely the object of her active search. The first clause suggests that she "belongs" in the home, with her man, and the "streets" establish her as open season. If she is looking to get raped, she is looking to become the property of some other, and this objective is installed in her desire, conceived here as quite frantic in its pursuit. She is "running around," suggesting that she is running around looking under every rock for a rapist to satisfy her. (p. 18)

Because words and ideas can be harmful, deconstruction contributes to social justice by revealing the injustice that is perpetuated by language and ideas. Within criminology, postmodernism has been put to productive and (de)constructive use in the analysis of crime and justice by Arrigo (1995), Henry and Milovanovic (1996), Michalowski (1993), and Pfohl (1993, 1994), among others. Through the process of deconstruction, postmodernism "alerts us to what we do not know and subverts the comfortable structures of thought, images of reality, and certainty of thinking that underlie conventional criminal justice science" (Arrigo, 1995, p. 449).

Because so much deconstructive work has been aimed at literary texts, words and language have played a central role in this enterprise. As a result, reading some postmodern writing is like reading the writings of a first grader: many of the words are familiar, but the way they are spelled and their ordering is a little strange. Increasingly, though, some postmodern theorists, especially within the social sciences, have sought to make the central ideas of postmodernism accessible to a larger audience (see, for example, Rosenau, 1992). This has been done, in part, by writing about postmodernism in a style that is familiar to most readers. It has also involved efforts to identify the strengths of postmodern thought and to acknowledge its weaknesses. In the process some postmodern theorists have discovered that some of the weaknesses of postmodern theory can be responded to by consideration of feminist theory. In particular, postmodern theory is often viewed as relativistic and apolitical, a charge that is rarely leveled against feminism. By exploring points of convergence between postmodernism and feminism, both perspectives can be strengthened considerably.

As the girl left the playground and began again along the path, she saw in the distance a glint of metal through the trees, a shimmering of reflected sunlight. The girl left the path and walked toward the light. As she drew near, she saw that someone had hung a chain from one of the trees in the forest. The chain was unusual: its links were all different from one another—each one a different size and shape. In fact, the character of each link was so distinctive that it was amazing that they had ever been connected together in the first place. Although the chain looked like no chain she had seen before, when she tugged on it she was surprised at how strong the chain with the different links was. Yes, it seemed unusually strong.

As the child took a step toward the chain, she saw something move out of the corner of her eye. When she turned to look, she found that what had moved was a rope made from many cloths that hung from a nearby tree; the rope was moving slightly in the very slight breeze. The rope was also unusual. It had the feel of a quilt, each piece a square from a different piece of fabric. It was a rope that had obviously been made by human hands and human effort. It was beautiful, and strange, and also strong.

It didn't take the child long to see the magic in the gifts she had discovered. At first she swung from the rope, but soon she was dissatisfied with the height that the rope could travel. And to make the rope swing, the child had to continually push off from the ground. Then the child tried the chain, but it too was hard to keep going, and like the rope, it did not seem to go very high. The child was happy for her discovery, but she began to wish again for the easy swing, the conventional swing, that the children played on in the park. Wistfully, the child sat down to rest.

COMMON DESTINIES:
POINTS OF CONVERGENCE

Despite their unique histories, at least four important points of convergence between feminism and postmodernism can be identified: a critique of objectivity, a focus on process, the centrality of identity and difference, and a new conception of power (Wonders, 1996). These points of convergence provide the tools with which to forge a feminist and postmodern version of social justice. I will describe each of these in turn.

Subjectivity/Objectivity

Feminism and postmodernism both offer a powerful critique of the concept of objectivity. Many scholars who study justice issues think of themselves as social "scientists" who use the scientific method to objectively study the social world. This objectivity makes it possible to discover the "truth" about social reality. However, postmodern and feminist theorists recognize that what passes for objectivity and the "truth" is really just one possible story about reality. They use the word *contingent* to explain the way that truth varies by time and place and depending on who is telling the story. So, the truth that some women are witches deserving of punishment and incapacitation seemed like a fact at one point in time, but it was determined to be a story at a later point in time. The truth that slaves were not fully human was inscribed in the law as a fact, only to be revealed to be a story later. As Flax (1992) notes, "this does not mean that there is no truth but rather that truth is discourse dependent" (p. 452). She goes on to say:

> As a product of the human mind, knowledge has no necessary relation to Truth or the Real. Philosophers create stories about these concepts and about their own activities. Their stories are no more true, foundational, or truth adjudicating than any others. There is no way to test whether one story is closer to the truth than another because there is no transcendental standpoint or mind unenmeshed in its own language and story. (p. 454)

Similarly, feminist and postmodern theorists argue that the scientific method is no more objective than any other method; indeed, all methods rely on the subjectivity or perception of the investigator. Scientists of all kinds draw on their own opinions and personal perceptions when they decide what to study, what questions to ask, what methods to use, and what findings to report to others. Thus, truth is always contingent on historical understandings, particular circumstances, and individual judgments; truth, therefore, is temporary and partial—it can always change. Truth is also always political, privileging some perspectives over others. Thus, truth is like a story; indeed, for many postmodern and feminist theorists, truth *is* a story.

Identity and Difference

One of the reasons that feminist and postmodern theorists have been so critical of the concept of "truth" is because of the way some people have been able to have their opinions represented as truth at the expense of others. Both theoretical perspectives recognize that some individuals and groups do not participate in the construction of "truth" because they have been systematically excluded from access to the tools of science, the power of the state, and the writing of history. Instead, the truth has historically been determined by those with greater power in our society. Importantly, one of the primary ways that power has been achieved is through the construction of "difference."

Within both postmodern and feminist thought, difference plays a pivotal role in explaining the oppression of some groups by others. Difference is constructed when a continuum is turned into a dichotomy, such that one part of the dichotomy is represented as better than the other. So we take the continuum of age, create the categories of "adult" and "child," and privilege adults over children. We take the continuum of skin color, invent racial categories based how closely skin color resembles blackness or whiteness, and then privilege whiteness. Difference is a linguistic construction in which the *relationship* between the two halves of the dichotomous construction is ignored, while the binary construction is elevated in importance and portrayed as natural.

> When we identify one thing as like the others, we are not merely classifying the world; we are investing particular classifications with consequences and positioning ourselves in relation to those meanings. When we identify one thing as unlike the others, we are dividing the world; we are using our language to exclude, to distinguish—to discriminate. (Minow, 1990, p. 3)

In particular, postmodern and feminist theorists recognize the way that "identity" has been used to construct and maintain difference by creating divisions between people. They also argue that identity—difference based on race, class, gender, or other categories—is not a fact but is instead socially constructed by the larger society. Some examples may help clarify this point.

We tend to think of race as an identity category that is based on a single biological characteristic: skin color. But for postmodern and feminist theorists, race is understood to be a social construction; it is not a biological characteristic but instead a label used to distinguish people from one another as a basis for differential reward. Thus, race is produced and reproduced all the time; indeed, we are continually changing the meaning of race. For example, in South Africa the government changed the race of almost eight hundred people in 1987 (Uys, 1988). This was not because these individuals' skin color changed; instead, it was because the government decided to classify people differently as a way to accomplish certain political ends. In the process, race as a category is revealed to be an unnatural legal and political category rather than a reflection of a natural division. Race only has meaning because we choose to make it a mattering "difference" in a particular time and place.

Similarly, feminists have questioned gender identity. For most feminists, gender does not reside in biological sex but is something that is created and re-created in social interaction. In other words, we "do gender" every day through such mundane decisions as deciding what to wear, how to talk to others, and how to cross our legs (West & Zimmerman, 1987). What seems "naturally" associated with biological sex characteristics is a result of this kind of everyday decision making. In the early 1800s in England, doing gender for wealthy men meant putting on wigs, wearing tights and high heels, and taking care not to break their long nails. Now the same ritual applies for wealthy women. Thus, conceptions of gender also change over time and from place to place.

For feminists and postmodern theorists, all difference is constructed through a similar process. We are all "doing difference" all of the time (West & Fenstermaker, 1995). Identity is the result of complex relationships we each have with others in the external world. It reflects "positionality" (Butler, 1990, 1993). Positionality describes the ongoing process by which we attribute meaning to things, and then the things take on the meanings we have given them. Positionality is similar to the concept of a "self-fulfilling prophecy." If I claim that I am a criminal, or if others claim that I am a criminal, I "become" a criminal. Similarly, if the state claims that young people who use drugs are criminal (rather than "ill," as is done in many other industrialized countries), then the state has played an active role in shaping the identity of teenagers and others who used drugs—it has changed who they are. But positionality goes further by arguing that through this discursive process—through the use of language and words—the word *criminal* comes to be associated with who it is applied to. So, for example, even though whites are more likely to use all major drugs (except heroin) than are blacks, African Americans are disproportionately arrested and prosecuted for drug usage (Tonry, 1995). "African-Americans make up 12 percent of the U.S. population and constitute 13 percent of all monthly drug users, but represent 35 percent of those arrested for drug possession, 55 percent of those convicted of drug possession, and 74 percent of those sentenced to prison for drug possession" (Donziger, 1996). To appreciate the drama of these numbers, remember that 21 percent of all inmates in state prisons and a startling 58 percent of those in federal prisons are in for drug offenses (Donziger, 1996). As a result of criminal justice policy and differential enforcement of drug laws, increasingly the term *criminal* has come to be defined in the public's mind in relationship to black youth, (re)producing over and over again the identity of black and the identity of criminal. Butler (1993), then, defines positionality as "the reiterative and citational practice by which discourse produces the effects that it names" (p. 2). In a sense, then, our identity represents the unfolding of our own personal history. We are constantly in the process of being constructed and reconstructed through our own actions and those of others.

Process

In general, feminist and postmodern theorists believe that all aspects of the social world are always in the process of being created. For them, reality itself is a transitory, ever-changing process. This view is in marked contrast to many other social science perspectives that too frequently view society, institutions, and individuals as static, relatively fixed objects that can, therefore, easily be researched and studied. For postmodern and feminist scholars, the processes that create the social world are more often the subject of study rather than an object or fixed point in time. For this reason, feminist and postmodern methods of understanding the world typically do not rely on the scientific method or experimentation but instead utilize interpretive strategies that can reveal how the social world is created day to day, through interaction with others. Let me illustrate with an example.

It is common for those who study crime and criminal justice processing to focus on outcomes of criminal justice decision making. So, for example, researchers have frequently studied criminal sentencing as a single decision point within the justice process. Researchers will focus especially on whether judges make fair sentencing decisions. But sentencing is not a single decision point; instead, it is the result of a complex set of decisions made by other actors within the criminal justice system. Police officers must decide whether to arrest, prosecutors must decide how to charge the individual, and probation officers must make a presentence recommendation; all of these prior decisions are deeply embedded in "the case" that judges decide on. Thus, sentencing decisions are part of a larger process of decision making that includes sentencing but also plea bargaining, probation recommendations, bail decisions, arrest decisions, and even which behaviors are criminalized under the law. Postmodern and feminist researchers would devote less time to analysis of judges' sentencing decisions and more time to analysis of the ways that crime itself is constructed in our society, as well as the ways that officials interact with each other and with citizens to give meaning to crime and justice processing. Rather than focusing on sentencing decisions per se, it is more useful to reconstruct and deconstruct all of the small and large decisions and dialogues that lead up to the moment of sentencing (Wonders, 1996). Feminist and postmodern researchers would be more likely to use ethnographic and qualitative research techniques that allow them to participate more fully in these interactive rituals as a way to better understand the way that meaning is constructed through social interaction. In general, then, feminist and postmodern scholars are not very interested in the question "Are criminal justice outcomes the result of a fair and objective procedure?"; instead, they seek to understand and respond to a different question: "How does the inherent subjectivity associated with the process of constructing and reconstructing crime and the criminal justice system shape identities, experiences, and (in)justice?"

Power

Another point of convergence between feminist and postmodern thought is that both share a new and different understanding of power. Most social theorists look for power in hierarchies—institutions or interactions in which one individual or group is able to exercise control over another, usually through coercion or force. Feminists and postmodern theorists challenge this understanding of power by analyzing the power that resides in everyday interactions. They focus on the power attached to everyday behaviors and ordinary cultural symbols, including the power of ideas, nonverbal behavior, material objects, and, importantly, language. This is in part what feminists mean when they say that the personal is political. It is at level of the ordinary that much political life happens.

Let us use the problem of woman battering to illustrate. Violence against women within their homes was virtually ignored historically. The failure to take the harm that men caused to women seriously cannot be understood simply by looking at the government, law, or even the domination of important institutions by men. We must also look at the role everyday behaviors and cultural attitudes play in creating a climate of acceptance for violence. At a very young age, boys are taught to trivialize the pain and concerns of women by calling them "sissies." Because girls are discouraged from participation in rigorous physical activity and are likely to experience public harassment if they develop expertise in athletics (they will be called "tomboys," or worse), children learn at an early age that physical passivity and weakness are feminine and physical strength is masculine. Through everyday interactions with parents, the vast majority of children in the United States learn that people who love them hit them (Straus, 1991); in fact, they are told that it is the responsibility of the parent to hit them to show them how much they care for them and as a way to teach them to be better people. What makes battering prevalent in our society is not just the physical force that men use against women. At least as important is the power of everyday interactions and cultural meanings that reinforce the idea that women's pain is unimportant, that women should not develop or take advantage of their physical strength, and that people who love us hurt us. My point here is that feminists and postmodern theorists place just as much importance on language, ideas, everyday interactions, and culture as sources of power as they do on the use of force and coercion.

As the child sat, resting on the cool grass, she suddenly had an idea. Quickly she stood, then ran to a place between the two trees. By grabbing the rope in one hand and the chain in the other, the child was able to create a swing that could go higher than ever before. It was like a real swing, only the child's body was the swing itself, and by pumping her legs, she could make the swing go higher still. The child had filled the empty space between the rope and the chain; the child had become a bridge between the rope and the chain. Indeed, it was the child—the child—that made the rope and the chain go higher than ever before.

Although this swing was harder work than any swing she had ever been on, including the swing in the park, the child had never had so much fun in her life. Her arms ached and her legs throbbed from being held up over the ground, but the girl felt such pride in her swing, such ownership, that no other swing could compare. She played for a long time on the swing in the woods, and when the sun began to set, the girl went home exhausted but happy. And she did not think once about the swing in the park, the swing that never, ever seemed free for her.

POSTMODERNISM AND FEMINISM/
FEMINISM AND POSTMODERNISM

The points of convergence I have outlined represent important areas of agreement between feminism and postmodernism; the points of divergence represent unique contributions made by each perspective. Put together, these perspectives create what some have called postmodern feminism, feminism and deconstruction, or postmodernism/feminism. The reason that it has been so difficult to know what to call this new perspective is that it is not a single perspective, but is really two perspectives working together to create a new understanding. In fact, some argue that we should not combine them into a single phrase but continue to keep them separate, referring to feminism *and* postmodernism as I have done throughout this chapter. As Singer (1992) writes:

> The thematic and strategic interplay between paradigms, and their opposition, tends to work against any mechanism of unification. The "and" therefore keeps open a site for strategic engagement. The "and" is a place holder, which is to say, it holds a place open, free from being filled substantively or prescriptively. The "and" holds/preserves the differences between and among themselves. (p. 475)

Trying to force postmodernism and feminism into a single theory risks losing something from each perspective. Instead, it is more valuable to try to build bridges between the perspectives—to find points of convergence—which strengthens the story told by each perspective and creates a new vantage point from which to consider the social world.

Some of the most interesting work being done by either feminist or postmodern scholars is being done by those who are bridging the two disciplines. Nicholson's (1990) book *Feminism/Postmodernism* was one of the first to explore the advantages and disadvantages of a union between these two perspectives. Cornell's (1991, 1992) work on law and justice, Butler's (1990, 1992, 1993) and Bordo's (1993) analysis focusing on the social construction of gender, bodies, and sexuality, and Howe's work on punishment (1994) offer a small sample of those whose work falls into the category postmodern and feminist. Recent work by Elam (1994) and Hennessy (1993) explores the theoretical implications of feminist approaches that integrate aspects of postmodern scholarship. All of these scholars have found much common ground between these perspectives. They have also discovered that the union between these two perspectives helps address weaknesses in each. For example, because of feminism's primary focus on "women," many have argued that feminism is not inclusive of those who view their primary identity as black or Chicana or lesbian. Postmodernism's focus on "difference" in general is potentially more inclusive than many versions of feminism (Farganis, 1994). Similarly, postmodernism is frequently criticized for its apparent political neutrality; feminism offers a deeper sense of the political and has developed strategies for social change that do not reproduce oppression but transform it. Although conceptions of social justice are often more implicit in feminist and postmodern writing than explicit, much can be learned about social justice by attention to the work of these and other postmodern and feminist texts.

SOCIAL JUSTICE

The popular understanding of justice is that it emerges from the law, but for feminist and postmodern theorists nothing in the law necessarily links it to justice. Indeed, historically, many laws have intentionally promoted injustice and oppression, including slavery laws, laws sanctioning violence within the family, and laws declaring women and children the property of men. Law continues to promote injustice today. In 1994, "one out of every three African-American men between the ages of 20 and 29 in the entire country—including suburban and rural areas—was under some form of criminal justice supervision," and in some major cities over half of all black men were under justice supervision on any given day (Donziger, 1996, p. 102). It seems obvious that many African Americans would not find justice in either the law or the criminal justice system. Despite the overwhelming number of women who experience rape in this country (for example, in 1991, the National Crime Victimization Survey reported that 171,420 rapes had occurred), "only one in 100 rapists is sentenced to more than a year in prison," and "almost a quarter of *convicted rapists* are not sentenced to prison but instead are released on probation" (Buchwald, Fletcher, & Roth , 1993, p. 37). It seems obvious that many women would not find justice in either the law or the criminal justice system.

Some scholars have gone further in their critique of law and the criminal justice system to argue that, since state power relies on the threat or use of force, the law and the justice system are actually founded on (rather than opposed to) injustice and violence, creating a deep contradiction that is impossible to resolve (Taussig, 1996). From this point of view, because the criminal justice system relies so heavily on violence or the threat of violence, it cannot be depended upon for justice. As the videotape of the Rodney King beating portrayed, it is not always clear from the behavior of police officers or other officials that justice is a primary goal of the criminal justice system. It is evident that, at best, the criminal justice system and law have contradictory relationships to justice. Justice must be about something else.

Because postmodern and feminist thinkers do not believe in objective truth or reality, instead viewing truth as a social construction that is always being (re-)created, it might seem impossible to develop a feminist and postmodern conception of "justice." Is not justice different for everyone from this perspective? Does not any effort to define justice create a rigid boundary that necessarily benefits some people over others? But just because postmodern and feminist scholars recognize the limitations of *universal* definitions of justice (definitions that would be true for everyone for all time) does not mean that they believe that we can afford to ignore our responsibility to make the best decisions we can, for the moment. In fact, once we understand that we shape the world and can change it, we have perhaps a greater responsibility to make choices that construct the world in ways that we can live with and feel good about.

Elam (1994) calls this point of view "ethical activism." We have a responsibility—an obligation to ourselves and others—to understand our daily role in defining and creating reality and justice, and to do our best to make judgments that make the world a good place to be for all of us. This means that no single, overarching version of justice prevails. Instead, justice is always contingent, temporary, related to time and place and person. As Elam (1994) puts it:

One of the things that deconstruction and feminism do is make us aware of the necessity as well as the precarious status of ethical judgments. In the name of the ethical, the judgments that deconstruction and feminism make always contain a simultaneous questioning of their ethical status. At the same time they pass judgment they must also ask the question: "What's next?" In this abysmal scene, any question to the question will also necessarily lead to a reposing of the question. That is to say, just as there are no grounds for ethical judgments, there also is no end to judgment. (p. 115)

If we consider the conceptions of power and process that feminists and postmodern thinkers share, then it is also clear that social justice is not simply or even mostly created by legislators, judges, and justice officials. Social justice is created by ordinary people in the process of living their lives. Again, "the personal is political." The choices we make every day to help someone else or hurt them, to share resources or not to share, construct the world for others in ways that shape the realities that are available to them. Because we are social creatures and share a common planet, we have an obligation to consider our own role in defining what the world can be for others. In particular, we must appreciate that language is political and that it has the power to constrain people from being fully human. If we tell a child from the very moment that she is born that she is a "girl," with all of the cultural baggage that comes with that concept, are all possible life choices open to her as she goes through the developmental process? Or do some options disappear because of the choice to establish her identity as a girl so emphatically and so early in life? Similarly, if the state defines people who take television sets or use drugs as "criminals" but defines corporations who steal from people's retirement funds as worthy of government bailouts, does not the state profoundly shape identities and individual destinies?

Thus, we must be critically aware of our role in constructing identities and difference, since difference is so often the basis for inequitable treatment and differential reward. There are many differences between us, but we make some differences matter more than others. Social justice requires not that we do away with difference but that we think carefully about which differences we want to have matter and that we continually critique our own role in perpetuating differences that should not matter. We must understand that in the creation of identity, our "representations become understood as political practices which distribute unequally power and other goods" (Yeatman, 1994, p. 14). It also means that we have an obligation to consider the ways that the meaning attached to difference is inherited and not always of our choosing. We need to appreciate the extent to which individuals or groups are penalized in the present for meanings constructed in the past. In part, this means looking critically at many of the criteria we use to arrive at "just" decisions.

Too frequently, our conception of justice is linked with the concept of equality, but legal equality is of no value to people whose everyday lives are filled with the profound effects of economic and political inequality. This situation is equivalent to arguing that a foot race between two people is "fair" since both individuals are running the same distance, without acknowledging that one of the racers has only one leg. Who can argue that this is a fair race? As Farganis (1994) writes, "persons have different moral standpoints, different places from which they actually live and move and think, and justice requires not that we detach ourselves from individual particularities, but that we engage and sympathize with them" (p. 119).

In recognition of the ways that difference intersects with legal (in)equality, some postmodern and feminist scholars have formulated conceptions of justice that insert a recognition of difference into the legal system. Cornell (1992) argues that we should not focus on equality under the law but instead strive to develop "equivalent rights." Equivalent rights do not seek to treat people the same but attempt to recognize the ways that difference might need to be adjusted or accommodated to yield treatment that is "of equal value," although not identical (Cornell, 1992). Similarly, Young (1990) argues for "democratic cultural pluralism," which "requires a dual system of rights: a general system of rights which are the same for all, and a more specific system of group conscious policies and rights" since "some of the disadvantages that oppressed groups suffer can be remedied in policy only by an affirmative acknowledgment of the group's specificity" (p. 174).

Some who work from a feminist and postmodern perspective, however, are unwilling to even engage in the conversation about justice, arguing that the best we can do is to address injustice. Flax (1992), for example, writes that "claims about injustice can operate independently of "truth" or indeed "[can correspond to a] counterclaim about a transcendental good or (substantive) justice" (p. 459). She goes further to argue that overarching conceptions of justice are dangerous, because "they release us as discrete persons from full responsibility for our acts. We remain children, waiting, if our own powers fail, for the higher authorities to save us from the consequences of our own actions" (pp. 459–460). Essentially she, too, argues for ethical activism, for doing the best we can to act wisely, kindly, and peacefully in a world of too frequent conflict. For Flax, any conception of justice that is embedded within the state and law makes it too easy for ordinary people to lose sight of their personal responsibility for creating justice, preventing injustice, and making history.

Working individually and independently to achieve justice, however, does not guarantee that unjust institutions and social structures will be changed. Yet for many people today, it is difficult to work together with others because so many of the differences between us have been made to matter, whether it is skin color, sex, social class, sexual orientation, or the style of the clothes we wear. Difference separates us so much that it creates a barrier to collective efforts for social change. However, identity is not the only basis on which we can come together for a common purpose. Instead, Elam (1994) argues that we can come together based on what she calls "groundless solidarity." This solidarity is groundless because it is not based on identity politics or coalitions formed on the basis of shared physical or cultural characteristics. Instead, solidarity is achieved by building bridges across our differences to find common issues and concerns that we can work on together. So, for example, we need not be black to be concerned about the staggering growth in our prison population. We can build bridges between diverse sectors of the population by forging an alliance between taxpayers tired of wasting money on prisons, parents fed up with the trade-off between education and incarceration, underrepresented racial and ethnic groups who are angry about the disproportionate impact of criminal justice policies on their communities, medical professionals who view drugs as a health problem rather than a criminal justice problem, and numerous other constituencies who have other good reasons to support change.

In some places, coalitions of this type have already begun to be formed, as evidenced by the 1996 passage of referenda in Arizona and California that redefine drug use as a medical issue rather than a criminal one. The issues that confront us will be constantly changing and coalitions may not last, but they can be effective in the short term for responding to the problems that face us and for forging, for the moment, a more inclusive conception of justice.

CONCLUDING REMARKS

In the beginning of this chapter, I argued that a postmodern and feminist approach to social justice was more inclusive and more useful. It is important to remember that I also argued that it is more honest. Feminism and postmodernism suggest that justice is a story—a discourse—that has historically been written by just a few. I am not comfortable with the idea that we may not be able to arrive at a universal understanding of justice, but I recognize that it is infinitely more honest to admit that we cannot than to cling to a conception of justice that so clearly benefits some at the expense of many. Indeed, as Singer (1992) reminds us, "Part of the tradition of critical writing that postmodernism and feminism inherit, albeit in ways that are differentially specified, is a tradition of writing as a form of resistance, writing which works not to confirm cohesion, but rather to disrupt, destabilize, denaturalize" (p. 469). I write this chapter in the spirit of that tradition.

Ultimately, though, readers of this text need not agree with my story about social justice to appreciate the value of a feminist and postmodern approach. The wonderful thing about combining postmodernism and feminism is that it invites—no, it *challenges*—readers to disagree. It challenges readers to engage in ethical activism, to seek out solidarity with others, and to write their own story about social justice—to join the conversation and discourse about what social justice is and to actively participate in shaping what it will become.

Now, had she been a selfish child, the girl would have kept the magic of the swing to herself. But she was still young enough to understand that the more people with whom she shared her experience, the greater her own joy would be. So, the next day she brought several friends to see the swing in the woods. At first her friends thought the girl odd for bringing them to this place in the woods where the strange chain and rope hung down from the sky. But their happiness was profound when they discovered how high they could fly in this swing of their bodies and how far they could see from their new vantage point.

    The girl was a thoughtful child, and once again she sat on the cool grass, this time to watch her friends in play. As the girl watched her friends, an amazing thought came to her. She realized that not a single friend had actually been on her swing. They had only been on their own swing. For her swing was partly the rope and the chain together, but it was partly her body, her self, that made the swing real. At that moment, the girl laughed out loud, the pure and contagious laughter of a young child. For suddenly she saw that the real beauty of the swing was that it was a new swing, a different swing, for each of her friends. Because each person made the swing of rope and chain in their own unique way, it was each individual who could decide how high to go and how far the swing would help them see.

REVIEW QUESTIONS

1. How do feminism and postmodernism differ from one another?

2. What is deconstruction, and why is it so important within postmodernism?

3. What are the four points of convergence between feminism and postmodernism that are described in this chapter?

4. What new justice-related examples could help illustrate each of the four points of convergence mentioned in the chapter?

5. Does it make sense to keep postmodernism and feminism separate but connected with an *and,* or would it be better to come up with a new term that joins them together in some way?

6. Do feminism and postmodernism offer a different conception of social justice when they are together compared with the conception of social justice each

perspective offers on its own? (You may also want to refer to some of the other chapters in this book for comparison.)

7. What is meant by "ethical activism," and what are the strengths and weakness of this approach to social justice?

8 Why is equality a problematic concept for feminist and postmodern scholars, and how do they propose to alter the law to address these problems?

9. Postmodern and feminist scholars argue that justice does not depend on law. Do you agree with this point of view? What is the relationship between law and justice?

10. Feminism and postmodernism argue that justice is a story that everyone can help write. What is the story of social justice that you would author?

REFERENCES

Arrigo, B A. (1995). The peripheral core of law and criminology: On postmodern social theory and conceptual integration. *Justice Quarterly, 12*(3), 447–472.

Belknap, J. (1996). *The invisible woman: Gender, crime and justice.* Belmont, CA: Wadsworth.

Bordo, S. (1993). *Unbearable weight: Feminism, Western culture, and the body.* Berkeley: University of California Press.

Buchwald, E., Fletcher, P., & Roth, M. (1993). *Transforming a rape culture.* Minneapolis: Milkweed.

Butler, J. (1990). *Gender trouble: Feminism and the subversion of identity.* New York: Routledge.

Butler, J. (1992). Contingent foundations: Feminism and the question of "postmodernism." In J. Butler & J. W. Scott (Eds.), *Feminists theorize the political* (pp. 3–21). New York: Routledge.

Butler, J. (1993). *Bodies that matter: On the discursive limits of "sex."* New York: Routledge.

Caringella-MacDonald, S., & Humphries, D. (1991). Sexual assault, women, and the community: Organizing to prevent sexual violence. In H. E. Pepinsky & R. Quinney (Eds.), *Criminology as peacemaking* (pp. 98–113). Bloomington: Indiana University Press.

Caulfield, S., & Wonders, N. A. (1993). Gender and justice: Feminist contributions to criminology. In G. Barak (Ed.), *Varieties of criminology: Readings from a dynamic discipline* (pp. 213–229). Westport, CT: Praeger.

Chesney-Lind, M. (1989). Girls' crime and woman's place: Toward a feminist model of female delinquency. *Crime and Delinquency, 35*(1), 5.

Cornell, D. (1991). *Beyond accommodation: Ethical feminism, deconstruction, and the law.* New York: Routledge.

Cornell, D. (1992). Gender, sex, and equivalent rights. In J. Butler & J. W. Scott (Eds.), *Feminists theorize the political* (pp. 280–296). New York: Routledge.

Donziger, S. (1996). *The real war on crime: The report of the National Criminal Justice Commission.* New York: Harper Perennial.

Elam, D. (1994). *Feminism and deconstruction: Ms. en Abyme.* New York: Routledge.

Farganis, S. (1994). Postmodernism and feminism. In D. R. Dickens & A. Fontana (Eds.), *Postmodernism and social inquiry* (pp. 101–126). New York: Guilford.

Ferraro, K. J. (1989). Policing woman battering. *Social Problems 36*(1), 6.

Flax, J. (1992). The end of innocence. In J. Butler & J. W. Scott (Eds.), *Feminists theorize the political* (pp. 445–463). New York: Routledge.

Fraser, N., & Nicholson, L. (1988). Social criticism without philosophy: An encounter between feminism and postmodernism. In A. Ross (Ed.), *Universal abandon? The politics of postmodernism* (pp. 83–104). Minneapolis: University of Minnesota Press.

Hennessy, R. (1993). *Materialist feminism and the politics of discourse.* New York: Routledge.

Henry, S., & Milovanovic, D. (1996). *Constitutive criminology: Beyond postmodernism.* London: Sage.

Howe, A. (1994). *Punish and critique: Towards a feminist analysis of penality.* London: Routledge.

Martin, S. E., & Jurik, N. C. (1996). *Doing justice, doing gender: Women in law and criminal justice occupations.* London: Sage.

Messerschmidt, J. (1987). *Capitalism, patriarchy, and crime.* Totowa, NJ: Rowan & Littlefield.

Messerschmidt, J. (1993). *Masculinities and crime.* Lanham, MD: Rowman & Littlefield.

Michalowski, R. (1993). (De)construction, postmodernism, and social problems: Facts, fiction and fantasies at the "end of history." In J. A. Holstein & G. Miller (Eds.), *Reconsidering social constructionism* (pp. 377–401). New York: Aldine.

Minow, M. (1990). *Making all the difference: Inclusion, exclusion, and American law.* Ithaca, NY: Cornell Universtiy Press.

Pfohl, S. J. (1993). Revenge of the parasites: Feeding off the ruins of sociological (de)construction. In J. A. Holstein & G. Miller (Eds.), *Reconsidering social constructionism* (pp. 403–440). New York: Aldine.

Pfohl, S. (1994). A short history of the Parasite Cafe. In M. Ryan & A. Gordon (Eds.), *Body politics: Disease, desire, and the family* (pp. 97–103). Boulder, CO: Westview.

Rafter, N. H. (1985). *Partial justice: Women in state prisons, 1800–1935.* Boston: Northeastern University Press.

Rosenau, P. (1992). *Post-modernism and the social sciences: Insights, inroads and intrusions.* Princeton, NJ: Princeton University Press.

Singer, Linda. (1992). Feminism and postmodernism. In J. Butler and J. W. Scott (Eds.), *Feminists theorize the political* (pp. 464–475). New York: Routledge.

Straus, M. A. (1991). Discipline and deviance: Physical punishment of children and violence and other crime in adulthood. *Social Problems, 38*(2), 133–154.

Taussig, M. (1996). The injustice of policing: Prehistory and rectitude. In A. Sarah & T. R. Kearns (Eds.), *Justice and injustice in law and legal theory* (pp. 19–34). Ann Arbor: University of Michigan Press.

Tonry, M. (1995). *Malign neglect: Race, crime and punishment in America.* New York: Oxford University Press.

Uys, P.-D. (1988, September 23). Chameleons thrive under apartheid. *New York Times,* A-3.

West, C., & Fenstermaker, S. (1995). Doing difference. *Gender and Society, 9,* 8–37.

West, C., & Zimmerman, D. H. (1987). Doing gender. *Gender and Society, 1,* 125–151.

Wonders, N. 1996. Determinate sentencing: A feminist and postmodern story. *Justice Quarterly, 13*(4), 301–338.

Yeatman, A. (1994). *Postmodern revisionings of the political.* New York: Routledge.

Young, I. M. (1990). *Justice and the politics of difference.* Princeton, NJ: Princeton University Press.

Semiotics and
Social Justice

In this article, Manning examines the meaning of justice informed by a semiotic method of analysis. Semiotics is the study of language, language systems, and the evolving meanings contained in a given system of communication. Manning maintains that the concept of justice, although central to the criminal justice system, is rarely studied systematically in the literature. He claims this lack of attention is related to the ambiguous meanings of justice. He argues that justice is about individual perception and one's social position. Further, these factors are informed by and manufactured through the media, which, as Manning notes, provide mere images of justice. These images are sustained by television portrayals that compress and collapse reality into visually captivating appearances. These celluloid appearances function as reconstructions of justice. However, they are not synonymous with the concept of justice or the meaning(s) necessarily intended by the criminal justice system. Manning observes that at least three forms of justice are practiced and promoted within the criminal justice apparatus. He identifies them as "justice," *justice,* and JUSTICE. The meanings for each are often difficult to ascertain because of various denotative, connotative, and mythical interpretations that attach to them. Further, the level at which any one of these respective views operates complicates our understanding and can produce contradictory interpretations. Manning concludes by offering a semiotic analysis on the meaning of "justice," *justice,* and JUSTICE within and outside the legal system. These are conceptual and practical distinctions that are easily confused by citizens and often skillfully manipulated by the media. Thus, notions such as crime, law, and deviance are not only uncertain; they remain decidedly ambiguous.

7

Semiotics and Justice:
"Justice," *Justice,* and JUSTICE
Contradictions and the
Ideology of Criminal Justice

PETER K. MANNING

J ustice is the central concept that animates criminal justice studies. It is also
quite ambiguous, seldom defined, and rarely examined critically in research and texts (Souryal, 1992, in press). Thus, the literature contains virtually no careful consideration of the concept. Definitions of justice vary in
criminal justice including operational, due process, and pragmatic usages. Legalistic definitions, which rely on due process notions, are very commonly
used. Clearly, criminal justice is a practical and sensible field. Accordingly, it is
concerned with efficiency and effectiveness rather than "justice" or the quality of the experience of justice. In many respects, trust in the system and its
legitimation means that citizens—differentially, to be sure—believe that the
criminal justice system produces justice. This vague usage, or usage that is
highly determined by the context in which the word is used, suggests grounds
for discussing contradictions and associated ideological work that surrounds
the concept.

The focus of this chapter is the institutional context for the meaning of
justice. The chapter reviews some relevant aspects of justice, introduces semiotics as a technique for understanding, illustrates various justice contexts using
media materials, notes some key contradictions produced, and explains how
blindness to these contradictions is creatively sustained. In short, investigating
the concept of justice in the criminal justice system requires seeing it *in and
through* the media as well as through analytic procedures.

JUSTICE AND THE SENSE OF JUSTICE

Perceptions of justice, not surprisingly, are based on social position and perspective. People employed or deeply involved in the criminal justice system—
volunteers, civilian employees, and workers in police, courts, corrections, and
probation and parole—consider their work "doing justice." Democratic legal
ideology supports the notion that the criminal justice system produces "justice

for all." Periodic mistakes, public scandals, and acts of corruption are taken as unrepresentative—that is, as a function of "rotten apples," or exceptions to the rule of overall efficiency and scrupulous honesty.

Minority populations distrust the system and are much more sensitive to public scandals such as the Rodney King beating than are whites. The more contact with the system, the lower the opinion of those questioned. It is difficult to establish cause and effect here, whether low opinions came before or after contact; the role of third factors such as ethnicity, class, and education; or their interactional effects. Notwithstanding, primary experience does not increase trust (Baker, 1997). Finally, perhaps fortunately, the majority of citizens have secondhand knowledge of the criminal justice apparatus. They possess *knowledge about* criminal justice rather than experienced-based *knowledge of* its actual workings. The mass media are the principal source of criminal justice knowledge (Sparks, 1992; Surette, 1992).

In addition to perspective and social position, other grounds for defining justice include the philosophical, religious, legalistic, and operational. It would appear that the media and modern consciousness compress and combine various definitions and contexts in which the concept of justice is viewed. All of these bases are current. They are used in research, political debate, policy research, and everyday "bar talk." However, none has ultimate authority. Thus, discussions do take place and generalized notions embed the idea of justice. As a result, the context for one's use is very important.

Linguistic formulations (that is, how we discuss and attribute meaning to social events) have power. Legal language is not a mere tool, a neutral vehicle, because it is a means for classifying, controlling, and sanctioning citizens. Power sanctions legal language and expresses the interests of governmental agents of control, even while it remains an "open text," subject to interpretation. The discourse of criminal justice is complex and does not advance "only system-supporting declarations" (Arrigo, 1995, p. 457, n. 5). The discourse of the law—including civil, administrative, regulatory—and local statutes and ordinances contains quite diverse assumptions about motivation, proof, rationality, and deterrence. The focus of the law varies (for example, action, thought or intentions, the actors, social relations, market processes), as does the sanctioning mode employed (therapeutic, compensatory, penal, conciliatory) (Black, 1984, p. 8).

A dramaturgical principle can be employed to guide analysis in the uses of "justice." Conventional representations of justice are, in part, accomplished by careful manipulation of appearances and differential exploitation of practices and routines by those working in criminal justice. These take the form of suppressing information inconsistent with the appearance of justice being done— that is, elevating the counterfactual aspects of legal doctrine and case law (emphasizing that law obtains in spite of apparently anomalous outcomes and actions). It also includes the careful scripting and staging of legal scenes and settings (including props, costumes, and fronts) and control of the setting, the management of unfolding legal proceedings, and the stylized role performances of participants (McBarnet, 1979). This creates something of a "legal theater"—a mannered performance made possible when the penetrating gaze of the media is distracted, averted, benign, or tacitly cooperative with the tumed illusion of criminal justice.

The subsystems within criminal justice, however, differentially attempt to control and manipulate information, to provide misleading data, and to disseminate lies and half-truths. They are also differentially successful in maintaining tight control over information, damage control, and compliance from the media. For example, evidence is mounting that while police use public relations tactics, press officers, and media releases and willingly grant interviews on topical subjects, the media are more aggressively pursuing "backstage" insights, "cover-ups," and attempted cover-ups and are less willing to cooperatively maintain the legitimacy of state agencies generally. Until recently, the limits of technology (for example, the weight of the cameras, processing time for film, lack of satellite feeds, skills of editorial staff) also constrained the immediate capacity of the media to cover the widely disbursed workings of criminal justice. Nonetheless, to what degree does the penetration of the camera's eye into court and police practice alter the conventional circumstances or operational conditions? In other words, how does the media affect our sense of justice?

MEDIA EVENTS

Television is the quintessential medium and perhaps the single most important force shaping modern social relations. This is true because it is "domesticated," found everywhere, is the source of news and perspectives, and is the arena in which modern elections are contested. While television is present everywhere and a part of everyday life, it is set aside by artistic conventions that frame it as "presenting reality." It employs the realist conceit (namely, that what it presents is real), to probe into events immediately and up close. "You are there" is the metaphor for television's news coverage. This means that penetrating private relations, showing human error, illustrating force and fraud, and displaying the breakdown of the routine and the surprising force of the circumstantial has become equivalent to "the news." The principal allegory that drives news presentations is that "you never can tell" or "things happen," and these ironies, not the routine and banal, constitute "news." Uncertainty is more provocative than the predictable.

Television uses its unique perspective, "you are there." Its flexibility, mobility, fast-paced technology, and brilliant cinematography frames naturally occurring activities, sets them aside from everyday life, and then converts them into televised media events. This conversion may include media "looping" (media reframing of once framed events). These framed events have variable political power and social influence. These media images are often about crime, the staple of local news, special features, and "reality" television.

News during the last five years that dramatically fuses media images and politics often features the police. Consider the powerful and politically mobilizing "axial events" (those media-created events that transform natural activities into dramatic political realities; Manning, 1996a), such as the beating of

Rodney King by Los Angeles Police Department officers, the brutal killing of Malice Green by two Detroit cops, the 1995 double-murder criminal trial of O. J. Simpson, and the 1996 wrongful death civil suit against him. Further, consider the impact to the criminal justice system when a local television station filmed, by news helicopter, the chase and beating of a truckload of fleeing, illegal immigrant Hispanics in Riverside County, California (March 1996); the videotaping of a black women beaten by a South Carolina state trooper (April 1996); or the two videotapings in Lansing, Michigan, showing a death in custody and a raid on an after-hours drinking club, respectively (March 1996).

The Logic of Media Events and Transformations

Analysis of the aforementioned events illustrates how media transform experience and citizen perception of police and, by extension, of justice (Manning, 1996b). In the illustrations, several facets related to the media, reality, and justice are apparent. To be sure, the news reporting amplification process does have a logic.

First, the media focus public attention on the activity by announcements of its coverage, news stories, interviews, and features about the forthcoming event. These promotional activities are "news" and advertising for a show that is many genres in one—that is, a real-life show, entertainment, a feature show, and a documentary in the making. Television promotes itself and dramatizes that which it chooses to show in advance and "on-line."

Second, in significant enduring public events, "live" media is periodically present and, at times, broadcasts virtually continuous coverage (for example, two cable channels, CNN and Court TV, monitored the O. J. Simpson criminal trial for several months). Live on-site coverage was attempted in the Koon, Powell, and Brisnoe trials (officers charged in the King beating) and the second of the two Simpson trials. Television has a special use for the term *live*. Live in this context meant a reporter standing outside the courthouse talking into a microphone or experts offering their opinions on the meaning of reported recent developments and rumors.

Third, the media reshow themselves in different forms. A cable channel created daily "reproductions" or reconstructions of events using actors and prepared scripts in the Simpson civil trial (*Newsweek,* 1996). Media also looped or reused original film coverage to stimulate audience interest. They brought in experts to provide commentary, and encouraged audience participation via E-mail and phone call-ins on a CNN program, CNBC's *Rivera Live,* and the reconstruction. Media quickly produced various new loops, "spin-offs," and "infotainments." For example, *Rivera Live* reframed, in a new context with introduction and commentary by experts, videos of Simpson at play (drinking with a friend in a limousine), pictures of Simpson wearing shoes he denied ever owning, and news events surrounding the trial.

Fourth, through these actions, television transformed and amplified occurrences (the beating and the several trials) into media events that attained national and international status. Blending news as a genre or form with entertainment, they then reframed or looped images (often several times) in new contexts to collapse further the boundaries between "news," "politics," "justice," and "entertainment" (Cavender & Bond-Maupin, 1993; Manning, 1996b).

Fifth, in some cases, when the event shown takes on national meaning or lodges itself in the collective consciousness, a social activity, once filmed, amplified, seen widely, and discussed in the media, becomes an *axial media event*—that is, a dramatic marker and potentially a political turning point. The King beating, as an axial event, also generated a series of iconic typification or mini-scenarios for complex social processes.

Sixth, once the episode is captured, typified by labels, and associated with sharply framed visual scenes that include, when compressed, a number of diverse meanings, these media events can be strung together to form a media-produced pattern. Sometimes these are part of collective fear. Like all media events, they reflect, in some distorted fashion, perceived risks and fantasies, and have real consequences (Sparks, 1992, Chapter 1). Scenes of the Rodney King beating were typified and repeatedly linked to broad and explosive issues of race politics such as "police violence," "police accountability," "racism in America," "the jury system," "justice," and "fair trials." The King beating became a symbolic marker for a metaphorically linked series of events in the real world, attained a place in the collective memory, and may serve as an index of broad divisions and political tensions in America for many years (Hunt, 1996).

These now visible events were once believed to be rare. But media attention questions and makes problematic the routine, unseen, institutional activities that citizens assume sustain the fabric of justice in America. Axial media events, and the process of presenting visible evidence of crime and wrongdoing, are potentially revelatory breaks in the epistemological curtain. In other words, they may destroy previous symbolic barriers that prevent widespread citizen knowledge on the workings of the criminal justice system.

In some sense, by way of the framing and reframing of the media, axial events become political. They are representative of the wide range of unseen and complex institutional practices and of power and authority generally. They take part in the big theater of national politics. Although it is not precisely clear how this elevation in importance occurs, it is a feature of our times.

SOME EFFECTS OF
MEDIA EVENTS ON JUSTICE

Frequently today, once private behaviors by members of major institutions (for instance, the police, court, and correctional systems) are dragged from the backstage, to the wings, to the front stage of modern life. Keeping frontstage and backstage distinctive and controlling the "leakage" of information to the audience are abiding concerns of teammates (that is, participants). The potentially damning secrets teammates share are a basis for their mutually supportive efforts. As Goffman (1959) shows, teamwork requires that backstage understandings and shared secrets not be revealed routinely to an audience. Concealing and controlling information are essential to institutional power and authority.

Prior to the early 1970s, courts using the adversary system were represented as the essential democratic arena within which truths were uncovered, myths penetrated, conflicts revealed, and self-interests bared. Legal institutions, especially the courts, are now vulnerable, subject to rapid, incisive, and probative inquiries and dramatic revelations. Massive scrutiny of previously private legal practices in the criminal justice system is now under way. For example, consider the impact of the media showing selective video segments of brutal police actions as previously discussed axial media events. The media vigorously film chases, standoffs, and hostage situations that display indecision, ignorance, and error, as well as malice of forethought. Further, consider the often elaborate simulations of policing on such television shows as *Cops, Top Cops,* and *True Stories of the Highway Patrol.* These are edited, tightly orchestrated, and stylized versions of police work. Finally, consider news and feature programs on policing and crime, including the simulations and re-creations of violence on such popular shows as *America's Most Wanted* and *Crime Stoppers.*

Court proceedings, both live and filmed, are available nationally on the Court Television Channel with critical and, at times, malicious expert commentary. Citizens can become interactively involved in media justice by calling, E-mailing, or faxing their opinions to ongoing shows, providing clues to unsolved mysteries, or abetting hunts for "America's most wanted" (Cavender & Bond-Maupin, 1993). Citizens now provide videos as evidence in court cases and bring crime to the attention of the police using home videos. Even executions are semipublic in some states. For example, an execution in late 1996 was attended by the son and daughter of the murder victim.

The media now create scenes. They do this not only by reenactments and reconstructions using actors, simulated sound, and invented dialogue but also by instructing interviewees to repeat a scene for cameras, paying for stories, and paying individuals to entrap others to make news. Two recent and rather famous examples come to mind. The *Dallas News* made payments to a woman to entrap football player Michael Irving, and a tabloid paid a woman to be photographed with ABC Sports commentator Frank Gifford in a hotel room.

Media looping of news and situating feature events into new contexts obscure natural activities, intentions, and how and why they were framed by participants. Media interviews with "key players," especially members of a jury after a trial, erode the private nature of the decision, may be paid for by the media, and could lead to public dissonance about decisions after the fact. These interviews allow jurors to produce alternative versions of the events, their reservations, and their criticisms, especially if the questioned jurors were in the minority, asked to leave the jury, or were otherwise seeking publicity. Examples of this phenomenon include the many televised appearances in the Simpson criminal case by detectives, defense and prosecution lawyers, jury members, and distinguished lawyers (such as Arthur Miller and Alan Dershowitz of Harvard

Law School), passing comment on the judge, jury, and lawyers in the trial. Many of the prominent lawyers and notable police officers in the O. J. Simpson criminal trial—including Darden, Clark, Furman, Shapiro, and Cochran—had, by June 1997, published books presenting their versions of the frontstage and backstage events of the trial. These commercially driven ventures collapse the symbolic barrier between public and private actions that is central to the dramatic control of occupational image and mandate.

Each of these changes in meaning alters the political environment or structure of practices, roles, and beliefs within which sociolegal work occurs. The workings of justice takes place behind closed doors in many respects, but once it is made visible to a mass audience, social consequences can be expected. The work of justice is symbolic. It concerns the *representation* of fairness and equality of citizens before the law. The governing cliché is that "justice should be done" or that "justice should be seen to be done." But what is seen and what is concealed are controlled by judges and the court staff. How, then, are we to make sense out of justice? One formal vehicle for looking at the workings of justice and its contradictions is semiotics. Before proceeding any further with our investigation of justice, some description of semiotics and its unique method of analysis is warranted.

SEMIOTICS

Semiotics is the science of signs and how they create meaning. Semiotics contains assumptions and operating concepts that permit methodical analysis of symbolic systems. The Swiss linguist Ferdinand de Saussure (1857–1913) founded semiotics. Saussure's (1966) lectures, writings by the American pragmatists Charles S. Peirce (1931) and Charles Morris (1934), and the Italian novelist Umberto Eco (1979), are some primary sources for semiotic theory.

Let us begin with the concept of the sign and then proceed to explore the meaning of a sign system. A *sign* represents or stands for something else in the mind of someone. It is anything that can be taken to represent anything else. A sign is composed, in the first instance, of an *expression* (for example, a word, sound, or symbol) and a content (that is, something that is seen as completing the meaning of the expression). A lily (an expression) is linked conventionally to cigarette smoking and, by extension (or association), to cancer. Madonna is linked to music and, by extension or association, to sexuality. Each of these connections is social and arbitrary. Some associations made can carry us far semantically from the point of origin.

A *sign system* is a set of signs and a means to encode and decode them. A code helps us attach meaning to messages. Think of the criminal law as a sign system containing many kinds of signs, carried by many vehicles (the substance of the sign), words, settings, costumes, and other material objects, performed by role players. The criminal law contrasts with the civil law, and both contrast with everyday life. These differences (between everyday life and law and between types of law) produce, in context, meaning.

The connections between signs are variable, and the resultant meaning is also variable. It is conventional to restrict the range of meanings of a sign (an expression-content link) to three: denotative, connotative, and mythical. *Denotative* meaning is seen in the arbitrary equivalences between, for example, a numerical grade (expression) and school performance (content): 4.0 = excellent; 3.5 = very good, and so forth. *Connotative* meaning is created when "honors" are conferred on those scoring above a designated GPA. This status becomes mythical if the label, "honors," is taken to indicate "knowledge." The *mythical* level of interpretation (Barthes, 1972, p. 115ff) is sustained by routines, unexamined nonempirical or belief-based connections between denotative and connotative meanings. We see this at work in the legal system, and especially in the criminal justice system.

Complications appear in semiotics when the question of standpoint arises: who (or what group) interprets this sign or these signs in this or that fashion? How are the signs organized into discourse, narratives, or longer texts? To what degree does perspective or "standpoint" (Collins, 1991) pattern sign meaning? Consider how standpoint might pattern semiosis (the changing meaning of signs) as they are associated in a sequence. For example, a sequence can begin and end with Madonna. We might mentally associate the expression "Madonna" to a content such as Mary, mother of God, and then associate Mary as a content and link it to an expression relating to her son, "Jesus." If we mentally link Jesus as an expression to the content carpentry, and carpentry to nails, and then make a pun on nails—that is, change the referent from a piece of metal used to fasten things together to the hard covering on the end of human fingers—we can connect nails to the pop star Madonna's decorated fingers. We can play on this further to associate nails with the crucifixion and doubly link Madonna to Jesus. This is a semiotic journey, or wandering, from Madonna to Madonna.

Let us try another example. Think of "O.J." as an expression linked to orange juice as its content, juice as a kind of fluid, fluid as an expression linked to blood, blood to murder, and murder to O. J. (two separate contents are represented by one), and the expression "murder and O.J." linked to the name O. J. Simpson as a content. Once again, the illustration shows semiosis, or a series of associations that connect indirectly. The second example takes us from O.J. to O. J. We travel a long way in space and time. Many links exist between expression and content, and associations between a series of signs can extend the link further. How does semiosis occur? What sort of abstract model can guide analysis of these connections?

Language has a utilitarian aspect and acts as a constraint. Social life is often so complex that its immense detail escapes us. If we wish to analyze it and to communicate well with others, we must employ metaphors, analogies, and stories to convey our own mental images. Likewise, semioticians see social life, group structure, beliefs, practices, and the content of social relations as functionally analogous to the units (and rules) that structure language. They use semiotics to talk about (analyze more precisely) social functions. Thus, to extend this argument, all human communication is a display of signs, something like a text to be "read" or interpreted. That is, we understand social life like a sentence—as an unfolding statement and as a symbolic or representational exercise that can connect speakers to social life.

Typically, these connections are shared and collective and provide an important source of the ideas, rules, practices, codes, and recipe-knowledges (shorthand comments, clichés, aphorisms, and epigrams) termed "culture" (Culler, 1966). Culture is a comforting reference point when we try to sort out meaning. Culture is a means by which one comes to believe in the reality of the expression (Eco, 1979, pp. 71–72). In short, because the meaning of signs is "motivated" or arbitrary, we must read off other people's readings for cues to understand how signs work. While historically culture is passed on interpersonally, modern media create an engaging and entertaining source of realities and "cultural" readings whose source and veracity are intentionally problematic. The media play with meanings as entertainment, often confusing readers and viewers by providing misleading or confusing cues to what is being framed.

Clusters of similar signs, such as an arrest file, a court document, and a prison record, are types of social texts or *paradigms.* Signs are grouped because they differ from each other yet resemble others given the same social function. Several paradigms or domains of meaning, when collected, constitute a *field* (Bourdieu, 1977, p. 47). A field may be created or constituted by discourse— for example, in an artistic or scientific field by practices or material objects. The legal field is a specific field structured by subjective things such as beliefs and objective forces such as personnel, resources, records, rules, and physical settings. The legal field includes paradigms, or collections of like signs, that organize its practices and routine procedures.

Sign functions are important in social analysis because signs, and signs about signs that represent social differentiation, mark and reinforce social relations. The functions of law are symbolic and serve to order and constrain differentially. Within a given field, power and authority stabilize "floating" or arbitrary expressions to establish structurally dictated choices. Of course, the "full force of the law" is directed generally to the powerless. Legal labels serve to pattern life opportunities by class, race, and gender. To some degree, the potentially volatile and contextual meaning of such terms as *criminal* is reduced by shared knowledge, rules, and codes employed within a culture to make sense of signs. More often, understandings are a function of "knowledgeability," or tacit, nonverbal meanings, taken for granted and unrecognized even by participants (Giddens, 1984). These remain as powerful constraints on meaning even though they may not be fully shared or articulated within a group. Much of what is learned by watching television is knowledge about, or knowledgeability, rather than direct information of a factual or referential character. For example, in watching the NBA finals, one hears more and learns more about Michael Jordan as a symbol, a cultural icon of courage, success, and skill than what he knows, including technical knowledge about how to make free throws or a three-point shot, how to draw a foul, or the subtle aspect, the aesthetics, of basketball.

A NOTE ON NOMENCLATURE
AND PROCEDURE

Any given item in a set of signs (a cultural repertoire), can function as an expression, a content, a full sign, or the basis for an ideological statement. It can cling with other items in a mythological canopy. In the following analysis of the criminal justice system, justice, when used as an expression, will be indicated by quotes as "justice." When justice is used as a content, or something linked to an expression, it will be italicized as *justice*. When justice is used as a full sign—that is, as a link of expression and content—it will appear in capital letters as JUSTICE. *Justice* (here italicized only as an editorial style point) like any other term, can be used in at least three ways: (1) as an expression that lacks specific content, as in the phrase, "All men seek justice" (to be read following the nomenclature used here as "All men seek 'justice'"); (2) as content, as in the phrase "The consequence of imprisonment is justice" (to be read as *justice*); and (3) as a full sign "Justice results when a fair trial is provided" (to be read JUSTICE). The sentence "Justice means a fair trial" indicates that the full sign (JUSTICE) results when an expression, *justice,* and the content, *fair trial,* are combined in a sentence. This iconic device (using print fonts to convey information) will be useful when discussing meanings of "justice."

There are at least three ways to proceed with a rudimentary semiotic analysis of the concept of justice. One can venture into the world and ask people to respond to the question "What does 'justice' mean to you?" and try to create a code that enables one to sort, classify, and categorize the answers into similar groups. This empiricism is illustrated by social survey research. One can alternatively use "self-elicitation" to explore a range of associations. Self-elicitation, or "mind games," is most popular with philosophers. A third alternative is to use the *Oxford English Dictionary.* This is a massive, thirty-six-volume compendium of English usage developed in the late nineteenth century. It cites quotations in primary sources for selected words and classifies the nature of the context in which the word is used. In the following analysis, all three sources of meaning are used.

Criminal Justice

The institutions, practices, occupations, and organizations that produce "criminal justice" are referred to collectively as the criminal justice system. Within it, decisions are made. These choices, usually described as discretionary (that is, an unreviewed decision) (Reiss, 1974), link transactions among and between constituent subsystems. For example, think of the flowchart for the criminal justice system first used in the President's Crime Commission (1967a) *Final Report,* now reprinted in nearly every criminology and criminal justice textbook.

Clearly, the idea that the messy complexity called criminal justice constitutes a "system" is a function of applying a metaphor or way of thinking about one thing in terms of another. The organized properties suggested by the label, "system," are actually quite diverse, intricate processes that link agencies with quite different goals, procedures, and ideologies to facilitate the transaction of legal cases. The various agencies making up the criminal justice system do not constitute a coherent, integrated whole with clear boundaries and comparable transactions. At best, they are diagrammatic and linguistic contrivances as if they formed a system for purposes of simplification and explanation. Unlike natural systems such as the weather, the tides, or the planets orbiting around the sun, the "criminal justice system," as a social construction, is a creation of language. The system metaphor has strengths and weaknesses as a tool.

The system metaphor has very appealing policy utilities. It enables plotting how context or subsystems affect decision making and how such decisions have cumulative consequences; charting movement; noting official options and decision outcomes; developing semimathematical approaches to mapping inputs, transactions, outcomes, and rates because similar decision conditions are assumed to obtain across the several subsystems; and modeling system changes to discover the consequences of alteration in resources (for example, more or less personnel) or of reforms in decision-rules and practices. A researcher might ask, for example, what the effects are on selected system functions such as the number of arrests, the size of jail populations, the prosecutor's work load, and the hiring of 100,000 more police officers (as mandated by the Crime Control Act of 1994). The denotations of "system" are neutral in theory, just as the units (police, prosecutors, guards, judges) functioning to produce "output" have no valuational denotations. Alterations in one affect the functioning of others. Thus, reforms can be imagined.

However, each of these assumptions is problematic, and the label "justice system" actually carries a heavy moral freight. In *Report on Crime and Technology* (President's Crime Commission, 1967b), analysts asked, "What happens to the arrest rate if police response time is reduced?" They presented a model of response to crime, arguing for computer-assisted dispatching (CAD) to reduce response time. The position was that CAD, by decreasing response time, would increase arrests. Increased arrests, according to the deterrence model they adopted, would lower crime. This formulation reduced a morally loaded policy decision about crime control to a technical question. Many dubious assumptions were made about matters within the system: the validity of calls; the reliability and validity of coding and processing within the police computer system; the frequency of crime in progress or even "crime" calls relative to other calls; the reactive role of the police (as opposed to problem-solving or random patrol functions); and the relationship among arrest, charge, indictment, and further processing in the legal system. Without supporting data, this model and recommendation drove widespread "computerization" of policing from 1972 forward.

Let us consider the example of arrest. Arrest denotes holding for custody. However, following CAD, it was loaded with the connotation of crime control and even deterrence. Arrest has a wide range of meanings, uses, and connotations (Lefave, 1966). Rapid response was assumed to produce greater citizen satisfaction and increased arrests. These are nominal connotations of the expression "rapid response." These connotations of the denotative meaning for rapid response were the basis for policy recommendations. A political decision was made to emphasize some, and not other, denotations regarding the functioning of police dispatching. Thus, denotation and connotation for "justice," *justice,* and JUSTICE, are a function of perspective.

THE SEMIOTIC CONSTITUTION OF JUSTICE

The following section illustrates the meanings of "justice," *justice,* and JUS-TICE in the criminal justice system. It considers contradictory meanings with and across the criminal justice apparatus. It also examines some meanings outside the legal system.

Justice Within the Legal System

Let us assume that the expression "justice" can and does signify a number of referents and that these referents can be assembled into groups or paradigms in which denotations (various contents) share similar connotations. Consider, for example, "drug criminals" (DC) as an expression in the sentence "Let's wage a war on drug criminals." DC as an expression could be linked to various contents: African Americans, Colombians, Mexicans, Asians, Anglos, and Hispanics (clustered as "ethnic" connotations); cocaine, crack, heroin, alcohol, tobacco, amphetamines, and other chemicals (clustered as "drugs abused"); and user, dealer (retail), wholesaler, and big dealer (as clusters of market position). These three clusters have quite different connotations in the criminal justice system. For example, a Michigan law mandates a life sentence for dealing in amounts of cocaine above ten pounds. Conviction on this charge is dependent on how the deal was arranged, what the role of the arrested person was, how and under what specific law (federal, state, or both) the person was charged, acceptance of plea bargains by the defendant, prosecutors and judge, and available jail or prison space at the time of sentencing.

Having said this about "drug criminals," remember that the denotations of "criminal" change depending on subsystem, as do those of "justice." This is true because the expression denotes and connotes changing content. In this way, new signs are continuously created.

It seems plausible to identify and define several key legal subsystems within which "justice" is done (Reiss, 1974). The first broad division in Anglo-American law is between civil and criminal law. Within each are distinctions between substantive law, the fact of law and their assemblage, and procedural law or rules for processing cases. Criminal, civil, and administrative law are based on cases previously decided at various court levels, and these are published in law reporters, textbooks, and casebooks, and shaped into "case law." When cases accumulate into patterns around central issues (usually constitutional issues in American law), they are seen to cohere as a legal "doctrine." An example of doctrine is the "fruit from the poisonous tree" principle that states that evidence obtained by illegal means shall be suppressed or excluded from consideration in trials. Standing somewhere between case law and doctrine is "judge-made" or administrative law. Finally, city and county law, as well as municipal regulations, shape legal contingencies especially when used to control behavior (for example, using municipal housing codes to evict tenants from "drug houses" or fining landlords for unruly tenants). American law is a quilt of state, local, and federal law, civil and criminal law, as well as administrative law (often used in regulation of business and government). These laws cross-fertilize and intermingle in confusing fashion. Cases can be brought simultaneously in each of these fields of law.

Each subsystem contains distinctions or cognitive divisions—that is, denotations of "justice." In semiotic terms, the denotations of justice stand in metonymic relation (based on proximity or order based on a listing) to each other. They are bound together also metaphorically by their connotations (they are within the legal system). The denotations of justice found in the official discourse of criminal justice are only a sampling of the range of meanings of "justice." They include only "legal" or official and legitimized denotations of justice and exclude others. For example, they omit the view of the person in the street, group-based notions, ideas of natural justice, and anthropological or historical concepts of justice.

Reiss (1974) argues that the criminal justice apparatus, as a branch of the legal system, contains several relevant subsystems (for example, citizen law enforcement, public law enforcement [police], defendants, public prosecution, courts, corrections, and appellate judicial review). The internal laws and rules, tacit conventions, and ongoing practices and policies of these subsystems pattern discretionary outcomes. For example, within the police subsystem, the denotations of "justice" are, to a remarkable degree, "done on the street." The street is the stage and dramatic arena for the patrol officer. As Reiss (1974) aptly writes, "When an officer arrests someone, he or she has made a decision about the legitimacy of the basis for the arrest" (p. 37). Subsequent decisions by attorneys, courts, and juries are seen by police as independent of the police view of the culpability of the arrested "suspect."

However, the police view that an "arrest" is *justice* is not shared throughout the "criminal justice system." Each subsystem contains the seeds of injustice or justice (when compared with their baseline of "street reality"). Decisions at each and every point from review of the arrest, the charge, the booking, the indictment, the true bill, or even prosecution strategies can obviate previous police decisions and appear to reverse them. Interestingly, reversing decisions is revealing because it denotes that subsequent decisions take a step backward, moving away from justice.

These new connotations of arrest do not connote "justice" to the police. Prosecuting attorneys' responses to an arrest can be seen formally as a series of procedural steps that audit the quality of the arrest. One imagined ranking of the case (a connotation to the attorney) is in terms of the probability of a "win" (a conviction in this context). Here, one could imagine hypothetical rankings running from "dubious" to "sure winner." Depending on context, or subsystem, the denotations of "arrest" are either contradictory or complementary because a "good arrest" (satisfying to an officer in respect to "street justice" or occupational norms) may not be a "sure win" for a prosecutor. "Bad arrests" may, on the other hand, hold strong promise for prosecution. Belief in the practical value of the ideology of justice, especially the public's legitimation and the mutual dependency of the teams for results, unifies them in practice. Nevertheless, many conflicts arise as a result of beliefs that are thought to be shared but are not. These are ironies, or "shared misunderstandings."

Social Meanings of Justice Outside the Legal System

Let us consider three subsystems of meaning outside the legal system. These would included the social, the individual, and the political. Each one is a paradigm that assembles denotations of justice and differentiates those meanings from others in different contexts.

A group-based notion of "justice" has roots historically in Anglo-American criminal law, where Anglo-Saxon groups of a hundred people or more formed posses, selected sheriffs, and appointed juries. As a result of this diffusion of social relations, the official unit of justice became the city, county, or federal region. Thus, social justice, was (and is) not a shared idea in America beyond the ideological level. Attitudes are rooted in group perspectives and values. Claims that the justice system and the workings of "justice" are racist, sexist, or elitist, assume that *justice* and JUSTICE should somehow be distinct and mutually exclusive. These claims promote "perspectival truth"—that is, that the various positions are true from a given perspective.

Public opinion polls showed differences in the views of African Americans and whites on the justice of O. J. Simpson's trial and his innocence or guilt. These revealed perspectival truths. African Americans, by virtue of their experiences with and knowledge of the often violent workings of the criminal justice system, hold strong views of the quality of criminal justice in America. Research on plea bargains show quite different understandings of justice by the sentenced, the attorneys, and the judges (Blumberg, 1967).

A second, alternative social meaning of "justice" is "case by case." This use echoes the social construction of law and its workings held within the legal system. A case-by-case notion of "justice" (meaning JUSTICE) holds that each case is assessed by rules and procedures, carried out in light of the special particulars of the case, argued fully by lawyers taking "two sides," and weighed by a judge and/or a jury. Thus, any case can be defined as fair if it meets those criteria, regardless of other moral, political, or philosophical principles.

A second view of "justice" is that of the individual victim or arrested person. Of course, an individual view is a partial construction. Each individual will see a personal case in light of history, biography, past experience with the criminal justice system, and, especially, class, race, and gender location. These readings may or may not be consistent with the definitions of the legal system. They generally are correlated with extensive experience: the more experience with the police and courts, the more cynical the person is.

A third view of "justice" is political. Political meanings refer to the overlay of connotations of power and resource distribution that are attributed to a given case or a set of cases (for example, a doctrine or principle). Thus, some cases have had enormous political impact in changing the shape of criminal trials. Some cases have had doctrinal influence (for instance, *Miranda, Mapp v. Ohio*); some have had extralegal influence (such as *Roe v. Wade, Brown v. Board of Education, Furman v. Georgia*); others still have unfolding influence (for example, the trials of O. J. Simpson, the Menendez brothers, Dr. Jack Kevorkian). These are well-known, important, politically loaded decisions, woven deeply into the fabric of experience and memory.

Similar to axial media events, these cases and others like them influence affairs outside the legal system. They have a "ripple effect" and become part of the larger political spectacle. In this sense, they take on mythological or ideological meaning. For example, they are linked to "liberal" or "conservative" beliefs, patriotism, or racism. Ideologies are connotations of the connotation of JUSTICE. All legal decisions (even parking tickets) are political. They entail the reallocation of resources, opportunities, and life choices. Further, any legal decision may become broader in its influence and scope, a critical incident, or a "big bang" ruling. In each instance, however, the media add a very rapid, international, and explosive dimension to legal judgments.

CONTRADICTIONS

The sense of justice legitimizes the legal institution. The absence of justice seen to be done has social ramifications. Within the criminal justice system, as well as society, distinctive yet overlapping definitions of "justice" exist. At the extreme, they produce contradictions and internal denotations that border on inconsistency. Give this condition, how do we maintain a grounded sense of justice? Four major social factors serve to sustain the legitimacy of the legal institution in establishing the meanings of JUSTICE (or is it justice?), in spite of the variations noted here.

The first factor, "the counterfactual justification," is public belief in the idea of justice (Luhmann, 1986). This belief obviates, obscures, sets aside, or makes exceptional legal cases and factual disputes known to be "unjust decisions." Luhmann argues for the importance of the grounding assumptions of social communication in sustaining the legal system. The legal system is fundamentally differentiated from the social system, through language, by its faith in the just character of judicial decisions. Once legitimized, the legal system provides, in effect, a metadefinition that states, "Legal decisions are true!" Bourdieu (1977) calls this "institutional misrecognition." It works to convey truth or appropriate character to actions that might be seen as "self-interested" or antisocial. Further, it defines them as consistent with what is taken to be good practice. This conventional connection of ends and means becomes habitual—a routinely invoked perspective that sustains the power balance in society. Of course, language reflects these beliefs and contributes to the superiority of symbolic representations consistent with "justice."

A second factor is ideology. Ideology, or beliefs that resist empirical disproof (for example, belief in God), surround the American legal system. This system has come to stand for many valued things (including justice, liberty, civil freedoms, and the defense of property). The institution has its own ideological weapons and a highly developed, complex, and nuanced rhetoric of "justice" that is widely believed in Anglo-American societies. This includes not only the ideology derived from the Bill of Rights in the U.S. Constitution (equal protection, freedom of speech, right to a speedy trial, protection against cruel and unusual punishment, and so forth) but also the visible icons known to every school child (the statue of a blind women holding the scales of justice; the elaborate trappings, costumes, props, and roles found in the courtroom; the celebration of "Law Day" on May 1).

A third factor is ignorance. Ignorance is an excuse. When one examines the social distribution of knowledge (that is, who knows what), it is clear that most legal decisions and the procedures by which they are produced are not generally known. The social distribution of knowledge, even in this media age, is uneven. The barrier between public and private, although being eroded, remains and protects institutions from close scrutiny. Perhaps the most striking evidence of this is that victims of crime seldom hear the outcomes of justice system machinations, and it has taken a social movement in North America to create a lobby of "victims' rights" (Rock, 1986). As a result, there is little knowledge of outcomes and considerable difference between public expectations for punishment and actual decisions (Walker, 1991).

Fourth and finally, the media role is complex. The media act in ambivalent fashion, both sustaining the canopy of legalism and eroding it when it suits their interests. "News" is what is happening now. It is what attracts attention or what is unusual. Much of what is contained in the local news include crime stories focusing on the violent and bizarre taken out of context. Crime shows dominate current feature programming. They act to compress, combine, and confound various frames on reality or genres (for instance, live news, reconstructions, feature programs, gossip, investigative reporting). They deal in imagery, not fact. When it suits the media, they can adopt, on the one hand, the exposé approach to reveal malfeasance of courts, prisons, or the police. On the other hand, they can echo the conventional wisdom about crime and fear of crime.

This symbiotic relationship between the media and institutions seems to be changing. Ericson, Chan, and Baranek (1987) indicate that the media depend on the institutions (police, courts, prisons, prosecutors' office) for access, information, tips, quotes, and interviews that sustain their ideology of "being there." This dependency shapes what is taken to be news. However, a number of developments allow the media to rapidly simulate naturally occurring activities. Some of these include satellite networks that permit transmission and receipt of images almost worldwide; international news-creating networks such as CNN; mobile phone technology; citizens' video cameras; digital image transmission that obviates film shipping, developing, and editing; and laser-digital cameras that produce images for immediate reproduction via video screens. Space and time are less constraining on media actions. They can now rapidly enter and broadcast from public-private spaces such as parks, malls, and large-scale entertainment centers (for instance, stadia, parks, courts); share surveillance of public and quasi-public spaces with various forms of policing; reproduce the self-monitoring surveillance of criminal justice agencies that film jails, police stations, courts, and prisons; and buy and sell individual citizen's films of crimes in process. In this way, the media simulate "realistically" "justice," *justice,* and JUSTICE.

CONCLUSION

The field of criminal justice has failed to explore the concept of "justice" and its relevance for policy and practice. Justice has remained cloaked also because of the ostensibly practical nature of the criminal justice arena. The rise of an atheoretical, ameliorative, and practice-oriented field of criminal justice, and the erosion of systematic criminology, suggest that the conceptual and philosophical bases of justice are obscured. The emphasis on action and progress makes abstract musings unwelcome.

One of the most powerful forces that shapes modern concepts of justice is the mass media. Clearly, media penetration into the everyday workings of courts, policing, the defense and prosecution subsystems, and corrections makes the institutions vulnerable to new inside knowledge being produced. Semiotics, the science of signs and their evolving meanings, facilitates an analysis of this change by showing how media and close sociological analysis open up unexamined denotations and connotations, sometimes revealing the mystical aspect of our beliefs. Semiotics permits seeing sign work in new contexts, a "deconstruction" of the contexts, in which the "original meaning" was created. Many famous cases, for example, are now the basis for daily gossip across the country. The media play a new role in informal social control and actually participate in promoting (Black, 1984) the justice and sanctioning process. As a result, "justice," *justice,* and JUSTICE are not only easily confused by citizens; they are systematically manipulated by the media in an often invisible fashion.

REVIEW QUESTIONS

1. What uses of justice are dominant in criminal justice literature? Give several uses and examples of this as discussed in the chapter.

2. Why has the field of criminal justice not considered philosophical, ethical, and semiotic concepts of justice?

3. Define the following and give examples: (a) sign, (b) expression, (c) content, (d) sign system, (e) denotation of a sign, and (f) connotation of a sign.

4. Discuss the differences between "justice," *justice,* and JUSTICE.

5. What is the value of defining the criminal and legal structure and its functioning in system terms?

6. List and provide examples of contradictions for the concept of justice within the criminal justice system.

7. How are the contradictions of justice resolved in the system?

8. Comment on the claim: denotations and connotations are a function of perspective. Is this universally true?

9. The Simpson criminal decision was just. How would a semiotic analysis discuss this claim? (Clue: begin by defining the concept *just.*)

10. Justice is what the criminal justice system does. Comment on this claim, based on the arguments of this chapter. What sort of a definition of justice is it?

REFERENCES

Arrigo, B. (1995). The peripheral core of law and criminology: On postmodern social theory and conceptual integration. *Justice Quarterly, 12*(3), 447–472.

Baker, S. (1997). *Perceptions of policing among undergraduates.* Unpublished master's thesis, School of Criminal Justice, Michigan State University, East Lansing.

Barthes, R. (1972). *Mythologies.* New York: Hill & Wang.

Black, D. (1984). Social control as a dependent variable. In D. Black (Ed.), *A theory of social control* (pp. 1–36). New York: Academic Press.

Blumberg, A. (1967). *Criminal justice.* New York: Quadrangle.

Bourdieu, P. (1977). *Outline of a theory of practice.* Cambridge: Cambridge University Press.

Cavender, G., & Bond-Maupin, J. (1993). Fear and loathing on reality television. *Sociological Inquiry, 63,* 305–317.

Collins, P. (1991). *Black feminist thought: Knowledge, consciousness, and the politics of empowerment.* New York: Routledge & Kegan Paul.

Culler, J. (1966). *Structural poetics.* Ithaca, NY: Cornell University Press.

Eco, U. (1979). *A theory of semiotics.* Bloomington: Indiana University Press.

Ericson, R., Chan, J., & Baranek, J. (1987). *Visualizing deviance.* Toronto: University of Toronto Press.

Giddens, A. (1984). *The constitution of society.* Berkeley: University of California Press.

Goffman, E. (1959). *The presentation of self in everyday life.* New York: Doubleday Anchor Books.

Hunt, D. (1996). *Screening Rodney King.* Cambridge: Cambridge University Press.

Lefave, W. (1966). *Arrest.* Boston: Little, Brown.

Luhmann, N. (1986). *The sociology of law.* London: Routledge & Kegan Paul.

Manning, P. K. (1996a). Dramaturgy, politics, and the axial media event. *Sociological Quarterly, 37*(2), 261–278.

Manning, P. K. (1996b). Policing and reflection. *Police Forum, 6*(2), 1–5.

McBarnet, D. (1979). *Conviction.* London: McMillan.

Morris, C. W. (1938). *Foundations of the theory of signs*. Chicago: University of Chicago Press.

Newsweek. (1996, November 11). Periscope, 21.

Peirce, C. S. (1931). *Collected papers*. Cambridge, MA: Harvard University Press.

President's Crime Commission. (1967a). *Final report*. Washington, DC: Government Printing Office.

President's Crime Commission. (1967b). *Report on crime and technology*. Washington, DC: Government Printing Office.

Reiss, A. J., Jr. (1974). Discretionary justice. In D. Glaser (Ed.), *Handbook of criminology* (pp. 46–47). Chicago: Rand McNally.

Rock, P. (1986). *The view from the shadow*. Oxford: Oxford University Press.

Saussure, F. de. (1966). Course in general linguistics. New York: McGraw-Hill.

Souryal, S. (1992). *Criminal justice ethics*. St. Paul: West.

Souryal, S. (in press). *Justice in criminal justice*. New York: Longman.

Sparks, R. (1992). *Television and the drama of crime*. Buckinghamshire: Open University Press.

Surette, R. (1992). *Media, crime, and criminal justice*. Pacific Grove, CA: Brooks/Cole.

Walker, S. (1991). *Why punish?* New York: Oxford University Press.

❖

Constitutive Criminology
and Social Justice

According to constitutive criminology, concepts such as crime, law, and justice are coproduced. Police, court, and media agencies, for example, define what these concepts mean through institutional procedures, news-making images, and enforcement practices. But crime, law, and justice are also dependent on the language citizens, victims, suspects, and others use to define these abstractions. The words, phrases, or statements are shaped by the behavior of police, court, and media organizations as much as they are by the experiences each of us has regarding crime, law, and justice. In this chapter, Barak and Henry apply this thinking to the meaning of social justice. They begin by evaluating various conceptions of justice, emphasizing the "limits" of distributive, procedural, and criminal justice models. Building on these limitations, they then consider what social justice is. Barak and Henry suggest that a broader conception of social justice must include the constitutive nature of creating shared meaning, defining social and economic inequalities, and understanding personal harm and violence. The authors then link their position to postmodernist thought, referencing how the divergent ways of knowing and thinking in our society are reduced, through media-generated images, to a unified "culture of consumption." Barak and Henry maintain that a more precise definition of social justice must acknowledge the harm caused here—harm that distorts, masks, denies, or ignores the strength of our individual and collective differences seeking voice and legitimacy. Thus, they call for an integrated-constitutive theory of social justice. This is a theory that links the study of culture with the study of crime. It is a theory that maintains the diversity of vocabularies through which different people experience violence and different criminal justice organizations exercise their power. It is a theory that integrates each of these points of view into a more complete, more robust regard for law, crime, and deviance. According to the authors, it is this way of thinking that makes social justice possible.

8

An Integrative-Constitutive Theory of Crime, Law, and Social Justice

GREGG BARAK AND STUART HENRY

> [Parts] must be integrated into a whole or they remain abstract and theoretically misleading. . . . The point is that the totality is always part of something larger and the part is simultaneously a totality. . . . [T]he part cannot be abstracted from the whole and sociologically examined apart from it and then mechanically inserted again after analysis. (Swingewood, 1975, pp. 44–45, 57, on Marx's dialectical method)

The starting point for our critical theory of social justice is a brief consideration of the flawed liberal concept of justice. We believe that an adequate critical theory must take an active view of social justice oriented toward "passionately abhorring all forms of oppression, exploitation, and cruelty," actively "denouncing or combating them," thereby "preventing or remedying what would arouse the sense of injustice" (Cahn, 1968, pp. 342–346; see also Cahn, 1949). This position is akin to Marx's view on the need to struggle to abolish *all* conditions, processes, and relations that render humans "humiliated, enslaved, forsaken, and contemptible." Further, we see justice as the absence of all harm, exploitation, "plunder, subjugation, discrimination, and privilege at the expense of others" (Lang, 1979, p. 117). We argue that liberal theories of redistributive and procedural justice fail to confront the realities of injustice and that procedural justice and criminal justice contribute to, rather than ameliorate, the problems of injustice rooted in inequality. We contend that the way in which mass-mediated news and entertainment represent crime, justice, and order reinforces the moral authority and legitimacy of the dominant social order (Barak, 1994, 1996). We make the case that the central issue social justice needs to address is the inequalities born of modernity's social constructions of difference. We show that postmodern transformations enmesh in pain modernity's victims of inequality by conjuring up insatiable desires for the consumption of images and style. We believe that the fundamental task of a critical criminology, informed by a concern for social justice, is to expose and deconstruct the masked inequalities of the dominant order. We point out that to achieve this, an adequate theory of crime and social justice must take a holistic account of the production of modernism's inequalities. Thus, we advocate for an integrated perspective, not in the interests of advancing science or imposing an essentializing order, but as a basis to address the process whereby differences build to inequalities within social structures and how institutional practices coproduce the pain that is crime. We reject modernist criminology's recent attempt to provide integration, arguing that this fails to take a dynamic holistic perspective and is thereby unable to disentangle the coproduction of harms stemming from the diverse range of inequalities.

We turn to the contribution of postmodernist criminological integration, particularly constitutive criminology's reframing of the definition of crime to reflect the diverse and inclusive range of harms born of inequality. We then show how an integration of integrations, or a hyperintegrated theory of modernist and postmodernist criminology, allows for a criminology of difference whose policy implications for justice are far-reaching and futuristic. In short, then, we seek to demonstrate how the emerging integrative-constitutive theory of crime, law, and justice provides the kind of comprehensive analytical basis needed to deliver social justice.

FROM JUSTICE TO SOCIAL JUSTICE

Marx and Engels ridiculed the bourgeois and abstract use of the term *justice,* used by philosophers such as Plato, Aristotle, Aquinas, Kant, Bentham, and Mill. Nonetheless, more recent liberal and conservative philosophical contributions have continued to examine its meaning and substance, avoiding (perhaps compensating for rather than confronting) the central issue of justice—namely, the presence of inequality. Though this is not the place to explore diverse interpretations of justice, we need to offer some definition of it as well as point out the limits of existing interpretations, before showing how the integrative-constitutive theory of crime relates to our view of criminal and social justice.

At the risk of oversimplification, the liberal concept of justice relates to (1) how people are treated by whole social systems of which they are a part and (2) how subsystems or parts of the whole attempt to correct harms to which people have been subjected. This is similar to, though broader than, the Aristotlean distinction between distributive justice and corrective (remedial or commutative) justice. Distributive justice "[relates] to [one]'s allotment of honor, wealth, and other social goods," while corrective justice applies to "private, voluntary exchanges outside the law [or] courts" and to the functions of the judiciary (Cahn, 1968, p. 344).

Much of the philosophical discussion of justice focuses on the content of these distinctions and the criteria by which that content should be met. For example, while the issue of impartiality in procedural (formal) justice relates to corrective equality, much of the recent discussion by social philosophers has been about the content and function of distributive justice and about the achievement of harmony and equilibrium in the social body (for example, Nozick, 1974; Rawls, 1971). Our view is that these two aspects of justice are interrelated. Indeed, we accept that while procedural *in*justice (such as unnecessarily harsh rules or regulations) can accompany an oppressive system of substantive justice, we reject the view that "procedural justice . . . promotes advances in substantive justice" (Cahn, 1968, p. 344). Rather, we argue that procedural justice masks the inequities of substantive injustice and thus inflicts its own pain (Barak, 1980). The universal equality implied in the claims to neutrality of modern law are, as we shall argue, undermined by the law's integral relationship with other social forces (for instance, the economy, religion, mass media).

Central to our justice approach is the issue of difference and inequality. Aristotle observed that differences exist between people (whether naturally or socially created) and that justice requires equity between equals. He assumed that injustice arises when equals are treated unequally *and when unequals are treated equally.* The latter reflects Aristotle's endorsement of "natural" inequalities. Thus, for Aristotle, justice "consists of treating equals equally and unequals unequally, in proportion to their inequality" (Kamenka, 1979, p. 3). He further believed equal treatment should be embodied in the rules of law, though not so inflexibly to ignore the special circumstances of the individual and the concrete case.

What is crucial to the previous analysis is how equality and inequality are produced and how law deals with their production. If a social system generates inequalities between people, and if these inequalities produce harm, what should be done? Should a society (or its governing body) acknowledge the inequalities by treating some differently than others, or should the inequalities be ignored by treating people equally? In other words, should some be privileged over others in which the privileged have preferential access to rewards, benefits, honors, and so forth? Unequal treatment requires criteria of inclusion and exclusion. In various societies these criteria are based on birth, race, status, wealth, party affiliation, or any other condition of "merit," designed to identify members of the privileged group and to exclude those not part of it.

In liberal-democratic societies, the much broader notion of "civil justice" requires inclusion of all as equal individuals and provides for their equal treatment in the law, regardless of their social characteristics. Here the criterion of "competence" is designed to justify a greater or lesser degree of preferential treatment (Passmore, 1979, p. 26). Thus

> except by way of punishment or as a result of incapacity, no person ought to be excluded from participation in any form of desirable activity unless there is, of necessity, competition for entrance to it, when the more competent ought always to be preferred to the less competent. (Passmore, 1979, p. 26)

In the extreme, this merit/competency-based rationale leads to the libertarian concept of justice found in Hayek (1944, 1960, 1976) and to the more liberal-conservative version offered by Nozick (1974). In the case of Nozick, the only issue is one of corrective (commutative) justice. The function of corrective justice is to guarantee the freedom of choice to compete in a "free" market. Any inequalities in the distribution of goods and honors are viewed as the result of free and fair competition, provided they result from legitimate entitlement.

The theories of justice developed by Hayek and Nozick assume "that the capitalist system needs no moral justification" (Lang, 1979, pp. 134). Further, their views "are intrinsically linked with the concept of perfect procedural justice . . . [where] justice is identified with legal authority" (Lang, 1979, pp. 134–135). Legal authority here is conceived as "the pure, formal principle of legal impartiality" (p. 135). As Lang points out, free-market conservatives such as Hayek and Nozick accept that legal equality neither presupposes actual equality nor is challenged by a lack of it. They believe real inequalities born of nature or the competitive market are justified because the social worth of the economically successful is greater than the worth of others, such as the poor and the disabled (Hayek, 1960, 1976).

This extreme free-market position has been rejected in modern advanced industrial societies whose state administrations seek some amelioration of the inequalities of free-market capitalism through social policies (including progressive taxation and social welfare) designed to offset some of the inequities of the market (Barak, 1991c). Unfortunately, these policies are based on the limited concept of distributive justice.

The Limits of Distributive and Compensatory Justice

Liberal theories of justice, including those of Rawls (1971) and Barry (1973, 1989, 1995), argue that justice should not be based on principles of the market or on the utilitarian idea of "the general good." Instead, they should be based on principles of "justice as fairness" or "justice as impartiality." Rawls's (1971) basic notion is that justice prevails when people agree to be obligated to a system of rules without knowing whether they would personally benefit or lose as a result of the privileges or penalties conferred by that system. According to Barry (1989), what this means is that justice is "what someone with no stake in the outcome would approve of as a distribution of benefits and burdens" (p. 362). (This, of course, assumes that people care about what happens to others in the system, which, in a society based on social division and alienation, is unlikely).

Rawls's notion acknowledges that inequalities are produced by a capitalist economic system. Further, he only endorses the inequalities as long as everyone, including the worst-off group, is better off. This improved economic status occurs through a redistributive conception of social justice. According to Lang (1979), redistributive justice allows for

> a reduction of the range of differences in the distribution of social income within [a given economic] structure to [benefit] the least advantaged social groups. It justifies a transfer of social income from the top to the

bottom of society as a principle of social justice and . . . justifies the moral right of the least advantaged social groups to a growing participation in the distribution of social income and not merely to securing a social minimum. (p. 145)

In the context of modern administered, capitalist society, then, social justice results in "a set of policies and programs in which quality housing, health care, education, transportation, recreation are distributed on the basis of social status rather than or in addition to profit" (Young, 1995, p. 701).

Views on compensatory justice are even more egalitarian than distributive notions of justice. They are prevalent in some advanced capitalist societies that attempt to correct the inequalities of market capitalism by providing preferential treatment to disadvantaged groups (for example, by reversing unequal treatment, as in the case of affirmative action). Presumably, the groups are then able to regain equality of opportunity to compete in spite of historical and structural processes of exclusion. Another egalitarian liberal theory of justice argues that the principle of social justice requires that all "have equal claims to all advantages which are generally desired and which are in fact conducive to human perfection and happiness" (Honore, 1968, p. 91). This idea, too, is ultimately reduced to the insistence on actual equality of opportunity.

The major problem with these liberal distributive concepts of justice is that "[t]hey do not consider the fundamental problem of control of the means of production" (Lang, 1979, p. 148) and its role in the generation of inequality and injustice. For Marx and Engels the problem of injustice was in the source of inequality: the economic relations of production. Merely focusing on the inequalities and unfairnesses of distribution obscured the fundamental underlying exploitation of labor by capital. Calls for "social justice," defined in terms of distributive justice, were seen by Marx and Engels as dangerous because they masked capitalist exploitation via production. Further, as we shall argue later, in postmodern advanced industrial society the shift to consumption and styles of difference driven by capital and market expansion obscures not only the economic difficulties of the capitalist system but also the multiple dimensions of inequality constructed through the politics of difference. Redistributive justice fails to deal with these realities.

The Limits of Procedural Justice

Critics who see injustice in the inequalities born of capitalist market competition and who reject the arguments of redistributive justice as a solution assert that the reliance on pure procedural justice (that is, treating like people equally or treating like cases the same) contributes to the production of inequalities. According to the Marxist legal theorist Pashukanis (1924/1978), these laws actively make unequal social subjects into free and equal contracting individuals. Law reduces human social subjects, social organizations, and even the state to legal subjects; that is, to individuals with equal rights and duties. Pashukanis (1924/1978) maintains that the law does this by abstracting these subjects from their social contexts. Thus, abstract law and abstract bourgeois justice proclaim "a formal equality which, in the concrete social situation of class societies, amounts to real *in*equality . . . [that] conceals the 'Despotism of the Factory'" (Kamenka, 1979, p. 10). We note, then, that a direct interrelationship exists between law and the constitution of the economic structure of class society (Tigar & Levy, 1977) and, accordingly, between law and class societies' injustices.

If bourgeois legality is based on the material conditions of capitalist society and is constituted by them, then bourgeois legality shares in the production of capitalist societies' inequalities. How, then, is it possible for law to deliver justice? Treating people equally in law not only generates the illusion of justice, thereby serving an ideological function for an unequal society, but is constitutive of the inequalities that produce injustice. It is even arguable whether procedural justice in advanced capitalist society treats people equally in law. Nowhere is this more evident than in criminal justice.

The Limits of Criminal Justice

Criminal justice provides modernity a repository of ideological legitimacies and practical techniques with which state power controls those system "casualties" who resist or are different. Thus, "law is crucial to making convincing claims to moral authority because, in modern administered society, questions of legitimacy revolve around procedural norms, procedural propriety, and the search for and sanctioning of procedural strays" (Ericson, Baranek, & Chan, 1991, p. 343). However, the irrelevance of criminal justice in the quest for social justice is not born only of its ideological function but as a result of its active role in working against social justice.

The language of formal, procedural justice incorporates within it biases from conventional mass-mediated discourse that result in unequal treatment. Take, for example, the philosophy justifying punishment based on the concept of "just deserts." This purports to allow for the continuance of different value moralities and subjects all offenders, regardless of race, gender, and class, to punishments appropriate to their crimes. In theory, therefore, this basis for punishment is consistent with the neutral principle of rational procedural justice of treating like cases equally; the severity of the crime determines the sentence, nothing else. In effect, however, only one behavioral morality prevails, and differential treatment of offenders remains. This outcome occurs because the application of just deserts hides the various stories about punishment that define some offenders as redeemable and others as not.

The differential application is accomplished indirectly in two ways: (1) via the false distinctions contained in definitions of offense severity (or pain) and (2) via the implicitly held racist assumptions about "the nature" of African-American and Hispanic males as "others." Thus, imprisonment becomes appropriate for certain violent and drug-abusing offenders of color, while alternatives to incarceration become appropriate for women and male Caucasians (Sloop, 1996). The notion of what is a like case is negated here; that is, the criterion of similarity and difference becomes critical, but its supposed neutrality is undermined by being tied to conventional and media discourse. This is why the sentence "deserved" for using drugs varies by race rather than seriousness. Thus, the prison sentences for possessing crack cocaine, used by African Americans, are ten to fifteen years more than for possessing the same amount of powder cocaine, used by white middle-class Americans (DeKeseredy & Schwartz, 1996, p. 61; see also Tonry, 1995). This discretion still works its way within the supposedly socially neutral and universally applicable discourse of "three strikes and you are out." We ask the question, however, "Three strikes and who is out?"

The limits of criminal justice reside not only in false claims to impartiality but also in a less than universal scope. This means that even if criminal justice were impartial, it would be irrelevant to social justice, for several reasons. Criminal justice is an institutional fragment of state power whose scope is limited to processing "individuals" brought before the law for state-defined offenses. These offenses are restricted in their definition of what is criminal since the law defines crime narrowly. It does so not merely because powerful interests influence law but because social relations of power are the law and vice versa. The array of harms whose individual pain emanates from the invested structures of modernity results from discriminatory exclusions, subordinating hierarchies, and personal debasement, not only because these are rarely included in the realm of criminal justice but because the structural and cultural orders from which law is constituted embody these exclusions (Smart, 1992; Young & Rush, 1994).

The criminal justice system enforces these laws by dealing mainly with direct and obvious forms of naked power in which one party forcibly denies another its ability to make a difference. Street crimes of robbery, rape, theft, and homicide are obvious examples. Criminal justice is far less able to deal with indirect forms of denial such as domestic abuse, psychological manipulation, and economic coercion; rarely does it adequately confront hidden and subtle forms of coercive control that exist within the institutional structures of modern society based on class, sex, and racial differences. Moreover, the criminal justice system cannot confront these problems because it exercises some of these coercions. Indeed, rather than penetrate private institutions such as the family, the school, and the workplace, the law happily protects the right of these institutions to police themselves. These private control mechanisms preserve inequalities based on the differences embedded within the institution's own structure. Private justice mechanisms range from

> the practices of disciplinary bodies, boards and councils of industrial organizations, the tribunals of professional trade associations and unions, and the disciplinary committees of universities and colleges . . . [to] the peer sanctioning of relatively amorphous voluntary associations, such as self-help and mutual aid groups and the informal norms and sanctions operative inside more formal control institutions, such as the informal "code" governing police deviance or internal prisoner-to-prisoner control. (Henry, 1994b, p. xi; see also Henry, 1983)

Any attempt to deliver social justice must take account of all these private normative orders and the preservation of inequalities woven into their institutional structures (Henry, 1987a, 1987b). Moreover, these private forms of justice are not publicly accountable. While numerous refinements and endless energy is invested in public systems of criminal justice to protect the right to due process, to guard against excessive or abusive use of state power, rarely are limitations placed on arbitrary decision making and potential abuse exercised in the day-to-day working of nonstate social control. Yet more people are governed by and controlled through these numerous interwoven nonstate systems of justice than by their relatively distant involvement with state law. This private justice is rarely subject to procedural safeguards to protect against its abuses. It provides a partial justice because it is based on abstracting parts (individuals) from wholes (communities, societies, cultures) without addressing the whole from which the part came. Criminal justice is of limited scope in framing justice issues. To deliver social justice, private justice must be included in the realm of controls on criminal justice, but this, too, must be based on a system that stifles rather than generates inequalities.

In addition, an account must be taken of what former UNESCO legal adviser Karel Vasak referred to as the "third generation of rights." The third generation of rights goes further in its attempt to maximize the realization of human rights for all peoples of the world than did the first and second generations of rights. Each generation of structurally evolved rights has been the product of different historical struggles waged by peoples without sufficient rights to obtain them. With each new historical period, new notions have been expressed with respect to fundamental rights and to whom those rights pertain (Barak, 1991a). The first generation of rights were referred to as "negative rights" in that they called for restraint from the state. These rights were derived from the American and French Revolutions and the struggle to gain liberty from arbitrary state action. These rights may be found in the Civil and Political Rights of the International Bill of Rights. The second generation of rights were referred to as "positive rights" in that they required affirmative action on the part of the state. These rights are found in the Economic, Social, and Cultural Rights of the International Bill of Rights. They emerged from the experience of the late Soviet Union, and they also resonate in the welfare state policies of the West. Finally, the third generation of rights call for international cooperation.

> These rights are evolving out of the condition of global interdependence confronting humanity today. They recognize the human rights obligations can no longer be satisfied with individual states. In other words, the rights of peoples—independent of states—are required for a reduction in state violence, maintenance of world peace, protection of the environment, and global development on a massive scale. (Barak, 1991a, p. 280)

Hence, as presently constituted criminal justice cannot achieve social justice. Further, this has never been its intention. Criminal justice is both in and of modernity, diluted and mass mediated in postmodernity, and, as such, it contributes to the preservation and sustenance of inequalities. Flourishing postmodernity finds criminal justice a consumable commodity familiar through mediated images. These hawk an excitement born of fear feeding a popular desire for "infotainment." Representations of crime, law, and deviance marble our political conscience, fragmenting modernity's clear lines of structure and order, obscuring the reality of its control. Through the flickering images and sound bites of its process, we respond to parts, and images of these parts, without attending to the mosaic whole (Barak, 1996). We are skeptical that injustice is correctable. We stick to ideal rules of law and procedural justice and, thus, temporarily bridge the ideal-reality gap. We acknowledge corruption as inevitable and complacently withdraw into self-preservation. We do not follow through, and we feel powerless to counter the systemic malaise.

Glimpsing the Possibility of Social Justice

An adequate theory of social justice must address, rather than accommodate, the production of inequalities and law's part in their constitution. Rather than accepting the limited views of justice contained in distributive justice, procedural justice, and criminal justice, we argue that a broader definition is needed. This broader perspective should adhere to the postmodernist insight that people are not simply treated this or that way by whole social systems but are, instead, *constituted* as human subjects by them (Barak, 1997; Giddens, 1984; Henry & Milovanovic, 1996). Accordingly, social justice must deal with the harms stemming from the interrelationship between how people are defined by whole social systems and how parts of the whole system attempt to correct the harms in this constitutive process. This does not mean that law should compensate for inequalities, nor that the standards of equal treatment should be replaced with arbitrary standards of substantive justice. What it does mean, however, is that (1) the source and processes of injustice resulting from the production of society's inequalities need to be confronted, and (2) the principles of fair and equal treatment embodied in procedural law must be *extended* into the social body as part of the process whereby inequalities and their injustices are prevented. An ample theory of social justice, therefore, depends on a conception about the generation of substantive inequality and a related theory about the prevention of injustice through law. This notion of preventing injustice through law requires a working definition on the nature of harm produced within a postmodern capitalist society.

Marx's own solution to the first part of this problem proved to be no more helpful than Pashukanis's solution to the second—not least of which was because of the changing nature of inequality and society. Marx focused on the removal of what he saw as the fundamental injustice stemming from class inequality caused by the private ownership of the means of production. He believed that replacing capitalism with a communist system, in which producers of goods and services had full control over the means of production, the conditions of their work, and the decision as to what to do with the products, would solve the problems of inequality. Thus, Marx's two concepts of social justice became "from each according to his [her] capacities, to each according to his [her] work," and "from each according to his [her] capacities, to each according to his [her] needs."

These passages are related to different stages in the transition from capitalism, to socialism, to communism, respectively (Marx, 1875). The first of these quotes reflects the notion of desert based on the criterion of contribution to work in a still unequal socialist society where differences remain because, as Marx recognized, socialism is stamped with the birthmark of capitalism. The second excerpt relates to providing for people's basic elementary needs because they are human; however, it recognizes that one's higher needs may vary. Whether or not Marx's communist solution to the inequality of a class-based society was correct, it was not a solution to the production of inequalities in general. It largely dealt with inequalities produced by economic relations of capitalism. As a result, it did (and does) not deal with the problems of injustice stemming from other sources of difference. Further, it does not deal with the problem of the social construction of differences and how any social system builds inequalities based on such contrasts. This is what we call the *politics of difference.* Marx did not anticipate the effects of the politics of difference on the transition from capitalism to postindustrialism and their implications for injustice.

Similarly, Pashukanis overlooked the ways in which law and the absence of its protections can be coproductive of other categories of difference in which injustice is enshrined. His reliance on the revolution and socialist society to elevate administration, planning, and policy over the market, and his (and Marx's) insistence that with this transition bourgeois law would be undermined and would wither away, failed to account for other forms of injustice. As Kamenka (1979) correctly observes:

> The primary difficulty [with] the bureaucratic administrative view of justice . . . is that the equality it often claims to promote is at the same time most seriously undermined by the way in which its distributive aims require ever-more complex regulations and systems of distribution that *distinguish* between citizens and their activities in terms of social policies and social consequences, that substitute status rights for general and pervasive rights. (p. 12)

Thus, rather than the bourgeois law protecting the rights of the individual, albeit unequal ones, bureaucratic-administrative law excludes people from protection unless they are a member of a protected status group (for example, women, minorities, the unemployed, people with disabilities). An adequate critical theory of social justice necessarily requires that we confront *all* sources of injustice stemming from the production of inequalities based on any kind of difference, not that we compensate for the differences created and then enshrine these differences in law or its administrative surrogate. This approach simply leads to further injustice toward the newly excluded.

One radical alternative, presented in Harrington's (1989) *Socialism: Past and Future,* is understood as "visionary gradualism" and "free-market socialism."

This alternative is grounded in the global principles of feminist, antiracist, and ecologist communitarianism. It accepts the capitalist structure of accumulation (or economic growth) but advocates that accumulation be redirected toward qualitative living for all and away from quantitative consuming for a much smaller minority. In brief, Harrington's hope for human freedom and justice rests "upon the capacity of people to choose and implement democratic forms of socialization in the face of 'irresponsible,' 'unthinking' and 'unsocial' versions of corporate socialization" (West, 1990, p. 59). Moreover:

> Free-market socialism does not attempt to do away with all privileges and inequality, yet it does believe in the eradication of the social subjugation of people, and in the establishment of social justice for all. Because we live in a world without physical and technological shortages, free-market socialism believes that crimes of exploitation such as homelessness and poverty or the creation of dependent classes of people should be eliminated no differently than smallpox or hunger. Put a different way, free-market socialism believes that individuals should be limited by government to accumulating wealth only to the extent that accumulation does not deprive another coproducer or co-consumer of a minimal and humane share of the created wealth, based on what is commonly regarded as "fair" were their positions reversed. (Barak, 1991b, p. 181)

Similarly, when making sense out of such concepts as natural and social justice, Reiman (1990) contends that "real community exists among people in some interpersonal relationship, when each desires not only his own satisfaction but that of the others as well" (p. 211). More specifically, Reiman argues that justice is the precondition of true community: "the theory of justice as reason's *answer to subjugation* maintains that justice has primacy over all other ideals . . . because justice guards the boundaries between people" (p. 206). His theory of justice further insists that the principle of compatible liberty is the first rule of justice:

> The theory is deontological because it is not aimed at maximizing aggregate liberty (considered, say, as the total number of effective free choices) across people, but rather at maximizing liberty for every single person, even if this requires a lower aggregate liberty or aggregate anything else than might be obtainable otherwise. Accordingly, it holds the appropriate relations of non-subjugation to be prior in authority to any other conception of good. (pp. 207–208)

Building on the power and limitations of Rawls's theory of justice, Reiman articulates a new social contract capable of achieving social justice for all. Utilizing Rawls's "principles of difference"—the requirement that inequalities work to the greatest benefit of the worst off—Reiman examines how human beings and social order alike can be acquitted from the charge of subjugation. For example, regarding social and economic inequality worldwide or the distribution schemes that are principally responsible for the subjugation of homeless or hungry people, Reiman would argue that such relations are only justifiable if the shares of goods and services to the worst off cannot be improved by decreasing those inequalities.

These radical approaches are a considerable improvement over the liberal theories of distributive justice. They at least address social justice based on inequalities. Nonetheless, they fall short of a full social theory of justice because they do not challenge the need for inequalities. Rather, they accommodate inequality by restricting their impact again through redistribution. Further, they focus largely on economic inequalities without analyzing the process whereby differences are constructed and used as a basis for generating inequalities. We believe that they do not go far enough. Any attempt to deliver social justice must be grounded in an ongoing analysis of the politics of difference. By this we mean an analysis that exposes and deconstructs the sites of inequality based presently on class, gender, and race but that can only too readily be based on other socially constructed distinctions such as ethnicity, religiosity, style, age, physical or mental ability, and so forth.

Until the intertwined nature of the social construction of inequality based on the politics of difference is addressed, social justice will remain an unattainable ideal. Social justice can only be achieved when inequalities built on the imposition of difference are undermined. Social justice can only be achieved when a society comprehensively addresses the construction of difference, the multiple manifestation of inequalities that arise from them, and the investment in their preservation through societal and local controls.

An adequate social justice must be based on inclusiveness, not just of social categories and social types as presently constituted but of the knowledges whose assumptions make up their present legitimation. Put simply, an adequate theory of social justice cannot be based on the exclusion of some knowledges and the privileging of others, the marginalization of some people's actions at the expense of others. Instead, it must reconnect social types to their common humanity and human knowledges toward an integrated analysis of the social body. In short, the first task of an adequate critical theory of social justice is to identify the fundamental social processes that lead to inequalities in *any* society, but particularly in postmodernist societies because the transition to the postmodern era has reconfigured any simple analysis of the production of inequality.

POSTMODERNITY, INEQUALITIES, AND THE POLITICS OF DIFFERENCE

In a postmodern society, while the class relations of capitalism remain a central source of inequality contributing to injustice, these are intertwined with and accompanied by other sources of inequality, principally gender and race. To achieve social justice in such a society, it is necessary to understand how these inequalities are generated and how they interrelate with law and social control, media and popular culture. It is also necessary to understand the difference between a postmodern society (which some see as a higher form of capitalism) and earlier capitalist forms.

As Baudrillard (1981, 1983; see also Poster, 1988) has argued, under earlier stages of capitalist society the products of manufacturing were sold for exchange value, rather than use value. However, the exchange value was masked by the image of them as actually useful. In early capitalist societies, at least some reference was made to the object or to reality. With postmodern capitalist society, there is a shift from production and manufacturing to consumption, service, and information. These shifts occur as advances in information technology permeate the culture (Bell, 1976; Etzioni, 1968; Harvey, 1989; Jameson, 1984).

As Baudrillard points out, the growth of communication technologies and the media have become semiautonomous, serving the ideology of corporatism and promoting the *commodity form* rather than the commodity itself. The images of objects, as a facsimile or as a series, impose logic and order on social life. Advertising mavericks use symbols to code products to differentiate them from other similar products, thereby fitting them into a series with the product's own order (Poster, 1988). Consumption of a product is consumption of the image or the product's illusion, irrespective of the commodity's material function. For example, we purchase perfume for sex appeal, toothpaste for self-confidence, cars for eroticism, soft drinks for popularity (Baudrillard, 1981, 1983, 1985). "Consumers do not simply buy chocolate or perfume, but sensation, a drug experience: 'sweet dreams you can't resist' (Nestle ad)" (Henry & Milovanovic, 1991, p. 76).

For Baudrillard, the material product has its effect when it is consumed by transferring its symbolic meaning to its consumer (Poster, 1988). Again, it is the image that imposes its own logic, ordering society while providing the individual with an illusory sense of freedom and self-determination. Thus, consumer objects represent a system of "signs"—that is, a network of words and phrases with meanings, inexhaustible in their ability to incite desire (Baudrillard, 1983).

Baudrillard further argues that in the late twentieth century, signs become completely separated from that to which they really refer. "Emancipated" signs are extracted from their social context and float, emitting meanings that require no response, forcing a silence on the masses, signaling rather than symbolizing. This production of desire through ideology is consumed—whether we are talking about a personal computer, an Armani suit, or a pair of Nike shoes—by that clarion refrain of the marketplace: "Just do it!" However, the satisfaction is illusory, and it is supposed to be. The point is to generate an insatiable need for immediate gratification so that more and more consumption is necessary. Images replace real needs, and consumers orient their lives to endlessly obtaining the latest version of the product whose difference lies only marginally in its substance but substantially in its image.

As a result of these processes in postmodern capitalist society, social position and status appear even less tied to economic production and social class than under modern capitalism and its transparent illusions of mobility. In postmodern society, real social position is mediated and masked by the universal consumption of images. This is because

> "consumer freedom" requires that one's identity—and therefore consumer needs—evolves along the lines of market expansion. If increased consumption is only guaranteed by the recurrent "reinvention" of oneself, then the recurrent reinvention of oneself becomes a core democratic "right." (Cerroni-Long, 1996, p. 147)

In the context of constantly reinventing one's identity in a society geared to consumption, people are not only what they eat, drink, smoke, wear, drive, habituate, and so forth, but the image they provoke, the style they express, and the politics they reflect.

Baudrillard reveals that a third stage to this process suggests we are moving beyond a postmodern society toward a post-postmodern (ultramodern) one: the construction of *hyperreality*. In hyperreality we make models of the images (images of images) that imply that the illusions are the reality, that American society is real because Williamsburg and Disneyland are its imitations. Baudrillard contends that these images are counterfeit images and the everyday life in which we play is a fantasy, masked by the hyperreality. Everyday life is a simulation, made real by reference to the hyperreal. As a result, any possibility of real social relations and genuine meaning constructed to symbolize them is removed. Postmodern culture, says Baudrillard, involves social relations without content, fixed meaning, or substance.

Beneath this illusion of freedom and fantasy, however, are the forces of capital that generate both desire and division. In postmodern society an "opening up" of desire has emerged as the cybernetic ingenuity of "market sensitive" and "negative feedback" sensors appear increasingly able to capitalize on what had previously been repressed. As Pfohl (1993) concludes, "in a parasitic kind of way U.S. CAPITAL has thus gotten 'funky,' stimulating the once *outlawed styles* of African-Americans and claiming them as (if) their own" (p. 148). As the globalization of American culture escalated during the 1980s, for example, black music was given vast international importance (West, 1989). And Michael Jackson sang, "It really doesn't matter if you're black or white," unless, of course, you are neither white nor rich, but such distinctions are lost on the mass white-minded sectors of the U.S. economy. After all, rap music sells. So, "one marketing season after the next, white CAPITAL scans its borders and endeavors to appropriate and/or stimulate models that promise greater flexibility and adaptive expansion within its New World Order of cybernetic control" (Pfohl, 1993, p. 148).

Despite the mass-mediated message that race/ethnicity, gender, and class do not matter, they now matter even more. What is at work is the opening up of a multiple range of inequalities and profound differentiations, all of which enable mass and targeted marketing of an infinite diversity of consumer prod-ucts. An adequate critical theory of social justice, then, must be grounded in an appreciation of the diversity of differences that form the basis for a diversity of inequalities and through them a multitude of harms. How does this relate to crime and criminology? As we have already discussed, very concrete and direct illustrations are the differential applications of criminal justice and the practices of just deserts. More abstract and less direct are the connections be-tween the socialization of the consumer in mass society, the technological de-velopments in telecommunications, and the changing forms of crime and delinquency.

Postmodern Society, Crime, and Criminology

The "culture of consumption" has a profound relationship to crime through the ever expanding role of the "consumer personality." As Rosenfeld and Messner (1994) argue, consumption plays a major role in explaining crime, not merely in terms of causal significance of poverty or economic inequality but also in terms of the institutional significance of crime for the consumer role. Following "strain" and "anomie" theories, crime results from defective social conditions that interfere with the ability of persons or groups to con-sume at required or expected levels. However, as Rosenfeld and Messner (1994) correctly point out, "crime also reflects social arrangements widely viewed as normal and desirable—including equal and open access to the means of consumption, and fulfillment of the requirements of the consumer role" (p. 2). As they argue, the American Dream is fulfilled through consumption, and consumption is often not possible without crime.

Rosenfeld and Messner (1994) further argue that one's position as con-sumer in a capitalist society chiefly determines the likelihood for that society to experience cultural pressures to obtain certain consumable products. Whether the consumer's role leads to crime depends on the degree and inten-sity of the desire for consumption. In community-based societies like Japan, the pressures are subdued. Other noneconomic forces are at work that control and restrain behavior. In capitalist or market-driven societies like the United States, the economic "bottom line" pervades all institutional arenas, and social standing and personal worth are defined primarily in terms of individual ma-terial acquisition. Thus, there is greater stimulation to engage in crime.

Rosenfeld and Messner's argument about consumption and crime recog-nizes that acquisitive behavior is socially and culturally organized. In other words, the desire to own and possess things, though appearing natural, is actu-ally a commodified desire produced by market societies. In market societies, the individual possesses essentially two roles or sets of expectation: work and consume. Both of these roles embody "expectations and obligations that mo-tivate certain behaviors, shape their expression, and convey cultural values and beliefs" (Rosenfeld & Messner, 1995, p. 3). In sum, postmodern capitalist economies require that a large segment of the population be engaged in pro-ductive activity and that consumption continues to rise rather than drop or hold steady. Where these roles differ, however, is that the role of work exerts restraining power, whereas the role of consumption exerts liberating power.

In the role of work, we behave as we do because we have to; in the role of consumer, we behave as we are able to depending on our financial worth. Whereas Marx maintained that work defined the person, Veblen (1899/1953) argued that consumption also has great expressive significance for its members. In the postmodern advanced capitalist society, consumption often assumes priority over employment as a sign of social membership and status (Coleman & Rainwater, 1978). Further, "the expectations of the consumer role are highly permissive by comparison [to the role of employee] and provide considerably more discretion with respect to how, when, where, and with whom the role is performed" (Rosenfeld & Messner, 1995, pp. 4–5). Thus, "consumption offers powerful gratifications not easily matched by the intrinsic satisfactions or extrinsic rewards of work" (p. 5).

A strong orientation to consume the American Dream, then, may serve as a means of overwhelming the restraints associated with employment and of undermining cooperative bonds of social control. This may be as true for "criminals" as "noncriminals." It is also true for those crimes committed both against the state and by the state (Barak, 1991a). It is not argued here, however, that crime should be reduced to "mere" economics and self-determinism. On the contrary, it is not only the material-real expressions of the "freedom of consumption" but also the symbolic-ideal transference of one's social worth and self-esteem to an identification with a material measure driven by the processes of commodification.

An adequate theory of social justice, then, requires an expanded vision of criminology. The field of criminology must be cognizant of the multiple dimensions of social harm based on the politics of difference that emerge and are emerging in a postmodern, differentiated society. Modernist criminology is deficient in this task because of its failure to address the interconnections between the production of difference, inequality, and injustice. What is required is an integrated theory appropriate for a postmodern society.

Modernist integration—in all its different guises—is really aimed at the questionable objective of delivering some kind of positivist prediction of what causes criminal behavior (Barak, 1997). By contrast, with postmodernist integration, everything, at both the micro and macro levels, affects everything else, and these effects are continuously changing over time (Barak, 1997). Modernist integrative schemes, regardless of model, are propositional, predictive, particularistic, and static. They only use linear or multiple causality. Postmodernist integrative schemes, however, are conceptual, interpretive, holistic, and dynamic. They employ interactive or reciprocal causality. These holistic integrative models (for instance, "interactional," "ecological," "constitutive") of crime and crime control hold out the most promise for developing criminology (Barak, 1997). Further, the hyperintegration model attempts to integrate these integrations, arguing that bringing together both modernist and postmodernist sensibilities is necessary to capture the whole picture regarding the social reality of crime.

A hyperintegrated vision of criminology must start with an analysis of the harm of inequality based on an expanded definition of what counts as crime. This includes not simply crimes against property and person but all those harms based on the use of difference to create advantage at others' expense. A definition along these lines is found in constitutive theory (Henry & Milovanovic, 1991, 1994, 1996). It is part of the emerging postmodern school of thought (Barak, Henry, & Milovanovic, 1996).

A Constitutive Definition of Crime

The essence of the constitutive argument is that crime and its control cannot be separated from the totality of the ordered, structural, and cultural contexts in which it is produced. Constitutive criminology argues that unequal power relations, built on the construction of difference, provide the conditions that define crime as harm. Thus, constitutive criminology redefines crime as the harm resulting from investing energy in relations of power that involves pain, conflict, and injury. People taken to be in relations of "crimes" are in relations of inequalities as well. They are, as different human subjects, being disrespected—that is, reduced from what they are, prevented from becoming what they might be. Thus, a constitutive approach defines crime as "the expression of some agency's energy to make a difference on others, and it is the exclusion of those others, who in the instant are rendered powerless to maintain or express their humanity" (Henry & Milovanovic, 1996, p. 116). This agency may be composed of and energized by people, social identities (men, women, and so on), groups, parties, institutions, the state. Crime manifests a disrespecting power. Indeed:

> crimes are nothing less than moments in the expression of power, such that those who are subjected to them are denied their own contribution to the encounter and often to future encounters, [and they] are denied their worth . . . Crime then is the power to deny others their ability to make a difference. (Henry & Milovanovic, 1996, p. 116)

In our postmodern advanced capitalist society, the activities of many individuals working in institutions are premised on the exercise of their power over others—the witting or unwitting denial of others' right to make a difference. This is the root of why capitalism is criminogenic and why ours is a violent society. It is also why Party hierarchy state socialism is/was criminogenic. The activities of those who construct occasions for the deliverance of power is crime. It is crime because it takes from people any present dignity and, further, represses their attempt to change. Thus, a constitutive view of crime includes much of what currently stands for business practices, governmental policies, and hierarchical social relations. It includes a lot of what occurs in family life. It is why sexual harassment and violence against women (whether in emotional torment or physical beating from either spouse to the other or to dependents) are crimes. It is especially why child abuse is a crime. Indeed, it is why emotional terror by employers over employees through at-will employment is a crime (Henry, 1994a). Finally, it is why several of the actions or inactions of government agencies, such as neglect of health and safety in the workplace, are also crimes. It is why unaffordable housing and homelessness are crimes (Barak & Bohm, 1989). These arenas are each premised on the inequality of power relations that allow some to build their freedom on the backs of others denied (Barak, 1991b).

The constitutive definition of crime is highly appropriate for an integrative-constitutive criminology within postmodern society. The constitutive definition focuses on harm inflicted in all its guises, particularly how the disenfranchised, disempowered, and marginalized have had their voices denied or their desires quashed (Aronowitz & Giroux, 1991; Freire, 1985; Giroux, 1992).

Thus, in contrast to existing legal and modernist definitions of crime, this definition of crime is specific, but historically contingent. It includes victim categories that allow us to be aware of the changing nature of the emerging social constructions whose relations of power are relations of harm. Harm results "from any attempt to reduce or suppress another's position or potential standing through the use of power that limits the other's ability to make a difference" (Henry & Milovanovic, 1996, p. 13).

Thus, constitutive criminologists find it helpful to identify two aspects of the relations of domination that characterize crime. "Crimes of reduction" and "crimes of repression" refer to power differentials and to hierarchical relations that reinforce both types of harm (Henry & Milovanovic, 1996, pp. 99–100). Harms of reduction occur when offended parties experience a loss of some quality relative to their present standing. They could have property stolen from them, but they could also have dignity stripped from them, as in acts of hate against discredited groups. Harms of repression occur when offended parties experience a limit or restriction preventing them from achieving a desired position or standing. They could be prevented from achieving a career goal because of sexism or racism, or a promotional "glass ceiling." Considered along a continuum of deprivation, harms of reduction or repression may be based on any number of constructed differences. As presently defined within late twentieth-century Western industrial societies, harms cluster around the following constructed differences: economic (class, property), gender (sexism), race and ethnicity (racism, hate), political (power, corruption), morality, ethics ("avowal of desire"), human rights, social position (status/prestige, inequality), psychological state (security, well-being), self-realization/actualization, biological integrity, and so forth. Whatever the construction, these are harms either because they move the offended person away from a position or state she or he currently occupies, or because they prevent the harmed party from occupying a position or state that the person desires, whose achievement does not deny/deprive another (Henry & Milovanovic, 1996, p. 103).

As is evident, unlike the narrowly defined modernist definitions of crime, the constitutive definition is capable of accommodating an infinite range of harms as experienced. Our definition of crime as "the exercise of the power to deny others their own humanity" needs to be anchored to the specificities of endless substitutable, existent, and emergent social constructions. It is through these constructions that humanity is constituted and along these assorted dimensions that it takes shape. It is in this way that we are continuously made aware of the relations of crime and of the social space needed to replace these with less harmful forms.

To change the social construction of harm, it is necessary to change its social forms and its implied power relations. In this way, harm and victimization are not carried under the guise of law in the expression of power over others. To both comprehend and counteract the harmful outcomes of these interrelations, integrative-constitutive criminology points to the need to transcend modernist culturally produced images of crime and punishment. Further, integrative-constitutive criminology endeavors to see them more appropriately as mutually produced through social relations and various (mis)readings of both modernity and postmodernity.

An Integrated-Constitutive Theory of Crime

It has been argued (Barak, 1997) that an integrated vision of criminology must incorporate a cultural studies approach to the study of crime as harm. This view not only reflects a concern with the politics of difference and with identity politics, but it overlaps with postcolonial studies and uses concepts and vocabularies "that attempt to reflect the diversity, the plurality, the diffuseness, and the blurring of boundaries of academic disciplines and between disciplines and the external world" (Bloland, 1995, p. 546).

Contemporary cultural studies proponents argue for a historically mediated, culturally specific understanding of crime as harm and of social justice. As Dines and Humez (1995) posit:

> many dimensions of social stratification influence the unequal distribution of power and resources in our society. Racism, sexism, classicism, heterosexism, ageism, ableism, and others—each system of social domination has its own separate history, dynamic, conditions of existence and material and ideological components. (p. xviii)

Hence, in the multicultural world of late or postmodern society, each of the "isms" represents its own unique social experiences, movements, and consciousnesses. Each of them needs to be expressed and accounted for as they represent socially constructed inequalities built on differences. For example, Roberts (1993) examined what she terms the terrible intersection of crime, race, and reproduction and "the convergence of two tools of oppression—the racial construction of crime and the use of reproduction as an instrument of punishment" (p. 1945). She argues that the "technology of power" that links crime, race, and reproduction exemplifies how racism and patriarchy function as mutually supporting systems of domination, and how criminologists need to incorporate such awareness into their criminological analyses. As she puts it:

> It is most likely that this tactic of domination will be meted out through the control of black women's bodies. Discouraging black procreation is a means of subordinating the entire race; under patriarchy, it is accomplished

through the regulation of black women's fertility. In our effort to dismantle hierarchies of gender, race, and class, a critical initial task is to explore how each of these hierarchies sustains the others. (p. 1977)

Race matters so much that Roberts contends it identifies criminals. She further argues that race is not only embedded in the very foundation of the criminal law but that it helps determine "who the criminals are, what constitutes a crime, and which crimes society treats most seriously" (p. 145). Thus, to deliver social justice we need to deconstruct inequalities based on difference, while celebrating difference. To do this, we must understand the continuities and discontinuities in the social experiences of different groupings of peoples as these intersect *ideologically* across the horizons of individual and environmental development.

Although it is impossible for people (or "identities"), regardless of their race/ethnicity, gender, and socioeconomic backgrounds, to ever completely escape from the social and ideological parameters of which they are a part, the question of "difference" and "sameness" should not be simply reduced to modernity's one-dimensional social constructions of black/white, male/female, rich/poor, young/old, and so forth. There are differences within sameness and sameness within differences, especially as one examines the combination of social and physical statuses involved in identity formations. For example, Austin (1992) has commented about the black community and the dominant society. She claims that both are in a constant state of flux because of the challenges from without and within. In terms of the strains and multiple voices of "the black community" on crime, she writes:

> There are tensions at the border with the dominant society, at the frontier between liberation and oppression. There is also internal dissension over indigenous threats to security and solidarity. "Difference" is as much a source of contention within the "community" as it is a factor marking the boundary between "the community" and everyone else. (p. 1769)

Similarly, difference within is as important as difference between when it comes to crime and crime control among women, men, rich, poor, middle-class, straight, gay, old, and young alike. The central issue is the politics of how difference is transformed into inequality experienced as injustice.

Knowledge of these interactive relationships and how they impact on each other is fundamental to the development of more inclusive and integrated theories of crime. In a different way, and in relation to the development of more inclusive and integrated theories of crime and social control, each of these dimensions has been viewed as a source of a particular form of oppression or experience. Depending on which particular triad of race-gender-class identity is involved, for example, these forces may be reciprocal and reinforcing of criminal behavior, or they may be contradictory and resistant of such behavior.

The integrative-constitutive perspective also incorporates an appreciation of differences in the patterns of crime attributed to socialization, opportunities, and bias in the context that everyone's life is framed by inequalities of race, class, and gender. As Anderson and Hill Collins (1992) have written:

African-Americans and other racial/ethnic groups are not the sole recipients of differential treatment by race; racial politics also encompasses the experiences of whites. Women and men are both affected by gender, and the lives of the poor and their more affluent counterparts are intimately intertwined. By seeing that we are all part of one historically created system that finds structural form in interconnected social institutions, we gain greater insight about the actual and potential shape of our own lives. (p. 177)

CONCLUSION

An integrative-constitutive theory of crime, crime control, and social justice is steeped in postmodernism and cultural studies, and it is joined by gender/feminist studies, racial/ethnic studies, and media/communications studies. It is here that we find a convergence of interest in popular discourse and the social construction of reality. The integrated-constitutive theory, informed by a cultural studies approach to crime and its control, attempts to bring the intersection of class, race, and gender together with the dynamics of mass communications and identity formations. This integration attempts to address the issues of how the politics of difference translates into multiple inequalities, each with its own injustices. It assumes that crime, defined as harm expressed as the power to deny others a right to make a difference, is connected to the larger relations of the symbolic and social structures as these are expressed in the ideologically patterned practices of nonconformity and social control.

We see, then, that to fully understand criminal behavior, an integrative-constitutive approach to crime and its control in mass-mediated society must incorporate studies in political economy, textual readings, and audience receptions (experiences). Berger (1995), picking up on Weber's emphasis on the importance of both the "ideal" and the "material," writes, "Cultural understanding requires attention not only to image, sound, word, gesture, and the symbolic character of human things but . . . to the material as well as the ideal interests of persons and groups in those symbolic realms" (p. 12). The understanding of crime defined as social harm and its control requires no less if we are to deliver ourselves from the multiple injustices of postmodern capitalism.

REVIEW QUESTIONS

1. What is the difference among free-market, liberal-conservative, and radical theories of justice? Provide examples of each, and explain why these might fail to deliver social justice.

2. Discuss the difference between distributive and procedural justice. Why do free market theories of justice focus on procedural justice, and why do critical theorists find this approach too limiting?

3. Compare and contrast the different conceptions of modernist criminal justice and postmodernist social justice as exemplified by free-market capitalism, welfare capitalism, and free-market socialism.

4. Critically assess theories of distributive justice for dealing with the problems of inequality in a capitalist society. How and based on what criteria do you think inequalities should be addressed in such a society? How does the postmodern era change the nature of inequality, and how we might respond?

5. Why is it important to understand socially constructed differences when considering social justice in a postmodern society? Provide examples of how these differences build toward inequalities.

6. What social and criminal justice policy implications follow from an integrative-constitutive theory of crime and social justice? Why does social justice require more than fixing the criminal justice system?

7. How does an integrative-constitutive theory propose to redefine crime? What might be its policies for social control?

REFERENCES

Anderson, M. L., & Collins, P. H. (Eds.). (1992). *Race, class and gender: An anthology*. Belmont, CA: Wadsworth.

Aronowitz, S., & Giroux, H. A. (1991). *Postmodern education*. Minneapolis: University of Minnesota Press.

Austin, R. (1992). "The black community," its lawbreakers, and a politics of identification. *Southern California Law Review, 65*, 1769–1817.

Barak, G. (1980). *In defense of whom? A critique of criminal justice reform*. Cincinnati, OH: Anderson.

Barak, G (Ed.). (1991a). *Crimes by the capitalist state: An introduction to state criminology*. Albany: State University of New York Press.

Barak, G. (1991b). *Gimme shelter: A social history of homelessness in contemporary America*. New York: Praeger.

Barak, G. (1991c). Homelessness and the case for community-based initiatives: The emergence of a model shelter as a short term response to the deepening crisis in housing. In H. E. Pepinsky & R. Quinney (Eds.), *Criminology as peacemaking* (pp. 47–68). Bloomington: Indiana University Press.

Barak, G. (Ed.). (1994). *Media, process, and the social construction of crime: Studies in newsmaking criminology*. New York: Garland.

Barak, G. (Ed.). (1996). *Representing O.J.: Murder, criminal justice, and mass culture*. Albany, NY: Harrow & Heston.

Barak, G. (1997). *Integrating criminologies*. Boston: Allyn & Bacon.

Barak, G., & Bohm, R. E. (1989, September). The crimes of the homeless or the crime of homelessness? On the dialectics of criminalization, decriminalization, and victimization. *Contemporary Crises: Law, Crime and Social Policy, 13*(3), 275–288.

Barak, G., Henry, S., & Milovanovic, D. (1996). Constitutive criminology: An overview of an emerging postmodernist school. In B. MacLean & D. Milovanovic (Eds.), *Critical criminology* (pp. 93–99). Vancouver: Collective Press.

Barry, B. M. (1973). *The liberal theory of justice*. Oxford: Clarendon.

Barry, B. M. (1989). *Theories of justice: A treatise on social justice*. Oxford: Clarendon.

Barry, B. M. (1995). *Justice as impartiality.* Oxford: Clarendon.

Baudrillard, J. (1981). *For a critique of the political economy of the sign.* St. Louis, MO: Telos.

Baudrillard, J. (1983). *Simulacra and simulations* (P. Foss, P. Patton, & P. Beitchman, Trans.). New York: Semiotext(e).

Baudrillard, J. (1985). The masses: Implosion of the social in the media (M. Maclean, Trans.). *New Literary History, 16*(3), 577–589.

Bell, D. (1976). *The cultural contradictions of capitalism.* New York: Basic Books.

Berger, B. M. (1995). *An essay on culture: Symbolic structure and social structure.* Berkeley: University of California Press.

Bloland, H. G. (1995). Postmodernism and higher education. *Journal of Higher Education, 66*(5), 521–559.

Cahn, E. (1949). *The sense of injustice.* New York: New York University Press.

Cahn, E. (1968). Justice. In D. L. Sills (Ed.), *International encyclopedia of the social sciences* (Vol. 8, pp. 341–347). New York: The MacMillan Company and The Free Press.

Cerroni-Long, E. L. (1996). Ethnic expressive style and American public opinion: The O. J. Simpson case. In G. Barak (Ed.), *Representing O. J.: Murder, criminal justice, and mass culture* (pp. 140–150). Albany, NY: Harrow & Heston.

Coleman, R. P., & Rainwater, L. (1978). *Social standing in America.* New York: Basic Books.

DeKeseredy, W. S., & Schwartz, M. D. (1996). *Contemporary criminology.* Belmont, CA: Wadsworth.

Dines, G., & Humez, J. M. (Eds.). (1996). *Gender, race and class in media: A textreader.* Thousands Oaks, CA: Sage.

Ericson, R. V., Baranek, P. M., & Chan, J. B. L. (1991). *Representing order: Crime, law, and justice in the news media.* Toronto: University of Toronto Press.

Etzioni, A. (1968). *The active society.* New York: Free Press.

Freire, P. (1985). *The politics of education.* South Hadley, MA: Bergin & Garvey.

Giddens, A. (1984). *The constitution of society: Outline of the theory of structuration.* Cambridge: Polity.

Giroux, H. A. (1992). *Border crossings.* New York: Routledge.

Harrington, M. (1989). *Socialism: Past and future.* Berkeley, CA: Arcade.

Harvey, D. (1989). *The coalition of postmodernity.* London: Blackwell.

Hayek, F. A. von. (1944). *The road to serfdom.* Chicago: University of Chicago Press.

Hayek, F. A. von. (1960). *The constitution of liberty.* Chicago: University of Chicago Press.

Hayek, F. A. von. (1976). *The mirage of social justice.* London: Routledge & Kegan Paul.

Henry, S. (1983). *Private justice.* London: Routledge & Kegan Paul.

Henry, S. (1987a). The construction and deconstruction of social control: Thoughts on the discursive production of state law and private justice. In J. Lowman, R. Menzies, & T. Palys (Eds.), *Transcarceration: Essays in the sociology of social control* (pp. 89–108). Aldershot, U.K.: Gower.

Henry, S. (1987b). Private justice and the policing of labor. In C. Shearing & P. Stenning (Eds.), *Private policing* (pp. 45–71). Beverly Hills: Sage.

Henry, S. (1991). Introduction: The postmodern perspective in criminology. In B. D. MacLean & D. Milovanovic (Eds.), *New directions in critical criminology* (pp. 71–78). Vancouver: Collective Press.

Henry, S. (Ed.). (1994a). Employee dismissal: Justice at work. In *The annals of the American Academy of Political and Social Science* (Vol. 536, November). Thousand Oaks, CA: Sage.

Henry, S. (Ed.). (1994b). *Social control: Aspects of non-state justice.* Aldershot, U.K.: Dartmouth.

Henry, S., & Milovanovic, D. (1991). Constitutive criminology. *Criminology, 29*(2), 293–316.

Henry, S., & Milovanovic, D. (1996). *Constitutive criminology: Beyond postmodernism.* London: Sage.

Henry, S., & Milovanovic, D. (1994). The constitution of constitutive criminology: A postmodern approach to criminological theory. In D. Nelken (Ed.), *The futures of criminology* (pp. 110–133). London: Sage.

Honore, A. M. (1968). Social justice. In R. S. Summers (Ed.), *Essays in legal philosophy.* Berkeley: University of California Press.

Jameson, F. (1984, July/August). Postmodernism, or the cultural logic of late capitalism. *New Left Review, 146,* 53–92.

Kamenka, E. (1979). What is justice? In E. Kamenka & A. Erh-Soon Tay (Eds.), *Justice* (pp. 1–24). London: Arnold.

Lang, W. (1979). Marxism, liberalism and justice. In E. Kamenka & A. Erh-Soon Tay (Eds.), *Justice* (pp. 116–148). London: Arnold.

Marx, K. (1875). Critique of the Gotha programme. In K. Marx & F. Engels (Eds.), *Selected works.* Moscow: Progress.

Nozick, R. (1974). *Anarchy, state and utopia.* New York: Basic Books.

Pashukanis, E. B. (1978). *Law and Marxism: A general theory.* London: Ink Links. (Originally published 1924)

Passmore, J. A. (1979). Civil justice and its rivals. In E. Kamenka & A. Erh-Soon Tay (Eds.), *Justice* (pp. 25–49). London: Arnold.

Pfohl, S. (1993). Twilight of the parasites: Ultramodern capital and the new world order. *Social Problems, 40*(2), 125–151.

Poster, M. (Ed.). (1988). *Jean Baudrillard: Selected writings.* Stanford, CA: Stanford University Press.

Rawls, J. (1971). *A theory of justice.* Cambridge, MA: Harvard University Press.

Reiman, J. (1990). *Justice and modern moral philosophy.* New Haven, CT: Yale University Press.

Roberts, D. E. (1993). Crime, race, and reproduction. *Tulane Law Review, 67*(6), 1945–1977.

Rosenfeld, R., & Messner, S. F. (1994). *Crime and the American Dream.* Belmont, CA: Wadsworth.

Rosenfeld, R., & Messner, S. F. (1995). *Consumption and crime: An institutional inquiry.* Paper presented at the annual meetings of the Academy of Criminal Justice Sciences, Boston.

Sloop, J. M. (1996). *The cultural prison: Discourse, prisoners, and punishment.* Tuscaloosa: University of Alabama Press.

Smart, C. (1992). The women of legal discourse. *Social and Legal Studies: An International Journal, 1,* 29–44.

Swingewood, A. (1975). *Marx and modern social theory.* London: Macmillan.

Tigar, M. E., & Levy, M. R. (1977). *Law and the rise of capitalism.* New York: Monthly Review Press.

Tonry, M. (1995). *Malign neglect: Race, crime and punishment in America.* New York: Oxford University Press.

Veblen, T. (1953). *The theory of the leisure class.* New York: Macmillan. (Originally published 1899)

West, C. (1989). Black culture and postmodernism. In B. Kruger & P. Mariani (Eds.), *Remaking history.* Port Townsend, WA: Bay Press.

West, C. (1990, January 8–15). Michael Harrington, socialist. *The Nation.*

Young, A., & Rush, P. (1994). The law of victimage in urban realism: Thinking through inscriptions of violence. In D. Nelken (Ed.), *The futures of criminology* (pp. 154–172). London: Sage.

Young, T. R. (1995). *The red feather dictionary of critical social science.* Boulder, CO: Red Feather Institute.

❖

Critical Race Theory
and Social Justice

ritical race theory is a direct outgrowth of the critical legal studies
(CLS) movement. The CLS movement emerged in the mid-1970s.
CLS scholars incorporated Marx's insights on economic and political
power and oppression, and then applied them to law, legal reasoning, and legal
decision making. Critical race theory (CRT) was a response to the perceived
theoretical and methodological inadequacies within the CLS agenda. According to critical race theorists, the CLS critique simply did not explain the variable of race. At best, CLS scholars obscured race with class when examining
legal thought and legal practice. Critical race theory asserts that the "rule of
law" doctrine legitimizes white supremacy and oppresses people of color.
Critical race theorists seek an end to white racial supremacy as embodied in
the law and thus advocate for changing how the law is used to enforce such
victimization. In this chapter, Russell applies a critical race analysis to the
question of understanding crime and law and, more generally, to understanding definitions of deviance. She applies the critical race method of analysis
to two criminal justice problems: interracial crime and racial hoaxes. She
concludes that the critical race method of analysis—with its emphasis on per-
sonalized accounts of harm and other forms of storytelling—shows us the importance of redefining and reconfiguring legal analysis about race in the law.
For CRT scholars, this is what racial justice in the law must embody. The

CRT agenda, then, is one more step in the direction of social justice. This is a direction that seeks to undo the harm perpetrated by existing definitions of crime, law, and deviance. This is a direction that seeks to undo the harm advanced by prevailing notions of criminal justice.

9

Critical Race Theory
and Social Justice

KATHERYN K. RUSSELL

The goal of this chapter is to explore the relationship between critical race theory (CRT) and social justice. More pointedly, this essay will assess whether social justice is promoted by a critical race analysis. Attention is given to how a critical race analysis furthers our understanding of law, crime, and definitions of deviance. This chapter is divided into two parts. The first section provides an overview of CRT, its origins, basic premises, and operating principles. Relatedly, this section details the critical race method of analysis, including the framework that critical race scholars utilize and the challenges that have been raised to their research. The second part applies a critical race analysis to two criminal justice issues: interracial crimes and racial hoaxes. These issues are discussed to evaluate whether a critical race analysis, its theory and its goals, furthers the goal of social justice.

HISTORICAL OVERVIEW,
OPERATING PRINCIPLES, AND GOALS

Critical race theory is a direct descendent of critical legal studies (CLS). The CLS movement emerged in the mid-1970s. The movement was formed by a small group of professors at northeastern, elite law schools who sought to develop a new and critical method of analyzing legal doctrine. The group's express goal was to challenge the legitimacy of the mainstream method of legal analysis. Critical legal studies was formed around several basic principles, including *indeterminacy* and *antiformalism*. Scholars of CLS, including Duncan Kennedy and Roberto Unger, argued that legal doctrine is not systematic, it does not offer a definitive resolution for all circumstances, and there is no such thing as a value-free or autonomous legal method. This rebellious group of legal scholars concluded that all legal decision making is designed to reinforce the status quo.

For example, CLS scholars have analyzed several areas of case law, including civil rights, labor, and gender discrimination. The CLS critique establishes that the law cannot be relied on to protect the rights of those without power. According to CLS analysis, the law is not a bellwether for justice; rather, it is a bellwether for securing the positions of those already in power. Critical legal studies places economic and class structures at the center of its analysis. Both opponents and proponents of CLS have labeled it as a leftist or Marxist-Leninist critique of the law. It shares many of the same political assumptions and structural analyses as radical and critical criminology (see Chapter 1 on Marx and social justice for more).

A CLS critique of legal decision making, or "trashing," has been applied to several substantive areas of law, including antidiscrimination law, labor law, contract law, and the role of women in the law. Taub and Schneider (1991) analyze how early legal doctrine was used to keep women out of the workplace. They detail how the law expressly precluded women from the public sphere while, at the same time, it upheld differential treatment on the basis of sex. In their review of nineteenth-century Supreme Court doctrine (doctrine that barred women from voting and bar membership), Taub and Schneider write, "[T]he persisting separate-sphere ideology legitimized and reinforced women's marginal and secondary status in the work force. Working women were suspicious, inferior and immoral" (p. 151).

Although CLS scholarship is clearly a descendent of a long-standing tradition of legal critique (notably legal realism), it has been consistently maligned. The mainstream legal community's reaction to CLS is famous for its intensity—some have responded to it as though it constituted a personal affront. The very existence of the CLS critique prompted one law professor to suggest that CLS scholars, who are obviously cynical about the law's legitimacy, have "an ethical duty to depart from the law school" (Carrington, 1984, p. 227).

Others have discounted CLS as the work of a fringe group of law professors. However, CLS supporters and opponents share one common critique of CLS: that it is unnecessarily dense. Left-of-center academics, who largely welcomed the CLS critique, have questioned whether its turgid prose renders it inaccessible, thereby limiting its ability to effect change. Numerous other criticisms have emerged; CLS was dubbed elitist because it primarily reflected the work of Ivy League–educated white men, teaching at Ivy League law schools (Delgado, 1995). This led some to question the authenticity of the CLS critique—whether it was simply ivory tower theorizing rather than praxis. Another argument that surfaced was that CLS had failed to incorporate areas of analysis most in need of critique, including criminal law (see, for example, Russell, 1994).

Over several years, a more substantive critique of CLS surfaced from left academics. In short, the argument was that the CLS movement was not critical enough. In the mid-1980s, a small group of legal scholars of color, some of whom had participated in CLS scholarship, declared it wanting. These scholars expressed concern that the CLS critique did not adequately or accurately take account of race and the role it continues to play in the American legal system. Many of these legal scholars, primarily interested in exploring the role of race and the law, criticized CLS for confounding race with class. This fundamental criticism of CLS fertilized and solidified the growth and development of critical race theory (CRT).

Critical race theory centers around two basic goals: "(1) understanding how the rule of law has been used to maintain White supremacy and the subordination of people of color; (2) *changing* how the law is used to support White racial power" (Crenshaw, Gotanda, Peller, & Thomas, 1995, p. xii). Several assumptions underlie the basic principles and goals of critical race theory. First, CRT assumes that inequality exists between whites and all other racial groups. Specifically, the assumption is that nonwhites are treated as inferior to whites, in both covert and overt ways, and that this disparity is historically rooted. The inequality gap is most acute between blacks and whites.

Second, CRT assumes that the law is not self-correcting. The law is an arm of the prevailing economic order; therefore, it alone cannot correct the problems of racial inequality. Until fundamental changes are made in how race is tied with all social institutions, racial equality cannot be realized.

Third, following the tradition of CLS scholars, critical race theorists reject the notion that legal scholarship is value-free. Underlying CRT is the assumption that all legal analysis expresses a value, one that either promotes or rejects the status quo. This premise ties in directly with the CLS tenet of antiformalism. Critical race theorists believe that what passes for justice will depend on the race of the parties involved and the economic interests that are at stake.

The foundational premise of CRT is that understanding how the American legal system works necessitates an understanding of racism. This is true because race and the law are historically intertwined. Most important, critical race theorists seek to move beyond engaging in academic debate with other legal scholars. They work to transform the existing legal structure into one that addresses historical and contemporary injustices. Thus, there is a nexus between critical race theory and social justice.

Part of this transformation occurs by demonstrating the law's limited ability to ensure social justice. The critical race critique tells us at least two things about social justice. First, the methods for achieving social justice are shaped by the legal and political climate. This point is made most dramatically by comparing how differently the fight for social justice was structured during the pre–civil rights era, compared with how the fight is configured today.

Aside from the fact that the law on its face created racial double standards, pre–civil rights legal critiques also argued for the enactment of laws that would mandate equality of opportunity for minorities. However, neither of these conditions exists today—de jure discrimination is a historical fact, and the written law promises fairness and equality regardless of race. Today, the attempt to use the law as a means toward social justice requires a legal methodology distinct from the pre–civil rights era strategies. This is one of the defining characteristics of CRT scholarship. Critical race theory makes it clear that new and evolving paradigms are required to keep pace with the changing forms of racial and social discrimination. It offers a new legal method for assessing the law's promise to deliver justice. The old legal tools are not helpful in waging a battle today for social justice. Calmore (1992) observes that critical race theorists have "deliberately chosen race-conscious orientations and objectives to resolve conflicts of interpretation in acting on the commitment to social justice and anti-subordination" (p. 2189).

Second, achieving social justice necessitates the insights of those directly effected by social inequality. Working toward social justice, then, requires recasting and redefining legal analyses of race and the law. Addis (1993) refers to this as the need for a "corrective story"—an analysis of the law that incorporates the viewpoints and critiques of all racial groups, not just European Americans. Addis comments, "The rhetoric of white innocence and of black [deviance] are possible because African Americans have not been allowed to tell their story" (p. 527).

Critical race scholars write their corrective stories in a variety of forms. They use unconventional writing methods in addition to mainstream legal analysis to make their case. Critical race theorists frequently incorporate personal narratives and anecdotes to support and explain their legal arguments. Many CRT scholars refer to themselves directly, using "I" in their legal critiques. The first person is used to bridge the distance between the reader and the writer and to erase the unstated value-neutral premise of most legal scholarship.

For example, in her legal writing, Matsuda (1993) weaves in her experiences as a Japanese-American woman to explain how race-based hate speech inflicts injury. She writes:

> As a young child I was told never to let anyone call me a J_p. My parents, normally peaceable and indulgent folk, told me this in the tone reserved for dead-serious warnings. Don't let anyone call you that name. In their tone they transmitted a message of danger, that the word was a dangerous one, tied to violence. . . . This early training in vigilance was reinforced by what I later learned about violence and Asian Americans: that people with features like mine are regular victims of violence tied to a wave of anti-Asian propaganda that stretches from Boston to San Francisco, from Galveston to Detroit. (p. 17)

Matsuda shares her experiences, through personal accounts, to illustrate the impact of hate speech. This account is used to support her legal analysis of hate speech, the goal of hate crime legislation, and ultimately her argument that race-based hate speech should be made criminal.

Likewise, Williams (1987) uses personal narratives to buttress her legal arguments. In a critical race critique of how the media analyzes racial assaults, she describes how it feels to be barred from a store because of one's race. Williams, who is black, details an incident in which she attempted to gain entry to a Benetton clothing store. Entrance to the store was controlled by a buzzer. Williams, who saw several shoppers in the store, pressed the buzzer to gain admittance. A young, white store clerk looked her over and then mouthed the words, "We're closed." Williams writes:

> I was enraged. At that moment I literally wanted to break all of the windows in the store and *take* lots of sweaters. . . . In the flicker of his judgmental eyes, that saleschild had reduced my brightly sentimental, joy-to-the-world, pre-Christmas spree to a shambles. He had snuffed my sense of humanitarian catholicity, and there was nothing I could do to snuff his, without simply making a spectacle of myself. (p. 128).

Williams's writing style removes the distance and "objectivity" usually sought in legal writing. Similar to Matsuda, Williams uses the first person to describe what it feels like to be a member of a racial group that experiences discrimination, without legal recourse. Both anecdotes offer a compelling portrayal of how the law (or how the absence of law) impacts the human experience. In attempting to carry out the CRT goal of affecting change, the personal narrative shows the direct force of the law. This narrative form has become increasingly common in legal scholarship.

Storytelling is another writing method employed by some critical race theorists. Bell (1992) and Delgado (1995) have skillfully used this writing tool. Bell's "Space Traders" parable involves a proposal made by aliens to the U.S. government. The aliens offer to solve all of the nation's problems, including gold to bail out the bankrupt state and federal governments, special chemicals that will unpollute the environment, and fuel to relieve the nation's almost depleted supply. In exchange, the aliens want the United States to hand over its entire black population. Bell uses the hypothetical scenario to raise, discuss, and analyze questions about race, race relations, law, and justice.

In *The Rodrigo Chronicles,* Delgado (1995) creates an ongoing dialogue between a seasoned minority law professor and a newly minted minority law professor. The pair philosophize on a range of topics, including affirmative action, crime, race relations, and democracy. What is distinctive about their conversations is that they talk about these issues as people directly affected by them and not as observers from afar. The storytelling method of legal analyses has been used to a limited degree in mainstream scholarship (Fuller, 1949).

Critical race scholars employ radical writing styles in direct response to staid and "objective" mainstream legal critiques. As a general rule, mainstream analyses do not acknowledge any bias on the part of the writer—political or otherwise. The critiques are presented as objective and value-free, as if the writer (for example, U.S. Supreme Court justice or law professor) has no opinions or biases. The tacit assumption is that writers are not persuaded by personal biases or economic interests. In marked contrast, critical race theorists wear their biases on their sleeves. They offer no value-free pretense. Critical race scholars typically signal their readers by stating their biases and opinions at the outset. This makes for a difference in both style and substance between mainstream and CRT critiques. The critical race scholar's desire to affect social conditions shapes the form and core of the critique.

Another notable distinction between CRT and mainstream legal methods is the variation in length. Mainstream legal analyses—law review articles—typically involve lengthy prose. Some CRT analyses are long and detailed; others are succinctly written. This radical departure from the standard hundred-page law journal article makes CRT analyses accessible to a larger, non-lawyer audience.

Within its analysis of race, CRT scholarship has explored many other areas, including the roles of gender, patriarchy, and class. Early on, CRT focused almost exclusively on issues relating to blacks and whites. More recently, CRT has moved beyond a dichotomous treatment of race. For example, legal issues about the Asian-American experience with the justice system are part of the "race" that CRT explores (see, for instance, Lee, 1995). The expansion of the race critique also includes analyses of what race means and an examination of existing definitions of race. Several articles explore the definition of "blackness"—who is black and how this has been determined by the law (Floyd, 1995). Most notably, CRT explores overlapping social categories, including race, sex, gender, and class. These overlaps are referred to as "intersections." Critical race scholarship also includes analyses of sexual preference (Valdes, 1995).

As the ranks of CRT grow, so does the attention it receives. Similar to critical legal studies scholars, CRT advocates have encountered an avalanche of criticism. Three main criticisms of CRT have been raised. A recurring criticism is that CRT is not scholarly. Some have dismissed it as unscientific because some critical race scholars support their arguments with personal experiences. The variegations in writing style have also ruffled the feathers of some mainstream legal analysts. Some have suggested that CRT methods, including personal narrative, storytelling, and allegory, make it more like art and less like legal critique. A second criticism is that CRT amounts to academic whining by women and minorities (CLS proponents faced this criticism as well). A third issue has been accessibility, with some complaining that CRT is dense and difficult to understand at times.

Criticisms of CRT notwithstanding, it remains a rich, incisive, and vibrant method of legal analysis. The uniqueness of the CRT approach is that its proponents refuse to rely on the dominant paradigm to critique legal doctrine. As important, CRT provides a convincing counterapproach to value-free theory.

Critical race theory has been successful at avoiding some of the pitfalls of the critical legal studies movement. Unlike CLS, a sizable amount of the CRT critique has focused on the criminal justice system. In an analysis of the costs of street crime and white-collar crime, Delgado (1995) concludes that white-collar crime exacts a greater toll on American society. He evaluates and compares the cost of physical injury, death, and economic harm caused by both types of criminal activity.

Austin (1992) has explored how blacks are stereotyped as criminal and how this affects their participation in the open market. Specifically, Austin's analysis evaluates how blacks, compared with whites, are treated by staff and security in commercial businesses. She concludes that blacks regularly encounter subtle discrimination and that this harms blacks as well as whites.

Numerous other critical race theorists have written on criminal law issues. Beyond the CRT analyses that directly address criminal law and justice, a sizable body of work analyzes areas of law that impact the justice system. For example, critiques of the public discourse on "blackness" invariably raise issues of crime, deviance, and justice (for example, Addis, 1993; Williams, 1987). Likewise, analyses of antidiscrimination laws raise criminal law issues (for instance, Crenshaw et al., 1995).

Although CRT has developed a more thorough critique of criminal law than CLS, there is still room for a more comprehensive critique. Critical race theorists should examine criminal law and justice issues for at least two reasons.

First, minorities are overrepresented in the criminal justice system as both victims and offenders. Since one of the central goals of CRT is to effect change, analyses of the criminal justice system have the power to provide the biggest "bang" for the CRT "buck." Second, the criminal justice system is the legal arena that garners the lion's share of public and media attention. Because crime and justice are topics that are widely discussed, numerous opportunities are available for critical race analyses to affect public discussion.

In recent years, the CRT critique has expanded to explore other issues related to race and the law. It has been broadened to assess how the law impacts people of all racial groups. One of the criticisms of CRT has been that it frames race as a "black/white" issue and that its racial critiques focus almost exclusively on how blacks fare in the legal system. Today, however, a growing body of CRT literature looks at "whiteness." For example, in "Whiteness as Property," Harris (1994) examines the white skin privileges (including social, political and economic benefits) that accrue to whites. Critical race theory has also broadened its critique of "minorities" to include Latinos, Latinas, Asians, and Native Americans. This expanded analysis of race is partly due to the diversity of scholars who take part in critical race analysis. Additionally, CRT has tackled issues of sexual preference and how the law supports heterosexual privilege.

CRITICAL RACE ANALYSES: TWO APPLICATIONS

The following discussion is offered to further illuminate how a critical race critique can be used to analyze criminology and criminal justice issues. Similar to mainstream legal analyses, a CRT analysis can be applied to any area of law. Perhaps the most important contribution that CRT makes to legal analyses is that it creates new areas of inquiry. Critical race theory is not simply a twist on mainstream analysis. The critical race critique looks for missing links in dominant legal analysis. It seeks to resolve these gaps and explain why and how mainstream analysis does not adequately address them.

The Case of Interracial Crime

It is notable that many of the crime stories that reach national attention involve interracial offenses. Table 9.1 provides a list of some of the crime stories that have seized national headlines in the last decade. As the table indicates, many of these stories, now etched firmly into our public conscience, have an interracial face. More pointedly, many of the cases involve a black offender and a white victim. The O. J. Simpson case is only one case in a long history of cases that involves a black defendant and a white victim. Further, most of these cases involve a black male offender and a white victim.

Although official data establish that interracial crime is not commonplace, the picture of interracial criminality is overrepresented in the news. In turn,

**Table 9.1 Offender and Victim Races
in National Crime Stories**

	Minority Offender	White Offender
Minority Victim	Clarence Thomas	Jeffrey Dahmer
	Mike Tyson	Berhard Goetz
		Rodney King
White Victim	Reginald Denny	Ted Bundy
	Colin Ferguson	*Jenny Jones* murder
	Michael Jackson	William Kennedy Smith
	O. J. Simpson	
	Susan Smith*	
	Charles Stuart*	

*These cases were racial hoaxes (see the text). Initial reports about these cases involved a claim by a white person that he or she had been victimized by a black person. This claim was later determined to be false.

these images have had a disproportionate impact on our perceptions of race, crime, and justice. It is not surprising, therefore, that polls show that many whites wrongly fear that they face the greatest threat of victimization at the hands of a black offender. This widespread fear attests to the impact that news of interracial crimes have had on the public psyche.

The constant media attention given to interracial crimes, combined with the public's fascination with these offenses, offers a useful backdrop for a discussion of how perceptions of racial justice are influenced by the race of the offender and race of the victim. As noted earlier, issues of gender also play a role. If racial justice is at stake, larger issues of social justice also hang in the balance. The important issue is whether the media's disproportionate emphasis on interracial crime involving white victims and black offenders operates to impede racial justice and, therefore, social justice. Critical race scholars have examined the indicators of racial bias in the law, including the impact of race of the victim. Studies consistently show that criminal penalties are most harsh when there is a white victim and a black offender.

Race-of-victim analysis has been made most acutely in death penalty cases. This analyses is most notable in *McCleskey v. Kemp,* 481 U.S. 279 (1987). This case involved a black offender, Warren McCleskey, who was convicted and sentenced to death for killing a white police officer. McCleskey offered overwhelming data to establish that under Georgia law an offender convicted of killing a white person was substantially more likely to receive the death penalty than someone convicted of killing a black person. The United States Supreme Court, unpersuaded by the statistical data, upheld the sentence of death. The Court gave short shrift to compelling empirical evidence that showed that in 22 percent of the cases involving a black offender and a white victim, there was a sentence of death, compared with 3 percent for cases involving a white offender and a black victim. A critical race analysis of the research findings and the Supreme Court's holding have unmasked the Court's reluctance to accord black and white victims equal weight (Johnson, 1988; Russell, 1994).

Returning to Table 9.1, we might first ask whether the race of the victim and offender impacts our thinking about punishment. A critical race analysis suggests that because whiteness is more valuable than blackness, white victims will receive more heightened concern and media attention than black victims. Therefore, it is not surprising that interracial crimes with a white victim garner a sizable amount of media attention. Although these cases are by definition atypical, since most involve well-known, celebrity defendants/parties, they are useful at assessing societal attitudes about race and crime. Because the cases were played out on a national screen, they have become part of our national consciousness and imagery about race and crime.

Racial Hoaxes

Racial hoaxes offer another prism through which to view interracial crime—how it is treated by the media and the criminal justice system. Racial hoaxes occur when one person accuses another person of a crime because of that individual's race—when someone says that he fell victim to crime at the hands of a black person, for example. In some instances the racial hoax is used as a cover-up for an actual crime; in others no crime has occurred. The most well-known racial hoaxes are the Susan Smith and Charles Stuart cases. In the first case, Smith, the mother of two young boys, told police that she had been carjacked by a young, black man. According to Smith, the man forced her out of her car and drove off with her two young children. A massive search by federal and state officials was launched. Nine days later, Smith confessed to murdering her two sons by drowning them in a lake. She was later found guilty of the murders and sentenced to life in prison.

In the second case, Charles Stuart claimed that he and his wife, returning home from a birthing class, were shot and robbed by a black male jogger. Stuart's wife and unborn child died following the attack. It was later discovered that Stuart had committed the murders and fabricated the "criminal black man" story to conceal his crimes, scheming to cash in on his wife's sizable life insurance policy.

The Smith and Stuart cases are notable because of the press coverage and police attention they received. However, more than forty other racial hoaxes involving a white perpetrator and black victim have been reported. Some argue that because racial hoaxes cause numerous social and economic harms, they should be subject to criminal penalty (Russell, 1996).

The study of racial hoaxes provides a look at how the media simultaneously portrays, perpetuates, and creates deviant images of blackness. The rampant criminal images of blacks, particularly of young black men, are partly responsible for the acute level of fear that many whites experience when dealing with black men.

CONCLUSION

Critical race theory operates as a check on mainstream legal analyses. It provides more than an alternative viewpoint on legal doctrine; it seeks to raise questions about the law's operation and what this reflects. The CRT critique is valuable beyond its challenge to the dominant legal paradigm. Critical race scholars, using various methods of legal analysis, are committed to reducing bias and achieving social justice. This theory/practice link sets CRT apart from mainstream legal methods. Insofar as CRT works toward racial justice it moves us one step closer toward social justice.

REVIEW QUESTIONS

1. How is CLS different from CRT?

2. What are the goals of CRT?

3. Are there other, more preferable ways to achieve the goals of CRT?

4. What are some of the essential elements of the critical race method of legal analysis?

5. How does the CRT method of legal analysis compare with conventional legal inquiry?

6. Select one issue in criminal justice/criminology and state how a critical race analysis would be useful.

7. How does a CRT method of legal analysis advance our understanding of such criminal justice problems as interracial crime and racial hoaxes?

REFERENCES

Addis, A. (1993). "Hey man, they did invent us": The mass media law, and African Americans. *Buffalo Law Review, 41,* 523–626.

Austin, R. (1992). "The black community," its lawbreakers, and a politics of identification. *Southern California Law Review, 65,* 1769–1817.

Bell, D. (1992). *Faces at the bottom of the well.* New York: Basic Books.

Calmore, J. (1992). Critical race theory, Archie Shepp and fire music: Securing an authentic intellectual life in a multicultural world. *Southern California Law Review, 65,* 2129–2130.

Carrington, P. D. (1984). Of the law and the river. *Journal of Legal Education, 34,* 222–239.

Crenshaw, K., Gotanda, N., Peller, G., & Thomas, K. (1995). *Critical race theory: The key writings that formed the movement.* New York: New Press.

Delgado, R. (1995). *The Rodrigo chronicles.* New York: New York University Press.

Floyd, J. (1995). The other box: Intersectionality and the O. J. Simpson trial. *Hastings Women's Law Journal, 6,* 241–274.

Fuller, L. (1949). The Speluncean explorers. *Harvard Law Review 62,* 616–645.

Harris, C. I. (1994). Whiteness as property. *Harvard Law Review 106,* 1707–1791.

Johnson, S. (1988). Unconscious racism and the criminal law. *Cornell Law Review, 73,* 1013.

Lee, C. K. Y. (1995). Beyond black and white: Racializing Asian Americans in a society obsessed with O.J. *Hastings Women's Law Journal, 6,* 165.

Matsuda, M. (1993). Public response to racist hate speech: Considering the victim's story. In M. Matsuda, C. Lawrence, R. Delgado K. Crenshaw (Eds.), *Words that wound* (p. 17–51).

Russell, K. K. (1994). A critical view from the inside: An application of critical legal studies to criminal law. *Journal of Criminal Law and Criminology, 85,* 222–240.

Russell, K. K. (1996). The racial hoax as crime: The law as affirmation. *Indiana Law Journal, 71,* 594–621.

Taub, N., & Schneider, E. (1991). Women's subordination and the role of law. In D. Kairys (Ed.), *The politics of law* (pp. 151–176). New York: Basic Books.

Valdes, F. (1995). Queers, sissies, dykes and tomboys: Deconstructing the conflation of "sex," "gender" and "sexual orientation" in Euro-American law and society. *California Law Review, 83,* 3–337.

Williams, P. (1987). Spirit-murdering the messenger: The discourse of finger-pointing as the law's response to racism. *University of Miami Law Review, 42,* 127–157.

Chaos Theory
and Social Justice

C haos theory maintains that all systems, including social systems, are based on a mixture of order and disorder, predictability and unpredictability. In this chapter, Young considers how nonlinear dynamics or principles of chaos theory help further our understanding of social justice. Looking at complex, highly differentiated adaptive societies such as the United States, he argues that criminal justice efforts at control, regulation, order, and precision cannot account for the increasing degrees of disorder that exist in everyday life. Young demonstrates this in his account of police work, court procedures, and sentencing and probation decision making. He argues that notions of crime, law, and deviance need to move away from criminal justice toward social justice. According to chaos theory, uncertainty, randomness, flux, absurdity, chance, and irony are apart of living and being human. A nonlinear notion of social justice embodies these features of interactional life. These features, too, must be expressed through a society's laws and system of punishments.

10

A Nonlinear Theory of Justice

Affirmative Moments
in Postmodern Criminology

T. R. YOUNG

Chaos theory has much to offer as a framework for developing a philosophy of justice (Young, 1992, 1997). Contrary to both modern and the more nihilistic forms of postmodern thought, many features of chaos theory offer several possible foundations for a theory of justice. In this chapter, I look at some of these features and suggest what a distinctly affirmative, postmodern theory of justice might have to offer the quest for a peaceable and just society.

This exploration of chaos theory and justice contrasts greatly with modernist theories of the state since these latter are based on the enthusiasms of the Enlightenment for precise knowledge and tight control of both nature and society (Arrigo & Young, 1996). Political philosophy since the seventeenth century has been predicated on the Newtonian idea that physical, natural, and social science can reveal absolute, eternal, and universal laws of nature, life, and society on which to ground both law and justice. The great successes of Newtonian physics led and still lead many since Hegel to argue that the natural order of the universe carries over to human affairs. The quest for justice becomes a quest for conformity and control, precision and predictability, reason and regulation.

The Hegelian premise states the following: the state is to embody whatever rationality is possible in social life. Rationality becomes an instrument and is limited to the search for effective ways to ensure conformity to state law itself informed by enlightened social scientists. The postmodern critique of modern law sees the foundations of modern law and the use of state power as arbitrary exercises that benefit Euro-American culture in the first instance and the political economy of private ownership in the second instance.

Thus, postmodern concerns with the concept of justice are embedded in the larger questions of politics and political economy. In more affirmative postmodern groundings of the justice concept, distributive justice takes priority over retributive justice. In this chapter, I want to show how the quest for justice may, to some degree, be grounded on chaos theory and nonlinear social dynamics. The case is, in brief, that a mix of order and disorder is more congenial to the human project than is the modernist quest for, and only for, order. At the same time, I want to counter the postmodern tendency to dismiss the knowledge process as hopelessly contaminated by position and power. First let me offer a word about justice.

SOME ASSUMPTIONS OF CHAOS THEORY: ON COMPLEX ADAPTIVE SYSTEMS

Chaos theory upsets modernist claims of universal law with its predictability and possibilities of close control. This new science reveals a changing mix of order and disorder in all complex physical, natural, and social systems. In chaos theory, a complex system is one with three or more variables. The formal differences between simple and complex societies have not been worked out since research has not been formally undertaken. A complex society, however, would be one with four or more social differentiations (for example, class, age, gender, ethnicity, education, occupation).

Not only is disorder essential to all existing systems, but chaos theory further confounds modernist theories of politics and social life by revealing that disorder has many positive consequences, while order becomes a form of death in the present and future life of that system. In a word, complex societies require deviance, dissipation, and rearrangement of its social forms. The aim of this chapter, then, is to help build a well-tempered affirmative postmodern conception of justice on which political philosophy and practice can be judged and justified. To build a much more open and affirmative theory of justice, let us begin with the very concept of justice.

On the Concept of Justice

The root of the word *justice* comes from the Latin: *ius* = right or the law— that which is right and proper in terms of a given set of principles. For most of human history, justice meant rewards and punishments oriented to the requirements and proscriptions of a religious system. If one conforms to those divine laws, *jus divinum,* given by one's gods, then one can justify the rewards that ensue. Conversely, if one fails to conform to divine law, then one has no grounds for making claims for either social honor or material wealth. Simple societies, in a fairly stable environment, can solve the problems of survival by the use of negative feedback loops with which to discourage innovative behavior. Complex societies in a constantly changing environment require theory and practices of law and justice that embody nonlinearity.

In his theory of justice, Rawls (1972) comes close to the argument presented here. Rather than appeal to universal law, divine law, natural law, or historical codes, as do most legal theorists, Rawls asks people to put aside their own special statuses and privileges and consider grounding their theory of justice on a "fairness" principle. The principle is grounded, in turn, on the assumption that all social wealth is a collective legacy and should be distributed equally. The variation on a Rawlsian theory of justice, derived from chaos/complexity theory, is that variations in wealth, status, and power are tolerable—indeed, sometimes helpful to the general good. Rawls's (1972) theory provides for this inequality in his claim that "unequal distribution is justified [only] when it is in the interest of those 'least favored'" (p. 302).

In this theory of distributive justice, there is no particular need to justify inequality; the concern is with the magnitude of inequality. Ratios of 2, 4, 8, and even 16 to 1 in wealth or political power should have no adverse effect on the common good. However, when inequalities in wealth are greater, chaos theory suggests that greater and ever more unpredictable fluctuations in economic, political, and social life may well ensue.

According to one of chaos theory's principles of nonlinear dynamics, the preceding situation produces *bifurcations.* A bifurcation is a point at which two or more outcomes become possible for any given system. In the case of wealth, two distinctly different life chances emerge with the first bifurcation; life chances become ever more different with each successive bifurcation. Feigenbaum (1978) discovered that, with each bifurcation or doubling, there is a distinct change from one behavioral regime to a new one for all systems affected by one or more key parameters. After the third bifurcation in key parameter(s), the system tends to move in ways that fill the space available to it in an outcome basin. This latter state is a far from stable chaotic state. I assume that inequalities in wealth lead to greater disorder in the making and enforcement of laws. In chaos theory, a fourth bifurcation does propel a system toward deep chaos. As we shall see, whereas some disorder is helpful to a justice system, too much interferes with ordinary social processes essential to the human project.

On Justice in Complex Adaptive Societies

Rather than retributive justice procedures aimed at reproducing existing social forms, affirmative postmodern social policies are aimed at social justice. As Pepinsky and Quinney (1991) have put it, peacekeeping is the task of both criminology as a discipline and the justice system as a social institution. These processes are often called *distributive systems* or, in the language of those hostile to distributive justice patterns, *redistributive justice.* For conservatives, the idea is that some people possess wealth, status, and power as a natural right, that any state engagement in present patterns of distribution constitute interference with the natural/divine order of things.

Postmodern sensibility, on the other hand, is sharply critical of natural right theory especially when it is used to endorse domination or exploitation. Great inequalities in social honor, wealth, or social power are held to be the residue of past and present conquests, systems of domination, special privilege, and/or strategic advantage in the social location of time and space. In place of such prior advantages to given groups, classes, nations, or genders, affirmative postmodern justice claims are seen to be based on changeable, limited combinations of rights, obligations, needs, and desires. It is the ratio of inequality and the fixity of inequality that is of special interest to a postmodern theory of justice.

PRINCIPLES OF CHAOS THEORY: MIXTURES OF ORDER AND DISORDER

A complex adaptive society cannot afford magnitudes of disorder that exceed the capacity of human beings to share ideas, plan, act together, and judge and learn from successes and failures. Indeed, complex systems survive because they are learning systems. At the same time, too much order defeats communication, experimentation, innovation, and thus survival. The just society in a changing environment is a society that mixes order and disorder in those ratios permitting both dependable yet flexible processes. Postmodern expressions in the sociology of law and justice incorporate that mixture in its theory and practice.

For our purposes, one of the features of chaos theory is that the mixture of order and disorder comes in different packages. Figure 10.1 displays the patterns/mixtures of order/disorder on which we can build a postmodern theory of justice. For the criminologist, the middle three regions are of special interest. Each region has its own unique mixture of order and disorder marked by the bifurcation points clearly seen in this display (called, in the literature, a *bifurcation map*). As we proceed, we do well to remember that different routines in the justice system call for orientation to different patterns or regimes of order-disorder.

Chaos theory suggests that chaordic regimes with from four to sixteen dynamic regimes (called *attractors*) suffice to provide the necessary adaptive requirements of most social processes.* We will use the concept of "chaordic" to refer to those regimes that serve the human interest in both order and variety. These are found in a limited area around the fourth change point in the bifurcation map depicted in Figure 10.1. In this region, one finds from $4n$ to sixteen dynamic regimes (that is, some regimes have four regions of order; some have eight regions in which a given system may be found; some have up to sixteen outcome states). Preference for one and only one "natural" state in human affairs is not supported by the behaviors of actually existing systems. Indeed, order is very unusual in natural and social systems.

Social regimes in regions 1, 2, and often 3 do not provide the necessary variety for a complex system to adapt to the great variety found in its environment. Dynamic regimes in region 5, a region of deep chaos, do not entail the necessary order for planning, coordinating, understanding, and wisely using time and energy. Complex adaptive systems require both order and disorder in changing mix. Justice, in such a milieu, must accommodate chaordic regimes in politics, policing, and adjudication as well as rehabilitation.

---

*The term *chaordic* comes from Dee Hock, former CEO of the Visa Company. Uri Merry was kind enough to provide me with the idea. In this work, it refers to the regions of order/disorder between the third and fifth bifurcations on the map in Figure 10.1. This region includes a complex outcome basin with between two and sixteen wings/attractors.

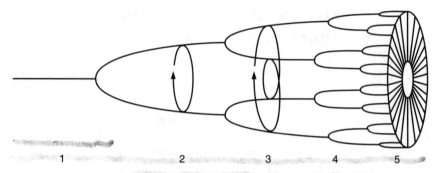

FIGURE 10.1 Mixtures of Order and Disorder for a Postmodern Theory of Justice

The need for chaordic regimes can be seen in language. Adaptability requires but four to eight meanings for the same word; fewer meanings than four explode the number of words required to communicate; more meanings than sixteen explode the amount of discussion necessary to explain oneself. Four to eight age grades suffice to ground the transition from childhood to adulthood; fewer age grades force young people into adult roles before they are quite prepared; more grades postpone adulthood far beyond the physical, mental, and psychological potentials of people. Four to eight genders serve the human need for pairing and intimacy; fewer limit desire and greatly expand the growth of underground structures, some of which can be very ugly to the human project. More than sixteen gendering nominations entail so much variety that the investment of love and desire escape the social process and become purely private matters.

CHAOS AND THE PRACTICE OF JUSTICE:
CRIMINAL JUSTICE APPLICATIONS

In chaos theory, then, one finds not one dynamic regime but, for our purposes, some five distinct and very different regimes. Contrary to modernist theories, one and only one outcome is not the natural state of a complex system, nor can theories of justice or deviancy be predicated on some one outcome pattern. Any legal system that presumes there is only one way to do marriage, sex, religion, economics, or politics flies in the face of the natural complexity of social systems.

In the map in Figure 10.1, the first two regimes are very ordered, but they apply only to very simple systems. For complex systems, though, there is a changing parade of dynamic regimes in which order gives over to uncertainty. However, even in the most complex dynamic regimes with hundreds and thousands of hidden patterns of behavior, still one finds order. With order comes the possibility of new ways of life and living that, in chaos theory, serve a most valuable role. In a complex world, only chaotic regimes can cope with chaos. Order becomes a distinct liability to individuals, organizations, groups, and whole societies. A theory of justice founded on the quest and imposition of order becomes itself a liability to the human project.

In the following discussion, I will use this basic idea to assess policies and practices in policing, courtroom deliberations, juridical dispositions, as well as selected institutions oriented to control and incarceration. Again, the idea is, in brief, that a postmodern theory of justice requires a changing mix of order and disorder in constitutions, codes, statutes, and judgments in court. Justice ceases to be the simple and rational application of given laws to given cases but becomes the explication of wisdom and judgment by both judge and jury.

On Criminal Justice Procedures

The first two regimes in Figure 10.1 constitute a model for a few processes in criminal justice procedures. The collection of evidence, the chain of evidence, the scientific analysis of evidence, and forensic testimony at trial are best done when they approximate the precision and exactitude of the point attractor found in region 1 of the map. It is this dynamic regime in which certainty of guilt or innocence can be determined. Other kinds of evidence fit the second regime. It is in the second regime that, for the first time, one meets a bit of uncertainty. Such things as fingerprints, blood types, genetic mappings, barrel riflings, tire prints, and/or fiber analysis can approach certainty but some small region for doubt remains. In the case of one's opportunity to commit a crime, regions of still greater disorder emerge.

Order is not the hallmark of postmodern juridical procedures. The specification of indictments, the organization of evidence, the presentation of a case to a court, the rulings by a judge, and the deliberations of a jury all exhibit disorder. When one leaves behind the simple dynamics of physical evidence and turns to the actions of human beings, chaordic regimes emerge. This is neither good nor bad; it simply is how things function in matters of legal procedure. In criminal and civil justice proceedings, one must expect and accommodate both law and sanction to the chaordic nature of this and other justice systems.

On Nonlinear Policing

Police officers have been, with the modernization of large urban departments, reduced to technical instruments of bureaucratic rules and routines. Policing philosophy, predicated on chaos theory, requires the officer to be much more insightful and flexible in his or her duties. Armed with court rulings about procedures, warnings, sequential actions, and prohibitions, police officers must stay in close contact with a hierarchical organization and check back and forth continuously to ensure rules are observed and policies are honored.

The postmodern police officer is very much like his or her premodern predecessor: flexible, open to explanation, able to turn a blind eye to much that, in a rational policing system, must be subject to official action. The difference is that while the premodern police officer is committed to given kin, ethnic, gender, and class arrangements, the postmodern police officer must look beyond status characteristics of the parties concerned and focus on questions of personal welfare and public peace. As long as the behavior in question is not immediately harmful to the police officer or others, tolerance takes precedence. As long as the person in question does not make a career of theft, public nuisance, or personal animus, patience is preferred.

To be sure, this flexibility means that "fairness" ceases to be central to the conduct of the officers concerned. One cannot treat each person exactly as one treats every other person. Each case, each behavior, occurs within a larger behavioral and social context that must be weighed by the officers concerned, who make a best guess on the spot. Wisdom and prudence mean that the officer concerned must know his or her precinct very, very well and know, to some extent, the persons within it.

Impersonality, exchangeability, rotations to other precincts, remote monitoring, rapid movement through large districts, close oversight by inspectors, detailed written records of every event at close time intervals, and so forth, are contrary to postmodern policing practices. These are the essence of modernist/rationalist efforts to control. However, strict applications, impersonal treatments, standardized responses, and uniform codes require an ever growing monitoring system and an increasing police presence. As a part of the whole society, control institutions come to require greater portions of community resources. And, as we shall see, they do not produce the kind of law and order for which they are meant.

Many thoughtful critics will protest that such discretion provides the opportunity for misfeasance of duty by the officer on the beat. That point is true enough, but what is said of the officer on the beat is also true of those who have close responsibility for the shift, the division, the precinct, and the department as a whole. Wisdom and judgment must be informed by intimate knowledge of the police officers concerned. Charges can be made against delinquent officers, but, again, such charges must be tempered with an understanding of the officer, the beat, and the history of both.

A CHAOTIC SYSTEM
OF (CRIMINAL) JUSTICE

On Fractal Policing Structures

A fractal policing system is a fuzzy system. It has loose and changing boundaries. It is open to and merges with other social institutions. In postmodern policing structures, the police function is shared out to taxi drivers, mail delivery persons, shopkeepers, freeway drivers, and others whose business takes them to the public domain. With high-tech communications capacity, each person in the public domain can be part of the process by which social behavior can be kept within the bounds marked by judgment and good sense.

The relocation of the policing function depends on cooperation. Policing practices that reproduce inequality, discrimination, and ethnic privilege are hostile toward cooperation. Social justice is key to the development of a fractal policing structure. Each cab driver, each citizen with a wireless phone, each truck driver, and each resident in an ethnic community must know that he or she is well served by both the criminal justice system and the social justice system. They are twinned sources of citizen participation in a peaceable society. They cannot be delinked by simply calling for cooperation.

On Chaos and the Prosecuting Attorney's Office

In most American cities and counties, the office of the prosecuting attorney is evaluated, in part, by its routines. In a modernist worldview, indictments must consistently follow given kinds of behaviors. In the quest for technical justice (that is, a just application of rules), procedural safeguards exist to protect the accused from arbitrary or personal use of social power. An affirmative postmodern criminology oriented to peacekeeping would respect such procedures and urge close compliance to them.

Where the office of the prosecuting attorney is elective, reelection often lurks behind prosecutorial decisions: weak cases are dismissed unless racism or ethnic pride fuels prosecution, and strong cases are deflected if wealth or power is brought to bear. A methodological stance close to the ordered end of the chaordic map seems appropriate to the ends of criminal justice.

On Chaos and the Courtroom

The court itself is caught up in several incompatible legal traditions that move the actual hearing toward deep chaos. A body of common law is based on precedent to which defense, prosecution, judge, and jury can refer. Statutory law may require entirely new procedures and groundings for judgments. Differing norms in every court, district, and state produce even more complex dynamics in the criminal justice system. Again, race, class, age, gender, and other status assignments compound that complexity. The situation is not that such complexity should be simplified but rather that wisdom and judgment should mediate the operation of such self-similar or qualitatively different legal norms.

In our legal system, the judge is the arbiter of what substantive rationality exists while in the courtroom. A strong norm permits the jury to take control of the proceedings and make judgments that are not within the range of those set by the judge, but most juries do not know, nor are they appraised of such regions in their deliberations.

It is the mechanical application of rules in the criminal justice system against which an affirmative postmodern criminology sets itself. Avenues for creative policing, legal rulings, and jury deliberations also serve the larger ends of justice and should not be lightly or routinely set aside.

On Chaos and Nonlinear Judgments

A modernist approach to both policing and sentencing would call for similar treatment for similar offenses. Postmodern sensibility calls for a short list of qualitatively different dispositions of similar cases. It well may be the case that for most decisions, similarity best serves concern for substantive justice. Yet, in some cases, creative disposition may work best for a peaceable society. Mercy, forgiveness, forbearance, forgetfulness, and compassion are embodiments of nonlinear disposition of wrongs, torts, and even serious crimes.

The assumption here is that learning is not linear and that increase in pain does not bring forth decrease in harmful behavior. Often, mercy is a better teacher to those who have yet to learn to honor the status given to them in a given social order. Learning often transcends both reward and punishment. Most religions around the world incorporate this insight into their theology. Chaordic systems would do well to do the same.

On Chaos and Dispositions of Offenders

The general question to which the postmodern court must address itself is which option, among a limited variety, is right and just for the case at hand. Again, two, four, or eight standard dispositions are preferable to one and only one, and this variety is preferable to sixteen or more. Standardized, mandatory sentencing ignores too much in the personal history of the offender, the social history of his or her family, and the larger social context that affects outcomes in disposition. A disposition chart with sixteen pathways through the criminal justice system is probably too complex and too susceptible to the kind of unfairness grounds (rightly so) appeals as well as existential anger for those whose lives are so determined.

It is the social context to which the well-tempered postmodern criminologist must give the most attention. Probation officers and social workers can best inquire into the personal history, social context, and family and friendship resources of a person adjudged guilty or responsible for a given crime. Criminologists have a larger task that is no less important. It is to work toward an equitable social peace. Generally, this means working for social justice.

SUMMARY: FROM CRIMINAL
JUSTICE TO SOCIAL JUSTICE

A recurrent theme in this chapter and this book has been that social justice is preferable to criminal justice as a pathway to a peaceable society. Social justice is more humane and less costly than the correction of crime. And it is more effective than the expansion of police, court, prison, and probation agencies. There is much merit in both conservative and liberal efforts to control crime within the existing structures of racism, growing class inequality, and a violence-driven patriarchy that both degrades and brutalizes the men and women caught up in it.

We know the structural features of low-crime societies. The short version of that agenda is that if we are to reduce crime, social policy must be informed by the kind of human rights and human obligations set forth by the United Nations Universal Declaration of Human Rights or some version of it (Kamenka & Erh-Soon Tay, 1978). If we are to reduce international crime in both its political and economic dimensions, foreign policy concerns in the Western countries must be informed by the same human rights and human obligations. The boundaries of social space must expand to include all peoples while aggressive nationalism must be reduced.

Yet the concept of a *universal* set of human rights does not sit well within postmodern sensibility. It would take a special, nonlinear declaration to accommodate the great variety of cultural practices now embedded in human societies around the world. Chaos theory does give us some guide in this endeavor. In brief, fractal and fairly autonomous social systems are the repository of such diversity.

The proper agenda of an affirmative postmodern criminology includes a transition to a peaceable, praxis-oriented society, and, ultimately, a just world system predicated on both change and tradition. This agenda is intrinsic to a democratic socialist program for crime prevention, crime control, and the repair of existing structures of crime that will, over the long run, help each child realize the fullness of his or her humanity; that will provide each adult with the social means to remain a respected and esteemed member of the human species; that will provide the ultrastability for even the smallest society. As we enter the twenty-first century, this is the proper study of criminology.

There will always be cases of murder most foul. There will always be theft and the privatized use of public goods. Rape, arson, bribery, and embezzlement will be with us to the end of human history. These are variables. They increase and decrease with the state of the social order. Many of the suggestions from conservatives and liberals are helpful as a short-term response to crime, whereas most of the democratic socialist proposals are designed to lower crime rates in the long term, well into the twenty-first century.

REVIEW QUESTIONS

1. What are the characteristics of conventional "modernist" models of (criminal) justice?

2. How does postmodern affirmative justice theory differ from modernist conceptions of justice?

3. What are the essential principles of chaos theory as presented in this chapter?

4. What do these essential principles of chaos theory tell us about post-

modern conceptions of social justice?

5. What are attractors, bifurcations, and fractals? According to chaos theory, what do these concepts tell us about social justice?

6. How can police practice, judicial procedures, and probation work advance the tenets of chaos theory?

REFERENCES

Arrigo, B., & Young, T. R. (1996). Chaos, complexity and crime: Working tools for a postmodern criminology. In B. MacLean & D. Milovanovic (Eds.), *Thinking critically about crime* (pp. 77–84). Vancouver: Collective Press.

Feigenbaum, M. (1978). Quantitative universality for a class of nonlinear transformations. *Journal of Statistical Physics, 19,* 25–52.

Kamenka, E., & Erh-Soon Tay, A. (Eds.). (1978). *Human rights: Ideas and ideologies.* London: Arnold.

Pepinsky, H., & Quinney, R. (Eds.). (1991). *Peacemaking in criminology.* Bloomington: Indiana University Press.

Rawls, J. (1972). *A theory of justice.* Cambridge, MA: Harvard University Press.

Young, T. R. (1992). Chaos theory and human agency. *Humanity and Society, 16*(4), 441–460.

Young, T. R. (1997). The ABCs of crime: Attractors, bifurcations and chaos. In D. Milovanovic (Ed.), *Chaos, criminology and social justice* (pp. 77–96) New York: Greenwood.

Catastrophe/Topology
Theory and Social Justice

C atastrophe theory originated in the natural and physical sciences, especially through geometry and other mathematical disciplines. It is a methodology for understanding how systems (for example, prisons, courts, hospitals) respond to changes or events, especially those that are more unpredictable, unplanned, and uncoordinated. Catastrophe theory is linked to topology theory. Topology theory provides several conceptual models through which the methodology unfolds and testable hypotheses develop. In this chapter, Milovanovic relies heavily on the science of catastrophe and topology theory to advance our understanding of social justice. Specifically, he considers how one topological construct (the "butterfly catastrophe" in five-dimensional space) is useful in mapping out a peace discourse that contributes to diffusing and "deescalating" situations of interpersonal conflict and/or violence. Milovanovic reminds us that he is not describing a macrolevel analysis akin to those found in broader Marxist critiques but, rather, a microlevel response to situational pain and suffering. The author is especially interested in developing a "third way"—that is, a method for creating stability during situations of relational violence when the disputing parties assume two very extreme, often hostile, positions. The author comments on the limitations of both the "accommodating" and "peacemaking" approaches. He then explains the elements of the butterfly catastrophe. Milovanovic particularly points out how a "pocket of compromise" can stably emerge, thereby promoting a "third way," or a sustainable option, to interpersonal violence. The author then applies the butterfly catastrophe formula to advances in postmodern criminology. This is what he means when describing the creation of a "peace rhetoric." These are discourses that transcend the limits of the entrenched "either/or" polarized positions that often end violently. These are discourses that seek to create new vocabularies of meaning when conflict occurs—multiple vocabularies more fully affirming of the different ways of knowing that people embody. Thus, these are languages that promote peace, social justice, and nonviolence through a critically aware topological consciousness.

11

Catastrophe Theory, Discourse, and Conflict Resolution

Generating the "Third Way"

DRAGAN MILOVANOVIC

Interpersonal violence often arises from spiraling emotional states that abruptly end in nonlinear ways. This article seeks to develop some vistas for an alternative. How does the "third way" develop out of seemingly mutually incompatible positions? Suggestive for how this might take place is catastrophe theory (Thom, 1975; Zeeman, 1976, 1977). Thom developed the mathematics and the topological diagrams for the various catastrophe models in the late 1960s early 1970s. Zeeman provided it with a more popular reception with his article on the subject in *Scientific America* (1976). Elsewhere we have argued that catastrophe theory is one of the constitutive threads of postmodern analysis, the other most prominent threads being psychoanalytic semiotics, chaos theory, and topology theory (Milovanovic, 1995).

There has been little applied scholarship on catastrophe theory in the social science literature; however, much can be learned by its topological portrayal of nonlinear developments in systems otherwise linear in orientation. This chapter explores and recommends possible alternative ways to "freeze" spiraling emotional states that often lead to abrupt violent endings. Topology theory, then, is useful for developing insights on how this may be. Elsewhere we have investigated how one topological construct in catastrophe theory, that of the "cusp catastrophe" in three-dimensional space (hereafter, 3D), can be used to gain understanding of the onset of some forms of interpersonal violence (Milovanovic, 1996). In this chapter, we want to develop and apply the "butterfly catastrophe" in five-dimensional topological space (5D) and indicate how it provides some clues to deescalation. We want to indicate how a peace discourse or peace rhetoric can offset, to some extent, the spiraling phenomena.

This chapter, then, endeavors to provide some advances in peacemaking and social justice. Thus far, the literature has been rather sparse as to the application of catastrophe theory, particularly the butterfly catastrophe model to the area of peacemaking and social justice. Conspicuously lacking has been any application to the onset and reduction of interpersonal violence. Zeeman (1977) did suggest an application of a cusp catastrophe model to prison disturbances. Others have applied it to management versus worker bargaining (Oliva, Peters, & Murphy, 1981). Still others have employed catastrophe thinking to the collapse of civilizations and the formation of new forms (Casti, 1994, pp. 73–80). It is time to explore the possibilities of applying a butterfly catastrophe model to methods of decreasing interpersonal violence. This will further the contributions in the peacemaking literature.

The use of catastrophe models in the social sciences cannot be used in an overly rigid manner. Algorithms underlying the geometry of the catastrophe models cannot be applied with all the precision of mathematics. At best we have a methodology—that is, critical topological thinking. The various topological constructions (for example, the Klein bottle, the torus, the borromean knot, and mobius band) offer methods for modeling theories, developing new ones, and generating further conceptual insights. Catastrophe theory is also a method for discovery and for the generation of researchable hypotheses. One of its core assumptions is that on the behavioral surface of the various catastrophe models, point attractors are said to exist, except in the folded regions where bimodal or trimodal behavior can take place. In other words, dynamic systems that are mostly linear (or sometimes referred to as continuous or "smooth") are those that are characterized by single outputs given some combination of input variables, except in an area known as the cusp region where more than one output can exist. Chaos theory (see Chapter 10 for more information), on the other hand, indicates that many dynamic systems are characterized by periodic, torus, or strange attractors; that is, given a combination of input variables, the output can have more than one result and indeed can have unpredictable results (Milovanovic, 1996). Although a pattern may exist (global stability), locally, at any instance, the results can be unpredictable. Therefore, in doing research in the application of catastrophe theory one must be very sensitive to the applicability of the various models.

Given that the political economy of our society has structural sources for the pervasive development of interpersonal violence, we make no claim that our suggestions will do away with *all* forms of violence. However, to the extent that catastrophe theory can make a contribution to alleviating some suffering, we find our exercise here quite useful. Social activists are in need of methodologies that advance new macro- and microsociological vistas by which to conceive of social justice. Focusing exclusively on some idealistic macrolevel societal plan by which to transform the political economy while neglecting suffering that continues at the microlevel is not prudent. We must work on both fronts.

BUTTERFLY CATASTROPHE, DISCOURSE, AND CONFLICT REGULATION: PEACEMAKING

Elsewhere we have applied the cusp catastrophe model in explaining how nonlinear dynamics may lie behind the development of various forms of crimes of violence (Milovanovic, 1996). Here we want to show how the butterfly catastrophe could be used to explain how, out of seemingly polarized positions, a "third way" could arise in various conflict situations. This would be an important addition for those who have focused on conflict regulation, mediation, and resolution (Harris, 1988, 1990; Kriesberg, 1991). In *The Behavior of Law,* for example, Black (1976) advocates a "conciliatory style of social control." More recently, a "peacemaking perspective" has been developed within radical criminology (Pepinsky & Quinney, 1991; see also the collection of essays on "peacemaking criminology" in MacLean & Milovanovic, 1996, and Chapter 3 in this volume). Neither the positions by Black nor the peacemaking criminologists, however, have made convincing theoretical forays into how "third positions" develop and how, perhaps, they may attain useful institutional status or a degree of stability in a social setting.

Ultimately, the particular repressive mode of production must change before genuine mediation and social justice can take place. However, we need not wait for the "revolution" while persons are harmfully affected in various interpersonal situations. The analysis that follows also has relevance for certain conceptions of a "superliberal" society envisioned by Unger (1987). His ideal would increase the occasions for conflict; in fact, in his model, conflict would not necessarily be a situation for violence but an opportunity for becoming sensitive to differences, a source of understanding, and an occasion for the development of solidarity. Missing from Unger's vision of the coming utopian society, however, are certain pathways to deescalating the more destructive forms of conflict that lead to spiraling dynamics and, in some instances, violent outcomes.

We have chosen the butterfly catastrophe because it has clear implications for explaining how "third positions" may theoretically develop. This model has been used to explain various results: (1) therapy for anorexia (Zeeman, 1976); (2) how a "chiefdom" could develop as a society moves from a centered to a noncentered type of society (Casti, 1994, pp. 76–77); (3) how compromise opinions emerge in the development of war policy as "hawks" and "doves" seek to achieve their respective policies (Zeeman, 1976, 1977); and (4) how alternatives are generated in the debates between those who advocate censorship versus those who advocate free speech (Zeeman, 1977, pp. 349–356). Clearly, this usage cannot be overly mechanistic. Instead, it serves as a tool for intellectual discovery for more viable alternatives. Critical topological thinking, therefore, provides a methodology for exploring given models, establishing new models, and developing testable hypotheses.

BUTTERFLY CATASTROPHE: ON CONSTRUCTION AND BASIC PRINCIPLES

The construction of the butterfly catastrophe contains several basic principles. Before proceeding, however, it is necessary to provide some background on the cusp catastrophe as it helps our understanding of how the butterfly catastrophe functions.

In deciding whether the cusp catastrophe model is appropriate for the modeling of some phenomena (that is, how systems or events behave), the researcher looks for the following characteristics. If one or more are present, there is a strong possibility that the cusp catastrophe model is the appropriate method to use. The five characteristics are *divergence* (small initial differences, or changes in the control parameter can produce dramatic changes in states or the behavioral surface such as the bifurcation); *catastrophe* (sudden discontinuous jumps in an otherwise dynamic system where point attractors are the norm); *inaccessibility* (the middle pleat in the cusp region indicating neutrality is a highly unlikely even); *bimodality* (periodicity of two, of bimodal behavior in the cusp region where for the same value on some control parameter two results could occur on the behavioral surface); and *hysteresis* (small decreases in a control parameter do not reverse the process when a trajectory has moved from one part of the M-surface, with a jump, to another part of it; a much larger value or magnitude is needed for the normal factor to reverse the process). These concepts are described in more detail later.

In the more simple catastrophe, the so-called *cusp catastrophe model,* we have two control parameters (also called factors or variables) producing a 2D control space (C-space) and one behavioral surface (M-space) reflecting the range of possible behavioral states (see Figure 11.1). Identification of the control variables may take one of two forms. In one form, we may have two control parameters consisting of the *normal factor* (*a*) and the *splitting factor* (*b*). The latter is seen as a moderator that "specifies the conditions under which the normal factor affects the dependent variable continuously or discontinuously" (Baack & Cullen, 1994, p. 214). In other words, as the splitting factor increases in magnitude along with an increase in the normal factor, a bifurcation may be produced called a *divergence.*

Alternatively, in the second form, our two control parameters could be normal factors that are conflictual influences on the behavioral dimension (Zeeman, 1977, pp. 332–333). The vertical axis (x) that runs perpendicular to the control surface represents various outputs, forming at the top a smooth 2D plane, the M-surface. We have identified four possible outputs: endure, escape, agitation, and violent attack. For example, for each intersection of the two control variables (normal factors), we have some state produced on the M-surface represented by a point. Chaos theorists term this a *point attractor.* The totality of points on the M-surface produces the smooth plane with a fold in the middle. Here we have a 3D cusp catastrophe model with a 2D bifurcation set projected onto the control space. The bifurcation set indicates divergence in outcomes. It exists on the M-surface, but can be projected downward onto the C-surface.

In the cusp catastrophe model (see Figure 11.1), we note bimodal behavior in the cusp region where the M-surface folds over itself. For a particular value on the C-surface, we may have two possible behavioral states on the M-surface. This is so because some trajectory along the M-surface (namely, line A to B in Figure 11.1), indicating linear movement toward various states as the changing magnitudes of the two control parameters are having effects, could move, alternatively as in C to D, along this M-surface until it reaches the edge of a curve. Trajectory A′ to B′ represents the intersections of the

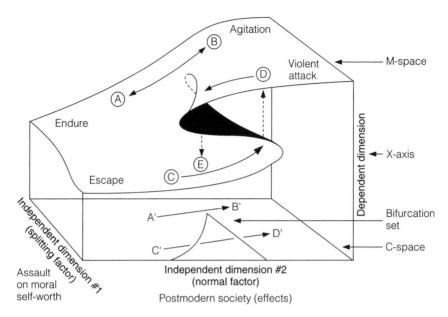

FIGURE 11.1 Cusp Catastrophe Model

control parameter values/magnitudes. A perpendicular line drawn upward from each point along this trajectory connects with the A to B trajectory on the M-surface.

So far there is linear movement and a smooth change from one state to another (that is, from "endure" to "agitation"). However, at the edge of the curve (called a "curve line") it will "jump" to the higher or lower plane (see the projection C to D, in Figure 11.1). The trajectory C′ to D′ on the C-surface represents the plots of the two control parameters as they smoothly increase in value. The "jump" is the catastrophe or discontinuity in an otherwise linear, continuous system. A person is no longer in the "escape" mode but engages in a "violent attack." Outside the cusp region we have one outcome for every interaction between the two control parameters.

Turning now to the butterfly catastrophe, we increase the control parameters to four and maintain one behavioral surface. We now may have trimodal behavior emerging within a "pocket" region. The intersection and interpenetration of several surfaces produces a "pocket" that suggests a butterfly—hence the name for this generic catastrophe. Here we have a 5D model, with a 4D projection of the bifurcation set. Or, worded another way, we have a 4D control space and an additional dimension for the behavioral surface, giving us five dimensions.

This catastrophe cannot be drawn, but we can do two things to simplify it. First, we can take slices, subsets, or sections of the bifurcation set, reducing it first to 3D and then with another slice, to 2D (see Figure 11.2). Second, two of the control parameters, for the sake of illustration, could be suppressed or held

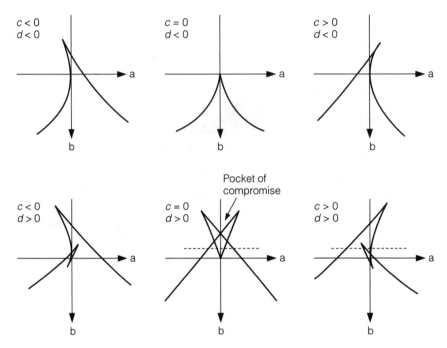

FIGURE 11.2 2D Sections of the Butterfly Catastrophe Bifurcation Set

SOURCE: Adapted from Zeeman (1977, p. 337).

constant (see Figure 11.3). One should note that the 2D slice of the "pocket of compromise" (for example, the third way) is located in the middle portrait of the bottom row of Figure 11.2, and it can be seen again in Figure 11.3 on the bottom 2D surface, the C-surface of the butterfly catastrophe in 3D.

The four control parameters of the butterfly catastrophe include *a*, the normal factor; *b*, the splitting factor; *c*, the *bias factor*; and *d*, the *butterfly factor*. The bias factor alters the shape and position of the cusp. It moves the cusp to the left or to the right, with the vertex pointing the opposite way in each instance (see Figure 11.2; note that in the top left portrait when *c* is less than zero, the cusp opens up, or swings toward the lower right quadrant, while the vertex points to the upper left; see also the upper portrait of Figure 11.4. When *c* is greater than zero, the cusp swings toward the lower left quadrant, while the vertex now points to the upper right; see Figure 11.2 and also the lower portrait in Figure 11.4). The bias factor also effects the behavior surface in an upward or downward direction (see Figure 11.2).

The butterfly factor is what is responsible for the third stable form of behavior; it is what makes the outcome trimodal. As the value for the butterfly factor increases, the cusp located on the M-surface develops into three cusp-like structures that together form a triangular structure, looking very much like a pocket (for example, the lower center portrait in Figure 11.2; see also the bottom C-surface in Figure 11.3). By varying *c* and *d*, we can enlarge,

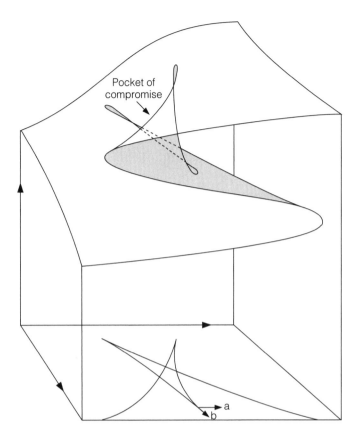

FIGURE 11.3 Butterfly Catastrophe Model

SOURCE: Adapted from Zeeman (1977, p. 338).

narrow, or delete this pocket. In other words, "space" opens up for the "third way" or third option. Between the top and bottom sheets of the behavioral surface of Figure 11.1 we see this additional triangular surface, the Pocket of Compromise in 3D in the M-space in Figure 11.3 (Casti, 1994, pp. 63–69; Zeeman, 1976, p. 80; 1977, pp. 336–339). Keep in mind that the 2D bottom plane (C-plane) shown in Figure 11.3 represents a projection of the bifurcation set onto the C-plane.

To actually envision this 5D structure, we can again, as *d* varies, draw various 2D slices of the control space (Figure 11.2). As Zeeman (1977) tells us, "each section is an (a,b)-plane drawn for (c,d) = constant" (p. 338). This indicates what the bifurcation set would look like. In Figure 11.2 note what happens when *c*, the bias factor, is less than zero; when it is equal to zero; and when it is greater than zero. In the top row of Figure 11.2, for each case *d*, the butterfly factor, is less than zero, and no pocket emerges. The cusp, again, swings to the left or to the right. Now consider what happens when we vary *d*, particularly when we make it greater than zero. A pocket of compromise,

Where $c < 0$

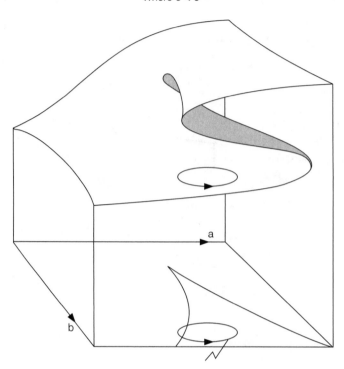

Where $c > 0$

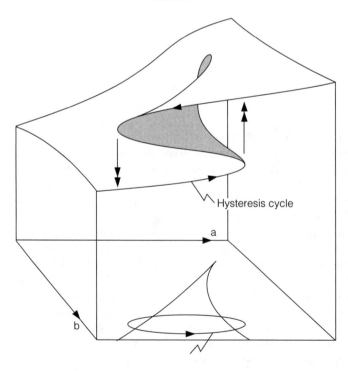

Hysteresis cycle

FIGURE 11.4
Cusp Catastrophe Bifurcation Set with Different Values of c

SOURCE: Adapted from Zeeman (1977, p. 37).

the third way or option, begins to emerge. Actually, when c equals zero, the effect is to produce three cusps (the bottom row of Figure 11.2). The lower center frame of Figure 11.2 shows a V-looking structure indicating three cusps forming a triangular pocket (we can visualize this in Figure 11.3). Again, this is the pocket of compromise.

Zeeman (1976) also notes that "the bias factor . . . tends to destroy a compromise" (p. 80). Note, for example, that the pocket is largest when c equals zero. When the values of d, the butterfly factor, are positive, then the pocket emerges and we have trimodal behavior. When d is positive and c is positive or negative, the pocket will move to left or right on the behavioral surface and indicate which "wing" of the butterfly is dominant (Casti, 1994, p. 76).

The illustrative picture is represented in Figure 11.3. Again, for demonstration purposes, factors c and d have been suppressed with their effects nevertheless being indicated. Comparing this with Figure 11.1, we see how a new "sheet" has materialized between the top behavioral surface and the bottom one. Note that as the butterfly factor increases above the value of zero, the pocket emerges and grows. Initially it is quite susceptible to perturbations and fragile, but as it increases in size the pocket of compromise grows in strength and stability; that is, it now remains stable even with ever larger perturbations (Zeeman, 1977, p. 32).

APPLICATION TO CRIMINOLOGY: PEACE RHETORIC (DISCOURSE)

We are now ready to apply the butterfly catastrophe model to doing postmodern criminology. Our goal is to provide some suggestions for how a "peace rhetoric," a peace discourse, could act as the "butterfly factor" in deescalating spiraling conflicts in various interpersonal situations and produce a "third way" or option—namely, nonviolence. This peace rhetoric has much in common with what Harris (1988, 1990) identifies as a "peace pedagogy." We are only too aware of the escalating nature of violence in domestic situations, in street corner encounters, with police-citizen transactions, with guard-prisoner exchanges, with prisoner-prisoner encounters, and generally with various interactions citizens have with the criminal justice system and its operatives. Offered here is a direction for providing further momentum in the development of the conciliatory style of social control, peacemaking, and social justice. With some modifications, we can see the relevance of our deescalation schema for management-worker disputes, international struggles, and other forms of conflicts.

In our example of the cusp catastrophe model, we saw that two control parameters would produce a continuum of behaviors (states) ranging from "endure" to "escape" to "agitation" to "violence." We use only four outcomes for purposes of simplicity. The forms of violence under investigation represent "righteous slaughter," as defined by Katz (1988). In the cusp region we had bimodal behavior: here escape and violence were likely occurrences given some value on the C-surface. In our example of the butterfly catastrophe model, we will maintain this range of possible behaviors (states) but indicate how, by the addition of two other control parameters, trimodal behavior could develop, an option to the polarized positions of "escape" or "violence." This option is located in the pocket of compromise, or at the intersection of three cusps.

Defining the Control Parameters

We need first to specify our four control parameters. In applying catastrophe theory to the social sciences, "[t]he problem is what kind of interpretation to give to these new inputs. What do these purely mathematical necessities really *mean*?" (Casti, 1994, p. 76). We shall define the normal factor, *a,* as the effects of postmodern society. The effects of postmodern society can be operationalized in terms of the negative consequences of alienation and the hyperreal, clocktime, and commodification (O'Malley & Mugford, 1994; see also Chapter 8 in this volume). Further, these effects include capital logic and the law of equivalence (Laclau & Mouffe, 1985).* Our example includes the full, integrative magnitude of these postmodern effects.

The splitting factor *b* will be defined as "perceived assault on moral self worth" (Katz, 1988). This includes the variety of attacks on a desirable identity or conception of self. The bias factor, *c,* will be identified as "perceptions of limitations on life chances." Numerous well-established sociological research indicates that life chances are differentially distributed and correlate quite well with structural location in a social formation in terms of socioeconomic indices. Thus, we can conceive of a scale ranging from perceptions of less limitations on life chances (c is less than zero) to greater limitations on life chance (c is greater than zero). Perhaps a score of c equals zero could represent a modicum of both where the net result cancels out placing this person as leaning in one direction rather than in the other. Our hypothetical scale for "perception of limitations on life chance," therefore, could be depicted as in Figure 11.5.

In an example used by Zeeman (1977), who was exploring how a compromise opinion could arise in military action, "average vulnerability" was defined as the $c = 0$ value (p. 344). As Casti (1994, p. 76) has informed us, we do not so rigidly define each of our parameters so that their interplay does not defy the precision demanded by mathematics. Thus, our $c = 0$ value could

---

*The notion of *alienation* follows Karl Marx's various statements concerning the effects of capitalism (see Milovanovic, 1989); *hyperreal* follows Baudrillard's (1993) various statements concerning the development of an imaginary reality, which then becomes the basis of contemplation and action; *clocktime* follows the ideas Marx, Weber, and others have indicated as being of an increasingly stronger value in certain forms of industrialized orders such as capitalism, often leading to the loss of freedom and the loss of meaning; *commodification* follows the notion of "fetishism of commodities" that is explained by Karl Marx (see Milovanovic, 1989); and *capital logic* and the *law of equivalence* follows the implications of commodity fetishism (Laclau & Mouffe, 1985).

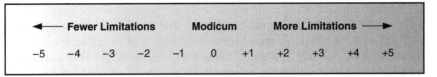

FIGURE 11.5 Perceptions of Life Chances

also be creatively defined as the moment when, as chaos theorists tell us, *far-from-equilibrium* conditions prevail. In other words, this is the moment when the notion of limitations on life chances is in flux. Here the perception of life chances waxes and wanes, and no clear-cut leaning one way or the other exists. Again, this is suggestive. Other interpretations are possible.

The butterfly factor, *d*, will be identified as discourse or a linguistic coordinate system. We may employ a discourse that has greater emphasis on peace, a "peace rhetoric" (*d* is greater than zero), or one that supports escalating violence, an "instrumental rhetoric" (*d* is less than zero). On many occasions, both may be operative, with one being more dominant.

Increasing values of the bias factor (for example, perceptions of less or more limitations on life chances[*c*]), given the effects of postmodern society (*a*) and assaults on moral self-worth (*b*), may contribute to the "escape" *or* the "attack" option on the M-plane in Figure 11.1 (respectively, the lower left and lower right areas on the M-surface). According to Katz (1988), "when tensions arise on the job, one may feel severe humiliation but there are possible escapes: other people, other times, other social places in which one can expect to be free of humiliation" (p. 22). The key, then, is an escape option. This can be an imaginary or a physical escape. At this point, with the three control parameters being employed (*a, b, c*), when *c* is less than zero (perception of fewer limitations on life chances), we would expect that in the case where the person feels an alternative place to escape is available, violence is less likely.

Note that in the upper portrait in Figure 11.4 the cusp opens up toward the lower right, while the apex points to the upper left. Note also the location of the "escape mode" on the M-surface. However, where *c* is greater than zero (perceptions of greater limitations on life chances), the perception also exists that there is nowhere else to go, and here a violent reaction would have a high probability of occurring. In the lower portrait in Figure 11.4, note that the apex is now pointing to the upper right and the cusp has swung over to the lower left encompassing the previous coordinates (or locus) for the "escape" mode. In this instance, the person would negotiate the edge of the bifurcation curve (right side of the drawn ellipse on the C-surface) and "jump" to the higher plane, indicating "violent attack." An oscillating cycle may also exist whereby a violent attack is followed by "escape" as the person moves left along the M-surface, once again negotiating the fold curve and jumping to the lower plane, signifying escape (for example, the "hysteresis cycle" in Figure 11.4, lower portrait).

At this juncture, three points need to be emphasized. First, those subjects who are the brunt of alienation, clock time, and commodification processes, coupled with an attack on moral self-worth, may find their "escape" option greatly limited. Second, as Katz (1988) tells us, there are "places of last resort" such as "casual life, affectionate relationships, the weekend and Saturday night, or drinking and cruising Main Street . . . for the pursuit of relaxed fun" (p. 22). Nonetheless, if one cannot make use of the escape option, the inescapable perception may be that there is nowhere else to go. The attack option may become an alternative consideration. Katz, for example, has shown how spiraling emotions may lead to humiliation, rage, and violent attack. As he explains: "[I]n some cases . . . the assailant's rage emerges so suddenly and silently that only when it appears does a preceding experience of humiliation become visible" (p. 22). This statement suggests a discontinuity and hence a catastrophe. Third, even though the most probable outcome of behavior for those generally confronted with an increase in the negative effects of the three control parameters would be "endure" or "escape," it is not a desirable end result. It is an undesirable outcome because it maintains the very conditions that reduce people as fully human and as having the capacity to actively confront and change oppressive structures. We shall return to this in the "Discussion" section.

As previously stated, the butterfly factor will be identified as discourse or the linguistic coordinate system employed. We follow Lacan's (1977) version of psychoanalytic semiotics (see also my explication in Milovanovic, 1992, 1994) for further elaboration. According to Lacan, we cannot separate the desiring subject from discourse. The "elementary cell of speech production" indicates how the person is intimately connected to discourse (Lacan, 1977). Lacan also developed the idea of four discourses (Bracher, 1988; Milovanovic, 1993) that indicate that the subject locates itself in structured communication (linguistic coordinates) whereby certain, greatly circumscribed narrative constructions are produced (see, for example, Arrigo's [1993, 1996] development of the discourse of the legally mentally insane; the practice of jailhouse lawyers [Milovanovic, 1988] and activist lawyers [Bannister & Milovanovic, 1990]). The person speaking is intimately connected to the discourse he or she inserts him- or herself into to construct and convey various, coherent meanings. In other words, when a person speaks, she or he takes up temporary residence in a language system (for example, law, engineering, psychiatry) that ensures the relative stability of that grammar and that discourse's limited meanings. Discourse, in this view, is *performative:* it produces effects in behavior (Lee, 1990), speaking through the subject (Arrigo, 1996) and speaking the subject (Milovanovic, 1996).

Forms of Discourse

Let us now briefly turn to forms of discourses and their effects, after which we will be in a position to operationalize more carefully the butterfly factor in our model. Consider the Schwendingers' (1985) discussion of the different and shifting "moral rhetorics" that are associated with juvenile life. The "instrumental rhetoric" "disregards egoistic standards of fairness" and "assumes people to be engaged in a vast power struggle, with the weak and the powerless as legitimate victims" (pp. 136–137). As the authors inform us, "[R]hetorical devices—words like Punk, Chump, Mark, and Mother fucker—incorporate sufficient meaning to justify illegal acts, especially personal victimization, all by themselves" (p. 141). This is the performative dimension of language. The juvenile, therefore, acquires words, some of which justify victimization. "The increasing adoption of these victim words signals the gradual acquisition of a working ethic, of motives, rationales for action, images of victimizers and their victims, and assumptions about reality" (p. 148).

Lacan's (1977) *Schema R* is especially well suited to indicate how images and symbols interact in the creation of possible victims (see also Milovanovic, 1996). Schema R is composed of various *Mobius bands* (take a rectangle, put one twist in it, join the edges, and you have a Mobius band). These are "cuts" depicting the relationship between, on the one hand, the various imaginary constructions of self (ideal egos) as a desirable person (ego ideal) and, on the other, the various specular constructions of the other as an object of desire having the ability to both reflect one's self and also being the basis of imaginarily fulfilling desire (Milovanovic, 1996, pp. 230–233).

An instrumental rhetoric provides material for the construction of allowable victims and for victimization. It objectifies the other as less than a complete human being and, in the process, allows victimization without remorse. A peace rhetoric undermines this process. It reinforces the conception of the other as a human being.

Other studies on discourses and their effects could also be cited: Cressey (1953) with embezzlers, particularly the "vocabulary of motives" such as rationalizations found in the work environment that justify or excuse embezzlement; Sykes and Matza (1957), with their idea of "techniques of neutralization"; Matza (1964) with his idea of neutralizations found in peer groups; and Arrigo (1996) in his research on discourses that justify legal commitment to psychiatric institutions, to name a few.

Given the negative effects of discourse, we want to now look at the positive potentials. We already have seen the importance of various television campaigns to curtail various forms of violence: a basketball TV commercial shows a potential flare-up between two high school students, and then the message "Just walk away"; an antidrug commercial says, "Say no to drugs"; an antirape commercial says, "No means no!"; an antialcohol commercial says "Don't drink and drive" or "Have you ever got a friend smashed?" while showing a demolished car. The effectiveness of these various rhetorics have yet to be fully understood. However, there does seem to be a link to the potential ceasing of otherwise spiraling phenomena that may lead to abrupt violent episodes. Future studies will surely test to what extent this is so.

Let us consider, for example, Katz's (1988) study of "righteous slaughter." Subjected to an attack on moral self-worth, with an ensuing feeling of humiliation, the subject may envision a future where the humiliation would no longer exist (for instance, the escape option), or he may also attempt to abolish it by conjuring up various culturally stable narratives (pp. 24–25). According to Katz:

> He tries to abolish the unbearable awful feeling by reciting folk recipes: "time heals all wounds"; "he's drunk, he doesn't mean it and won't remember it"; "she's upset because of her period"; "life goes on"; "I don't need him, I'll leave"; or "I'll move, and my new associates won't know about my past." (p. 25)

Katz also stresses that even these, at times, do not work, even when one may resort to "counting to ten," a form of a "time-out" rhetoric. We pick up on this theme to indicate that Katz's investigations are suggestive in indicating that (1) certain narrative devices may in fact curtail escalating or spiraling emotional states that abruptly end in rage and attack, and (2) at times even these narrative devices do not work. The latter notwithstanding, we nevertheless want to push ahead to suggest perhaps a form of minimizing much of this spiraling activity that, at times, abruptly ends in violence.

The implications drawn from the research on discourse and narrative constructions are that various rhetorics may be functional in minimizing some forms of escalating and sudden violence in various settings. I would therefore suggest the development of a "peace rhetoric" or a "peace discourse." Consider, for example, the suggestions by Harris (1990) as to the thrust of a peace pedagogy with its promotion of a peaceful disposition in persons. This has much to offer for the development of a peace rhetoric. As he indicates, "Such a disposition would orient a person toward caring for others, using compassion, respecting diversity, seeking nonviolent alternatives, and mediating conflicts" (1990, p. 255). This also has much to do with Buber's (1970) notion of "I-thou" relationships, a recognition of the other in oneself and vice versa. Campaigns, in the media and within the school system, could focus on these rhetorics with attached imageries that sustain them. For Harris (1988) "peace, a concept which motivates the imagination . . . implies human beings working together to resolve conflicts, respect standards of justice, satisfy basic needs, and honor human rights" (p. 7).

Dynamics of the Butterfly Catastrophe:
Developing Hypotheses

Returning to Figure 11.3, we could envision the butterfly factor, "peace rhetoric" or the "peace discourse," as offsetting, to some extent, the interactive effects of a violence-enhancing discourse (that is, the Schwendingers' [1985] identified "instrumental rhetoric"), the negative effects of postmodern society, attacks on moral self-worth, and diminished life chances. Let us explore the various states.

Critical topological thinking can lead to the development of testable hypotheses and novel lines of inquiry. It is an exercise conducive to discovery. Studying our developed butterfly catastrophe model, we can suggest the following hypotheses. We will consult Figure 11.2, focusing, in turn, on each of the six 2D bifurcation sets. We should not assume a rigid stance on the mathematical interpretations, for the various models can be seen more as ideographs, as generators of insights. Let us assume in each instance similar escalating postmodern effects (*a* is greater than zero) along with moments of attack on moral self-worth (*b* is greater than zero) (for example, *a* and *b* will remain constant). Next, let us look at the likely behavioral occurrences as the bias factor (*c*) and butterfly factor (*b*) vary.

Hypothesis 1: Where *c* and *d* are less than zero, the endure and escape quadrants would be likely behavioral occurrences (states).

Elaboration: Where increasingly fewer perceived limitations exist on life chances, even with the increasing prevalence of an instrumental discourse, endure and escape states are likely occurrences. There does exists another place to go, in an imaginary or physical way.

Hypothesis 2: Where *c* equals zero and *d* is less than zero, either the escape or violence quadrants would be likely behavioral occurrences.

Elaboration: Where the perception of life chances waxes and wanes, coupled with the increasing prevalence of an instrumental discourse, escape or violence is likely. Bimodal behavior is likely in the area of what appears very much like the cusp catastrophe bifurcation. Small changes in initial conditions can produce divergent results.

Hypothesis 3: Where *c* is greater than zero and *d* is less than zero, agitation and violence quadrants would be likely behavioral occurrences, with agitation often leading to violence.

Elaboration: With perception of life chances being more unfavorable and with the increasing prevalence of an instrumental rhetoric, the agitation and violence states are likely, with agitation more often moving on to violence. In Figure 11.4 we note how the swing of the cusp toward the left with the apex pointing to the right now encompasses the area where the determinants for the escape option were previously at play. In other words, there is now movement toward the cusp's curve at which point a jump to the top surface follows producing violence.

Hypothesis 4: Where *c* is less than zero and *d* is greater than zero, endure and escape quadrants would be likely behavioral states but with the beginning emergence of a third position that increases in size and stability.

Elaboration: With fewer restrictions on life chances and with the beginnings of a peace rhetoric, the endure or escape state would find a pocket beginning to emerge that signifies the pocket of compromise or the third way. This is still a precarious state. The danger of continuously enduring or escaping is that at moments where the perception of life chances may dramatically change to the worse, the enhanced probability exists that the fold curve will be reached and a jump to the violence state experienced. The pocket of compromise has not yet reached a sufficient degree of stability and strength and, with a slight perturbation, may quickly dissipate.

In other words, much sensitivity to initial conditions persists: slight perturbations may have dramatic effects. For hypotheses 4, 5, and 6, the bias factor determines which wing of the emerging butterfly is dominant. Where c is less than zero, endure and escape are probable; where c is greater than zero, agitation and violent attack become probable.

Hypothesis 5: Where c equals zero and d is greater than zero, a pocket of compromise would be the likely behavioral occurrence.

Elaboration: As a continuation of what has begun in hypothesis 4, space is increasingly opened up for a nonviolent option. The pocket has now reached greater stability and strength. Perturbations to the system would have to be greater than in the case in hypothesis 4 for the pocket to dissipate.

A minimalist position would be that any spiraling dynamic, often culminating in violence (for example, "righteous slaughter"), would be arrested. A maximalist position might see the "space" created as an occasion for the further development of alternative discourse, peace pedagogy, tolerance, and understanding of differences. What is problematic here is why the model assumes that the third way is more complete in hypothesis 5 (where c equals zero and d is greater than zero) than in hypothesis 4 (where c is less than zero and d is greater than zero).

It is at this point that the full creative capacities and potentialities of the model are at work. Let us speculate. We can conjecture by building a time evolution. In hypothesis 4 because of time/space being created through the enduring/escaping option and because of an increase in the perception of life chances simultaneous with the prevalence of the peace rhetoric, an alternative solution begins to evolve. Thus, could it be that the zero value, where a modicum of perceived life chances exists, provides the impetus for imaginary constructions of an alternative? Could there exist an oscillating reminder that life chances are precarious and therefore a third way is desirable? Or perhaps we can conceptualize c equals zero as being "far from equilibrium" conditions where perceptions of limitations on life chances wax and wane and alternatives spring forth, perhaps in a nonlinear mode of thought? Perhaps other explanations exist? Perhaps a "poetic spark" (Lacan, 1977) results during these conditions?

Alternatively, the four key parameters might demand rethinking. Perhaps an additional control parameter must be introduced, and/or perhaps the behavioral dimension must be expanded to two (for the latter, see the *parabolic catastrophe;* Zeeman, 1976, p. 78). Zeeman's (1977) own classic example of treating anorexia begins with the use of the butterfly catastrophe, but he then goes on to show that a more accurate model needs to increase the control parameters to five and the behavioral states to two (for example, an additional y-axis beyond the x-axis, which, in the 5D model, indicated outcomes), producing a 7D model (p. 364).

The model's strengths are that it stimulates the researcher to raise deeper questions about the nature of the interactive effects of life chances, discourse, and the third way. The apparent discrepancies among hypotheses 4, 5, and 6, after further thought, may be explained or become the basis of further hypothesis building. This fuels the thought-provoking nature of thinking topologically.

Hypothesis 6: Where c and d are greater than zero, the most likely behavioral occurrence would be agitation, with violence being secondary and with the existence of a smaller, unstable, and diminishing pocket of compromise.

Elaboration: With greater perceived limitations of life chances, even with the increasing prevalence of a peace rhetoric, movement toward the agitation state continuing toward a violence state is a likely occurrence. In Figure 11.4 we note that the lower portrait indicates that the previous probable behavior (escape) is now incorporated within the limits of the new bifurcation set. In addition, recall that the bias factor accounts not only for the left/right swing of the cusp but also for its movement up/down. Thus, for hypothesis 6 we suggest that probable behavior is more in the form of agitation than violence. Again, note in Figure 11.2 that the apex in the lower right-hand portrait has moved up and to the right. Some small space still exists for the third way, but it is diminishing in scope (for example, the size of the pocket) and is unstable. The pocket, in other words, is disappearing. Small perturbations to the system can quickly witness the disappearance of the pocket. However, the peace rhetoric is still having some effect in producing agitation (highly probable) rather than violence (less probable). Moreover, small perturbations, again, can quickly produce violence as the point attractor.

DISCUSSION

We cannot remain optimistic that most forms of violence will be curtailed in a society where structural sources of alienation, life chances, and various attacks on moral self-worth prevail. Clearly, the structural components of a postmodern society need to be addressed. Our suggestion is more limited—a short-range, crisis intervention tool that should not be envisioned as supporting the contemporary arrangements in society with its structurally defined life chances and vulnerabilities. We do not, however, subscribe to some romantic revolutionary's ideal of remaining idle, letting the system collapse with the various contradictions whereby the "good" society would presumably appear. To use Van den Haag's idea, we cannot wait while a barn is burning with children inside when we do have available buckets of water. Attempts at eradicating escalating violence in various interpersonal situations are worthy and should be developed.

Our synthesis suggests a number of things. Given the continuous emergence of localities of interpersonal communication where differences will appear, and given that these differences may be amplified by (1) the effects of the normal factor (postmodern society and its effects), (2) a splitting factor (assault on moral self-worth), and (3) a bias factor (the effects of differential life chances), a peace rhetoric sufficiently stabilized within various cultural spaces may militate against the spiraling nature of hostilities. This would be portrayed in Figure 11.3 as the pocket that emerges, the "third position." From seemingly polarized positions, we find that we may create a viable option. Bimodal behavior changes into trimodal forms.

The works of Katz (1988), Matza (1969), and others indicate that at a certain moment in the escalation process, the person finds him- or herself more object than subject. Creating time intervals or time lags may provide the pause or "space" necessary for returning the "pacified" subject to a reclaimed active position of agent.

Clearly, the question of the "escape option" remains somewhat problematic. Katz (1988), for example, says that "the lives of those who are higher in the social class system are likely to be so thoroughly different that not just the response but the emergence and shape of humiliation may also be radically different" (pp. 46–67). Thus, further investigations that focus on this issue are necessary. It may be, in the end, that for a peace rhetoric to work, it will need to be culturally sensitive and socioeconomically targeted. Doing ethnographic work with teenagers in the schools and their hangouts would help, for example, in understanding negative rhetorics and escape options and in devising effective peace rhetorics. These peace rhetorics would be in the form of "contingent universalities" (Butler, 1992)—that is, subject to continuous examination, change, deletion, and substitution. Equally significant are life chances. They would need to be changed allowing those further down the economic ladder greater opportunities for self- and community actualization.

We also wish to say a few words as to the assumed desirable point toward which our butterfly catastrophe model applied to peacemaking and social justice points: endure and escape. Clearly more is needed. We are not advocating that, confronted with structural sources of alienation, assaults on moral self-worth, reduced life chances, and instrumental rhetorics, one should (continuously) simply escape or endure. This is resignation and abdication. The development of a pocket of compromise or the third way that our model predicted needs to be further researched. During the space created by the butterfly factor, it is likely that the person may momentarily regain his or her faculties, recover the self as subject rather than object, reintroduce the other as a "thou" rather than an "it," recognize the escalating nature and absurd point having been reached, and entertain a nonviolent alternative.

We can foresee a continuum of possible results: a minimalist position would have it that the escalating or spiraling nature of the emotions may have a heightened probability of being arrested or suspended whereby "cooler heads" may then prevail. A middle position would see the beginnings of an understanding of the external forces at play (structural sources of alienation, diminished life chances, assaults on moral self-worth, and instrumental rhetoric). A maximalist position would see the conflict as an opportunity for the development of a critical consciousness and for the stabilization of a "border pedagogy" (Giroux, 1992). Rather than intensities of emotions taking a destructive turn, they would be "refracted" (see Henry & Milovanovic, 1996, 22–23), or turned back on themselves providing the energy and focus for the development of a critically aware consciousness. After all, permanent consensus on most issues that confront us is a highly dubious ideal.

In Unger's (1987) well-developed model of a more sensitive and fulfilling society, there is a clear indication that the possible zones of conflict would substantially increase. New social movement theory, commentary by Laclau and Mouffe (1985), and Giroux's (1992) studies of contemporary society predict an ever increasing amount of differentiation and differences. As Giroux tells us, the new "borderlands should be seen as sites for both critical analysis and as a potential source of experimentation, creativity, and possibility" (p. 34). We also add, however, that momentary suspensions of destructive spiraling emotions may also need an external catalyst in translating the newly directed energies. Elsewhere, we have integrated the works of Jacques Lacan and Paulo Freire in indicating that "cultural revolutionaries" may be a key in the collaborative development of new discourses that better reflect the unique desires of diverse human beings (Milovanovic, 1993, 1996, 1997; Henry & Milovanovic, 1996, pp. 203–211). Further analysis of the butterfly catastrophe in mapping out a third way would do well to consider and integrate each of these perspectives.

CONCLUSION

Lyotard (1984) has identified catastrophe theory as one of the elements of doing postmodern investigations. Few commentators in postmodern research, however, have incorporated this perspective. In this chapter we have pursued this call by indicating how postmodern criminology can be advanced with these conceptual tools of inquiry. Certainly, further refinement is needed. Additional hypothesis development and testing are necessary. The efforts here, however, have been to demonstrate applications to both an understanding of certain forms of crime as well to the development of a third way during occasions of interpersonal violence.

REVIEW QUESTIONS

1. Explain why language is an important consideration in conflict deregulation.

2. Life chances are said to be differentially distributed in the socioeconomic class structure. Explain the importance of life chances in

the sudden (discontinuous) onset of violence in interpersonal situations.

3. The butterfly catastrophe model incorporates a number of interacting variables. Substituting a new one for any of the ones that are

used in the chapter, explain how it could interact with the other variables in the deescalation of violence. (You will need to think creatively through an important variable that might be an important contributor to deescalating violence.)

4. Take any two of the six hypotheses offered in the chapter, and elaborate, in your own words, how violence may be deescalated.

5. The chapter notes that there are limitations to using catastrophe

theory, especially the butterfly catastrophe model, given the prevalence of a political economy that systematically generates violence. Explain. Make a distinction between "short run" and "long run."

6. What suggestions could you provide, given your reading of this chapter, as to possible media commercials advocating short peace rhetorics and as to the extension of life chances to many of the disenfranchised in society?

REFERENCES

Arrigo, B. (1993). *Madness, language and the law*. Albany, NY: Harrow & Heston.

Arrigo, B. (1996). *The contours of psychiatric justice: A postmodern critique of mental illness, criminal insanity, and the law*. New York: Garland.

Athens, L. (1989). *The creation of dangerous violent criminals*. New York: Routledge.

Baack, D., & Cullen, J. B. (1994). Decentralization in growth and decline: A catastrophe theory approach. *Behavioural Science, 39*, 213–228.

Bannister, S., & Milovanovic, D. (1990). The necessity defense, substantive justice, and oppositional linguistic praxis. *International Journal of Sociology of Law, 18*(2), 179–198.

Baudrillard, J. (1983). *Simulacra and simulations*. New York: Semiotext(e).

Black, D. (1976). *The behavior of law*. New York: Academic Press.

Bracher, M. (1988). Lacan's theory of the four discourses. *Prose Studies, 11*, 32–49.

Buber, M. (1970). *I and thou*. New York: Scribner's.

Butler, J. (1992). Contingent foundations: Feminism and the question of "postmodernism." In J. Butler & J. W.

Scott (Eds.), *Feminists theorize the political*. London: Routledge.

Casti, J. (1994). *Complexification*. New York: Harper Perennial.

Cressey, D. (1953). *Other people's money*. Glencoe, IL: Free Press.

Giroux, H. (1992). *Border pedagogy*. New York: Routledge.

Harris, I. (1988). *Peace education*. Jefferson, NC: McFarland.

Harris, I. (1990). Principles of peace pedagogy. *Peace and Change, 15*(3), 254–271.

Katz, J. (1988). *The seductions of crime*. New York: Basic Books.

Kriesberg, L. (1991). Conflict resolution applications to peace studies. *Peace and Chance, 16*(4), 400–417.

Lacan, J. (1977). *Ecrit*. New York: Norton.

Laclau, E., & Mouffe, C. (1985). *Hegemony and socialist strategy*. New York: Verso.

Lee, J. L. (1990). *Jacques Lacan*. Amherst: University of Massachusetts Press.

Lyotard, J. F. (1984). *The postmodern condition*. Minneapolis: University of Minnesota Press.

MacLean, B., & Milovanovic, D. (Eds.). (1996). *Thinking critically about crime.* Vancouver: Collective Press.

Matza, D. (1964). *Delinquency and drift.* New York: Wiley.

Matza, D. (1969). *Becoming deviant.* Upper Saddle River, NJ: Prentice Hall.

Milovanovic, D. (1988). Jailhouse lawyers and jailhouse lawyering. *International Journal of the Sociology of Law, 16,* 455–475.

Milovanovic, D. (1989). *Weberian and Marxian analysis of law: Structure and function of law in a capitalist mode of production.* Aldershot, U.K.: Gower.

Milovanovic, D. (1992). *Postmodern law and disorder: Psychoanalytic semiotics, chaos, and juridic exegeses.* Liverpool: Charles.

Milovanovic, D. (1993). Lacan's four discourses, chaos and cultural criticism in law. *Studies in Psychoanalytic Theory, 2*(1), 3–23.

Milovanovic, D. (1994). The postmodern turn: Lacan, psychoanalytic semiotics and the construction of subjectivity in law. *Emory International Law Review, 8*(1), 67–98.

Milovanovic, D. (1995). Dueling paradigms: Modernist versus postmodernist. *Humanity and Society, 19*(1), 1–22.

Milovanovic, D. (1996). Postmodern criminology: Mapping the terrain. *Justice Quarterly, 13*(4), 567–609.

Milovanovic, D. (1997). Visions of the emerging orderly (dis)order. In D.

Milovanovic (Ed.), *Chaos, criminology and social justice* (pp. 195–211). New York: Greenwood.

Oliva, T., Peters, M., & Murphy, H. (1981). A preliminary empirical test of a cusp catastrophe model in the social sciences. *Behavioral Sciences, 26:* 153–162.

O'Malley, P., & Mugford, S. (1994). Crime, excitement, and modernity. In G. Barak (Ed.), *Varieties of criminology.* Westport, CT: Praeger.

Pepinsky, H., & Quinney, R. (Eds.). (1991). *Criminology as peacemaking.* Bloomington: Indiana University Press.

Schwendinger, H., & Schwendinger, J. (1985). *Adolescent subcultures and delinquency.* New York: Praeger.

Sykes, G. M., & Matza, D. (1957). Techniques of neutralization: A theory of delinquency. *American Sociological Review, 22,* 664–670.

Thom, R. (1975). *Structural stability and morphogenesis.* Reading, MA: Benjamin.

Unger, R. (1987). *False necessity.* New York: Cambridge University Press.

Zeeman, C. (1976). Catastrophe theory. *Scientific America, 234,* 65–83.

Zeeman, C. (1977). *Catastrophe theory: Selected papers, 1972–1977.* London: Addison-Wesley.

Queer Theory
and Social Justice

Q ueer theory developed as a reaction against homophobia. Homophobia is discrimination, prejudice, bigotry, and oppression that gay, lesbian, bisexual, and transgendered persons experience. In this chapter, Stockdill examines some of the social injustices that members of the AIDS Coalition to Unleash Power (ACT UP) confront. Understanding AIDS activism is a cornerstone for this investigation. Stockdill begins his analysis by providing background material on "queer politics." A central theme of queer politics is challenging socially held beliefs that dehumanize the lives of gay, lesbian, bisexual, and transgendered people. Queer politics celebrates queer identities and resists heterosexist thoughts and norms. According to queer advocates, traditionally held convictions about sexuality are social constructions that must be contested in both theory and practice. Stockdill then considers how ACT UP, in the context of the AIDS crisis and epidemic, deals with social injustice. ACT UP chapters throughout the country continue to debunk questionable health care practices, housing initiatives, educational policies, and media images, exposing them for the homophobic oppression they represent and the unfounded fear of AIDS they promote. Stockdill also examines how ACT UP organizations wrestle with intimidation and harassment from government authorities, especially agents of the criminal justice system. He demonstrates how governmentally sponsored social control efforts are designed to undermine the political agenda of ACT UP chapters and criminalize the behavior of queer/AIDS activists. Police brutality, FBI surveillance, and court sanctions are standard methods that promote these objectives. Stockdill particularly reveals the demoralizing impact such control mechanisms have for sustaining queer politics for people of color. This leads him to question the "justice" of the criminal justice system. Stockdill's conclusion is that a queer political framework allows us to see the deep-seated marginalization of the poor, women, nonwhites, and nonheterosexuals. Notions of crime, law, and deviance are saturated within a culture that represses such constituencies. Queer social justice and queer social activism, then, is about agitating for change in which the construction of sexuality is ultimately recast. As the slogan puts it: "We're queer; we're here; get used to it!"

12

AIDS, Queers,
and Criminal (In)Justice
Repressing Radical AIDS Activism

BRETT STOCKDILL

A group of activists—mostly in their twenties and thirties—begins each of their meetings by asking if any police officers are present. If they are, they are asked to leave. Members of the group report strange things happening with their phones. Women in the group receive harassing phone calls and death threats. At several nonviolent demonstrations, members of the group are verbally abused, physically brutalized, and arrested by police officers. Some spend time in jail, and some face lengthy criminal trials. The FBI maintains surveillance of the group, amassing thousands of pages of files.

What kind of activism would warrant such attention and action from the criminal justice system? The introduction to this chapter refers to a group called "ACT UP"—the AIDS Coalition to Unleash Power—a primarily lesbian, gay, and bisexual group that uses direct action protest (for example, sit-ins, rallies, civil disobedience, activist art and video) to combat the AIDS crisis. However, many other kinds of progressive groups (see Glick, 1989) have faced similar forms of government repression in recent years. Confrontational groups such as ACT UP that expose and challenge systematic injustice perpetuated by the government, corporations, and other dominant social institutions have often found that their efforts are met with repression. Other AIDS groups—especially groups working in communities of color—have sometimes decided not to use direct action because of fears of repression. This essay will examine the kinds of repression that have targeted ACT UP as well as expectations of repression held by many AIDS activists of color—some of them in ACT UP, some of them in other groups. Before looking at the topic of AIDS activism and political repression, I will briefly discuss the idea of "queer politics" and provide an overview of ACT UP, a queer AIDS group.

I would like to thank all the activists who generously agreed to be interviewed for this research. I am indebted to the other members of ACT UP/Chicago's Prison Issues Committee and the Legal Defense Committee for teaching me so much about AIDS, criminal (in)justice, and activism. I would also like to thank Aldon Morris, who challenged me to think more critically about the topic of repression; Michelle Vannatta and Vensive Lamb, who helped me think more rigorously about queer theory and action; and Shana Krochmal, who thoughtfully read the chapter and offered excellent editorial advice.

QUEER POLITICS: OVERVIEW, ASSUMPTIONS, AND PRINCIPLES

Queer people and queer politics occur within a particular social context. Over the past century, lesbians, gay men, bisexuals, and transgendered people (collectively referred to as queers in this chapter) have faced prejudice, job discrimination, police harassment, arrest, institutionalization, imprisonment, violence, and other forms of homophobia (see D'Emilio, 1983; Duberman, 1994; Freedman & D'Emilio, 1988; Kennedy & Davis, 1994). Queers today continue to face oppression. Federal civil rights legislation prohibiting discrimination based on sexual orientation is nonexistent. In 1996, President Bill Clinton signed into law the Defense of Marriage Act, which effectively restricts the right to marriage to heterosexuals. In many cases, the government continues to take away children from their lesbian and gay parents. Homosexuality is criminalized by sodomy laws in nearly half the states. The mass media trumpets negative stereotypes, and gay bashings (physical attacks against queers) occur regularly across the nation. During the past fifteen years, homophobia has been the driving force in the AIDS crisis, which has claimed over 300,000 lives—queer and straight—in the United States alone.

In the face of this systematic bigotry, lesbians, gay men, bisexuals, and transgendered people have fought back—by surviving and supporting each other, by educating the broader public, and by protesting the institutions, practices, and laws that constrain their lives. A central aspect of these collective struggles has been challenging collective beliefs that dehumanize queer lives. One vocal protest to homophobia is queer politics—theory and action that challenge heterosexist thought, defy heterosexist norms, and celebrate being queer (see essays in Warner, 1993). Though in this essay I use the word *queer* to refer to lesbians, gay men, bisexuals, and transgendered people, it is important to point out that not all these individuals refer to themselves as queer. In fact many believe that the term and accompanying politics are counterproductive. The word *queer* is a term used by those who do not consider themselves heterosexual. It is typically derogatory when heterosexuals use it, and thus pro-queer heterosexuals may want to think about the implications of their using the word.

So just what are queer politics? On the one hand, there are just as many conceptions of queer politics as there are people who think of themselves as queer. On the other hand, many queers see some important themes as essential to their political perspectives. The following four points will help us understand the concept of queer:

1. Queer theory rejects the idea that sexuality is merely a private, personal matter confined to the bedroom. Queer theory maintains that sexuality is public and has everything to do with power in our society (and other societies also). From this perspective, marital heterosexuality is reinforced in our society as the only valid expression of sexuality, and those that deviate from this norm are often excluded, ostracized, and/or punished.

The Defense of Marriage Act, sodomy laws, and gay bashing are all vivid reminders that the area of sexuality is regulated by both individuals and institutions in our society. Queer theory unmasks the powerful ways in which the (hetero)sexual order shapes our lives as individuals and groups.

2. Queer theory rejects dominant notions of sexuality by questioning gender and sexuality categories. Queer theory challenges the idea that sexuality that is good, natural, and normal is heterosexual, monogamous, and re-productive. Queers have sex that is seen as bad, abnormal, and/or unnat-ural, insisting on their right to perpetuate these practices. Furthermore, queer theory asserts that sexuality—hetero and homo—is socially con-structed; that is, the categories of homo and hetero are not universal, god given, or transhistorical but occur within a particular historical and socio-logical context. On a strategic level, the goal of queer activism is to take apart identity categories (gay, straight, and so forth) and blur group boundaries.

3. Queer politics optimally challenge the limiting construction of homosex-uality as white, male, and middle class, allowing for the inclusion of race, gender, and class. This point is not to imply that queer groups do not suffer from conflicts around race, gender, and class. Most queer groups do. For example, many ACT UP chapters have been divided as to whether to deal explicitly with race and gender issues in relation to the AIDS crisis. However, acknowledging difference and diversity is integral to the agenda of queer politics.

   Queerness is also more inclusive of bisexuals and transgendered peo-ple. An important objective for many queer activists is to expose the in-terconnectedness of different forms of oppression. For example, from this perspective, access to health care is an issue not just for people with AIDS but for women, people of color, and poor people—whether they have AIDS or not. During the campaign to end the ban on gays in the military, queer activists criticized mainstream gay and lesbian activists for failing to be critical of the racism and sexism entrenched in the military.

4. When it comes to collective action, queer politics reject assimilationist strategies. Queers do not try to fit into the heterosexual world. They defy it. Rather than saying, "We're just like you, please tolerate us," queers say, "We're here. We're queer. Get used to it." The very use of the term *queer* is evidence of this perspective. Queers take a pejorative term and reclaim it, asserting their right to be different and simultaneously reducing the power of homophobes in using the term as a weapon. Queers challenge the heterosexist idea that they must keep their sexual identities quiet. They refuse "closeting" strategies of assimilation and assert their sexuali-ties publicly. This leads to such tactics as "in-your-face" public displays of homo-affection at shopping malls, bars, and other places. Queer activist groups include organizations with chapters across the nation such as ACT UP, Queer Nation, the Lesbian Avengers as well as ad hoc/local groups such as Queers United Against Strait-acting Homosexuals (QUASH).

These groups tend to prefer to work outside conventional politics (such as the Democratic Party) and often question the long-range utility of mainstream strategies. For example, although many queers believe that they should have the right to marry, they challenge the idea that married people—of any sexuality—should be entitled to benefits such as health insurance and tax breaks not available to all people.

Queer theory and action help us better understand the social construction of sexuality and gender, the emergence of gay and lesbian communities, bisexuality, transgender issues, gender roles, and other topics. Queer politics enable us to expose the ways in which dominant notions of sexuality and the institutions that perpetuate these notions are used to constrain the life chances of women, queers, and anyone who deviates from heterosexist rules of play.

The case of the AIDS crisis provides a tragic example of how society treats people who are different. Homophobia has been at the core of the terrible injustices suffered by queers and others living with HIV/AIDS. In turn, the work of ACT UP provides a vivid illustration of the use of queer politics to struggle against these injustices.

AIDS AND ACT UP: EXAMPLES OF
AND RESPONSES TO SOCIAL INJUSTICE

After we kick the shit out of this disease, I intend to be alive to kick the shit out of this system, so that this will never happen again.

THE LATE VITO RUSSO, FILM SCHOLAR AND ACT UP/NEW YORK MEMBER (CRIMP, 1993, P. 302)

During the early and mid-1980s, tens of thousands of people died of AIDS in the United States. Yet in the face of this incredible loss of life, the government, the mass media, the medical establishment, and other institutions in U.S. society were virtually silent. When AIDS did receive attention, the HIV virus was often seen as punishment for sin, crime, or pathology (Padgug, 1989; Patton, 1990). This nationwide neglect reflects the fact that the vast majority of people with AIDS were members of marginalized groups—gay men, injection drug users, and people of color. Rather than compassion, these people were often seen as deserving of the terrible disease.

In the face of this inaction, a predominantly queer group called AIDS Coalition to Unleash Power (ACT UP) formed in New York City in 1987. Within a short time, ACT UP chapters sprang up in various cities across the country. ACT UP is self-described as:

A diverse, nonpartisan group of individuals united in anger and committed to direct action to end the AIDS Crisis. We meet with government and health officials; we research and distribute the latest medical information. We protest and demonstrate; we are not silent. (Carter, 1992, p. 1)

ACT UP represents the coalescence of queer consciousness in the face of the AIDS crisis. By the time ACT UP started, members of the group had watched while friends and lovers had died of AIDS. Many people in ACT UP were living with AIDS themselves. They refused to merely sit back and die. Patton (1990) writes, "[P]eople living with AIDS would not stay quiet for long. Their discourse shifted to a critique of the oppression of early death and unnecessary infection resulting from treatments delayed and education denied" (p. 130).

Over the past decade, ACT UP has utilized creative, confrontational direct action tactics targeting multiple aspects of the AIDS crisis, including exorbitant drug prices, inadequate government funding for research and prevention, sluggish medical research, inaccessible clinical drug trials, negligent AIDS service organizations, and biased media coverage. These tactics include phone and fax zaps (bombarding an agency, corporation or other group with phone calls and faxes), marches, rallies, die-ins (sit-ins in which people symbolically die to call attention to the ever increasing number of AIDS deaths), office takeovers, art, video, and agit-prop (agitational propaganda).

A key part of ACT UP's work has been exposing the homophobia and heterosexism that have fueled the fires of AIDS. The vast majority of AIDS fatalities in the United States have been gay and bisexual men, and perceptions of homosexuality as sinful, unnatural, and so forth, have been at the core of our society's response to AIDS—a response marked by inaction and victim blaming. Padgug (1989) observes that measures proposed to combat AIDS, such as expulsion, quarantine, mandatory testing, and the removal of Persons With AIDS (PWAs) from schools, jobs, and housing, have been patterned on historical forms of homophobic oppression. The hysteria related to AIDS— fueled by the fusion of anti-queer sentiment and fear of disease—has catalyzed homophobic violence and discrimination that targets gay men, lesbians, bisexuals, and transgendered people regardless of HIV status.

Members of ACT UP realized that to fight AIDS, they would have to fight the homophobia that undergirded the epidemic. In true queer fashion, ACT UP has not just exposed anti-queer bigotry but publicly embraced the right to be queer. This includes speaking openly and explicitly about lesbian and gay male sex, publicly displaying homosexual affection, distributing thousands of condoms and dental dams, and unfurling banners promoting safer sex at major league baseball games, the Republican National Convention, and other public events (Gamson, 1989). ACT UP has often used video and art to expose the injustice of the AIDS crisis and boldly promote positive images of homosexuality (see Crimp, 1990). ACT UP popularized the pink triangle, which queers were forced to wear in Nazi concentration camps during the Holocaust, as a symbol of queer pride. Notably, the pink triangle has been reversed to point upward to symbolize hope and resistance. The organization's mission to emphasize the value of queer lives and vocally defy the status quo is encapsulated in the slogan "SILENCE = DEATH," which appears below the pink triangle.

A central element of ACT UP's work has been forcing government agencies such as the National Institutes of Health to develop more rigorous research programs on HIV/AIDS, to improve treatments and make these treatments more affordable. One early success of ACT UP was to force the Food and Drug Administration, a federal agency that approves drugs and sets prescribed doses, and Burroughs Wellcome, one of the largest pharmaceutical manufacturers in the world, to acknowledge (after a year's delay!) studies showing that the antiviral drug AZT was just as effective at 600 milligrams/day as 1,200 milligrams/day. This cut the price of AZT in half and reduced the likelihood of the often toxic side effects of the drug.

Whereas some ACT UP members (typically, but not exclusively, white gay men) have been reluctant to focus energy on fighting racism and sexism, other members have argued strongly that systemic racial and gender oppression are part and parcel of the AIDS crisis. People of color caucuses were formed in many ACT UP chapters to do educational outreach in communities of color. These caucuses have put together educational workshops to challenge racism within the organization, sponsored conferences on AIDS in communities of color, and worked with community-based organizations to improve AIDS services. Most of these caucuses are now defunct, with many of the members having left the organizations to do work elsewhere.

One of the primary goals of ACT UP has been to expose the distorted, and often bigoted, coverage of AIDS by the mass media. For example, in 1988, ACT UP/New York's art group, Gran Fury, produced a chilling poster printed in English and Spanish in response to a *Cosmopolitan* article (January 1988 issue) that asserted that heterosexual women had little to fear from AIDS (Crimp, 1990, p. 42):

AIDS: 1 in 61

One in every sixty-one babies in New York City is born with AIDS or born HIV antibody positive.

So why is the media telling us that heterosexuals aren't at risk?

Because these babies are black.

These babies are Hispanic.

Ignoring color ignores the facts of AIDS.

STOP RACISM: FIGHT AIDS.

Many women involved in AIDS activism have critiqued perceptions of AIDS as a solely gay male disease, pushing for more research on, and services for, women with HIV/AIDS (see Corea, 1992). Women in ACT UP, particularly lesbians, led several protests—disrupting conferences and sitting in at the Centers for Disease Control (CDC)—against the CDC definition of AIDS, which did not include the primary manifestations of AIDS in women for several years. Women's caucuses have challenged the portrayal of women as "vectors of transmission" (to men and to children) rather than people actually at risk for HIV infection themselves. Creating programs for women has meant simultaneously reconceptualizing women as whole people rather than just child-bearers and wives and confronting the male-centered health care system. Significantly, lesbians in many ACT UP chapters have stimulated internal dialogues on race, class, and gender and have played a central role in pushing for collective action around these and related issues, such as AIDS among prisoners and injection drug users.

In one action illustrating ACT UP's creativity and determination, ACT UP/Chicago led a protest against the failure of the Cook County Board of Commissioners to establish an AIDS ward for women at Cook County Hospital. ACT UP's Women's Caucus, supported by the People with Immune System Disorders (PISD) Caucus and the People of Color Caucus, created a symbolic AIDS ward by placing sixteen mattresses, wrapped in sheets covered with slogans about women and AIDS, in the center of a busy intersection, blocking traffic. The women lay down on the beds and refused to move. Over one hundred people were arrested in the demonstration. The AIDS ward was opened the next day.

ACT UP's queer political response to the AIDS crisis has been very successful. The combination of extensive educational programs and social protest has been integral in raising awareness in the queer community and broader society, increasing government AIDS budgets, opening up experimental trials, initiating needle exchanges, and making treatment more accessible for PWAs (ACT UP, 1992; Arno & Feiden, 1992; Carter, 1992; Corea, 1992). ACT UP has played a crucial role in the empowerment of PWAs and queers. They have exposed the inefficiency and greed of pharmaceutical companies and the insurance industry as well as the calculated negligence of the government. On a broader level, ACT UP has provided a model for confrontational queer political struggles against homophobia and other oppression.

Within the context of queer politics, ACT UP has exposed the concrete ways in which homophobia has driven the AIDS crisis; challenged the idea that being gay, lesbian, bisexual or transgendered is bad; and linked AIDS to other issues such as housing, incarceration, sexism, racism, poverty, and militarism. ACT UP challenges not only the specific institutions and policies that fuel the AIDS crisis but also the underlying beliefs that promote neglect and allow hundreds of thousands to die. Exploding myths about homosexuality, asserting members' queerness, and making links to other communities hit by AIDS have been key parts of ACT UP's work.

ACT UP has faced considerable resistance from different groups. Some members of the gay and lesbian community consider its "in-your-face" tactics to be excessive and counterproductive. The mass media has often painted ACT UP as irrational and extremist. In addition, ACT UP's strong critique of the oppression entrenched in U.S. social institutions and culture has alarmed political authorities at various levels. This alarm has sometimes translated into government attempts to destabilize the organization.

INTIMIDATING ACT UP: THE POLICE,
THE FBI, AND THE COURTS

They [the Chicago Police] went right through the middle of us with horses and they just started hitting people right in the crowd. . . . I'm very afraid of them, and that's their strategy.

JEANNIE, ACT UP/CHICAGO

Elites may respond in different ways to challenges to authority. They may approach protest with facilitation—negotiations, concessions, support, co-optation, and coalition development. Authorities may also respond to opposi-tional movements with repression (they often use both simultaneously). Uekert (1994) defines repression as "the use or threat of use of coercion by governing authorities to control or eliminate opposition" (p. 4). For the pur-poses of this discussion, this definition will be expanded to include any actions taken by authorities to impede mobilization, harass and intimidate activists, divide organizations, and physically assault, arrest, imprison, and/or kill move-ment participants. Repression may take the form of job loss, surveillance and harassment, threats, police violence, arrest, criminal prosecution, imprison-ment, and murder.

The United States has a long history of political repression targeting progres-sive social movements. During the late 1800s and early 1900s, large railway, coal, and other corporations used federal troops, the National Guard, the Pinkertons, private militias, and hired thugs to put down strikes and crush unions (Fantasia, 1989; Zinn, 1980). For example, on April 20, 1914, in Ludlow, Colorado, the National Guard attacked a camp of striking miners and their families with ma-chine gun fire. Later that day, the Guard set fire to the tent camp, killing eleven children and two women. Thirteen more people were gunned down as they fled (Zinn, 1980). Other forms of repression used against the labor movement include infiltrating of unions, firing union leaders, making bribes, red-baiting, and publicly accusing union leaders of serious crimes (Fantasia, 1989).

The criminal justice system, particularly the Federal Bureau of Investiga-tion (FBI), which is responsible for upholding federal law, has been a key part of controlling political dissent. During the 1950s, the FBI formed its Counter Intelligence Program (COINTELPRO) unit to disrupt the Communist Party USA and the Socialist Workers Party. In the sixties and seventies, COINTEL-PRO targeted a wide range of movements and organizations including the Black Panther Party, the antiwar movement, the American Indian Movement, the Puerto Rican independence movement, the women's movement, the gay liberation movement, and the Chicano movement. It used wiretaps, burglar-ies, live "tails," and mail tampering to gather information and, perhaps more important, to induce paranoia among liberal and radical activists. It also fabri-cated correspondence between members of targeted groups and distributed false information misrepresenting organizations to other political groups and the press. The FBI also worked with the judicial system to arrest, prosecute, and imprison hundreds of activists during the 1960s and 1970s. This involved fabricating evidence, intimidating witnesses, and making harassment arrests. Hundreds of activists, especially members of the Black Panther Party, were imprisoned and/or killed (for more information, see Churchill & Vander Wall, 1990; O'Reilly, 1989).

In his cogent analysis of historical and contemporary political repression in the United States, Glick (1989) shows that government harassment of activists persists and currently creates "a climate of fear and distrust which undermines our efforts to challenge official policy" (p. 5). Targeted groups include the Puerto Rican independence movement, Committee in Solidarity with the People of El Salvador (CISPES), the New Jewish Agenda, and the Maryknoll Sisters. As a queer group working to challenge the bigotry of the AIDS crisis, ACT UP has been confronted with harassment and intimidation from government authorities.

Using data collected from interviews with members of ACT UP in Los Angeles, New York, and Chicago, participant observation in ACT UP/ Chicago, and published writings on the organization, I now turn to the use of social control to undermine the political work of ACT UP. This repression has contributed to the deterioration of the organization in recent years. Though not nearly as severe as the repression targeting movements of the 1960s and early 1970s, ACT UP has faced police violence, FBI surveillance and harassment, and the criminal prosecution of its members. For ACT UP members, this repression has been exacerbated by the stress related to living with a life-threatening disease and/or working in a group in which a significant number of members are often ill and many have died. This repression has drained time, energy, and resources away from fighting AIDS; contributed to burnout; and discouraged people from participating in protest actions. ACT UP/New York member George M. Carter (1992) writes:

> [I]ncidents of police brutality include physical assault and verbal abuse sustained by AIDS activists in Chicago, Philadelphia, New York and elsewhere. This affects AIDS activism directly. The point of AIDS demonstrations is lost in the story of violence while activists continue to face the threat of police brutality. (pp. 18–19)

Interviews with members of ACT UP chapters in New York, Chicago, and Los Angeles as well as published documents on ACT UP reveal numerous instances of police harassment and the use of excessive force at ACT UP demonstrations. In one instance, Chris Hennelly was beaten in front of New York's Midtown South police precinct by police officers on February 11, 1991. Hennelly was a marshal at an ACT UP demonstration protesting police brutality during the arrest of three lesbian and gay activists a week earlier. As the protest was ending, the police attacked the demonstrators without provocation. According to Carter (1992):

> Mr. Hennelly was videotaped trying to crawl out from under swinging billy clubs. He was further beaten at the station. The brain injuries, in-

cluding epilepsy, that he sustained are permanent. Typically, the police charged him with severe crimes, including assaulting an officer, even though Hennelly was clearly the one assaulted. (p. 19)

In 1990, ACT UP/Chicago organized a national demonstration to demand an AIDS ward for women at Chicago's Cook County Hospital. Ferd, a former member of ACT UP/Chicago, describes the protest:

It was a very big, very militant demonstration. It was probably the most militant demonstration that had taken place in Chicago since the sixties. People were charged by the police on horses. A number of people were seriously injured.

Steven, a member of ACT UP/Los Angeles, who has been arrested "a couple times" and has been hit by police officers, remarked, "The police hate us." He described a sit-in at which ACT UP/Los Angeles members locked themselves to each other around a tree in the atrium of the State of California's Ronald Reagan Building. Their arms were linked together with mountain climbing carabiners and rope inside fiberglass tubes—a tactic used to thwart any attempts to cut them apart. When the police tried to pull their hands apart, the activists explained how they were connected and told the police they would undo themselves. The police kept pulling, however, causing "excruciating pain. . . . That's part of their strategy." Steven had marks on his wrists for weeks. "They beat the shit out of us and then arrested us."

In some instances, the police have attempted to end protests by arresting leaders. During a protest against the city of Chicago's failure to put safer sex messages on city buses, ACT UP/Chicago members got on city buses, gave presentations on safer sex, distributed condoms, exited the buses, walked back and boarded another bus. The Chicago police mounted a camera on top of a store near the bus stop, and according to Saundra, one of the group's members, proceeded to arrest "people who were telling other people what to do. . . . It was just like they knew who to go for." Without leaders to direct the action, the remaining activists found it difficult to continue. The group ended up at the police station trying to bail out those people who had been arrested.

ACT UP/Chicago members report that police reaction was particularly severe at a 1991 action targeting the American Medical Association (AMA). According to ACT UP/Chicago member Jeff, the Chicago police came up from behind the protesters and started beating and arresting people. Many of the people arrested were people who had never been to a demonstration before and had not planned on doing civil disobedience. ACT UP/Chicago member Jeannie recalls the demonstration: "I saw them [the police] abuse Debbie. I was there when they stood on her back." She continues:

I never want to get arrested in Chicago. I've been arrested everywhere but Chicago for ACT UP. I'm afraid of them. I'm very afraid of them, and that's their strategy. If I thought everybody was gonna get arrested, maybe I'd overcome my fear, but I'm just very fearful of Chicago Police because

I've seen what they've done. . . . So their strategy is effective. People dread getting arrested in Chicago.

Jeff comments on the effect of police violence at the AMA demonstration:

It had a real chilling effect and ACT UP never did anything like that since then, until World AIDS Day [in December 1992]. . . . That got a lot of publicity. I sort of feel like it was supposed to 'cause it made it clear that nobody could go to an ACT UP demonstration and not feel like they're gonna get arrested. . . . Meeting attendance and interest in demonstrations really fell off after that.

Marvin, a former member of ACT UP/New York, who traveled to Chicago to participate in the 1990 Cook County Hospital action, remarks, "I was arrested in Chicago, and that was enough to make me say that I would never do it again anyway." He states that the scars on his wrists are still painful. After the 1990 Cook County and 1991 AMA demonstrations, ACT UP publicized the police brutality in hopes of gaining public sympathy. However, Jeff believes that such publicity "was a mistake. It drew attention to all the costs of participating with ACT UP."

Several respondents report being subjected to homophobic slurs such as "faggot" and "dyke" made by New York, Los Angeles, and Chicago police. Roberto, who worked with ACT UP/Chicago, also described an incident that demonstrates homophobia on the part of the police and how one activist used humor to defy the police. According to Roberto, after arresting several demonstrators at an ACT UP protest, the police were "nasty" and "more physical" with "one guy from Radical Fairies [a gay men's organization] wearing a funky dress, cat glasses, and a tasteful wig." In an elevator at the police station, the police officers harassed him by saying:

[H]e wasn't a man, he wasn't a woman, he wasn't a human being, something very condescending like that. He just kind of laughed at them and said something. I can't remember what he said, but he said something really witty. I find gay humor to be so appealing. I really think that we as gay people have a culture that make us really distinct from straight people and this comes from a whole different set of experiences, and I think that our humor is something that is so much a part of that.

One other notable aspect of police behavior at ACT UP demonstrations across the nation is the use of plastic gloves. The gloves—which serve no practical purpose—highlight the stigma targeting PWAs and the ignorance on the part of the police and other segments of mainstream society. The gloves reinforce the popular image that PWAs, and by association all AIDS activists whether HIV positive or not, are diseased, deserving of ostracism and punishment rather than compassion and fairness.

Other forms of police intimidation were reported. Juan states that the Latino Caucus of ACT UP/New York experienced harassing phone calls, phone taps, and infiltration. The caucus would plan demonstrations in secret, and when they arrived at the site of the protest, the police would already be there. Jose, another Latino Caucus member, notes, "We were followed by them [police] when we were planning [a large action]." In some instances, police patrols were stationed outside the ACT UP office. At one point, a police officer called Jose's house and asked him if he knew of any upcoming demonstrations. Other members of ACT UP/New York and ACT UP/Chicago reported similar occurrences.

Rita, who worked with ACT UP/New York, states that the police are not acting alone and warns that the United States and other capitalist nations are organizing to stop any potential radical organizing that might lead to revolutionary movements. She maintains that governments are putting resources into controlling, neutralizing, and stopping actions. As part of this repressive strategy, antiterrorist forces are being sent to ACT UP protests dressed as regular police. Churchill and Vander Wall (1990; see also Glick, 1989) report that in New York the Joint Terrorist Task Force, a "FBI police amalgam," has worked to suppress political dissidence, including the framing and arrest of eight New York City black activists in 1984 and the harassment of the Puerto Rican independence movement. Similar operations exist in Chicago and Los Angeles. FBI files released under the Freedom of Information Act show that ACT UP has been the subject of "Domestic Terrorism" and "Civil Unrest" investigations since its birth in 1987 (Carter, 1992; Wolfe, 1993). A campaign of harassing phone calls and death threats that targeted ACT UP women nationally in the early 1990s is speculated to be a part of the FBI's harassment of ACT UP (Wolfe, 1993).

The harassment and abuse of activists by authorities impacts on collective action. Echoing the work of Marx (1974) nearly two decades before, sociologist Ruud Koopmans (1993) concludes in an article on protest waves in West Germany, "The repression and marginalization of these [radical] groups also stimulates sectarian conflicts and distrust among activists, which diverts energy from external activities and discourages outsiders from participating" (p. 655).

The testimonies of AIDS activists support Koopmans's argument. Experiences with the police and the FBI as well as knowledge of past COINTELPRO activities have promoted fear and mistrust in many ACT UP chapters. At the beginning of every ACT UP/Chicago general body meeting, police officers and journalists are asked to identify themselves and leave. New members are sometimes suspected of being police informants. Fearful that committee members' apartments were bugged, members of ACT UP/Chicago's Prison Issues Committee established the practice of writing down protest times and dates rather than saying them out loud.

In addition to the police and the FBI, the judicial system has been involved in containing the activism of ACT UP. Across the nation, ACT UP members have been arrested, spent time in jail, and faced lengthy and costly legal battles. In one instance, multiple felony charges were filed against the Houston Three (members of ACT UP/New York) for their participation at a protest at the 1992 Republican Party Convention in Houston, Texas (Wolfe, 1993). One particular case involving the grand jury indictment, extradition, and subsequent trial of three members of ACT UP/Denver provides a concrete example of government repression. The following analysis of the Denver case is based on newspaper articles, ACT UP/Chicago Defense Committee literature, and discussions with committee members.

On August 12, 1993, on the eve of the pope's and the president's arrival in Denver, a grand jury in Colorado indicted three members of ACT/UP Denver, charging them with two felony and two misdemeanor counts that hold prison terms of up to twenty-six years. The charges stemmed from a January 14, 1993, action in which AIDS activists draped plastic bags bearing the word *AIDS* over tombstones in a Catholic cemetery. The goal of the action was to dramatize the AIDS-phobia and homophobia of the Catholic Church. ACT UP/Chicago's Legal Defense Committee literature states, "Their message painted a picture of what a cemetery will look like in the not too distant future if the Catholic Church continues to oppose the use of condoms to prevent the spread of HIV: a cemetery in which tombstones relay AIDS as the cause of death."

Several elements of the Denver case demonstrate that the indictments, charges, and prosecution were not part of a typical vandalism case but a repressive political strategy. These elements are instructive for the study of political repression and further support the perspective that repression is a key force shaping social movement development.

The first important aspect of the case is the aggressiveness with which the state of Colorado (and perhaps the federal government as well) pursued the case. The charges are certainly severe considering the relatively mild nature of the action. It is hard to imagine a grand jury being convened and charges carrying sentences of twenty-six years being filed in similar cases involving cemetery vandalism. The activists were also treated harshly on a personal level. All three activists spent at least a week in jail. Two of the three were interrogated by the U.S. Secret Service and thrown into Cook County Jail where guards announced to other inmates that they were "faggots with AIDS" and "pope killers." These two were subsequently extradited to Colorado. All three were interrogated by law enforcement officers without the presence of their lawyers. Two of the activists are HIV-positive gay men whose T-cell counts precipitously dropped to about 500 during the months following their arrest. (T cells, the primary target of the HIV virus, typically range from 800 to 1,200 in people with healthy immune systems.) The third activist, a lesbian, was held in Los Angeles and transported in a van to Colorado where she spent several days in jail before being bonded out.

Second, the timing of the indictments suggests ulterior motives on the part of the state of Colorado as well as the Catholic Church, which pushed aggressively for prosecution. An initial investigation in January 1993 was dropped because of a lack of evidence. Yet eight months later, a grand jury was convened and indictments issued. The indictment coincided with the arrival of President Clinton and the pope in Colorado. At least one police officer alleged that the defendants were conspiring against the pope—despite the fact that all three were out of the state for several months before the indictments. ACT UP/Chicago's Legal Defense Committee literature states:

> The fact that the indictments and arrests occurred simultaneously with the arrival of the Pope and the President in Denver reveals Colorado's absurd attempt to paint those indicted as dangerous people who posed a threat to the Pope and the President.

The third critical aspect of the case is the fact that it occurred in the state of Colorado, home of Amendment 2—a state law that prohibits civil rights protection for lesbians and gay men and, in effect, legalizes discrimination and violence against lesbians and gay men. Significantly, the Catholic Church, which opposes equal rights for queers, was instrumental to the passage of Amendment 2. Further, the Catholic Church opposes the use of condoms and dental dams as a means of preventing the transmission of the HIV virus. Thus, the Church demanded the prosecution of the activists.

The fourth and perhaps most telling event in the case is the fact that a grand jury was convened. Historically, the grand jury has been used by the government as a tool to divide and conquer social movements (Churchill & Vander Wall, 1990; Glick, 1989; Wolfe, 1993). Grand jury proceedings are secret, and people who refuse to testify can be thrown in jail for contempt. Activists and others are interrogated about organizations, demonstrations, and civil disobedience. Grand juries have been used to attempt to destroy movements such as the Catholic Left, the Puerto Rican independence movement, the black liberation movement, the American Indian Movement, the women's liberation movement, the anti–Vietnam War movement, and others. According to Defense Committee literature:

> A grand jury was used to divide the lesbian, gay, and AIDS activist movement in Colorado. The state's attorney was able to intimidate members of the lesbian and gay community and gather testimony pointing fingers at radical activists to produce indictments against the three ACT UP members.

Approximately twenty of forty-six grand jury witnesses were reportedly lesbians and gay men (the others were all police officers). One former member of ACT UP/Denver initially implicated in the action testified—apparently after the state threatened to take her child away. On May 6, 1994, the three activists pled guilty to one deferred felony (which is expunged from criminal records after two years barring further convictions) and one misdemeanor. They were placed on probation. In addition, they were ordered to pay a fine of $2,900, perform community service, and write a letter of apology to the Catholic Church.

The severity of the charges, the allegations of a conspiracy against the pope, the political climate fostered by Amendment 2, and the grand jury support ACT UP's claim that the Denver case represents the criminalization of queer/AIDS activism. The Defense Committee writes that the activists were targeted to:

> punish them for their activism and discourage others from vocally opposing the Catholic Church's policies and fighting the AIDS crisis with direct action protest. . . . The members of ACT UP/Denver were targeted not for putting plastic bags on tombstones, but for being outspoken, queer AIDS activists.

Overall, the Denver case had a debilitating effect on ACT UP. On a financial level, tens of thousands of dollars had to be raised for bail—most of it by ACT UP/Chicago and other ACT UP chapters. Thousands more were spent on the defense campaign over a period of nearly a year. Perhaps more significant was the intimidation of AIDS/queer activists in Denver. According to one Defense Committee member:

> The homophobic hysteria which fueled Amendment 2 had already led the three activists to move from Denver to Los Angeles and Chicago. The grand jury had the effect of intimidating and dividing Denver activists, decimating what was left of ACT UP Denver.

ACT UP/Denver no longer exists. The case itself sowed bitter conflict between different activists and organizations in the Denver gay and lesbian community. Some activists in Denver lashed out against the indicted ACT UP members. According to one defense committee member:

> The grand jury caught people off guard. The movement was quickly swept up in divisive arguments about ACT UP's tactics, the cemetery action, and so on, rather than the despicable actions taken by the state of Colorado and the Catholic Church.

In the long run, ACT UP members felt that the case served to weaken the movement.

The data demonstrate that repression has worked to impede mobilization around the AIDS crisis. Police brutality often frightens both participants and potential participants. FBI surveillance and harassment create an atmosphere of fear and distrust. The Denver case and similar legal cases take time and energy away from combating AIDS and promote divisions within the queer/AIDS movement.

It is important to note that other factors have also contributed to the gradual weakening of ACT UP chapters across the country. Some members of ACT UP have moved into paid positions in the expanding AIDS bureaucracy. In many cases, they have not continued their involvement in ACT UP. Several ACT UP members have died of AIDS. Others have grown less active as a result of physical and emotional burnout. It is hard to sustain an organization in the face of such widespread illness and death.

Stress has a peculiar role to play with respect to repression in the AIDS movement. Although many HIV-infected activists joined ACT UP to fight for their very lives, the stress of living with HIV serves as a weapon that heightens the risks of AIDS activism. The various costs of activism exacerbate the already precarious physical health of activists with HIV disease. Burnout—common in any social movement—takes on a new meaning in the AIDS movement. When contemplating the consequences of participation, many AIDS activists have to assess the impact participation will have on their health. Fear of FBI surveillance, police abuse, arrest, loss of employment, and so forth, coupled with a compromised immune system, undoubtedly discourages confrontational activism. Thus, the natural repressive force facing HIV-positive activists creates difficult dilemmas for activists.

It is important to point out that HIV-negative activists are also not unaffected by death and illness. Some members of ACT UP/Chicago have been involved for nearly a decade and point out that it is difficult to keep struggling after watching so many of their fellow activists get sick and die. The costs of activism—naked repression, bureaucratization/co-optation, burnout, death, and internal conflict—feed on each other and have certainly taken their toll on ACT UP.

COINTELPRO, COMMUNITIES OF COLOR, AND THE LEGACY OF FEAR

Our protests are limited to the civil rights thing. . . . We ain't goin' out there and throwin' no blood on nobody and chain linking ourselves to no fences to be shot and killed. That's not happenin'.

WENDELL, AIDS PREVENTION TEAM, AN AGENCY SERVING AFRICAN-AMERICAN COMMUNITIES IN LOS ANGELES

What about other groups protesting the injustice of AIDS? More mainstream AIDS organizations that do not rely on confrontational tactics have faced considerably less scrutiny and coercion from authorities. In addition to ACT UP, other progressive groups have used direct action to call attention to the injustice of AIDS. In communities of color, small gay and lesbian groups such as Teatro Viva in Los Angeles and Black AIDS Mobilization (BAM) in New York City have developed grass-roots strategies to fight HIV/AIDS, including direct action. However, interviews with members of these and other groups indicate that collective memories of past repression along with contemporary expectations of brutal treatment by the police and the courts discourage confrontational AIDS protest among people of color, especially African Americans. This finding indicates that, in some cases, political repression may have long-term effects, stretching across decades and instilling fear in present-day activists.

Knowledge of historical political repression and present-day perceptions of the criminal justice system as racist and classist are factors that shape the strategic and tactical choices of many AIDS activists of color. Queer AIDS activists of color interviewed report that the expectation of repression—violence, arrests, and imprisonment—is one variable that weighs into deciding whether to participate in civil disobedience. They also express a belief that organizations composed primarily of people of color face higher risks than predominantly white groups such as ACT UP. The respondents link this fear of repression to racial oppression.

In speaking about expectations of repression, a majority of the African Americans, Latinos/Latinas, Asian Americans, and Native Americans refer to the historical government repression of antiracist movements. Comments about the potential for repression against AIDS activism are placed within a larger historical context. Saundra, a member of ACT UP/Chicago, states, "History has shown us that they're not gonna show us any mercy. And there's nothing that I or anybody else can do to lessen that fear because that is a reality. That is a reality."

In the interviews, we see collective memories that have been produced by the extreme trickery and violence used by the federal government and other authorities to crush the radical movements of the 1960s and 1970s, particularly those led by people of color (see Churchill & Vander Wall, 1990; Glick, 1989; O'Reilly, 1989). The two primary examples discussed by activists were the Black Panther Party and the Puerto Rican independence movement. Several respondents specifically mentioned the FBI's COINTELPRO, as mentioned earlier, exerted its greatest efforts in the 1960s to crush the Black Panther Party, fabricating evidence, infiltrating organizations, forging correspondence, conducting surveillance, and killing dozens of radical activists.

Repression was a critical factor in the demise of Black Power groups such as the Black Panther Party. Violence, intimidation, harassment, and surveillance increased risks of participation, making it difficult to recruit new members. Fear of government informers generated a climate of suspicion and distrust that triggered serious internal problems. Legal assaults on leaders led to costly and time-consuming legal battles. Overall, repression led to a shift from community organizing to defending the organization from outside attacks that served to undermine support within the larger black community (Allen, 1992; Churchill & Vander Wall, 1990; Helmrich, 1973; Killian, 1975; Marable, 1991).

While discussing the role of direct action, Wendell states that a large group of black people "makes people nervous" and leads to negative reactions. The following quote reveals how knowledge of past repression influences expectations of repression today:

> If we had been the ones who formulated the ACT UP model, it wouldn't be as successful as it is today because what would happen is we would be still in jail. A lot of us would be dead. And drug companies and other folks who have listened to people who have been a part of those kinds of models would not have taken us seriously. We're fortunate in that we do have the ACT UPs to go out and do it. 'Cause if it wasn't for fear that we would get knocked in the head and beat up or whatever, we would be doing the same thing, but what's real historically for us is that when we

act up we get shot and killed or we get institutionalized for the next twenty-five, thirty years. I don't think people are at that point with AIDS and HIV that they're willing to take that risk.

Respondents of color base such statements not only on collective memories of historical repression but knowledge of contemporary racist police abuse and racism in the criminal justice system. Activists' perceptions of a greater possibility of conviction and longer sentences for people of color are borne out by research on the criminal justice system (Bridges & Crutchfield, 1988; Gray, 1991; Mauer, 1990; Reiman, 1995). These patterns impact on strategic choices in activism. Gil, who works as a consultant for various AIDS agencies across the country, states:

I think it's important to say . . . that there sometimes has been an expectation that people of color ought to be protesting in ways that we're supposedly not doing. But I think that one needs to look at the way the criminal justice system deals with people of color and to recognize what role that plays in people's decisions as to how they're gonna participate, whether they're gonna participate.

Virtually all of the respondents of color expressed negative attitudes toward the police. Several respondents reported being the victims of police abuse, during both political demonstrations and routine interactions on the street. My first interviews were conducted in Los Angeles in the wake of the rebellion following the acquittal of the police officers who brutalized Rodney King, a young African American. Several respondents stated that inadequate health care, including AIDS care, was one factor in the discontent that erupted into violence the day of the acquittal. Carla, a case worker at an AIDS agency serving Latinos/Latinas in Detroit, links police brutality to social protest:

Not being able to trust the police is a big problem in the Latino community. There is a sense of betrayal. The police represent protection, but they've violated this. . . . I think people are afraid of protesting 'cause of the police.

Fear of police brutality was prevalent among the activists interviewed. As a consequence of such fears, individuals and organizations are often reluctant to engage in sit-ins and other confrontational tactics. There were very few instances in which activists risked conflict with the police. As discussed elsewhere (Stockdill, 1996), this is also due to the intracommunity focus of much of the AIDS activism in black, Latino/Latina, and Asian communities. This dynamic extends to non-AIDS events. One respondent notes that immediately following the first verdict in the trial of the Los Angeles police officers who beat Rodney King, heated discussions ensued about whether blacks should go to Simi Valley to protest the verdict along with ACT UP/Los Angeles. Some members of black lesbian and gay organizations felt the "danger was much too great" for blacks to engage in civil disobedience. Others spoke in favor of civil disobedience. Ultimately, a decision was made to go ahead with civil disobedience, and those who had a problem should just not come. As it turned out, no one was arrested.

The overwhelming sentiment among the respondents is that a group of blacks or Latinos would be treated quite differently by the police than a group of whites. For example, Darrell believes that if the People of Color Caucus of ACT UP/Chicago had been larger and stronger, it would have been repressed by authorities. This perception is supported by the extensive documentation of past and current police repression targeting black, Latino/Latina, and Native American activists as well as people of color in other situations such as the unorganized rebellion in Los Angeles in 1992 in which dozens of blacks and Latinos were killed by police and National Guardsmen (for more research on police brutality, see Davis et al., 1971; Marable, 1983; Stockdill, 1991).

Activists place race-based political repression and police abuse within a larger context of racial oppression that turns people of color away from direct action. The social conditions of people's lives figure prominently into people's decisions as to whether or not to participate in social protest. Jose, a member of ACT UP/New York's Latino Caucus, states that it is difficult trying to get people to do civil disobedience in a community that is constantly being subjected to police abuse and drug-related arrests and has more immediate concerns such as housing and food. Consequently, there is a need to create new ways to do outreach and protest. Suzanne, cofounder of the Black AIDS Mobilization (BAM) in New York City, says that in addition to government repression and police brutality:

> [BAM] also encountered the very real material constraints on people that kept us from doing massive CD [civil disobedience] . . . because we didn't have the same sort of access to people who could get four days off. . . . [S]ome of the people we had were not citizens of the United States. I think we ran into more obstacles that were related to our identity as people of color than ACT UP.

Respondents state that it is more difficult for poor and working-class people to come up with bail money and get time off of work for court dates and so forth. Because of racial bias in the criminal justice system, people of color are more likely to have arrest records than white people and, as a result, are likely to face harsher sentences if arrested during a demonstration. The consequences of arrest weigh even more heavily for undocumented immigrants— disproportionately people of color—who face the possibility of deportation. John, a member of the Asian and Pacific Islander Coalition on HIV/AIDS (APICHA) in New York City, comments that much of the power in the AIDS arena lies with the government:

> AIDS again is connected to the INS [Immigration and Naturalization Service]. And so people aren't gonna be in droves wanting to get arrested because people could get deported. . . . What bothers me about the typical gay white male ACT UP work is that they don't live in the communities where they do direct action. It's like "Why don't you do direct action

in Chinatown?" These people live there, they're different, they're ghettoes, much different sociologically—different community dynamics. The privilege isn't the same.

Thus, social inequality—in different forms—works as a form of repression. The price of activism weighs more heavily on economically and racially marginalized groups.

Although expectations of repression—including violence, police abuse, arrest, imprisonment, deportation, loss of unemployment—are key in understanding the reluctance to engage in direct action, the interviews suggest that the picture is more complex. Some AIDS activists of color maintain that there is a need to "reclaim" confrontational tactics; African-American and Latino activists stressed that direct action has been a cornerstone of historical antiracist struggle. Interviewed respondents also explained that though AIDS is a terrible crisis, it is not in and of itself enough to engage in direct action. From this perspective, political strategies need to incorporate the myriad social problems that are connected to AIDS. Finally, as mentioned earlier, within the data, a small number of direct action protest actions around AIDS were held in communities of color. These actions provide culturally appropriate models for AIDS organizing in communities of color (see Stockdill, 1996).

Nevertheless, the data for this study indicate that the expectation of repression is a factor in many AIDS activists' decisions not to engage in confrontational forms of collective action. Tactical discussions include assessing the potential for violence. Fear of repression—especially police brutality and imprisonment—makes political organizing around AIDS especially difficult for those activists who advocate direct action. Many activists expressed frustration with developing social protest methods that will be successful in mobilizing people and effecting change. According to activists of color interviewed, racial and class oppression are important forces increasing the risk of repression, thereby diminishing the likelihood of participation among poor people of color. What is particularly important is that knowledge of repression of earlier movements promotes fear of repression decades later. Along with contemporary social positioning—namely, the police and the criminal justice system—the collective memory of historical repression has a dampening effect on AIDS activism.

CONCLUSION

In his introduction to the anthology *Fear of a Queer Planet: Queer Politics and Social Theory,* Warner (1993) writes:

From the most everyday and vulgar moments of gay politics to its most developed theoretical language, the sexual order blends with a wide range of institutions and social ideology, so that to challenge the sexual order is sooner or later to encounter those other institutions as problems. (pp. x–xi)

LIBERTY AND JUSTICE FOR ALL*

*Offer not available to anyone with AIDS

SOURCE: Adapted from a flier by Ken Woodard for ACT UP/New York's U.S. Civil Rights Commission demonstration in 1988 (Crimp, 1990, p. 67).

Perhaps more than any other group in recent years, ACT UP has challenged the sexual order—exposing the perversion of homophobia and AIDS-phobia embedded in federal agencies, pharmaceutical companies, scientists, and the mass media. ACT UP has conceptualized health care, clean needles, and safer sex (however and with whomever one chooses) as basic rights, and its members have fought for these rights. These and other campaigns for social justice have put them into direct conflict with the criminal justice system.

A queer analysis of the repression targeting ACT UP as well as the deep-seated fear of repression among many AIDS activists of color presents us with an alternative perspective of the criminal justice system—a perspective frequently glossed over in academic research. Paralleling the actions of local, state, and federal authorities in the 1960s, government authorities have used considerable resources to undermine the only radical, mass-based organization fighting AIDS—ACT UP. Police brutality and other forms of repression have intimidated movement participants and potential participants and contributed to the ongoing decline of the group. FBI surveillance has added to the fear of repression and fomented mistrust within many ACT UP chapters. The use of the judicial apparatus to prosecute AIDS activists has drained away resources and robbed ACT UP of valuable time and energy. The stress and uncertainty facing HIV-positive ACT UP members raises the stakes of taking part in social protest.

Among AIDS activists of color, expectations of repression—rooted in collective memory and present-day experiences—have the effect of diminishing the prospects for more disruptive protest methods. Familiarity with widespread racist police abuse and racial bias in the judicial system dims the prospects of confrontational political struggle. It is not just contemporary threats of coercion that shape decisions to participate but collective memories of past repression. Given the extent of COINTELPRO's efforts to crush social movements in the 1960s, continuing government harassment and surveillance targeting ACT UP and other progressive organizations, and marked patterns of racial and class inequality in police abuse and the criminal justice system, expectations of repression on the part of activists of color make complete sense. Together with existing repression facing ACT UP, the overall effect has been to divide the movement, inhibiting coalitions between different communities and organizations.

The intimidation, harassment, brutalization, and prosecution of queer AIDS activists—actual and expected—calls into question the "justice" of the criminal justice system. The interaction between AIDS activists and state authorities illuminates the role of the police, the courts, and the FBI as mechanisms of social control. Militant queer AIDS activism helps reveal the root causes of hundreds of thousands of AIDS-related deaths and millions more infected in the United States—systemic homophobia, a health care system driven by profits rather than human need, and a government beholden to corporate interests. Warner (1993) writes:

> [Being queer] means being able, more or less articulately to challenge the common understanding of what gender difference means or what the state is for, or what "health" entails, or what would define fairness. (p. xiii)

Queer AIDS activism rejects the idea that we are ruled by a "fair" government. It threatens the balance of power. As queers using confrontational and disruptive tactics, ACT UP members are vulnerable to sanctions from heterosexual social institutions. Homophobia and AIDS-phobia work against radical AIDS activists, facilitating stigma, harassment, and violence. As ACT UP expands it political strategies to incorporate race, gender, and other issues, the potential for coercive responses from elites is heightened.

Carter (1992) links repression to ACT UP's move to embrace a broader and more radical set of political concerns:

> As ACT UP broadens its base to be more inclusive of different views and people in true coalition, there is the potential for broad-based, radical change that threatens the inimical power base of both government and the giant pharmaceutical industry. (p. 19)

This increasing radicalism is seen in ACT UP's efforts in the areas of housing, clean needle exchanges, prisoners' rights, women and AIDS, political prisoners, the group's strident opposition to the United States' war on Iraq, as well as coalitions with health care workers, the Puerto Rican independence movement, and environmental, labor, and other groups.

The queer politics of ACT UP highlight contested conceptualizations of "crime" and "criminal." From a queer perspective, homosexuality is not criminal or sinful. Rather, discriminating against queers and sitting idly by while they die is criminal and sinful. Distributing clean needles to reduce the likelihood of HIV transmission is against the law in virtually all jurisdictions in the United States, but ACT UP members and others working with needle exchanges often break the law to save lives. In this case, a strong argument can be made that the law (against needle possession and distribution) is the crime. In turn, from this vantage point, the criminalization of addiction is the crime—not addiction itself.

A queer analysis encourages making links between AIDS and other social problems such as incarceration. In addition to political repression, other key aspects of the criminal justice system are intertwined with the AIDS crisis. In recent years, the prison population in the United States has soared above one million—the largest prison population in the world. The majority of these prisoners are poor people of color. They come from and return to communities severely impacted by HIV. As welfare and other programs (including AIDS services) that help people survive are cut, the prison industrial complex continues to grow. However, despite large amounts of funds for building prisons, few prison systems have adequate AIDS prevention and intervention programs. In fact, the rate of HIV infection has skyrocketed in prisons and jails in the 1990s (Stockdill, 1995). Thus, when prisoners reenter their communities (as most do), they are more likely to be HIV infected and less likely to be educated about HIV/AIDS. Thus, the prison system actually exacerbates the AIDS crisis.

Using a queer political framework, we can also critique the ways in which the legislative system sustains an environment that is hostile to the needs of HIV-impacted communities. It is no coincidence that as more and more poor African Americans and Latinos are warehoused in prisons, we are also witnessing racist attacks on affirmative action and civil rights legislation (such as Proposition 209 in California). Assaults on economic and educational opportunities further increase the vulnerability of communities of color to poverty, AIDS, and a host of already severe social ills. As queer bashing continues on an individual level, we see efforts to further codify homophobia on the state level (Amendment 2 in Colorado) and the national level (the Defense of Marriage Act). This legal homophobia perpetuates anti-queer bigotry, creating an open season on queers and, in many cases, people with AIDS. A queer analysis enables us to see these and other patterns as connected.

A queer analysis of the repression targeting AIDS activism challenges the notion that those arrested at AIDS demonstrations are "criminals." In turn, such analysis begs the question of how "just" the justice system is. Within the context of the AIDS crisis, the criminal justice system has worked against providing the most effective and humane forms of prevention and care. We can apply this lesson to other social problems such as homelessness, drug addiction, police brutality, and so on. We can reevaluate other perceptions of "criminal." Perhaps those identified in the mass media and popular culture as criminals are not as criminal as those whose job it is to dispense "justice." Queer politics encourage us to think more critically about basic concepts such as crime, justice, democracy, and family values as well as the alleged benevolence of dominant social institutions. This critical thinking is invaluable as we seek to understand and combat social injustice and forge struggles to move toward a more equitable and humane world.

REVIEW QUESTIONS

1. What are some of the ways that sexuality is regulated in our society?

2. How does queer politics respond to this regulation?

3. How is social inequality linked to AIDS?

4. What are some of the concrete ways in which the criminal justice system has responded to radical AIDS activism?

5. What other organizations or movements have used civil disobedience? What are the pros and cons of such tactics?

6. Why would the U.S. government have an interest in undermining ACT UP and similar organizations?

7. What are other examples of controversial social problems? Are there conflicting perceptions of (in)justice with respect to these problems?

REFERENCES

ACT UP (Aids Coalition to Unleash Power)/New York: Women and AIDS Book Group. (1992). *Women, AIDS and activism.* Boston: South End.

Allen, R. (1992). *Black awakening in capitalist America.* Trenton, NJ: Africa World.

Arno, P. S., & Feiden, K. L. (Eds.). (1992). *Against the odds: The story of AIDS drug development, politics and profits.* New York: HarperCollins.

Bridges, G. S., & Crutchfield, R. D. (1988, March). Law, social standing and racial disparities in imprisonment. *Social Forces, 66,* 699–724.

Carter, G. M. (1992). *ACT-UP, the AIDS war and activism.* Westfield, NJ: Open Magazine Pamphlet Series.

Churchill, W., & Vander Wall, J. (1990). *Agents of repression: The FBI's secret wars against the Black Panther Party and the American Indian Movement.* Boston: South End.

Corea, G. (1992). *The invisible epidemic: The story of women and AIDS.* New York: HarperCollins.

Crimp, D. (1990). *AIDS demographics.* Seattle: Bay Press.

Crimp, D. (1993). Right on, girlfriend! In M. Warner (Ed.), *Fear of a queer planet: Queer politics and social theory* (pp. 300–320). Minneapolis: University of Minnesota Press.

Davis, A., and other political prisoners. (1971). *If they come in the morning.* New York: Okpaku.

D'Emilio, J. (1983). *Sexual politics, sexual communities: The making of a homosexual minority in the United States, 1940–1970.* Chicago: University of Chicago Press.

Duberman, M. (1994). *Stonewall.* New York: Penguin.

Fantasia, R. (1989). *Cultures of solidarity: Consciousness, action, and contemporary American workers.* Berkeley: University of California Press.

Freedman, E. B., & D'Emilio, J. (1988). *Intimate matters: A history of sexuality in America.* New York: Harper & Row.

Gamson, J. (1989, October). Silence, death, and the invisible Enemy: AIDS activism and social movement "newness." *Social Problems, 36*(4).

Glick, B. (1989). *War at home: Covert action against U.S. activists and what we can do about it.* Boston: South End.

Gray, J. (1991, June 5). Panel says courts are "infested with racism." *New York Times,* B1.

Helmrich, W. B. (1973). *The Black Crusaders: A case study of a black militant organization.* New York: Harper & Row.

Kennedy, E. L., & Davis, M. D. (1994). *Boots of leather, slippers of gold: The history of a lesbian community.* New York: Penguin.

Killian, L. M. (1975). *The impossible revolution, Phase II: Black power and the American Dream.* New York: Random House.

Koopmans, R. (1993, October). The dynamics of protest waves: West Germany, 1965–1989. *American Sociological Review, 58*(5), 637–658.

Marable, M. (1983). *How capitalism underdeveloped black America: Problems in race, political economy and society.* Boston: South End.

Marable, M. (1991). *Race, reform and rebellion: The second reconstruction in black America: 1945–1990.* Jackson: University Press of Mississippi.

Marx, G. (1974). Thoughts on a neglected category of social movement participant: The agent provocateur and the informant. *American Journal of Sociology, 80,* 402–442.

Mauer, M. (1990, February). *Young black men and the criminal justice system: A growing national problem.* Washington, D.C.: Sentencing Project.

O'Reilly, K. (1989). *Racial matters: The FBI's secret file on black America, 1960–1972.* New York: Macmillan.

Padgug, R. A. (1989). Gay villain, gay hero: Homosexuality and the social construction of AIDS. In K. Peiss & C. Simmons with R. Padgug (Eds.), *Passion and power: Sexuality in history.* Philadelphia: Temple University Press.

Patton, C. (1990). *Inventing AIDS.* New York: Routledge.

Reiman, J. (1995). *The rich get richer and the poor get prison: Ideology, crime, and criminal justice.* Needham Heights, MA: Allyn & Bacon.

Stockdill, B. (1991). *Racial violence: A structural analysis.* Unpublished master's thesis, Northwestern University, Evanston, IL.

Stockdill, B. (1995). (Mis)treating prisoners with AIDS: Analyzing health care behind bars. In J. J. Kronenfeld (Ed.), *The sociology of health care* (Vol. 12, 49–77). Greenwich, CT: JAI.

Stockdill, B. (1996). *Multiple oppressions and their influence on collective action: The case of the AIDS movement.* Unpublished doctoral dissertation, Northwestern University, Evanston, IL.

Uekert, B. K. (1994). *State terrorism and armed conflict: Is terrorism an effective strategy?* Paper presented at the Annual Meeting of the American Sociological Association, Los Angeles.

Warner, M. (1993). *Fear of a queer planet: Queer politics and social theory.* Minneapolis: University of Minnesota Press.

Wolfe, L. (1993). Denver grand jury. In *Queer women and men in support of political prisoners.* Unpublished work.

Zinn, H. (1980). *A people's history of the United States.* New York: Harper & Row.

Critical Social Justice: An Integration

This chapter attempts to develop an integrated theory of social justice informed by critical criminology in an effort to distinguish it (social justice) from conventional definitions of criminal justice. Each of the previous chapters in this anthology contributes to this undertaking. Individually, they represent unique perspectives on social justice. Arrigo explores what the thematic points of convergence and divergence are across the chapters. The author begins his analysis by returning to the forms that social justice can assume as identified in the book's introduction. The position taken by each author is identified and examined. Next, he develops those joint areas of similarity and dissimilarity that reappear in the respective chapters. The author contends that these thematic notions represent an outline for an emerging and integrative theory of critical social justice. Arrigo then broadly contrasts his appraisal of social justice with standard accounts of criminal justice. He argues that typical definitions of law, crime, and deviance, as the basic blueprint for the operation of the criminal justice apparatus, are not consistent with an integrated theory of social justice as informed by critical criminology. According to Arrigo, an integrated theory of critical social justice recognizes that the criminal justice system does not promote socially just outcomes and practices. Further, critical social justice theory shows us how much the criminal justice system works to thwart such possibilities. Arrigo's conclusion is that not only are the two concepts (social justice and criminal justice) not compatible, they are fundamentally opposed to one another. If social justice principles are to be valued in criminal justice contexts, then future explanations of law, crime, and deviance will need to be more consistent with an integrative theory of critical social justice.

13

In Search of Social Justice

Toward an Integrative and Critical (Criminological) Theory

BRUCE A. ARRIGO

ach of the preceding chapters in this anthology tells us something about what social justice is based on a particular theory situated within the critical criminological tradition. As stated in the introduction, the various theories do not represent all critical perspectives. However, they do represent some of the more "cutting edge" approaches to understanding crime, law, and deviance. Further, it is somewhat difficult to construct an integrated theory of critical social justice when relying on chapters written by one or two people who then speak for that critical criminological point of view. Nevertheless, this is exactly what I will be attempting here.

Generalizing from this kind of data can be inherently suspect. The assumption made, however, is that the authors who speak for and write within the critical traditions described in the respective chapters are recognized "experts" on that school of thought to which they claim allegiance. Thus, it is reasonable to advance a provisional, integrative theory of critical social justice based on their analyses.

To describe a consolidated theory of social justice informed by critical criminology, it is important to recall the forms that social justice assume in relation to criminal justice. Clearly, each of the chapters' authors believes there is something called social justice. Thus, the question that remains is how social justice is envisioned in light of the various frames of reference presented within this text.

The introductory chapter outlines four possibilities on the association between criminal and social justice (see the introduction, Figure 2). Briefly, they include the following:

1. Social justice is the point of origin, and the criminal justice system seeks or fails to advance principles of fairness, equity, reasonableness, and so forth, through police, court, and correctional practices.

2. Criminal justice is the starting place, and, when the system is working effectively, it reflects the collective sense of social justice that American citizens embody.

3. Social justice exists, but it is neither dependent on nor related to criminal justice.

4. Both social and criminal justice models exist but in a more dynamic, interactional state where system demands and public needs are, on occasion, equally ensured.

This chapter will assess what position each of the anthology's contributors take on the form that social justice assumes given the critical criminological perspectives studied. Further, this chapter will identify and examine those core areas on which the respective authors generally agree or disagree. These core areas represent thematic points of convergence and divergence. Collectively, they depict a developing and integrative conception of critical social justice. This overall theory will be provisionally contrasted against conventional criminal justice notions. This contrast will specifically focus on standard definitions of law, crime, and deviance. Further, this assessment will make it possible to comment on how an integrated social justice, based on critical criminological theory, is or is not related to conventional police, court, and correctional practices.

REVISITING THE FORMS OF
SOCIAL JUSTICE: CONTRIBUTIONS
FROM CRITICAL CRIMINOLOGY

Table 13.1 lists the various theories examined in this anthology. The position each contributor took on the form that social justice assumes is also identified by the symbol X. Interestingly, there is no complete agreement. Depending on the particular critical criminological point of view in question, social justice is a starting point, a destination, a separate condition, or is simultaneously a beginning and end point depending on the crime problem in question.

Based on Table 13.1, several trends can be identified. Socialist feminism, peacemaking criminology, prophetic criticism, critical race theory, and topology theory maintain that social justice is the point of origin. That is, given the assumptions of the particular perspective in question, criminal justice concerns are (and ought to be) dealt with through socially just principles. In addition, radical criminology, queer theory, and chaos theory assert that social justice is the goal. It is the direction toward which society should move. This means that criminal justice is the point of origin and that, to achieve social justice, certain systemic changes must occur or several fundamental conditions must be present. Finally, one critical theory argues that social justice interacts with criminal justice on a dynamic and fluid basis. This is anarchist criminology. This means that, depending on the crime, law, or deviance event, there are occasions when social justice precedes criminal justice and vice versa. Further, according to anarchist criminology, the interests of both the system and of society can be, at times, concurrently achieved.

A few theories indicate that social justice assumes different forms simultaneously. Semiotics, for example, maintains that social justice can be a starting point, an end point, an autonomous state, or much more interactive with criminal justice. Postmodern feminism and constitutive criminology argue that social justice exists independent of criminal justice but can also be extremely interactive with it. In my subsequent discussion on thematic areas of convergence and divergence, these matters will be explored in greater detail. For now,

Table 13.1 Revisiting the Forms of Social Justice

Theory	Social Justice as Starting Point	Social Justice as End Point	Social Justice as Independent	Social Justice and Criminal Justice as Interactional
Radical criminology		X		
Socialist feminist criminology	X			
Peacemaking criminology	X			
Prophetic criticism	X			
Anarchist criminology				X
Postmodern feminist criminology			X	X
Semiotics	X	X	X	X
Constitutive criminology			X	X
Critical race theory	X			
Chaos theory		X		
Topology theory	X			
Queer theory		X		

however, I simply wish to indicate that several critical criminological perspectives view social justice as concurrently operating from a myriad of forms.

Identifying the relationship that social justice shares with criminal justice is important. As this anthology demonstrates, there is a great deal of confusion surrounding the meaning of both terms. Establishing the association helps us understand two things. First, we can begin to recognize how the various orientations presented in this book generally view social justice. This is particularly revealing when examining each perspective's unique position on law, crime, and deviance. Second, we can increasingly identify what a critical and integrative theory of social justice looks like. Settling on the parameters for this theory is significantly enhanced when areas of similarity and dissimilarity are described. It is to the matter of core themes that I now turn.

IDENTIFICATION OF CORE THEMES ON SOCIAL JUSTICE: CONTRIBUTIONS FROM CRITICAL CRIMINOLOGY

Before presenting a thematic overview of social justice, some clarification is warranted when speaking about points of "convergence" and "divergence" as employed in this chapter. Convergence refers to a theme (for example, the role of power) that all of the theories address in some way. The manner in which the core area is described across the critical criminological orientations may vary significantly or only nominally. Divergence refers to clear contrasts where some perspectives adopt one position on a given theme and where other theories adopt an entirely different view on that same theme (for instance, micro- versus macrolevel of analysis). The difference between convergence and divergence as used here, then, is a function of *how* the theme is incorporated into the respective theories and not whether a particular frame of reference does or does not embrace the identified core area. The more readily all the theories assume a similar position on a theme, or all the theories assume vastly different points of view on a theme, is the degree to which a point of convergence rather than divergence has been identified. The more readily individual perspectives can be grouped into thematic categories given a core area is the degree to which a point of divergence rather than convergence has been identified. Admittedly, this process is a bit arbitrary. However, the aim is to give some additional clarity on how social justice is generally envisioned by critical criminology. Further, the aim is to distinguish it (social justice) from criminal justice. The strategy employed here facilitates these goals.

Table 13.2 presents a summary of the themes identified across the various critical criminological perspectives. They are listed as points of convergence and divergence. This cataloging is not exhaustive. Only those core areas most prominently featured within and throughout the critical criminological perspectives are identified. Thus, what is presented here is preliminary; that is, more detailed analysis is encouraged and is necessary.

I previously attempted something of an integration relevant to theoretical concerns in crime and justice. This synthesis explored contrasts among conflict, radical, and postmodern criminology (Arrigo & Bernard, 1997), as well as compared modernist and postmodernist themes pertinent to law and justice studies (Arrigo, 1995). The integration undertaken in this chapter will, in part, be guided by the insights developed in my earlier work. Organizationally, I will first examine all themes of convergence and then consider all areas of divergence. This process should make the integration easier to follow. In other words, by beginning with what is consistently maintained across the criminological perspectives and proceeding to what is differentially asserted, we can see what is most evident with critical social justice to what is increasingly complex about it.

Critical Social Justice and Points of Convergence

1. Social Justice Is Valued over Criminal Justice According to critical criminology, social justice is viewed as something of considerable value. In fact, each perspective believes that the concerns of social justice are, in many fundamental ways, more significant than the problems of criminal justice. Broadly defined, the interests, needs, and rights of individual people and citizen groups are of substantial worth. Let us examine how critical criminology assumes this position.

Radical Marxists take this position when asserting that the economic needs of people must be met such that everyone experiences similar life chances and

Table 13.2 Convergence and Divergence in Critical Social Justice

Convergence	Divergence
1. Social justice over Criminal justice	1. Type of theory (structural vs. agency)
2. Importance of power	2. Basic assumptions (modernist vs. postmodernist)
3. Source of crime	3. Level of analysis (macro vs. micro)
4. Goal(s) of justice	4. Nature of crime, law, deviance (absolute vs. not absolute)
5. Creating social change	5. Nature of social justice (absolute vs. not absolute)

opportunities. Socialist feminists maintain this same view; however, they draw specific attention to the interests of women and the manner in which they are invalidated through a highly exploitive and deeply patriarchal system of social and economic inequality. Peacemaking criminologists argue for the rights of individuals in their steadfast commitment to mutual respect, open communication, and genuine care for all citizens, including those who offend or otherwise victimize. Proponents of prophetic criticism promote social justice over criminal justice by emphasizing the connection between who we are as people (for example, lawyers, police officers, correctional administrators, defendants) and who we ought to be as humane, emancipatory, and empowering contributors to a just society. Anarchist criminologists recognize the importance of social justice by rejecting the state-regulated criminal justice system altogether. In its place, anarchists support decentralized, nonauthoritarian, and community-based initiatives that promote self-growth, inclusivity, and local autonomy. Critical race theorists affirm the importance of social rather than criminal justice by drawing attention to how legal doctrines and criminal statutes obscure race. Racial justice is about exposing and challenging the presumed superiority of white standards as applied to all persons, especially people of color. Queer theory advocates acknowledge the importance of social justice rather than criminal justice by insisting that American culture, particularly in its construction of sexuality, marginalizes nonheterosexuals. The effect of such oppression is the criminalization of gay, lesbian, bisexual, and transgendered persons.

These theories emphasize everyday contexts (for example, economics, morality, ethics, gender, race, sexual orientation) in which social justice needs are viewed as more valuable than criminal justice demands. The remaining theories, however, address the merits of social justice from a different vantage point. Postmodern feminists, constitutive criminologists, semioticians, chaologists, and catastrophe theorists recognize the importance of social justice through the variable of language. In other words, what we say and how we say it has considerable impact on whether the goals of social justice are being met. Let us consider how this works for these theories.

Postmodern feminism addresses the significance of social justice in two ways. First, it identifies where and how gender (male) biases infiltrate the practice of criminal justice. In this regard, the theory is compatible with socialist feminism. Second, however, it recalls what "*stories*" structure our lives (male-dominated narratives about crime, law, and deviance, and so forth) and, thus, color our vision of justice. Integrative-constitutive criminology insists that a media-induced "culture of consumption" masks, distorts, denies, or ignores alternative forms of justice. Thus, the enduring difference that multiple conceptions of reality, truth, and knowledge contribute to the process of *articulating justice* for various citizen groups is obstructed. Semiotics understands the value of social justice by recognizing its essential role in *defining the various meanings* of crime. Chaos theory values social justice by explaining how complex systems behave both predictably and unpredictably. Contrary to the position of conventional criminal justice, this mixture of order and disorder, as a facet of social life and human interaction, cannot be rigidly controlled. Thus, the *language we employ* to discuss this essential unpredictability must be open to chance, flux, randomness, inconsistency, and spontaneity. Catastrophe theory recognizes the importance of social justice in its effort to establish a *peace rhetoric* that reduces the escalation of violence, harm, and victimization between opposing factions or parties.

2. Importance of Power Critical social justice is about power and the extent to which individuals, groups, institutions, and societies exploitively exercise it over and against others. Critical social justice seeks to reconceptualize how power is expressed such that imbalances are minimized or eliminated. This reconceptualization entails a closer look at how individuals and groups are treated within and throughout the criminal justice system. Critical social justice recognizes that the exercise of exploitive power is the will to harm. This harm can be economic (for instance, radical Marxist), gendered (socialist feminist, postmodern feminist), moral/ethical (prophetic criticism, peacemaking), political (anarchist, queer theory), and discursive (semiotics, constitutive criminology). In this regard, then, power is always social; that is, its effects are real and its harm is deep.

3. Source of Crime Critical social justice recognizes that crime exists. However, the source(s) of crime are more directly linked to how the criminal justice system operates. In other words, the problem of crime, to a large degree, is a function of how arrests are made, which felons are prosecuted, who determines criminal culpability, where sentences are served, why some jurors are selected and others are not, and so forth. Critical social justice maintains that individuals bear responsibility for their actions; however, the actions of the accused cannot be completely understood without first examining the political, economic, ideological, psychological, and interpersonal conditions giving rise to this behavior.

In this regard, the presence of crime is fundamentally the absence of some necessary social condition or combination of basic influencing factors. These conditions or factors, when present, help ensure that illicit conduct is kept to a minimum and/or does not otherwise reoccur. Radical criminology maintains this position through its critique of the capitalist economic system. Socialist feminism supports this view in its assessment of the patriarchal economic system. Peacemaking criminology affirms this perspective by stressing the importance of educating for peace *with* as opposed to *over* others. Prophetic criticism embraces this outlook in its vision of a more humanistic, ethical framework through which to effect justice. Anarchist criminology endorses the position that the source of crime is essentially linked to the criminal justice apparatus itself when calling for the system's complete dismantling. Postmodern feminism supports this viewpoint when questioning masculine-based stories about crime, law, and deviance and challenging them as the *only* narratives through which to understand justice. Integrative-constitutive criminology maintains this view in its insistence that media-driven images of crime and delinquency, as an unfolding drama, exclude certain voices and, thus, ways of knowing justice. Semiotics supports this notion through its decoding of the multiple interpretations that exist for the sign "justice." Critical race theory acknowledges this perspective by drawing attention to how nonwhite points of view are invalidated in legal codes or criminal statutes. Chaology assumes this perspective by recognizing that the tight and rigid control the criminal justice system seeks to establish essentially denies the unpredictable, unstable, irrational, and so on, aspects of being fully human. Catastrophe theory embraces this point of view when arguing for new and liberating vocabularies of meaning in which to resolve interpersonal violence. Queer theory endorses this outlook when resisting the homophobic basis on which sexuality is socially constructed.

4. Goals of Justice Based on the first three principles, critical criminology aims to create a certain type of "just" society. Broadly defined, the purpose of social justice is to ensure that individual or group *difference* is not criminalized, stigmatized, or otherwise devalued. In other words, each criminological perspective uniquely draws attention to the rights, interests, and needs of various citizens or collectives that are underrepresented or without voice in the criminal justice system. Some theories promote this agenda by addressing specific class (for example, radical Marxists, prophetic criticism), gender (socialist feminists and postmodern feminist), race (critical race theory), and sexual identity (queer theory) dynamics. Other orientations, however, are broader in application. They advance this same goal by indicating how different ways of knowing and various forms of being are denied expression given the language constraints of prevailing crime, law, and deviance discourse (semiotics, constitutive criminology, catastrophe theory). Thus, the goal of justice is about restoring this representation or reclaiming this voice within and throughout police, court, and correctional practices. It is through this humanistic and emancipatory process of recovering individual and group difference that social justice can be achieved.

5. Social Change Critical social justice seeks change. The change that it longs for is of considerable scope. Altering existing relationships between individual citizens and the criminal justice system is seen as absolutely essential for establishing a more just society. How this change is to come about varies from theory to theory. What is constant, however, is that change, although creating some instability, is healthy for society and productive for its members. Society benefits because no one group can unleash indefinite, indiscriminate, and unchecked power against other groups or citizens without eventually succumbing to the evolving will of the people. Members benefit because they are active contributors in the process of creating and reexamining the extent to which their unique life experiences are reflected in the unfolding script that is justice.

Each critical criminological lens distinctively promotes social change. Radical criminologists advance this position in their commitment to shared ownership over the tools, machines, and resources responsible for economic production in society. Socialist feminists endorse this point of view when calling for an end to the forces of capitalism and patriarchy that produce social and economic inequality and lead to a gendered (male-centered) form of crime and justice. Peacemaking criminologists foster social change by insisting on how the process of educating for peace can function as a restorative mechanism that mediates power imbalances among warring nations as much as between domestic violence participants. Proponents of prophetic criticism champion the need for social change by recalling the transcendent dimensions of our existences—that is, by transforming our daily lives into a journey of self-discovery rooted in history yet demanded by God. Anarchist criminologists promote social change by endorsing flexible, non-state-regulated, and neighborhood-based initiatives that promote local participation, direct action, and self-governance. Postmodern feminist criminologists support the role of social change by demonstrating how the discourse of crime, law, and deviance is always provisional, positional, and local. Constitutive criminologists advance the importance of social change in critical social justice by calling for replacement discourses. These are affirmative and liberating ways of speaking about crime, law, victimization, and so forth, such that people, in all their humanity, and the system, in all that it represents, interact on a more dynamic basis subject less to the constraints of commonplace ways of making justice. Semioticians embrace social change in their recognition that the meaning of justice is never fixed or static; rather, it is always evolving linked as it is to historical context, political economic conditions and other structural forces. Critical race theorists promote social change in their attempt to reconfigure and redefine legal analysis so that it is more consistent with the experiences of people of color. Chaologists advance social change when drawing attention to the nonlinear and fractal dimensions of our existences. These (dis)ordered facets of daily life require a new vocabulary of social exchange, particularly if the fullness of our identities are to be more completely embodied in such institutions as the criminal justice system. Topologists embrace social change when seeking, through discourse, different ways by which to establish peace and nonviolence in society. Gay/lesbian theorists support social change by agitating for queer activism. This type of engagement facilitates a new construction of sexuality with implications for recasting the criminality or delinquency of gay, lesbian, bisexual, and transgendered persons.

Critical Social Justice and Points of Divergence

1. Type of Theory Critical criminological theories can be loosely divided into two categories. Some emphasize the importance of social structure to account for the problem of crime and delinquency. Others stress the role of agency to explain the presence of these forces in society. This categorization is neither complete nor total. In other words, it is something of an overstatement to classify critical criminological theories into this "either-or" approach. Notwithstanding, the distinction is important. It sets the stage for how social structural perspectives versus agency-based orientations varyingly understand what social justice is, especially given the other thematic areas of divergence.

Critical criminological theories that primarily focus on social structure identify specific factors in society that shape or determine how crime and delinquency are conceived. Perspectives adopting this position include radical criminology, socialist feminism, peacemaking criminology, prophetic criticism, anarchist criminology, and queer theory. The specific factors identified differ a bit depending on which of these critical theories is invoked. However, it is clear that these perspectives rely on social structure as the model through which to understand the problem of crime and the need for justice.

Radical criminology is a social structural theory because it emphasizes social class and class structure in its explanation of crime, law, and deviance. Social class refers to an individual's position (for example, owner, manager, worker) in relation to the means of production. Class structure refers to how the distribution of societal interests (such as economic and political power) are disproportionately and consistently controlled by a few powerful groups (say, corporations).

This consolidation of resources produces inequalities. Examples of inequality include determining who will be prosecuted, who will be convicted, who will be sent to prison. Socialist feminism is a theory of social structure. It emphasizes the same dynamics as radical Marxism but draws specific attention to how the economic arrangements in capitalist society are steeped within a male culture that victimizes and exploits women. Gay/lesbian theory endorses the argument made by radical Marxists. It examines the organization of capitalism and explains how it is saturated within a homophobic economic reality that dismisses or marginalizes nonheterosexuals.

Peacemaking criminology, prophetic criticism, and anarchist criminology are social structural theories consistent with radical criminology. However, each offers a different recipe for changing the conditions that give rise to injustice. Peacemaking advances the humanistic principles of love, mutual respect, and empathic regard for others. Prophetic criticism promotes the humanization of work, the democratization of the economy, and moral accountability. Anarchist criminology supports the collapse of the criminal justice apparatus, the rise of local sites of community, and the adaptable process of justice making.

Critical criminological theories that primarily rely on an understanding of agency to account for crime and delinquency recognize the profound inability of individuals to regulate events in the world on their own, given the impact of language. In other words, agency-based theories maintain that who we are as people is, to a significant degree, determined through discourse. Agency-based theories or theories of subjectivity argue that implicit values and assumptions are embedded within the words that we use to describe people, interpersonal exchanges, and situations we encounter. If meaning insists within and throughout language, then the question becomes whose concealed voice and disguised way of knowing saturates the discourse that we use. Is it the person who speaks, or is it someone (or something) else?

Consider the following example. Police officers interact with and speak to citizens they detain in a certain way. This interaction and speech is different from how inmates in a prison engage one another, how attorneys in a courtroom argue a criminal case, how mentally ill persons present themselves before an administrative hearing board, or how juvenile gang members speak about crime. In each instance, certain parameters of meaning are embedded within the words, phrases, gestures, sounds, and silences employed by the respective individuals. These definable boundaries of sense structure how each person communicates. Police officers tend to be authoritarian, direct, in control. Attorneys tend to be persuasive, confident, passionate. Prison inmates seem hard, rough, cold. Mentally ill persons sound incoherent, confused, out of control. Juvenile gang members appear cool, street smart, tough.

How each person conveys his or her thoughts, feelings, beliefs, and so forth, is profoundly linked to the words each individual employs. Indeed, we can identify many words and phrases that have special meaning when used by police officers ("Book him"), prison inmates ("tossing salad"), attorneys ("Objection, your honor—leading the witness"), psychiatrically disordered persons ("flight of ideas" or "loose associations"), and youth gang members ("Crips versus Bloods"). Notice how all of the words or phrases are familiar to us. However, the context in which they are used by the identified speakers creates unique meaning that is most especially understood when invoked through the language of policing, imprisonment, lawyering, psychosis, and gang jargon, respectively.

More than creating limits for what is said and how it is uttered, however, is the extent to which language speaks on behalf of or in place of the one who utters the words or phrases. According to the critical criminological perspectives embracing theories of subjectivity, it is as if the discourse that is used often speaks *through* the one who speaks; that is, the language invoked is a stand-in for the person him- or herself.

What this means, then, is that we are never completely in control of what we say, how we say it, or its impact (intended or not) on others. Because of language and its powerful effects, we are made out to be, to a considerable extent, unstable, determined, spoken, and regulated. All of this is not to imply that we cannot find freer, more liberating forms of expression when interacting with others. Critical criminologists continue to explore this in some conceptual detail (for example, Arrigo, 1995; Henry & Milovanovic, 1996, pp. 185–243; Milovanovic, 1996a, 1997), and in different applications (for instance, Arrigo, 1993, 1994, 1996a, 1996b, 1997, 1998; Milovanovic, 1996b; Young & Arrigo, 1998). Again, though, the question remains whose voice (or what voice) speaks on our behalf even though we utter the words that we do? This is where agency-based theories in critical criminology vary considerably.

Perspectives adopting the agency-based approach outlined here include postmodern feminism, constitutive criminology, semiotics, critical race theory, chaology, and topology theory. Postmodern feminists identify the link between language and subjectivity by pointing out how crime, law, and deviance concepts are saturated within a masculine grammar that invalidates the voice of women. Constitutive criminologists adopt a similar outlook on language but draw attention to the duality of meaning created between human agents and the social structures (for example, sheriff departments, juvenile probation centers, jails) of which they are a part. Semiotics recognizes the role of language particularly in its effort to extract the assorted meanings conveyed by words and phrases used by agents of the criminal justice system. Critical race theory sees language as pivotal to the sense-making process and the construction of identity in its critique of case law and other legal narratives that exclude the voice of nonwhites. Both chaos and topology theory recognize the power of language when calling for new, replacement vocabularies with which to speak about crime, law, justice, community.

Of the theories inclined to the agency-based approach, constitutive criminology is the most problematic. In many ways, it is also a theory of social structure (Henry & Milovanovic, 1996, pp. 45–98). Constitutive criminologists are only now just exploring how agency and social structure are intertwined through language such that an understanding of subjectivity does not exist without reference to the social or institutional forces of which agency is a part (Milovanovic & Henry, 1998). Even in these investigations, however, language is the central factor. Clearly, the articulation of social structural dynamics (for instance, working in a police department, living in a jail, being selected as a juror in a capital case) proceeds only through the naming of such processes by humans. Thus, this local, and relational activity is what makes constitutive criminology a theory of subjectivity.

2. Basic Assumptions Understanding how best to classify each critical criminological theory (social structure versus agency based) sets the stage for all subsequent discussions on thematic areas of divergence. The most significant of these additional points of contrast involves basic methodological assumptions. Two general constellation of assumptions are found in critical criminology. Some theories adopt one set of assumptions, while other perspectives support the second clustering of presuppositions. Broadly speaking, these constellation of assumptions can be placed into either a *modernist* or a *postmodernist* frame of reference. Although some theories overlap a bit, it is evident that each theory more closely aligns itself with one or the other approach. The modernist/postmodernist split tells us something significant about a given theory's understanding of the world, events in it, and individual actors. Further, this divide is important because, depending on the critical perspective in question, the position taken on social justice will vary.

Theories advancing a modernist orientation include radical criminology, socialist feminism, peacemaking criminology, prophetic criticism, anarchist criminology, and queer theory. Essentially, these theories maintain that events in the world are retrievable, reducible, quantifiable, knowable, and controllable. In other words, all crime-related phenomena can be thoroughly studied. Given enough analytical rigor and methodological sophistication, precise and accurate scientific truths can be discerned. These truths will create objective and impartial knowledge about such things as criminal offenders, correctional officers, probation counselors, defense attorneys, the selection of jurors, the organization of prisons, drug use among juveniles, the criminal enterprise in Central America, violations of human rights, and the process of making justice itself. These knowledge claims can then be used as definitive statements about crime, law, and delinquency. These powerful statements substantially contribute to setting social/public policy, controlling criminal behavior, and redefining justice. Modernists believe that this process maximizes prospects for social justice in society.

Of the critical criminological theories identified within the modernist camp, anarchist criminology is the most problematic. Anarchists reject any kind of permanence or prescriptive control, believing that these forces minimize the diversity that people represent, erode the possibility for creating community, and impede the process of living humanely. Notwithstanding, anarchist criminologists believe that there is an objective basis to reality and knowledge. For them, people and places are real and certain. Thus, we can fundamentally know things about people and their engagement with the criminal justice apparatus. More important, according to anarchists, we can affect permanent, long-lasting solutions to the problems afflicting the system.

Theories promoting a postmodern attitude in critical criminology include postmodern feminism, constitutive criminology, semiotics, critical race theory, chaology, and topology theory. Essentially, these perspectives challenge and reject the position that basic, identifiable structures govern various aspects of social life. The study of crime and justice is one facet of social life. Contrary to the view espoused by modernist critical criminologists, postmodernists argue that it is not possible to ascertain with complete certainty what causes crime and delinquency, why some officers use excessive discretion, when sentencing decisions are racially motivated, why prisons are overcrowded, and so forth. These and other questions can never be answered completely because of the intervening variable of language. Reality is observer created, according to postmodernists. Moreover, the reality that is identified assumes the form of a language. As was previously described, speech always communicates embedded values and implicit assumptions about people and events. According to postmodernists, these meanings "get in the way"; that is, they color or encode our experiences. Thus, there is no such thing as reality per se. Instead, there are only approximations or versions of it that take form depending on who speaks about it and how it is spoken. Thus, social justice exists but does so from multiple-languaged points of view.

Postmodern critical criminologists are not skeptical, nihilistic, or fatalistic. They believe it is possible to promote greater possibilities for experiencing dignity, freedom, humanity, equality, being. This requires a twofold process. First, it is important to expose the layered dimensions of exploitation, victim-ization, and marginalization contained deep within the typical language that is used when speaking about law, delinquency, harm, and punishment. Second, it is also important to articulate where and how other, more complete, expres-sions of one's identity could be embodied in the stories about crime and jus-tice. Further, these narratives are themselves never finished. They are forever in process; that is, they are contingent, incomplete, positional truths produc-ing a partial knowledge about the self in relation to society. Postmodern criti-cal criminologists, then, believe that social justice is not rooted in absolute or totalizing statements; rather, it is contained in relational, positional, provi-sional observations that remain in a constant state of flux or becoming.

3. Level of Analysis Given the type-of-theory distinction and the basic-assumption dichotomy contained within critical criminology, it is evident that there is a split with the level of analysis that is intended within these various theories. By level of analysis, I am referring to a perspective's essential focus in its investigation of social justice. This focus is global, societal, macro-oriented or local, situational, micro-oriented. This macro versus micro divide is not absolute. Again, what is identified is the general tendency found within the respective theories.

Perspectives sympathetic to more macrolevel analysis include radical crimi-nology, socialist feminism, peacemaking criminology, prophetic criticism, an-archist criminology, and queer theory. This cataloging should come as no surprise given that they were previously identified as theories of social struc-ture. Again, what is at issue for these theories are the assorted social condi-tions and/or influencing factors that, if present, would maximize the likelihood for social justice. How each critical criminological orientation would accomplish this was described earlier in the thematic core area of diver-gence identified as type-of-theory.

Perspectives inclined to a more microlevel analysis include postmodern feminism, constitutive criminology, semiotics, critical race theory, chaology, and topology theory. These are theories of human subjectivity. What is at stake for these orientations is the intervening effects of language that structure thought in ways that are not neutral. Social justice exists when multiple ex-pressions of difference find embodiment in the narratives of crime, law, and deviance. The manner in which each theory advances this agenda was previ-ously described.

4. Nature of Crime Critical criminology takes two vastly different positions on the nature of crime. The "nature of crime" refers to how we can best understand it in relation to people who engage in criminal or delinquent behavior. One point of view claims that crime is absolute. In other words, certain acts can be defined as wrong or illicit by everyone all the time. The other point of view argues that crime is not absolute. In other words, social acts of wrongdoing are at best "contingent universalities," subject more to the local and relational interpretation of the behavior given form and substance through language.

Radical criminology, socialist feminism, peacemaking criminology, prophetic criticism, queer theory (and to some extent anarchist criminology) maintain that crime is absolute. The reason that some individuals or groups (for example, entrepreneurs, white-collar criminals, government leaders) are not as readily found guilty of engaging in criminal wrongdoing by the justice system is because they have the economic power to protect themselves from most forms of criminal sanction. This "absolute basis of crime" philosophy is consistent with both the social structural approach and the modernist assumptions previously explored as additional core thematic areas of divergence.

Postmodern feminism, constitutive criminology, semiotics, critical race theory, chaology, and topology theory assert that crime is not absolute. Crime *is* real and the harm it produces *is* deep; however, determining which acts are criminal, under what circumstances, for how long, and by whom is not certain. In other words, according to these nonabsolutist theories, much about crime is subject to the organizing principles of language.

Let us consider the example of homosexuality. Today, gay/lesbian mutually consenting sex is not considered criminal in most jurisdictions. Twenty-five years ago it was considered criminal in *all* U.S. jurisdictions. One of the important things that changed within this span of time was how gay/lesbian practices were envisioned and how we talked about them. Both thought and speech were therefore significantly intertwined and of consequence for the sense-making process regarding nonheterosexual behavior. The same can be said about people of color, the mentally ill, juvenile gang members, and even rock 'n' roll music! The emphasis given to language is not to dismiss political and economic forces that help change social views on these matters. The point is that even the impact of political and economic forces must be expressed. It is this very expression that assumes a certain form, a certain grammar.

Given that language always and already embraces hidden values and concealed assumptions, defining crime as absolute is just not possible, according to some critical criminologists. At best, we can speak of crime as real for particular individuals or groups, in given circumstances, for a specified period of time, based on the governing language principles of crime and justice, for that period. This is not the same as total relativism or an "anything goes" philosophy. Rather, what is affirmed are the incomplete and unfolding dimensions of our existences as situational, relational, and provisional. The position enunciated here is consistent with the agency-based and postmodernist themes previously identified as core areas of divergence.

5. Nature of Social Justice The nature of social justice is also the product of two vastly divergent perspectives for critical criminology. Following the logic of the fourth principle outlined, social justice is both absolute and not absolute. For those perspectives endorsing a social structural, modernist, macrolevel orientation, social justice is about coming to terms with the singular, objective, and absolute reality of crime. These theories have been consistently identified throughout the core thematic areas of divergence. For those perspectives embracing an agency-based, postmodernist, microlevel orientation, social justice is about coming to terms with the multiple, discordant, polyvalent realities of crime. These theories have also been routinely identified throughout the core thematic areas of divergence.

INTEGRATIVE CRITICAL SOCIAL JUSTICE AND STANDARD CRIMINAL JUSTICE PRACTICES: TOWARD A SYSTEMATIC COMPARISON

Thus far, an analysis of the forms of social justice, as understood by each critical criminological theory, has been identified and explained. Further, a detailed assessment of thematic areas of similarity and dissimilarity, across the respective theories, has been provided. Figure 13.1 summarily presents these findings in a much more integrative and comprehensive fashion.

To follow Figure 13.1, it is best to start with the various theories, asking two questions when considering them. First, what form of social justice does that theory espouse? As previously explained, there are four forms: (1) social justice is a beginning point, (2) it is an end point, (3) it exists independently of criminal justice, or (4) it dynamically interacts with criminal justice. The forms of social justice are identified at the left of the figure, with each theory's respective form noted.

The second question is, What position does each critical criminological perspective take on several core social justice themes? The figure indicates there is general agreement on several core areas (themes of convergence), and there is also some considerable disagreement on other cores areas (themes of divergence). Again, the thematic points developed are general statements. It is a bit of an oversimplification to pigeonhole any one theory this way. However, the aim is to bring an integrative overview of critical social justice into sharper focus.

The commentary developed on critical social justice throughout this text and integrated within this chapter can also be provisionally compared to customary criminal justice practices. In other words, what are the standard accounts of law, crime, and deviance embraced by police, court, and correctional agents, and how are these understandings related, if at all, to critical social justice? The answer to this question may appear somewhat obvious. Indeed, many

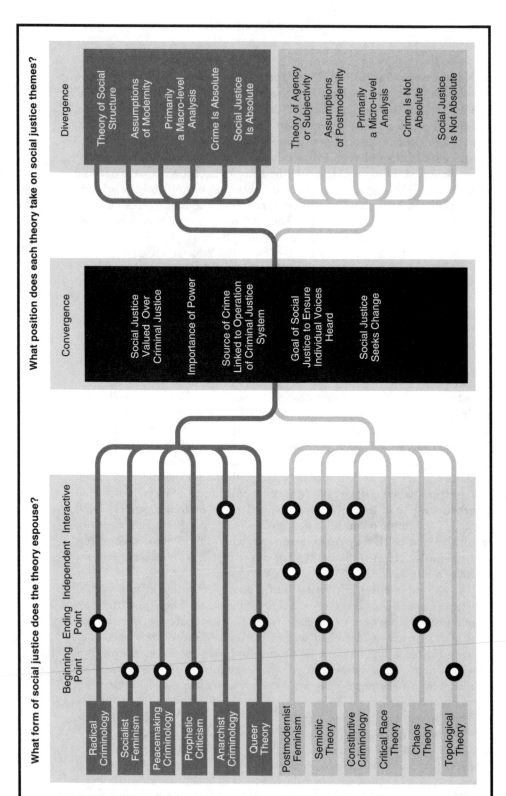

FIGURE 13.1 Justice: An Integrative Overview of Critical Social Justice

of the contributors based their analyses on the inadequacies of the existing system to address the needs, rights, and interests of everyday citizens or groups ignored, harmed, or otherwise brutalized by the criminal justice apparatus.

The point being made here, however, goes to the very essence of how crime, law, and deviance are acknowledged as such in American society and the extent to which they are compatible with critical social justice goals. The criminal justice system exists as a response to behavior deemed unacceptable. Police, court, and correctional work endeavors to ensure that social acts of wrongdoing are dealt with effectively and efficiently. Arrests are made, suspects are prosecuted, felons are convicted. Interestingly, the social justice problems associated with these decisions are not so easily identifiable. On the surface, we typically speak about such things as too much police discretion, too much plea bargaining, and too many prisons. If we could correct or change these matters, then efforts at establishing justice would be increased. Granted, police discretion, plea bargaining, and the growing number of prisons in our society are problems. However, specifically focusing on these issues misses much of the more critical attitude argued for throughout this reader.

It is one thing to identify the *symptoms* of the criminal justice system's failure to promote a more just society, and it is another to identify *root causes*. The presence of overcrowded prisons, racial disparities in sentencing, police use of excessive/deadly force, jury tampering, prosecutorial misconduct, excessive juvenile waivers to the adult system, parole board delays, and the like, have little or nothing to do with the system's inability to promote social justice. They are symptoms of a larger malaise that is endemic to how we understand criminal justice.

Given that the justice system is a response to crime problems, and given that social justice is about creating a climate in which individual and group differences can thrive, neither model speaks the same language. In other words, police, court, and correctional practices represent an entirely different set of rules about human social behavior than those envisioned by advocates of critical social justice. In a general fashion, each critical criminological theory describes what these rules presently are and suggests what they ought to be.

Granted, conventional mechanisms such as community policing, victim-offender mediation boards, prisoner rights advocacy groups, and so forth, exist to promote the interests, rights, and needs of citizens. However, these are typically components *of* the criminal justice system. Moreover, where such entities exist independent of the system (for example, as nonprofits), these agencies can only work from *within* the existing strictures of the criminal justice apparatus. Thus, to effect meaningful change, advocates of social justice must turn to those very subsystems (the police, the courts, the jails, the psychiatric hospitals, the juvenile boot camps, the prisons, and so on) all too often responsible for the very oppression and victimization that proponents seek to resist and denounce.

An integrative theory of critical social justice explains what is troubling about this appeal to the system in its consideration of the role of power, the source of crime, and the goals of justice. What we are to conclude, then, is that the criminal justice apparatus does not and cannot promote socially just outcomes. It is not equipped, in its present configuration, to do so. Nothing short of a massive, fundamental, and thorough overhaul, from subsystem to subsystem, would make it more consistent with critical social justice in theory and, as well, in practice.

In addition, given the organization of the criminal justice system and the formal/informal socialization of police, court, and correctional agents, the possibility for promoting more emancipatory, humane, and enlightened principles of justice rendering are, advertently or inadvertently, thwarted. Again, the system exists as a reaction to harms done or harms that might be done, in a very narrowly prescribed fashion. Critical social justice exists as a prism through which the myriad of interests and rights of all citizens can be protected and affirmed. This tension between system demands and citizen needs is not easily reconciled. In the end, it is often the criminal justice apparatus that prevails. Based on these observations, the conclusion that follows is that not only are the two concepts (social justice and criminal justice) not compatible; they are also fundamentally opposed to one another.

This opposition is a very big problem. Clearly, it is not enough simply to identify it, although this is certainly a necessary start. Further, by providing something of a systematic analysis regarding where and how this tension manifests itself, a potential direction for meaningful resolution emerges. The fundamental question that remains is to consider creative avenues by which criminal justice practices can be more consistent with critical social justice goals. How this can be accomplished will vary among the critical criminological perspectives. This anthology has taken the first step in articulating the dilemmas inherent in achieving social justice based on critical criminological theories and principles. The next step, the step that awaits, is for scholars, educators, policy analysts, practitioners, students, lay professionals, and everyone interested in the intersection of crime and justice, to insist on a society that understands acts of transgression in ways that ensure the dignity and humanity for all parties involved. This task is not an easy one. It is, however, the only chance we have of making peace with crime and restoring justice in our lives.

CONCLUSION

This chapter returned us to the basic question examined in this reader; namely, what is social justice? To answer this question, an integration, of sorts, was attempted. To foster this integration, the position taken by each critical criminological perspective regarding the form that social justice assumes was identified. Similarities and dissimilarities across the various theories were examined. Further, a detailed assessment on core themes of convergence and divergence were also described. This analysis, coupled with the previous investigation, established a comprehensive cataloging of what a critically inspired theory of social justice included. This comprehensive integration was summarily presented in Table 13.1.

Some attention was also given to the relationship between critical social justice and the practice of criminal justice. It was argued that conventional police, court, and correctional practices impede the progress of critical social justice. Further, the two were shown to be fundamentally at odds with one another. Although these dilemmas were acknowledged as serious, they were not depicted as insurmountable.

The project that lies ahead, in both theory and practice, is to liberate law, crime, and deviance principles from the constraints of conventional wisdom and understanding. The practice of criminal justice needs to be more consistent with the philosophy of critical social justice. How this occurs will vary from perspective to perspective; however, this is the only way by which to reduce the harm caused by crime and to enhance the prospects for justice in our society.

REVIEW QUESTIONS

1. What are the forms of social justice, according to critical criminology?

2. What are the five points of convergence and divergence as identified in this chapter?

3. Select one theory and explain how it addresses a theme of convergence.

4. Select one theory and explain how it addresses a theme of divergence.

5. In your own words, what is an integrative theory of social justice?

6. What are the basic differences between critical social justice and criminal justice practices?

7. If you could change something within the criminal justice apparatus so that the system was more consistent with critical social justice principles, what would it be? Why?

REFERENCES

Arrigo, B. (1993). *Madness, language and the law*. Albany, NY: Harrow & Heston.

Arrigo, B. (1994). Legal discourse and the disordered criminal defendant: Contributions from psychoanalytic semiotics and chaos theory. *Legal Studies Forum, 18*(1), 93–112.

Arrigo, B. (1995). The peripheral core of law and criminology: On postmodern social theory and conceptual integration. *Justice Quarterly, 12*(3), 447–472.

Arrigo, B. (1996a). The behavior of law and psychiatry: Rethinking knowledge construction and the guilty-but-mentally ill verdict. *Criminal Justice and Behavior, 23*(4), 572–592.

Arrigo, B. (1996b). *The contours of psychiatric justice: A postmodern critique of mental illness, criminal insanity, and the law*. New York: Garland.

Arrigo, B. (1997). Transcarceration: Notes on a psychoanalytically-informed theory of social practice in the criminal justice and mental health systems. *Crime, Law, and Social Change: An International Journal, 27*(1), 31–48.

Arrigo, B. (1998). Theories of crime and crimes of theorists: On the topological construction of criminological reality. *Theory and Psychology, 8*(2), 219–253.

Arrigo, B. (in press). Constitutive theory and the homeless identity: Discourse of a community deviant. In S. Henry & D. Milovanovic (Eds.), *Constitutive theory at work: Agency and resistance in the constitution of crime and punishment.* New York: State University of New York Press.

Arrigo, B., & Bernard, T. (1997). Postmodern criminology in relation to radical and conflict theory. *Critical Criminology: An International Journal, 8*(2): 39–60.

Henry, S., & Milovanovic, D. (1996). *Constitutive criminology: Beyond postmodernism.* London: Sage.

Milovanovic, D. (1996a). Postmodern criminology: Mapping the terrain. *Justice Quarterly, 13*(4), 567–610.

Milovanovic, D. (1996b). "Rebellious lawyering:" Lacan, chaos, and the development of alternative juridico-semiotic forms. *Legal Studies Forum, 20*(3), 295–321.

Milovanovic, D. (1997). *Postmodern criminology.* New York: Garland.

Milovanovic, D., & Henry, S. (Ed.). (1998). *Constitutive theory at work: Agency and resistance in the constitution of crime and punishment.* Albany: State University of New York Press.

Young, T. R., & Arrigo, B. A. (1998). *Chaos and crime: From criminal justice to social justice.* Albany: State University of New York Press.

Glossary

Activism The process by which ACT UP members challenge the status quo on matters of sexual orientation (queer theory)

ACT UP (AIDS Coalition to Unleash Power); a group consisting of primarily lesbians, gay men, and bisexuals that uses direct action protest to combat the AIDS crisis (queer theory)

Affirmative action legislative programs or steps implemented for the purposes of remediating a group's lack of access to opportunity within a society (radical criminology)

AIDS Acquired Immune Deficiency Syndrome (queer theory)

Alienation situation in which control over the product of one's labor is usurped by those who control the means of production within the capitalist system (that is, the employer) (radical criminology)

Ambiguity uncertainty; the possibility that something can be interpreted in more than one way (anarchist criminology)

Anarchism the belief that no government is the best government and that people will mutually cooperate voluntarily if left alone (anarchist criminology)

Anarchists critical scholars who believe the "political" system should be dismantled, consist of stateless and classless societies, and promote mutual aid and shared responsibility among communal members (introduction)

Anarchy the absence of government or law (anarchist criminology)

Animus hostility (chaos theory)

Antiformalism the absence of formalism in law. Formalism holds that persons similarly situated will receive identical treatment under the law. (critical race theory)

Attractors see **Chaordic regimes.** (chaos theory)

Axial media event media-created events that transform natural activities into dramatic political realities (semiotics)

Backstage the use of mannerisms, behaviors, experiences, rituals, props, and so forth, that disclose the real "performance" (identity) of a person; contrast with backstage performances; see **Dramaturgy**. (semiotics)

Base in Marxist thought, the economy (introduction)

Bias factor within the cusp catastrophe model, the factor that alters the shape and position of the cusp both to the left and right, and in upward and downward directions (catastrophe/topology theory)

Bifurcation division of the whole into two equal halves that emerge spontaneously creating a new pattern; an order-out-of-chaos phenomenon (chaos theory)

Bifurcation set within the cusp catastrophe model, a set of points that indicates divergence in outcomes; exists on the M-surface but can be projected downward onto the C-surface of the cusp catastrophe model (catastrophe/topology theory)

Bigotry holding blindly to a particular opinion; narrow-minded; excessive prejudice (queer theory)

Bimodality within the cusp catastrophe theory, bimodal behavior in the cusp region where for the same value on some control parameter, two results could occur on the same behavioral surface (catastrophe/topology theory)

Bureaucracy an organization with the following characteristics: a chain of command with fewer people at the top than at the bottom, well-defined positions and responsibilities, fairly inflexible rules and procedures, and delegation of authority downward from level to level (anarchist criminology)

Butterfly catastrophe the utilization of the cusp catastrophe model (a topological construct in five-dimensional space) to model how systems or events behave over time (catastrophe/topology theory)

Butterfly factor within the cusp catastrophe model, the factor that is responsible for the third stable form of behavior; it is this factor that makes the outcome trimodal. (catastrophe/topology theory)

Capital logic Marxists Marxists who recognize that many forces (for example, politics, the media, culture) determine the functioning of our society, and conclude that those in economic power cause, administer, and sustain the operation of it (introduction)

Capitalism an economic system in which all goods and services are competitively sold as commodities in a given marketplace (prophetic criticism)

Capitalist justice equates equal justice with the formulation and administration of positive law; is made concrete in the establishment of legal order; based on the survival needs of the capitalist system (prophetic criticism)

Catastrophe within the cusp catastrophe model, sudden discontinuous jumps in an otherwise dynamic system where point attractors are the norm (catastrophe/topology theory)

Catastrophe theory a methodology for understanding how systems respond to changes or events, especially those that are more unpredictable, unplanned, and uncoordinated

Causal analysis assumes no problem is adequately addressed unless its causes are eliminated (prophetic criticism)

Chaordic regimes graphic representation of amounts of disorder within a system of human interactions according to chaos theory (chaos theory)

Chaos theory theory of social systems predicated on the concept that human behavior and interaction are unpredictable and that a minimal amount of unpredictability is required for the relative health of the group

Citizenry crime control citizens that have been enlisted into the criminal justice system by organizing together in an effort to fight crime (prophetic criticism)

COINTELPRO: Counter Intelligence Program (queer theory)

Commodity exchange the idea that when a commodity enters the marketplace, the intrinsic, use value is replaced with an equivalent exchange value (introduction)

Commodity-exchange Marxists the belief held by structural Marxists that economic value plays a more important role in determining how society functions (introduction)

Complex adaptive systems any social or physical system that is highly specialized and organized in which the behavior of that system, although intricate, can be identified and plotted to form a less than completely predictable pattern (chaos theory)

Complexity theory a theory that indicates that given the combination of input variables within many dynamic systems, the output can have more than one result and thus unpredicted results (catastrophe/topology theory)

Constitutive crime harm or violence resulting from unequal power relationships, assuming a discursive linguistic form (constitutive criminology)

Contemporary in or of the current time; sociohistorically, the time period immediately following the modern age begun around the end of World War I (radical criminology)

Contingent the manner in which truth varies by time, place, and storyteller (postmodern and feminist criminology)

Corporate downsizing reduction of workforce by commercial entities for the purpose of minimizing labor costs and maximizing profits (radical criminology)

Corrective justice theory of justice that emphasizes the freedom of choice of people to participate in a free market (constitutive criminology)

Crimes of reduction in constitutive criminology, loss of quality or capability as a result of being on the less powerful end of the power relationship (constitutive criminology)

Crimes of repression a limiting of potential achievement as a result of an uneven power relationship (constitutive criminology)

Criminal justice in regard to law and order, it also recognizes the emphasis being placed on maintaining the existing order through the tools and agencies of the capitalist state. (prophetic criticism)

Critical legal studies a critical method of analyzing legal doctrine by challenging the legitimacy of the values embedded in the language of mainstream legal thought, and identifying what interest groups are reflected in those values (critical race theory)

Critical race theory a theory that takes race into account and the role it plays in the American legal system

C-space a 2D (two-dimensional) control space that is part of the topological construct referred to as the "catastrophe model" (catastrophe/topology theory)

Curve line the edge of the curve in the cusp catastrophe model (catastrophe/topology theory)

Cusp catastrophe model a model composed of two control parameters (factors or variables) that produce 2D (two-dimensional) space and one behavioral surface that reflects the range of possible behavioral states (catastrophe/topology theory)

Cusp region within catastrophe models, an area where more than one output can exist (catastrophe/topology theory)

Decentralization the act of breaking up the centralization of authority, as in government or industry (anarchist criminology)

Deconstruction the careful analysis of all language (written, spoken, or otherwise) regarded as a "text" in which the manifold conflicting meanings in the text are exposed to reveal the essential ambiguity and the subjective nature of reality (postmodern and feminist criminology)

De jure discrimination legal discrimination (critical race theory)

Democratic cultural pluralism a concept that requires a dual system of rights: a general system of rights that are the same for all, and a more specific system of group conscious policies and rights that provide affirmative acknowledgment of oppressed groups in an attempt to remedy inequality (postmodern and feminist criminology)

Deontological   a philosophy of ethics in which one looks at the act or behavior itself to determine wrongfulness; opposed to teleology, which looks at the intent or purpose to determine moral or civil blameworthiness (constitutive criminology)

Deterrence   punishment implemented with certainty and swiftness in an effort to deter crime (prophetic criticism)

Deviance   term used to denote behavior that a society finds unacceptable; specifically, crime (chaos theory)

Direct action   a term used by anarchy theorists to refer to individuals doing things for themselves (anarchist criminology)

Discrimination   making unreasonable, false, or unnecessary distinctions on the basis of preference or prejudice (critical race theory)

Discursive process   using language and words to attribute meaning to items, individuals, or situations (postmodern and feminist criminology)

Disorder   natural state of human interactions in which behavior is unpredictable (chaos theory)

Distributive justice   theory of social justice based on the goal of an equitable distribution of material and conditions (constitutive criminology and chaos theory)

Divergence   within the cusp catastrophe mode, when small differences or changes in the control parameter produce dramatic changes in states or the behavioral surface such as the bifurcation (catastrophe/topology theory)

Divine law   codes of human behavior dictated by religious precepts (chaos theory)

DIY   "do it yourself"; the anarchist philosophy that individuals should do things for themselves (anarchist criminology)

Dogma   a belief; doctrine, opinion (anarchist criminology)

Doing gender   engaging in rituals that are based on stereotypical gender-based behaviors (postmodern and feminist criminology)

Dramaturgy   an explanation of human behavior and human social interaction based on an understanding that people live out performances; that is, the theater of life is a stage. People adopt rituals, employ mannerisms, embody beliefs, use props, and so forth, that reflect a living, unfolding, incomplete performance. (semiotics)

Dumping up   the process of listening to the oppressed, personally confronting the oppressor with your concerns, and inviting a response (peacemaking criminology)

Dynamic regimes   see **Chaordic regimes.** (chaos theory)

Economic base   foundation of Marxist theory composed of class, means of production, and mode of production (radical criminology)

Economic injustice   the uneven distribution of wealth through exploitive means inherent in the capitalist system (radical criminology)

Economic structure   see **Mode of production.** (radical criminology)

Economic system   the interaction among the mode, means, and relations of production (radical criminology)

Empirical evidence   evidence obtained through observation, experiment, and practical experience (critical race theory)

Epistemic uncertainty   multiple interactions and perspectives with none certain or final (anarchist criminology)

Equivalent rights   attempt to recognize the ways that difference might need to be adjusted or accommodated to yield treatment that is of "equal value," though not identical (postmodern and feminist criminology)

Ethical activism   a point of view advocating personal responsibility to make choices and engage in behaviors that positively affect ourselves, others, and the world around us (postmodern and feminist criminology)

Exploitation   the process wherein the worker who produces an item is remunerated for a small fraction of its worth, resulting in a large surplus value retained by the owner of the means of production as profit (radical criminology)

Far from equilibrium   according to chaos theory, the moment where the notion of limitation, closure, certainty, finiteness, permanence is in flux; opposite of equilibrium conditions (catastrophe/topology theory)

Feminism   a set of theories about the oppression of women; a social movement to create social, political, and economic equality for women (postmodern and feminist criminology)

Feminist   (adj.) of or pertaining to viewing events, situations, and relationships from the perspective and perceptions unique to women; (n.) type of feminist advocate who pursues societal change within and among existing social structures (socialist feminism)

First generation of rights   set of "negative rights" protecting populace from power of government bodies secured through the American and French Revolutions (constitutive criminology)

First wave feminism   sociopolitical movement during late nineteenth and early twentieth centuries in which women advocated for political reforms, especially the right to vote (socialist feminism)

Forgiveness   according to peacemaking, the act of forgiving an individual but not forgetting what has been done (peacemaking criminology)

Fractal   system in which the goal of the whole is achieved through the interaction of its parts (chaos theory)

Free-market socialism   economic concept that advocates accumulation of wealth and goods, but toward the betterment of and qualitative living for all members in a society (constitutive criminology)

Frontstage   mannerisms, beliefs, rituals, behaviors, and so forth, that represent a less than completely honest presentation of the self to others in society; contrast with backstage; see **Dramaturgy.** (semiotics)

Gay bashing   physical attacks against queers (queer theory)

Gender inequality   disparity of sociopolitical power or influence between the two sexes (socialist feminism)

Gender role socialization   process by which individuals are taught behavior and expectations of their gender within a given society from the point of view of the dominant culture of that society (socialist feminism)

Global stability   according to catastrophe theorists, an identified pattern of results found when applying theories to topological constructs (catastrophe/topology theory)

Groundless solidarity   solidarity that is achieved by building bridges across our differences to find common issues and concerns that can be worked on together (postmodern and feminist criminology)

Hate crime   committing a crime against a person(s) because of his or her race, religion, beliefs, and so forth (critical race theory)

Hate speech   (racially based): derogatory remarks toward an individual based on his or her race (critical race theory)

Healthy order   according to a capitalist society, the order that primarily benefits the capitalist class—the class that owns and controls the productive process (prophetic criticism)

Hegelian   of or relating to the philosophy or writings of Georg Hegel (chaos theory)

Heterosexism   the systematic oppression of lesbians, gay men, bisexuals, and transgendered people on both institutional and ideological levels and the simultaneous legitimation of heterosexuality as the only valid form of sexuality (queer theory)

Historical materialism   effects of industrial development and mechanization of labor on society viewed from a historical perspective (socialist feminism)

HIV   Human Immunodeficiency Virus (queer theory)

Homophobia Discrimination, prejudice, and other forms of oppression facing transgendered people, bisexuals, gay men, and lesbians (queer theory)

Human community according to anarchism, a sense of community that develops not from regimented patterns of predictable behavior or common bonds or similarity but from a loose and inclusive federation of difference (anarchist criminology)

Human relations according to anarchy theorists, relations among people work best when they are emergent, open to possibilities, and devoid of inflexible roles. (anarchist criminology)

Inaccessibility within the cusp catastrophe model, the middle pleat in the cusp region indicating neutrality is a highly unlikely event (catastrophe/topology theory)

Indeterminacy in law, the principle that the meaning of case holdings, state statutes, and so forth, are never fixed or permanent (critical race theory)

Infrastructure see **Economic base.** (radical criminology)

Injustice according to the prophets of the Old Testament, injustice occurs in the form of crime and corruption or in the wretched condition of the poor. (prophetic criticism)

Instrumental Marxism the belief that the economy, or base, determines how laws are enacted, how crimes are constructed, and how deviance is defined (introduction)

Instrumental rhetoric provides material for the construction of allowable victims and for victimization by objectifying others as less complete human beings, thereby allowing victimization without remorse (catastrophe/topology theory)

Integrated–constitutive theory of crime a blend of constitutive thought, media studies, race/class analysis, and political-economic theory (constitutive criminology)

Interracial crimes crimes that involve a victim and an offender of different races (critical race theory)

Jump within the cusp catastrophe model, the catastrophe or discontinuity in an otherwise linear, continuous system (catastrophe/topology theory)

Jus divinum: "given by God"; refers to divine law (chaos theory)

Justice as distribution according to need assumes that human beings behave (or are capable of behaving) cooperatively and altruistically without the use of financial rewards or penal sanctions (prophetic criticism)

Legalese the code, or language, of the court used for communication within the court (introduction)

Legally battered when the courts allow individuals to enter or remain in situations that are abusive (peacemaking criminology)

Linguistic formulations the manner in which people use words to express and form our understanding of social events (semiotics)

Localism the state or condition of being local; the influence that a locality or particular place exerts; the narrowness or limitation of thought or feeling growing out of such affection (anarchist criminology)

Looking down listening to those who are the least heard and most isolated and violated (peacemaking criminology)

Marxist of or pertaining to a view of sociological phenomena from the socialist point of view as espoused by Karl Marx (socialist feminism)

Marxist criminology theory of criminology drawing on Marxist views of control and exploitation of labor as causes and motives for criminal behavior (socialist feminism)

Material feminism branch of feminist inquiry that examines the relationship of feminist philosophy on a material level, especially focusing on the issue of production/reproduction (socialist feminism)

Means of production the physical objects with which humans construct consumer items within a capitalist system (radical criminology)

Mechanization the conversion of human-performed processes to machine-performed processes (radical criminology)

Mental constructs conceptualizations of abstract concepts or objects within the mind of an individual according to how that individual perceives them (radical criminology)

Milieu the environment in an all-encompassing sense (chaos theory)

Mitigated alleviated; moderated (postmodern and feminist criminology)

Mobius bands "cuts" depicting the relationship between the various imaginary constructs of self as a desirable person and the other as an object of desire having the ability to both reflect one's self and be the basis of imaginary fulfilling desire (catastrophe/topology theory)

Mode of production method by which goods are produced, primarily manually versus mechanically (radical criminology)

Modern theoretical paradigm in which topics, issues, and phenomena can be objectively analyzed according to the scientific method (constitutive criminology)

Moral comprehension sense that justice goes far beyond our modern liberal and legal notions of justice (prophetic criticism)

M-space a behavioral surface that acts as one of two control parameters within the catastrophe model, reflecting the range of possible behavioral states that may result (catastrophe/topology theory)

Mutual aid interchangeable or reciprocal aid in which like duties and obligations are exchanged (anarchist criminology)

Narrative the art or practice of relating stories or accounts in writing or in speech as the preferred method of conveying one's meaning (postmodern and feminist criminology)

Natural law codes of behavior predicated on a society's perception of the rules governing nature apart from human (chaos theory)

Natural right that which is conferred on the state and individual by virtue of their place within the natural order (chaos theory)

New justice model justice dispensed for the purpose of preserving the capitalist social order and according to what the offender deserves in the pursuit of rational action (prophetic criticism)

Newtonian of or referring to Isaac Newton and the scientific method of analysis with which he has become associated (chaos theory)

Nonlinear literally, not in a straight line; referring to the theory that behavior of individuals and groups of individuals is not predictable (chaos theory)

Nonlinear policing philosophy and practice of responding to crime that accommodates the chaordic nature of human behavior (chaos theory)

Normal factor conflicting influences on the behavioral dimension of the cusp catastrophe model; one of the two control parameters found within this model (catastrophe/topology theory)

Nozick's theory of justice consists of a world of separate individuals, with individual rights, who exist and act irrespective of being in society (prophetic criticism)

Objective idealism method of perceiving one's environment based on a worldview dictated by an all-encompassing philosophy (radical criminology)

Oppression the act of keeping individuals or groups down by using cruel or unjust power or authority (postmodern and feminist criminology, queer theory)

Paradigm (1) an example that serves as a pattern or model (critical race theory); (2) patterns, examples, or models (postmodern and feminist criminology)

Parameters factors, or variables (catastrophe/topology theory)

Patriarchy social system in which the male gender is viewed as more powerful and controlling than the female (socialist feminism)

Peacemaking the process of weaving and reweaving oneself with others into a social fabric of mutual love, respect, and concern, thereby creating an atmosphere of safety and security (peacemaking criminology)

Peace rhetoric discourses that transcend the limits of the entrenched, polarized positions that often end violently (catastrophe/topology theory)

Performative producing effects in behavior (catastrophe/topology theory)

Phone/fax zaps bombarding an agency, corporation, or other group with phone calls and faxes (queer theory)

Pink triangle a symbol queers were forced to wear for identification in Nazi concentration camps during the Holocaust, now worn as a symbol of queer pride (queer theory)

Pocket of compromise within the cusp catastrophe model, a sustainable option to interpersonal violence; see the definition for **Third way** for cross-reference. (catastrophe/topology theory)

Point attractor the movement toward which a system tends or behaves can be specified at a particular point or limit. (chaos theory)

Point of convergence conceptual similarities identified between feminism and postmodernism (postmodern and feminist criminology)

Policy analysis used to address those conditions that can be manipulated to produce the desired change (prophetic criticism)

Politico type of feminist advocate who approaches the oppression of women as a form of class exploitation within the greater capitalist society (socialist feminism)

Positionality the process by which contingent meaning is attributed to objects (postmodern and feminist criminology)

Positivist the belief that social phenomena can be identified, quantified, and controlled, through scientific measures, with exactness or precision (socialist feminism)

Postmodern theoretical paradigm maintaining that objective study of a topic is impossible because all human language used to express thought is itself value laden (constitutive criminology)

Poststructural a philosophy that rejects the existence of definitive, underlying "structures" or foundations that therefore explain how social and physical phenomena function; beyond structuralism (socialist feminism)

Powerholders those who have an imbalance of power over others and achieve this power by systematically using violence and/or abuse (peacemaking criminology)

Praxical/praxis the blend of both theory and action as a method for understanding how social systems behave and for promoting change (chaos theory and socialist feminism)

Prejudice negative feelings toward persons based exclusively on their membership in certain groups (critical race theory)

Primary means of production the actual physical tools or machines for producing consumer goods (radical criminology)

Private justice informal justice where conventional methods of regulation are nowhere to be found, usually resulting in some form of exploitation (constitutive criminology)

Procedural justice a plan of justice based on treating like people equally with no regard for individual differences or circumstances (constitutive criminology)

Prophetic of or pertaining to the theological, philosophical, and moral dimensions of understanding human existence (prophetic criticism)

Prophetic justice conveys the idea that people are in a covenant with God and are responsible for the character of their lives and society, for the pursuit of righteousness, justice, and mercy. The social and moral order is consequently rooted in the divine commandments; morality rests on divine command and concern rather than on the relativity of reasonableness. (prophetic criticism)

Public psyche the public spirit or soul (critical race theory)

Punitive justice a system of justice that uses the infliction of punishment or penalties as both a consequence and form of crime deterrence (anarchist criminology)

PWA   Person with AIDS (queer theory)

Queer   an individual who is lesbian, gay, bisexual, or transgendered (queer theory)

Queer politics   theory and action that challenge heterosexist thought, defy heterosexist norms, and celebrate being queer (queer theory)

Racial discrimination   discrimination on the basis of race (critical race theory)

Racism   practice of discrimination, persecution, and/or segregation based on a person's skin color or ethnic heritage (critical race theory)

Radical criminology   branch of criminology that posits that replacing the current social structure is a necessary step in remedying current social injustices

Radical feminism   type of feminist philosophy focusing on the need to eliminate existing social structures that foster feminine oppression and replace them with more egalitarian ones (socialist feminism)

Rawls's theory of justice   considers the principles necessary to govern the distribution of the means to achieve individual goods; the modern welfare state assures and regulates this distribution. (prophetic criticism)

Regionalism   the division of a country into small administrative regions (anarchist criminology)

Representational democracy   the vesting of authority and power in others who claim to represent us in worlds well beyond our control (anarchist criminology)

Repression   the use or threat of coercion by governing authorities to control or eliminate opposition, including any actions taken by authorities to impede mobilization, harass and intimidate activists, divide organizations, and physically assault, arrest, imprison, and/or kill movement participants (queer theory)

Reproduction requirements   an individual's material needs to sustain him- or herself and the family (radical criminology)

Reproductive expenses   the cost to the worker of meeting the material needs of him- or herself and the family (radical criminology)

Reproductive labor   according to Marxist philosophy, the childbearing function of females that is exploited by the capitalist and patriarchal systems (socialist feminism)

Retributive justice   concept of justice based on the goal of exacting a punishment or penalty for specific behaviors (chaos theory)

Schema R   Jacques Lacan's conceptual model composed of various mobius bands ("cuts" depicting the relationship between the various imaginary constructs of self as a desirable person and the other as an object of desire having the ability to both reflect one's self and be the basis of imaginary fulfilling desire) (catastrophe/topology theory)

Second generation of rights   set of rights possessed by the people that require affirmative action on the part of the state to protect the safety and welfare of the people (constitutive criminology)

Second wave feminism   period of great feminist activity occurring in the late 1960s through the 1970s commonly referred to as the "women's liberation movement" (socialist feminism)

Semiosis   the evolving process, through language, in which the meaning of words, as signs, are created; see **Sign.** (semiotics)

Semiotics   the study of language, language systems, and their evolving meanings; see **Sign.** (semiotics)

Sign   the link between the expression and content for a word, phrase, gesture, or nonverbal cue. Signs are composed of an expression (or signifier) and a content (or signified). The *expression* is the word, gesture, or nonverbal cue. The *content* is the meaning assigned to the word, gesture, or nonverbal cue. (semiotics)

Signified   the content assigned to words, phrases, gestures, and so forth, thereby communicating specific meaning (semiotics)

Signifier   word, phrase, gesture, and so forth, that conveys meaning (catastrophe/topology theory and semiotics)

Social control the sense of greater trust and social safety among others grounded in honesty and truth; a state realized through feelings of happiness and security greater in this moment than the last (peacemaking criminology)

Social criticism an analysis or critique of social factors or social issues that are negatively affecting a segment of the population (postmodern and feminist criminology)

Social discrimination discrimination on the basis of social class (critical race theory)

Social justice perspective of justice that evaluates how a society provides for the needs of its members and the extent to which it treats its subgroups equally (radical criminology)

Socialist feminist sociological framework that identifies oppression of women as a dual function of the qualities of capitalism and patriarchy (socialist feminism)

Spheres of influence in Marxist thought, forces that shape and/or determine how society functions, such as politics, morality, personal beliefs, and education (introduction)

Splitting factor a moderator that increases in magnitude along with an increase in the normal factor in the cusp catastrophe model; one of the two control parameters found in this model (catastrophe/topology theory)

State of peace a state that manifests itself as harmony or resonance in human interaction (peacemaking criminology)

Status the position one assumes that dictates what rights will be honored in law and elsewhere (introduction)

Storytelling see **Narrative** for a cross-definition. (postmodern and feminist criminology)

Structural interpellation Marxists Marxists who maintain that the effects of the superstructure's spheres of influence (for example, political, ideological, and economic) codetermine the economic relations of our society (introduction)

Structural Marxism the belief that autonomous forces (spheres of influence) operate in society and shape and/or determine how society functions (introduction)

Superstructure (1) according to Marxist thought, the totality of the spheres of influence (introduction); (2) Marx's term for the social system when viewed as a whole (radical criminology)

Surplus labor the labor produced by a worker in a job minus the labor produced by the worker required to meet his or her reproductive requirements, the result of which is a product possessing surplus value that is retained by the controller of the means of production (radical criminology)

Surplus population the persons in a society not required to produce the labor required to produce the products necessary to sustain that society; namely, those persons no longer required by the controller of the means of production because of mechanization (radical criminology)

Surplus value the monetary value of a product minus the cost to produce it, retained by the controller of the means of production (radical criminology)

Technical justice disposition of criminals and criminal behavior with primary emphasis on the letter of the law (chaos theory)

Texts a term used by postmodern theorists that refers to written works such as books and poetry, as well as events in the world that create an established context of meaning through which individuals "read" meaning into experiences (postmodern and feminist criminology)

Third generation of rights concept that all citizens are due human rights in which the responsibility to provide for them reside with state governments on a collective level (constitutive criminology)

Third way within the cusp catastrophe model, a method for creating stability during situations of relational violence when the disputing parties assume two very extreme positions; see **Pocket of compromise** for cross-reference. (catastrophe/topology theory)

Topology theory a theory that provides several conceptual models through which methodology unfolds and testable hypotheses develop

Traditional criminology a more conservative school of thought aimed at remedying social injustice by repairing the current social system rather than replacing it (radical criminology)

Victim blaming the act of finding the victim at fault for his or her predicament instead of recognizing the true (societal) cause(es) for the situation (queer theory)

Violence according to peacemaking, all imbalances of power over others (peacemaking criminology)

Vocabulary of motives rationalizations found in the work environment that justify or excuse embezzlement (catastrophe/topology theory)

Warmaking winning wars against personal enemies by identifying, isolating, and subduing for personal and loved ones' safety (peacemaking criminology)

❖

Index